DICK CONNOR
REMEMBERED

COMPILED AND EDITED BY
MARY KAY CONNOR

FULCRUM PUBLISHING
GOLDEN, COLORADO

Library of Congress Cataloging-in-Publication Data
Connor, Dick.
    Dick Connor remembered / compiled and edited by Mary Kay Connor.
      p.   cm.
    ISBN 1-55591-216-8
    1. Connor, Dick. 2. Sportswriters—United States—Biography.
    3. Newspapers—Selections, columns, etc.—Sports. I. Connor, Mary Kay.
    II. Title.
GV742.42.C65A3   1995
070.4'49796'092—dc20
[B]   94-37940
                                              CIP

Printed in the United States of America
0 9 8 7 6 5 4 3 2 1

Fulcrum Publishing
350 Indiana Street, Suite 350
Golden, Colorado 80401-5093

For Mya, Matt, Cassie, Zach, Megan, Caroline, Nick, Andrew, Erin, Connor, Alex and any future "draft choices," so all of you can better remember a wonderful Grandpa

TABLE OF CONTENTS

INTRODUCTION

Dick Connor thought he was rich.

He was. But he wasn't wealthy.

He wrote about athletes who made millions of dollars, owners of professional sports teams and high-salaried coaches.

But he didn't envy their bank accounts. When he was offered a contract to write a four-times-a-week column for the *Denver Post* in 1988 toward the end of his 30-year career, he was far more concerned about the parameters of the job—what he would cover, his editorial freedom and how the column would be displayed in the paper—than he was of the numbers on his paycheck.

He counted himself among the world's luckiest people because he was paid to write about and attend sports events all over the country and a few times outside this country.

"I get paid to go to places other people pay to go. So many people when they work, don't see what they do. Every morning I pick up the paper, and there's what I did. It's kind of nice. It makes your work more frightening, though. You think, good lord, my grandchildren may see this. I don't want to embarrass them."

The quotes are from an interview with Dick on the occasion of the *Denver Post*'s centennial in August 1992.

Writing became a passion, pastime and hobby very early in his life. In fact on our first date—a blind date at that—he told me that's what he wanted to do. Be a writer.

On our third or fourth date, he showed me a short story he'd written and asked for a critique. I told him it was great. Good description. Good character development. Good mood setting. Realistic dialogue. But it had no plot.

He wasn't thrilled with my editorial comment, and we discussed the relative necessity of plot for some time. Still, he accepted my opinion with good humor. Later he showed me a rejection slip from a magazine for that same story. The editor complimented him on his writing skills and concluded with, "The story has no plot."

We laughed about that many times in the 38 years that followed.

Dick became an award-winning sportswriter and columnist. I became the editor of a weekly suburban newspaper, but not until our five children were pretty well grown.

While going through drawers, boxes, files and footlockers after Dick's death from cancer on Dec. 30, 1992, I found some early examples of his writing skills. His aunt, Mary Connor, saved many of his letters and cards from age 10 on. She also saved copies of *The Eagle,* a paper he started while a student at Sacred Heart grade school in Columbia, Missouri. Much of the news in *The Eagle* was related to Boy Scouts. They were progressive enough to include the Girl Scout news, too. Even before that, at age 8, Dick said he started a mimeographed neighborhood "news" paper that featured items such as birthdays, who had visitors and who got a new dog or cat.

But it was a letter written to Aunt Mary Connor on Feb. 21, 1943, when Dick was 12 years old, that convinced me his talent surfaced early. Dick's family had moved to Columbia from Iowa City earlier that month. He wrote:

> Yesterday, Terry Reise—a 12-year-old boy who lives next door, and Jimmy [Dick's next younger brother] and I went on a four or five mile hike out to Rollin's Springs. We all had a good drink and boy was it ever cold, and sweet, too. It comes out from under a tree and forms a small pool about two feet deep before it enters into the creek which in turn empties into a larger creek which in Iowa would be a river. Just as I was going to take a drink, Terry threw a rock into the pool in front of me, but it didn't get me wet at all. This rock disturbed a small frog which was sitting on a rock about three feet from my head. It jumped into the pool and I think it swam into the main stream, but I took a drink anyway because I was awful thirsty. Then we hiked around the creek over to the other side, climbed the cliffs, found two caves and climbed up to balancing rock which is a rock balancing itself on a pillar of stone like in "Lil' Abner."
>
> We are going to Sacred Heart School, and like it very much. They serve hot lunches at noon, but they taste like slop! Friday we had sauerkraut and beans, doughy rolls, not at all like grandma makes, and apples with worm holes in them at school.
>
> The R.O.T.C. riding stables are just over and up a hill to the southwest as is the stadium. To the southeast about four blocks over an open field is the swimming pool. Just across the street is the R.O.T.C. Armory and catty-corner to that is the university [Missouri] gym where I play basketball. Across from that is the baseball field. Here's a map of it.

Dick included a hand-drawn map for his maiden aunt. She was a favorite of his and his three brothers and two sisters. Aunt Mary was also tops among our five youngsters and other grandnieces and grandnephews as well. We found this letter, along with other letters and copies of newspaper clippings about the Connor children, in her apartment after she died.

Probably Dick's earliest newspaper entry was this letter to the editor. There was no date or indication of which newspaper, but he couldn't have been more than seven or eight.

> Dear Santa—I hope you are coming to our house. I want an electric train, bedroom slippers, bathrobe, high-top boots, skates to fit the boots,

boot pants and a jack-in-the-box. My brother, Jimmy, wants a jack-in-the-box, a horn and animals, a toy gas station, a rocking horse, slippers, robe and a play coal chute. My sister, Betty Ann, wants slippers, robe, horn, jack-in-the-box, doll, play doll house, a set of dishes. If this is asking for too much, just bring us what you can.—Your friend, Dickie Connor, 534 South Dodge Street.

I love the last line. And jacks-in-the-box must have been big that year. The coal chute certainly dates it, too.

Dick was born in Iowa City on June 7, 1930. He was the oldest of seven children. The next oldest, a sister, Kathleen, died tragically of pneumonia complicated by an adverse reaction to medicine at age 4.

The others in the family are James, Elizabeth Ann, Daniel, Robert and Pauline. Their parents were Richard Sr. and Pauline. The family moved to Columbia in 1943 and then to Denver in 1949. Both moves were due to job changes for Dick's father, who was a hospital administrator for about 30 years.

Dick's grades in grade and high school were good but not spectacular. He was a typical kid who loved sports, reading and exploring the Missouri hills. He graduated from Hickman High School, Columbia, in 1948.

He was accepted at the University of Missouri and planned to major in journalism. In the first semester, he pledged a fraternity and won a slot on the freshman football team. He broke his collarbone during a football scrimmage, and it had to be pinned. That ended his college football career, but probably saved him academically. He said he partied the first semester, and his grades showed it. He did much better the second semester.

That summer (1949) his family moved to Denver, and in the fall he enrolled at Regis College. Regis didn't offer a major in journalism, so he concentrated on English and American literature and creative writing. During the fall semester of his junior year, a friend from Missouri called to tell him they were about to be drafted into the army. It was 1950, and the Korean War, or Conflict, as we were told to call it, was just a few months old. Both Dick and his friend decided they would rather serve four years in the Air Force than two in the Army, so they enlisted.

Dick applied for Officers' Candidate School, but was turned down because of his vision—even though he memorized the eye chart and passed the first round of the exam.

He said his four years in the Air Force were good ones, and he laughed about defending his country from behind a typewriter in California. It wasn't long after boot camp that an officer learned he could type well and put him to work in an office. A short time later, he was assigned to the base newspaper, and that's what he did at both Parks and Hamilton Air Force bases in northern California.

His editor at Hamilton was John Sinor, who later became the major cityside columnist for the *San Diego Tribune*. After John's stint as editor of Hamilton's *Scramble* ended when he was discharged, Dick was named editor. Many years later, Dick was offered a job as assistant sports editor at the *San Diego Union* on Sinor's recommendation. He turned it down to stay at the *Denver Post*.

Dick was interested in cartooning as well as writing. A couple of his cartoons were used by the University of Missouri's *Show Me* magazine during his student days. Many of his cartoons were printed in the *Scramble* and later in the Regis College *Brown and Gold* when he was co-editor of that paper. He occasionally used cartoons for greeting cards and to ask for a date.

Dick and I met at the end of his second year in the Air Force when he was home in Denver on leave for Christmas. He and a couple of friends from Regis wanted dates to attend a University of Denver hockey game. One of them had a date with a classmate of mine at Loretto Heights, then an all-girls Catholic college located as far south on Federal Boulevard as Regis was north. It was essential for Elaine to get a date for Airman Dick Connor, because only he had access to a car. I hated blind dates, but since Elaine insisted I owed her a favor, I went.

Dick and I didn't go out again until after he was discharged from the Air Force in December 1954. We were married in August 1956, a couple months after he graduated from Regis.

I told Dick later that I married him because he made me laugh. Dick had the most marvelous, sometimes quirky sense of humor. But you had to pay attention or else you'd miss it. It was subtle.

When Dick graduated from Regis, he was already working full-time there as public information director at the princely wage of $300 a month. I was making a little over that as a teacher.

We lived in a second-floor, three-room flat for about 18 months, then bought our first house—a small, three-bedroom, brand-new bungalow in the Denver suburb of Westminster. We needed a larger place because Kathy was about a year old and we were expecting another baby. We lived in only four places during our entire 36-year marriage, including 30 years in Arvada, another Denver suburb.

The years Dick worked at Regis were pleasant; we made some wonderful friends and saw the Jesuit priests as co-workers and compatriots after having known them only as professors. Dick started an alumni magazine, the *Regis Roundup,* which is still published there.

But Dick was growing restless. What he really wanted to do was write—for publication, not just press releases and newsletters. He was doing a lot of sports releases by now because the Regis basketball team under Joe B. Hall was becoming a force to be reckoned with. Joe went on to fame and fortune as one of the winningest coaches at the University of Kentucky, his alma mater. But during those Regis years when Joe and Katherine and Dick and I and our children hung around together, a big night out was dinner at someone's house. Money was as scarce as children were plentiful.

Dick had a lot of contact with the Denver sportswriters, among them Irv Moss, Ralph Moore and Bob Collins. Bob was assistant sports editor under the legendary Chet Nelson at the *Rocky Mountain News.* After much arm-twisting and pestering from friends, Bob said he'd give Dick a trial at the *Rocky,* even though he didn't have a degree in journalism or any sportswriting experience, other than at the *Scramble*.

The *Rocky* offered Dick less than what Regis was paying. Granted, Father Richard Ryan, president of the college, had given Dick a couple of raises, but by this time we were a one-income family. And "family" is the correct term. We had three children and I was expecting our fourth when the offer came from the *News*.

I told him, "Take it." I figured we couldn't lose despite the cut in pay, because Dick would be much happier at a newspaper.

It was one of his—or I should say our—best decisions. Dick learned a great deal working with Bob Collins. But it became apparent, after a couple of years, that all the beats were taken at the *Rocky*, and Chet Nelson, Leonard Cahn and others were firmly entrenched in their jobs. There was little chance to move up or be assigned a college beat on a regular basis, let alone cover a professional team.

By now our family was complete with two daughters and three sons. Kathy, our oldest, is only six years older than Mike, the youngest. In between are Mark, Patrick and Sharon. Dick's hours were 3 p.m. to midnight. For me, it meant being alone a lot with no help.

Dick started talking to friends at the *Denver Post* and made the switch in June 1965. He stayed at the *Post* that first tour for 17 years. It was the break he needed. I was pleased, because at that time the *Post* was an afternoon paper and Dick's hours were something like 6 a.m. to 3 p.m., unless he was covering an evening game. Then he was home until a few hours before game time.

His assignment to cover the Denver Broncos was something of a fluke.

The Broncos were truly awful during the first years of the franchise. Bob Bowie, a sportswriter and cartoonist for the *Post,* asked to be taken off the beat. In addition to the poor public relations the team had at the time and the fact that the team got absolutely no respect from anyone, Bowie hated to fly.

The Bronco beat was then offered to Frank Harraway, who had covered Colorado University football for years during fall months and the Denver Bears baseball team during the summer. He preferred to stay where he was.

Dick was the newest member of the sports staff. Sports editor Chuck Garrity told him the beat was his if he wanted it. He did, and it gave him the opportunity to be in the paper regularly and to give up a recreation column that he really hated.

Those who follow sports know the rest. The Broncos' won-loss record didn't improve overnight, but it seemed as if some controversy or other was always brewing: coaches were fired; there were player revolts; a general manager was canned; ownership changed. All were good stories. And because Dick was the only reporter covering the beat, he got all the good stories.

It meant, though, that during football season—and that extended from training camp to after the draft, then held in midwinter—he wrote almost daily, sometimes more than one story a day. In the November 1974 issue, for example, Dick had 36 articles in the *Post*. He didn't mind. It meant travel, meeting interesting people and writing.

This book is an attempt to collect the best of Dick's articles and columns. It has chapters on football, baseball, basketball, golf, Super Bowls and other sports. There are examples of columns Dick wrote about our family. He also wrote very personal columns about having cancer.

The columns about people are the ones he remembered most and seemed to like best. In an interview in August 1992 for the 100th anniversary of the *Denver Post*, he said, "The people columns stand out more than event columns."

About his work in general, he said, "I pay attention to little details. I try to take the reader there. I do it with minutiae."

When I told friends, acquaintances and others about this project, I was a bit surprised at which columns they remembered and said they would like to read again.

At least six people mentioned a piece Dick wrote when my father died. My dad was not a prominent person, the column was not about sports and it appeared in 1982. I don't know why it struck a nerve. But it is included.

※　　　　※　　　　※

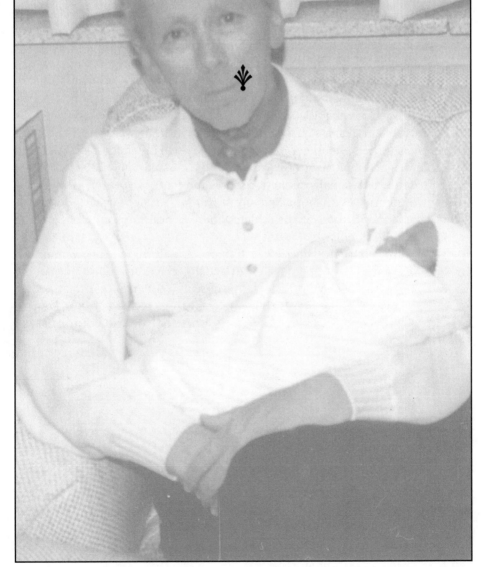

CHAPTER ONE

THE PERSONAL
AND THE FAMILIAL

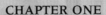

✣   ✣   ✣

In an era when commentators slay heroes and villains alike with poisonous prose in the manner of journalistic gunslingers, Dick was remarkably unique. His typewriter and computer were not weapons firing cynicism and know-it-all opinions to enhance his own reputation.

I will not remember Dick Connor primarily as Colorado's greatest press box Boswell in the past quarter of a century, which he was, according to his peers. I shall remember him as a true gentleman whose moral code set him apart from the greedy pursuers of fame and money. Dick took some shots, occasionally, at inept coaches and franchise owners who regarded themselves as sports Solomons. But he was not venal. He even had some kind words for the athletes and coaches short on talent and long on self-esteem. ...

I'm sure I embarrassed Dick because praise made him uneasy ... I told him I envied him, not because of his acclaimed writing talent, but because he was such a loving, loyal, caring husband, father and grandfather.

—Harry Farrar, author, retired *Denver Post*
sports editor and columnist

✣   ✣   ✣

Dick didn't write about himself or our family very often. He said he didn't subscribe to the Tom Sawyer school of journalism. Tom Sawyer, you remember, got Becky Thatcher's attention by walking on top of the fence. "Look at me, look at me," some writers seem to be saying, a la Tom. That wasn't Dick's style.

Occasionally, he would let his readers know what he was like—what kind of person he was—through a column or article. The following are examples of this.

Dick started at the *Denver Post* in June 1965 and was assigned to the Broncos beat in 1966. He covered the team for more than 10 years. During those years, he was the only reporter for the *Post* on the beat.

Football season lasted until late December. There were no playoff games or postseason appearances during that decade. The Broncos weren't good enough. Dick was also assigned to cover the University of Denver hockey team. Although hockey started before football ended, he would pick up the Pioneers as quickly as he could—sometimes juggling both teams. The Hilltoppers are the DU freshman hockey team.

March 3, 1968, *Denver Post*

WHAT IS HOCKEY FOR?
IT'S FOR GETTING ENOUGH OF POPCORN, POP AND STUFF

What do American youngsters think who see hockey for the first time? All I can vouch for are unsolicited impressions Saturday afternoon at DU Arena as Mark, Pat and Mike Connor, 9, 7 and 4, respectively, and a neighbor, 9-year-old Jerry Duquette, watched the University of Saskatchewan play the Hilltoppers. Here's how the game went from their vantage point in Row 10, Section F: Sat down at 2:44, Mark informed group "guys in red suits are Denver." At 2:46, Jerry asked if "the guy with the candy comes up here."

"Oh, yeah," Mark informs. "He especially comes up here."

Players leave for dressing room. Ice machine begins to lay new surface. Boys in scientific mood, wonder what will happen if it runs into end of rink. Explained machine was called Zamboni. Female seatmate heard only part of explanation. Thought driver was Zamboni. "He looks Italian." Agreed. Very Italian-looking Zamboni driver.

"How many rounds before halftime?" Mark wondered. General approval when he learned three periods separated by two "halftimes." Jerry dredged quarter from pocket. No concessionaire in sight. Teams return to ice. "The Canadian guys all have hats on," one said.

"Why aren't you in the press box?" Pat asked.

Game begins. Hilltoppers turn loose hard shot. Saskatchewan goalie Neal MacNevin gloves it. "Rats," Jerry says.

"How come he's wearing a baseball mitt?" Pat asks.

"It's a faceout," reports Mark. Note-taking observer misses private joke, hears tantalizing phrase, "Can't you see those guys on roller skates out there?" Observer shudders. MacNevin makes another desperate stop. Sprawls on ice. Gets up, skates to Saskatchewan bench for equipment repair. "The coach probably wanted to tell him about laying on his stomach," Mark decides. Saskatchewan scores. Boos from crowd. Boys join.

"Now we're going to win after all. All we need is one point more."

"Dad, today there's not very much people." Mike is confirmed crowd counter. Third and fourth goals missed due to business transaction. Bought popcorn during one, looked for "Coke" man during other. No difference. Booed anyway when learned "the Canadas" did it. Period ends, all four instantly to feet. Much of second period spent worrying whether roof is in imminent danger of collapsing—heard strange sounds from overhead girders. MacNevin to bench again when stopped hard shot with stomach. "I hope they get a lousy goalie for him," one offered. Nine-year-olds lack compassion?

Now 4:20. Pat hungry. "You couldn't be," female seatmate says. Cites menu to date: candy bar, popcorn, six cookies, "Coke" for each. Not yet second-period intermission. Now third period. Hilltoppers close to 4-3. Crowd excited. Boys bored, join crowd in jumping up and down. Mike confused over how Canada pronounced. Yells "Down with Kennedy." Must spend more time on his diction.

"Sort of like soccer," Jerry decides.

"Exactly like it," Mark agrees, "except they skate on ice. And they have a stick. And they use a puck. But they wear shorts like soccer guys." Decide good way to pass time is imitate push and shove of players on ice. Interesting result. Female seatmate now watching clock more than boys. Mike begins to cry—thinks boys cheering for Canada, such disloyalty shocking. "I hate hockey." Public address man announces "One minute to play."

Pat announces, "Can we get something to eat before it's over?" Game over. "Kennedy" wins 6-3.

February 3, 1970, *Denver Post*

DAD CUTS NO ICE AT HOME

One of the joys of parenthood, they tell me, is the unchallenged faith one inspires in one's offspring. It's rewarding, fulfilling. Like the episode at the dinner table the other evening. Monday evening, I casually announced I planned to skate during one of the Denver Spurs' games in the near future. "You?" my 12-year-old daughter, Kathy, shrieked. I could see I could have impressed them more only by volunteering to fix a faucet or paint the gutters. There was a moment of silence. Unfortunately, it was followed by several moments of raucous snickering. Mike (6) giggled. "Oh, no," said Sharon (8). More silence. And snickering.

"Can you skate?" Mike asked.

"Of course I can skate. I used to be an excellent skater." More silence. "Don't let them announce your name," Kathy said. There was a good deal of thoughtful food stirring.

"Are you going out there by yourself?" Mark (10) asked.

"No, there will be other guys, too. We're going to have these two hockey teams ..."

"Hockey?"

"Yes, we're going to play hockey between periods."

"Well, that won't be so bad. You'll have that pole to lean on." Kathy said reassuringly.

"It's a hockey stick. Besides, I get a free sweatshirt with my name on it."

"It will probably be that icky orange," she said. Kathy is in her first year at junior high and very conscious of ick. Pat (9) convulsed in laughter. "I thought you were going to ice skate in one of those belly suits like a figure skater."

"That's a ballet suit and it's hockey and besides that's not ... Oh, never mind." I said with superior dignity.

"Can you see Ray Jacobs playing hockey?" Mark asked.

He and Pat broke up. (*Note:* Ray Jacobs once played defensive tackle for the Denver Broncos and shook hands with Mark and Pat four years ago. He wore a cowboy hat and weighed 290 pounds at the time. It was an impressive handshake. They did have a point there, though. The thought of Ray Jacobs, on skates ...) But, I digress.

"He'd jump on the goalie and squish him."

"Can you keep your ankles straight? ... Are you going to wear your glasses? ... Why don't you put that black stuff on your hair so it won't be gray? ... What if they knock you into the wall? ... What if you break both your ankles? ..."

So curse you, Bill Bennett, you publicity director you. And curse the day you went to Salt Lake City and saw 7,000 persons regale themselves between periods at the plight of poor, hapless sportswriters marooned on the ice—and not in belly suits, either—and came home and lured Denver scribblers into the same harsh fate for your game here Sunday, Feb. 15. And fie on me for accepting. And I hope Ray Jacobs falls through the ice. On you. And if you announce my name, I'll take my double runners and go home. You can keep that damn orange sweatshirt, too. Kathy's right. It doesn't go with my gray hair. And Mary Kay, if it's not too much trouble, I'll take dinner in my room tonight, ALONE.

❀   ❀   ❀

This letter was written to daughter Kathy when she was a junior in high school in 1974. It was in response to a batch of pamphlets she had left on his desk at home. It was a time when she, like many teenagers of the time, was questioning almost everything. It was published in the *Denver Post* two days after Dick died.

January 1, 1993, *Denver Post*
LETTER TO KATHY, 1974

Kathy: I've just read those pamphlets you left and would like to offer an opinion. I found each extremely exaggerated and unfair. They also are totally wrong in their overall view of teenagers. That does not mean I can't agree with some isolated parts. I do. I simply can't buy their theme that today's teenagers are corrupt as a generation and bankrupt as a source of future leadership. In most cases, it is just the opposite.

Teenagers today must live with a conflicting fact: They are growing into adulthood in a more worrisome, tension-filled, technologically advanced world than their parents found at a similar stage. But this is merely a fact. I suspect some teenagers use it as an excuse. True, today's society and frantic pace pose more problems, choices, judgments and temptations. Some of the things that have glued our society together for generations are becoming dry and cracking, much as the caulking does around the tile in the tub. That doesn't mean that bathing is bad, or that the tiles are imperfect. It merely means it is time to redo the job, and this will be your task, yours and your friends, in the years ahead.

So, while there are many more pressures on you, there are also many more possibilities and exciting opportunities. You have, in a very real sense, a chance to help remake our way of life, perhaps for hundreds of years, if you do the job right. So that's the conflict. It might be too easy to mistake a temptation for an opportunity, to confuse real values with false, drying ones. There is a greater burden on the emerging young woman or man to be certain you sort them out correctly.

I feel a sense of great idealism among young people, but I also sense a companion strain that veers toward despair. There is a minimum of tolerance and real sense of personal responsibility. You want things changed, perfected, but only as you wish, and often without regard to the effect such change—if it isn't tempered—can have on others. There is little respect. You can argue, and often be right, that many segments of our society are not worth respect. I agree, to the extent we seem to reward hypocrisy and cheating at many levels.

But the fact remains that the world you are inheriting is by no means all bad, either, and you must learn to distinguish. It won't be easy. History, a practical knowledge of what once happened and the causes and effects, can help you interpret what is happening today. But too many are too willing to dismiss everything in the past. That's wrong. They may be becoming aware of the world for the first time, but the world and its good and bad parts has been here long before any of us and will be here long afterward. There is very little new.

Science and technology have perfected new gadgets, but man will wind up using or abusing them as he has others in the past. Yes, I'm overlooking one huge exception—the atom. For the first time, we can soar into the deep reaches of space, or possibly simply reduce ourselves to a monstrous cloud of dust filtering endlessly through that space. The stakes, I agree, are higher.

The tactics, unfortunately, must still be worked out and practiced by men.

And this is where you and your generation can make your contribution just as most previous generations have made theirs in one form or another. You will have to learn to think very clearly, to be yourself and not what someone else would have you be for their convenience.

Retreat, historically, has been for the defeated. Dropping out is, I feel, a retreat. It is much more demanding, and more rewarding to stay and attempt to change and improve than to simply say, I'll go do my thing and forget the rest.

There is courage in the person who does stay and remains true to himself or herself. Retreat is easy. Quitting is easy. Being angry at something is easy. So is a lack of tolerance and understanding for differences, human frailty, age, other ways of thinking or doing things. I see too much of this among young people today. It is wrong. It is selfish. And if they persist in it, they'll wind up making the same mistakes as those they criticize.

The other main lack I see too often among young people is a sense of personal responsibility to go along with the freedom they enjoy and insist on. You don't get one without the other, and both are costly. You are NOT entirely your own person. You owe parts of your life to others, just as they do to you.

So, Kathy, I disagree with those writers on the big things. You and your friends are capable of much more than they think. But, if you prove them wrong, you must work at it. If not, whose fault will it be?

Dad

May 17, 1981, *Denver Post*

SCHOOL'S OUT AS LAST GRADUATES, AND FRIDAY NIGHTS TURN EMPTY

We graduate today. That's not the regal we. Nor is it the journalistic we. It's the marital we. Mary Kay and me. After nine years, we're leaving high school behind us. Mike gets his diploma from Holy Family High School this afternoon, and we're through.

No more PTA. No more report card nights. No more Booster Club. No more going to the Junior-Senior Prom because one of them's an attendant or king. No more chorus recitals, or spaghetti dinners, or working the summer bazaar, or car pooling to a game, or trying to figure out how to find a field in an unfamiliar town on a Friday night.

"Oh, let's just drive until we see the stadium lights. Then all we have to do is find a street that aims that way." And it always worked out.

No more.

We're through. Dammit.

I'll miss it.

Ever since Kathy began the parade when she entered Arvada High in 1972, we've been high school parents. If you've played the role, you understand. If you haven't, just wait. And don't snicker. Your turn is coming. We should have it down pat by now. Mike is the fifth to get a diploma in that stretch. First Kathy. Then Mark. Then Pat. Then Sharon. Now Mike. I don't think Brutus the dog is going to qualify, but he's been there during the whole stretch, too. His lone distinction is getting thrown out of obedience school.

It all came home this week when we went to the annual athletic awards banquet at old H.F., down in the cafeteria in the basement, the one they repainted purple and gold a few years ago. It was, I think, our sixth. "I'd just like to thank ..." Lord, I'd just like to have one blue-chip oil stock for every time I've heard that phrase at an athletic awards dinner the past years. Just one. Blue.

We've thanked teachers and coaches and parents and sometimes, it seemed, just people whose feet we could see through the windows high on the cafeteria walls. We've bought—and blackjacked friends into buying—pancake breakfast tickets, chances, cookies, coupon books. I shudder to think how many miles we've put on several automobiles during that stretch. But some Arab sheik somewhere is smiling. We've shortened our lives shivering on October nights on an ill-lit field, or suffered hearing loss crammed into the H.F. or Denver Christian gyms on winter evenings where you couldn't hear yourself shout for help if you needed it.

And we'll miss it. "I'd just like to thank ..."

We started when you still could buy gasoline for 30 cents or so, and they gave you glasses for buying at their station. We've had flat tires in Leadville, lunch in Granby, breakfast in Frisco. All in the line of duty. We've hauled kids all over this state and loved it. Most of the time. I'd just like to thank our kids for bringing their friends along. That's been—still is, in fact—the best part. In this business, you tend to get a little discouraged at the human race. Then the kids come home with somebody and it's OK again. We're gonna be in good hands. We've had postprom breakfasts at 3 a.m. We've watched Kathy shivering at 6 a.m. swim team sessions and Sharon up for pom-pom practice at that hour and the three boys trying to survive two-a-days in the August heat.

I never did find out who holds the throw-up record.

From 1975 through 1979, we had at least three in high school at once. There just aren't enough Friday nights in the world to take care of that. I have no idea how we're going to fill weekends next year. Is there life beyond high school? "You can only write one Holy Family column a year," my boss ordered early on.

"That's your limit." I've stuck to it, even though I was tempted. The Tigers belong to a league I admire greatly, the Metropolitan League. It may be one of this nation's most distinctive. It sprawls geographically from the last remnants of the Great Plains, through the metro area, and up and over the Continental Divide to include Summit High in Frisco and Middle Park in Granby. It embraces public schools and private ones like Holy Family and Christian.

And, in a time of great change, it offers some anchors. Christian, it seems, is never going to run out of Forseths. Holy Family has some third-generation kids. Sheridan always has a Dudley playing. After a while, you don't even need programs. And you wind up sitting next to families from the other schools you've seen for years. "Where's Eric now? How's he doing?"

"I'd just like to thank ..."

So Mike will walk up to get his diploma this afternoon, and for the fifth time we'll hope to hell the flash cube works and I've got it in focus, and that's it. We're out. Finished. And what do grown-ups do on Friday nights in the fall? I guess we'll have to look it up. The only thing is, Kathy has two children, now, and Mya may start at Holy Family grade school this fall, and Matthew will be along four years after that. Save those purple and gold cushions, Mary Kay. We may need them in the 1990s. As I said. "I'd just like to thank ..."

TRIP HOME TO TIGER TERRITORY
PROVES SOME THINGS NEVER CHANGE

COLUMBIA, Mo.—Thomas Wolfe was partially wrong: You can go home again, but it doesn't change anything. I went back to Columbia Tuesday to start the Big Eight Skywriters Tour on a nostalgic note. I grew up here, went to high school here, even enrolled at Missouri. When I left several wars ago, crewcuts were in, drugs were out and the Tigers of Missouri were relentlessly chasing the Sooners of Oklahoma.

"Nothing's changed, has it?" Missouri Coach Warren Powers asked, laughing.

Hinkson Creek was far past the southern edge of the city in those years. And, except for the stadium up the hill, Hinkson probably drew the biggest crowds in town on autumn afternoons. Now, it has buildings and a softball field, and a name—Research Park. Appropriate. Meanwhile, up the hill, the stadium has been expanded to Mile High Stadium proportions, and Powers presides over an athletic complex that sprawls over what I remembered as some magnificent woodlands just west of the stadium. We used to hunt arrow-heads there. Powers hunts Sooners. ...

I borrowed a car. We had finished the interviews with Powers and players. Wolfe, I was determined, was wrong. You can go home. I just couldn't remember the address. And nothing looked right. Where I remembered fields, there were shopping centers, streets, homes. But Greenwood Avenue was out there, to the west side of town. Hell, in those years, it was the west side of town. And in those years, Don Faurot was at the height of his power with his split-T offense and a largely homegrown team that annually knocked off one or two top-10 clubs only to finish second or third or fourth—while Bud Wilkinson and Co. (Oklahoma) went to another stratosphere.

Ah. Yeah. It had to be. Only now, the house is painted a light green, and the trees we had as saplings are huge and the empty field across the road is full of other houses now. "I know this sounds idiotic," I told the young woman who answered the door, "But I used to live here a long time ago."

Dee Fabacher and her husband, David, bought our house a year ago. He's in cancer research. "I think we're the fourth to own it since you," Dee said.

There have been more people owning our old house than owned the Big Eight football crown of recent years. ...

"I firmly believe we are the caliber football team that can compete with Okla-homa. ... I am firmly committed to believe Missouri can get on top," Powers said.

And I firmly believe that if I sit here on Greenwood Avenue long enough, all those houses on the east side of the street will disappear, and the trees will shrink back to sapling size, and if I get tired of wondering if the Tigers can ever beat the Sooners, I can get a blanket and a girl and head for Hinkson Creek. ...

BRUTUS IS NO CAESAR AMONG 1981 HAPPENINGS

Here we are, only 361 days left until Christmas.

It may be just enough time to recoup.

I hope your Christmas was a nice one. Ours was. Most of it. Oh, there were the small problems created when Brutus the dog and Cinnamon the Wonder Chow disgraced themselves before the whole extended family. Brutus you may know if you've read this space before. He has terrorized the neighborhood for almost 11 years. To him, the Ten Commandments are a challenge, a standing checklist of possible pleasures.

A quick drive around some surrounding blocks shows at least a half-dozen brown and black semihound types, all of them suspiciously similar. Brutus roams. Or did, until his little operation a few years back made him hate vets and forget why he tries to get out in the first place anymore. Unless, of course, his goal is a garbage can. He leads the league in garbage cans.

He added to his list on Christmas Eve, foraging through ours. It always produces the same result: He gets sick.

On Christmas Day, son Mark brought his chow, Cinnamon, to keep Brutus company. They played in the backyard, then Cinnamon got too excited when she was let into the house, raced through the kitchen, skidded, slipped, slammed into the wall and sprained her shoulder. It hurt. We finally decided to give her a couple of aspirin. Mistake. So we spent part of Christmas watching Brutus and Cinnamon throwing up. I'm just bringing all this up as a way of getting into the obligatory year-ender. We call them that in the trade, the little summaries of what went on, and ranking them. The highs, the lows, the greats and the only-think-they-ares ...

AMAZING GRACE WILL MISS PERFECTLY GOOD WAKE, HIS

The only trouble with John Dominic Grace's wake this Saturday is that the guest of honor is going to have to miss it. He never did want a funeral. Just an old-fashioned Irish ending. So we're going to give him that. Right after the funeral. The funeral is for the record, and acquaintances. The wake is for us. And for him. And when we're finished, a family name will have finished, too. He was the last male in the Grace line. So the name stops. I'm just sorry you never got to know my father-in-law. If you'll pardon the pun on a popular hymn, John Dominic was the Amazing Grace. He was born in Liverpool, England, of Irish immigrant parents. It always caused him problems on applications.

"I see you're English."

"No, Irish. I was born in England, but my parents were Irish."

"But you were born in Liverpool."

"If you were born in a stable, does that make you a horse?" he'd shoot back.

So Jack Grace and the Beatles got their start in roughly the same neighborhood. Jack's dad was a dock worker, and before Jack's mom died and he was sent for relatives to raise outside Belfast, he could name you every ship in every line that sailed from Liverpool. In fact, he was standing on the dock when the *Titanic* sailed. Years later, working on an assembly line during World War II in the Midwest, he bet a whole week's wage against a penny that the *Titanic* sailed with the British Union Jack flying from her mast. He won. And so did his wife and three daughters, who blessedly didn't know he had wagered on a 30-year-old memory. Jack Grace, you see, was a man of conviction, even though he'd proudly proclaim that "I'm John D.—without the millions."

He will be buried Saturday at Mount Olivet—on his 85th birthday. Actually, he wasn't even supposed to have a first one. He was stillborn there in the Liverpool suburb of Boodle, but those Irish midwives dipped him alternately in cold and hot water and his fighting spirit took over.

He was smoking a couple packs of cigarettes a day by the time he was 10, and he spent his 20th birthday in the freezing mud of a French trench. Maybe all those little pockets of stale gas locked in some rainwater-filled shell hole leaked into his lungs to start it. Or maybe it was the cigarettes. Or maybe just the chronic Irish lungs. Years later, he spent a year in Colorado General Hospital with tuberculosis.

He was told, at 62, he wouldn't live another two years if he didn't quit smoking. So he did. And he defied every medical theory.

At 19, he enlisted in the British Army, a wisp of an Irish kid with flashing blue eyes. But why the British Army? (There still are relatives in Ireland who won't speak to him, but that's their problem). "If you enlisted in the Irish Regiment, they used to send them out ahead, to test the mine fields," he'd say, laughing. He laughed often, just as he was the most unprejudiced man you could hope to meet. He could even find kind things to say about the British. But, of course, you'd have to ask.

So why enlist at all? Irish lads didn't have to, certainly. "It was the only way I could get out of Northern Ireland." This time he was serious.

He never went back. Wounded, he recuperated in England, then came to the United States in the early '20s, joining two sisters in Chicago. He enrolled in the Chicago Art Institute, but didn't pick up a brush again for 35 years after he met and married Mary Phelan and went to work on the Chicago Elevated as a trainman.

In classic fashion, Jack and Mary and three daughters migrated west in 1945, towing the family heirlooms in a homemade trailer behind an old Ford, and settled in North Denver. One of his daughters found him on the couch in that same house Tuesday morning, the TV still running from the night before.

Jack Grace was a self-taught scholar, a man who could do enormous sums mentally and probably beat a modern pocket computer in the process. He could also beat the *New York Times* crossword, or any other you challenged him with. And he needed no batteries. He could recite every Irish folk song he had ever heard, all 150 verses. He had the most retentive mind I've ever encountered. I've often wondered what the world might have inherited if he had been permitted a university education some-where along the way.

He never threatened 140 pounds in his entire life, but he had that street-tough build that lasts. And outlasts. He was in the trenches of the Somme, and he survived.

He survived a voyage from England on a captured German freighter that listed badly all the way across the North Atlantic. He survived the Depression, and the Chicago of Al Capone, the move west, the raising of three daughters, and survived to see 17 grandchildren and seven great-grandchildren.

And, when he was forced to retire at 62 because of those lungs, those daughters, remembering, gave him a set of oil paints. It was like tossing a thimbleful of gasoline on a long-smoldering ember. In the next 20 years, Jack Grace churned out more than 300 oil paintings, many of them Irish scenes from half a century ago. He sold some, gave many away, saw them hanging in art shows and restaurants and bank lobbies. And he had a final one, the rare early stages of a brilliant flamingo, already sketched and started. We don't really know how many he actually finished. He retired like I want to. He bowled three times a week—the last time only a week ago—painted, went to dinner with friends and, until a couple of years ago, fished as often as the mood seized him. "Put this brush in his coat pocket," granddaughters Kathy and Sharon urged Tuesday after the shock of finding him had worn off a bit. It was fitting. So he'll wear a turtleneck—he hated ties—and that paintbrush in his inside coat pocket. And he would have loved the session at the mortuary, where we had to go through the formalities of choosing a coffin.

I can hear him. "What's this? Lloyd's of London? A warranty for a coffin? How will anybody know if it doesn't work? Who knows when to make a claim?"

So I asked the mortuary man for him. He seemed a little nonplused. "I see where you are coming from," he said, nodding. No. It was where Jack Grace would have come from.

"Last occupation? I presume, at his age, he was retired?"

My wife thought a moment. "Put down artist," she said. Perfect.

Jack Grace never did retire. He just moved on. And I'm damn sorry he's going to miss a perfectly good wake Saturday. His.

December 23, 1983, *Rocky Mountain News*

ROOKIE'S READY FOR HIS FIRST CHRISTMAS

Dear Mya: I thought I'd write you another Christmas letter because it's been awhile, and because you have a new brother and two new cousins since the last time.

And also because you're the only one that can read.

So you can tell Matt, and Cassie, and now Nicholas Richard that you all have a grandpa who gets to write for a big newspaper and who gets to put their names in his space every once in a while. Just because.

But that's not really why I'm writing this. It's Christmas. That's why. And Christmas is special, just as you are, and your brother is, and your new cousins are. In my business, you see, we spend all year watching and writing about people who do things with their bodies. They run fast, or jump high, or throw, or catch. They may throw a basketball through a basket more often than anybody else, or score more touchdowns, or run faster than anybody has ever run. So we write about that, and put their picture in our paper. And a lot of times, they mistake what God gave them for what they gave themselves. ...

I was in Dallas for a football game when you were born. They called me early in the morning with the news. You have always been impatient. You were then, six weeks early. I'm usually somewhere else when the important things happen, like you, or your brother Matthew, who was three months early, or your cousin Cassandra who now lives in Oklahoma and, perish forbid, will probably grow up to be a Sooner fan. She's only 13 months but she already sounds like Barry Switzer.

Ah, well, I suppose that's better than growing up to be a Husker fan. Now we have Nicholas Richard. He's definitely a rookie, but one of great promise. He showed up Tuesday night at eight pounds, two ounces, and I think we have another lineman in the clan. We've had two, plus a defensive back, a swimmer and a cheerleader. ...

I started out just wanting to say how important you are, and your brother, and your cousins. This is your season, you know. Truly. That Denver is flying to Seattle Friday, that Los Angeles has to fly to Dallas on Christmas Day, that somebody wins or somebody loses, really isn't as important or even as necessary as the look on your face Sunday morning.

A lot of adults and promoters and leagues have messed with your season. They schedule bowl games and playoffs, and run around trying to compete. They can't. Nobody needs a public relations man or cheerleaders on NBC to interpret Christmas. Statistics aren't necessary on Christmas morning. They aren't even possible.

The reason I'm writing you today is because on Christmas morning I'll be like all of us adults. I'll be writing about how the Broncos did in Seattle, and why, or who. And while you open presents on Christmas Eve, we'll all be up there in the rain forest, wishing we were here ... I keep thinking of you not long ago at the shopping center, finally working your way up to the front of the line and Santa's lap.

"You're not Santa Claus," you told him in your best 7-year-old voice. All down the line behind you, the mothers gasped and then glared at your mother.

"You're an elf," you continued, and they sighed in relief while their children listened intently.

"You didn't tell me he was an elf," one said to a mother who had no answer.

"You just help him. He's too busy making toys at the North Pole," you said rather haughtily. "Santa" didn't say anything. The mothers just sighed ...

What Dan Reeves needs most right now is what you found in the shopping center, an elf. He needs one that comes in during the night while we're all snug asleep, one who whistles while he makes a line that lets Sammy Winder and Gerald Wilhite run, and a passer that can find Steve Watson and Clinton Sampson and not the guys in the wrong-colored shirts, and defenders who keep Seattle way out on the field.

And when Dan Reeves walks into his workshop in the morning, he finds all these things lined up on the shelf and claps his hands. Then he can live happily ever after, or until New Year's, whichever comes first. And you and Matt and Cassie and I can get on with the important stuff, like wondering if Nicholas understands what his first Christmas means and how worms know which of their ends is the front one.

Love, Grandpa

SMALL SCHOOLS STILL PUREST OF ALL

We spent all morning driving there. The notion of multilane superhighways was still just a 2001 idea in the years after World War II. So Springfield, Mo., meant about as much as mentioning Frankfurt, Germany, to most of us Kewpies.

Yep. It may be the worst team nickname in the history of sports. We did or died for a doll. But it was all we had at Hickman High in Columbia, Mo., and it was enough we qualified for State. Everybody had crewcuts. Nobody had a jump shot. There was not a single jump shot, in fact, the whole next weekend at State, which may tell you something about the state of things in Missouri in those years. There was not a single black player in the tournament, either. Which may tell you something about the state of the nation in those years.

Our league took us into such exotic places as Jefferson City, which was the state capital, and Hannibal, which is where Mark Twain wove Tom Sawyer into our nation's literary fabric. When we played in Hannibal, we always drove by Becky Thatcher's house before we ate scrambled eggs for the pregame meal. There was never time to tour the caves.

The rest of the world was just datelines in the paper.

So qualifying for State against teams from the big schools in St. Louis and Kansas City, which most of us had never even visited, that was a thing of dreams. The fieldhouse seated something like 7,000 fans. It was the biggest structure any of us had ever ventured into, let alone thought of playing in. We gawked, standing there holding our equipment bags, looking at the expanse of seats climbing up from courtside. We sneaked looks at the teams from St. Louis, from the schools of 3,000 enrollment, doubting down deep that they ever bothered to pull on their uniforms one leg at a time as we did. They looked awesome just walking out the door to the court.

There was no way we were going to win. In those years, little schools and big ones were dumped into one final pool of 16, the survivors. We had survived, somehow, so we were reasonably good. But we were not that good, not good enough to beat teams that showed up in matching travel jackets with matching equipment bags that even had their school names and their individual names and numbers on the side, for Pete's sake.

Besides, our first glimpse of the arena, our first peek at the 6-foot-5 monsters from St. Louis, and we were so thoroughly psyched we couldn't have won an intrasquad scrimmage. But the trip was worth it. We had piled into parents' cars and driven there on winding two-lane highways, and coach Bob Ruark had let us all tug our warmup jackets out of the bags and walk around town. "Walk" is the wrong verb. We swaggered.

Here we were at State, with matching warmup jackets just like the big schools. We swaggered. And we lost. Big. And drove back to discover spring had come to Columbia in our absence, a warm, cheek-brushing spring that had somehow made the buds explode and losing didn't matter as much. We drove through town, horns honking, waving, having people wave back, and for most of us, that was the last time we ever wore a team uniform unless you count the one the United States issues a few years later.

It was worth it.

The whole thing came to mind again because my favorite week on the sports calendar is here. State ... State is the last true bastion of amateurism, and the small schools are the purest of all. They ought to have a moment to swagger down 16th Street and gawk at the upper tiers in McNichols Arena. If their jackets match, all the better.

Go Kewpies. Take State.

March 18, 1984, *Rocky Mountain News*

WHAT'S THIS WORLD COMING TO IF A MAN CAN'T LIGHT UP?

I am sitting here on a snowy Friday, blissful amid a sea of desks, puffing contentedly on a cigar. It may be my last. Yes. It has come to that. Actually, it came to that years ago, but enough of life in a smoke-filled closet. It is time to emerge, cough and defend the rights of cigar smokers against the onslaughts of the Philistines and joggers.

Nothing is sacred, there are no sanctuaries. Even the press box has become a showcase for those who nibble on lettuce and sip Perrier and frown ever so delicately when someone touches flame to the God-given gift of a finely wrapped panatela. Cigars were once the badge of writers, as commonplace as suspenders and eyeshades and stubby copy pencils. Now, we are beset from all sides.

"I was sitting over there looking around. I could smell the thing but I couldn't tell where it was coming from," said our distinguished art critic, Irene Clurman. "It carries clear across the office." She is blessed with several languages, English among them, but is much too refined to use any of them in outright denunciation. But obliqueness has a force of its own, doesn't it? "You're a nice guy, but that has to go," said Sandy Graham on another memorable afternoon. Sandy is our science/energy editor. Buried deep in her mental processes, no doubt, are all kinds of data about the effects of smoke on the lungs of man—and woman. Directness is one of her virtues.

The city room with cigar butts littered across a tile floor, smoke snuggled invitingly in the overhead lights, companionable coughing among comrades, ah, those were the days. Now they arrive in silk running shorts, the sweat of a morning run still fresh on their brows, bragging about pulse rates and body fat ratios. They order spinach quiche and white wine and sneer. They would deny the rest of us our little worldly pleasures.

"That thing's vile," said a much-cherished—otherwise—companion of these many marital seasons.

"But we're sitting outside. The wind is blowing it away."

"It is blowing it away right into my face." There is nothing subtle about her feelings in this matter. If a man's home is truly his castle, it now has a "No Smoking" sign dangling from the drawbridge door. Somehow we should organize, we smokers of the tobacconist's finest product. Not for us the certain infirmities of cigarettes, even those with filtered ends. Not for us the affectation of the pipe man, he of wise mien and evil thoughts. Those incendiary devices are almost socially acceptable. A cigarette, for some reason, does not bring out the worst in smokees. Only lung cancer in smokers. The pipe makes its operator appear wise and benign even as he plots unmentionable deeds that should haunt him forever. There is something judgelike about pipes of any shape. But tug a cigar from a coat pocket, and the world grimaces.

"Open the window," comes now even in the press box. It used to be a court of final resort, the last place a man could safely light up. No more. The quiche-eaters and pulse-takers lurk even there these days.

"It's going to discolor your teeth," faithful companion protests.

"They'll fall out anyway."

"If you don't quit, they may not be the only thing missing around here." Ah. You see. The pressures grow. There are threats from every quarter. ...

What the politician once said, that what this country needs is a good five-cent cigar, is only partially true. The other part it needs is a place to smoke it. ...

May 12, 1989, *Denver Post*

CHALLENGED CHILDREN DON'T ABUSE DRUGS

He will be there this morning.

Running. Throwing. Jumping. Laughing.

Each of those things, in itself, is a miracle. "Vegetable," the learned physicians had said some eight winters back, bending over his incubator. "I don't ever want to hear that word again!" his mother said fervently, teeth clenched, eyes flashing.

He spent the first four and a half months of his life wired to oxygen and other life support things in the special section at Children's Hospital. The first year and a half, he took oxygen. The first six months, nobody knew if he would move or see or think, let alone become the happy little boy he has.

"Look, Grandpa," he had shouted a year ago. He was holding up two blue ribbons for his granddad's proud inspection. No Olympic winner was ever more welcomed.

"We don't know," the doctors had said. He had been born three months prematurely, weighing just under two pounds. Even doll clothes hung grotesquely oversized on that tiny frame. Quickly, his weight dropped to a pound and a half. The tubes and other paraphernalia stuck into his miniature body weighed more than he did. There was corrective surgery for a heart problem. The scar still shows across his back.

"We don't know," they said when his mother asked if he would see. The oxygen that was keeping him alive was also damaging the optic nerves. One of his—and her—first triumphs was the morning somebody brought one of those shiny balloons that come with flowers into the living room, and he seemed to be tracking it with his eyes.

Maybe, she thought. Already, she had begun tying him to her stomach, binding his tiny hands and legs to hers so that when she crawled, the motion was duplicated for his system. It is called "patterning" in the learned texts. She was too young, too inexperienced, too frightened to know that. She just knew she had to try something. Instinctively, she tried the right thing.

Matthew is 8 now. He is finishing his second season on a soccer team that has not lost in two years and has given up just one goal. His mother has just enrolled him in a summer baseball league. He started ski lessons at Winter Park two years ago.

"I ski the black diamonds," he claimed with boyish exaggeration. Actually, he did once with his father. For the record, normally it's the blue trails, but they have to watch him or he'll dart off into the trees. "It's more fun," he tells them. His mother is afraid of going where he does.

One eye is, indeed, not working. The oxygen that saved his life took part of his vision. Why it didn't take both, they don't know. The remaining one has little peripheral vision. But, compared to what it might have been, it's a blessing.

So, this morning, he'll join hundreds of others in the annual Colorado Tournament of Champions on the Metro campus. I'll be there, just to flush my psyche of the residue of what those in my business deal with daily.

Steroid use may infect as high as 75 percent of the NFL, one player claims. You can't read the paper without an almost daily report of some other athlete being on drugs. These are men and women blessed with superb bodies and reactions and vision. Nothing is impossible for them physically. They are the chosen in that respect. And yet they choose—choose—to impose their own handicaps. It's a shameful waste, and one for which I have no tolerance, no sympathy. Nobody forces them, and I don't buy the claim "Others do it, I have to respond."

I see, instead, the kids around Matt, chattering, excited, anticipating, oblivious to the chairs in which they sit, the crutches on which they lean, awaiting a starter's gun or inspecting ribbons already won or talking about a race to come. I wonder sometimes, did God somehow take from these kids and give that borrowed share to the ones who make the NBA and NFL and major league baseball? Don't they owe us what these kids give us? And I see somebody like Mary Carpenter, a Jefferson County Schools physical therapist who gives her life to these kids.

There are no steroid abusers here, and Mary Carpenter has never been accused of betting $16,000 a day. She couldn't if she wanted to. These kids didn't choose their handicaps. "Colorado Sports for the Physically Challenged," the program is called. Not handicapped. Challenged.

Matt has this one good eye, see? It's enough. And a little cerebral palsy that you can notice only if you look very closely, and only when he is tired. He goes after each day with a zest I envy—and pros should imitate. This morning, Matt will compete in four or five events, and he'll win some.

Today, a whole bunch of kids will. They'll be able to say, "I was a winner for a day." And my grandson, Matt, will be one of them. Vegetable? Like any 8-year-old, he hates 'em.

BIRTHDAY BOYS CELEBRATE AT BASEBALL GAME

It was just the seven of us. Oh, and a few parents. We were celebrating our birthdays, grandson Zach and me. Zach was 4 yesterday. I wasn't. But our natal day is the same, and what better way to observe it than with the special birthday boy package the Denver AAA team offers.

For $85 you get one of the boxes on press level, hats, a visit to the dugout, Crackerjacks, a hot dog, a soft drink and bubble gum. It's an advance peek at heaven.

We got it all. Except me. I don't celebrate birthdays anymore. Not since the fiftySomething one. I view them now mostly as you would the last day of vacation. Zach, grandson No. 3, still celebrates.

He started yesterday sitting on Joey Meyer's lap in the Denver dugout. He got a broken bat, pine tar still fresh on it. ...

"He gave me this," said Zach. He could barely lift the redwood-sized Louisville Slugger. Zach was listed in the program, right under pitcher Mike Birkbeck. Zach Connor, bats right, throws right, 3-foot-2, 33 pounds, age 4. So far, it's the closest any of us have come to the majors.

Zach's the family's designated hitter. He will stand for two hours and let anyone handy toss baseballs at him. I figure by 2002, he'll be listed in the regular part of the Denver lineup sheet.

I watched him sit on Meyer's lap. Joey hits them longer. Zach hits them more often. So Andrew, Nick, Matt, Zach, Cassie, Nick and Craig and I all sat in box 243 at 12:30, and watched. Wrong word. I watched. They ... well, watched is not the operative way to describe it.

"What happened?" one asked.

"A strike."

"Who did it happen to?"

"Don't open anything," Zach's mother, Denise, said, in that voice mothers use just before something bad happens. So we didn't.

"Not 'til more people come," said Zach.

"Then we start eating."

More came. We started.

One of the things Denver gives out in this birthday boy package is a balloon with a whistle on the end. Blow it up, let the air out, the whistle takes over. By the time the Tides took the early lead, our booth sounded like an NBA game.

"Yaaay!"

"Why are you cheering?"

"Somebody did something."

Sounded reasonable. We lasted to the bottom of the second before the first mass potty break, and to the fourth before the first tears. By the fourth, of course, everybody's hands were sticking to walls, chairs, clothing and each other. It must have helped. Denver took the lead.

"Dad," Zach said.

"What?" his father answered.

"Why can't we go down and play the video games?"

If he can't hit, he doesn't want to watch much.

"Can we go home?"

"No. But we're ahead 5-4."

"Who's losing?"

"They are."

He had his 4-year-old cheek stuffed with bubble gum. He looked like Don Zimmer of the Cubs. By the fifth inning, the mothers in the booth were using full, complete Christian names. That's always a bad sign.

Third baseman Joe Mitchell hammered a 410-foot homer in the fifth, a two-run shot into the south stands. It was memorable mostly because he had posed for a picture with Zach. But Zach at the moment was hiding in one of the cabinets in the back of the booth and somehow missed the whole thing.

The Tides changed pitchers. The whole infield stood on the mound, arms folded. The three outfielders assembled in center, arms folded. Up in 243, if anyone folded his or her arms, they would never come unstuck.

"Did you push him?"

"Well, he pushed me first."

Denver persevered. So did fiftySomething.

"It's over?" Zach asked as we looked under chairs, in the cabinets, behind seats to make sure nothing was left behind.

"Yup. Denver won."

"Good. Now do we get cake?"

We do. And maybe a cold cloth, and drawn shades, and an aspirin, and soothing music for the oldest birthday boy? All strings, please. No loud drums. And especially no whistles.

June 10, 1990, *Denver Post*

WITH THIS JOB, WHO WOULD WANT TO GROW UP AND START WORKING?

Dear Zach:

Happy Birthday, bub. Me, too. It's kind of nice, both of us having the same birthday. You, a grandson, now 5. Me, a grandfather, no longer 5. Hell, no longer 50 or 55. If I forget my birthday—and God knows I'm trying—you're always there to remind me.

I kind of envy you, Zach.

At 5, with all those years left, it's entirely possible you will see major league baseball in Denver in your lifetime. I didn't say "probable," note. I said "possible." My chances are slimmer. We'll know more on the Ides of August.

Anyway, like I said, it would be nice to try 5 again. Or 50 again. In ancient societies, man actually honored the older members of the clan. They got to sit closer to the fire and people listened to them.

Now, it was like Friday. I took some of your cousins to McDonald's for lunch. And when I went back for a second coffee, the nice lady said, "Do you have your Golden Arches Card?" I didn't know I'd been leading a deprived life, Zach. No, I didn't have such a card. Never heard of it.

"It's our senior citizens' discount," she said proudly.

"Don't you want to see my driver's license to be sure?" I asked. "I mean, aren't you going to card me, like they do minors in a bar?"

She gave me my card. And a free coffee. It's come to that. Now I know why Gene Amole on That Other Paper rants and rails against AARP, the American Association of Retired People (persons? personas?).

It's tough, Zach. You get to go to school next year. I get to go back to writing about the Denver Broncos and the World Series and the University of Colorado. I'll have more fun.

My mother, your great-grandmother, died at 83 a few years back, still wondering what I was going to be when I grew up. She was never quite convinced the writing game was a real job. Every once in a while, even after I'd been at it for some time and gotten bylines and my picture on the column, she'd say, out of nowhere, "Have you ever thought of going to law school like you once planned?"

This starts my 30th year at this crazy business. Impossible, I keep thinking. Whose is that strange face I keep shaving each morning? I don't think differently. I don't view the world with any less hope, or even any less despair. About even, about like always, I think.

But things change. Why, I remember when Snow White was flat-chested. True. Look at the ads for her newest movie. She's, well, um, grown up over the years. When I first started in this business, we used to actually staff softball games at City Park, and the stock car races at Lakeside every Saturday night.

The Broncos were just beginning, and nobody quite knew what to make of them. So nothing has changed in that respect. ... The city was anxiously awaiting word it would get a major league baseball team. We've gone from softball to— again, maybe—major league baseball; from stockers at Lakeside to the Gran Prix; from Dal Ward and his CU single wing to Bill McCartney and, however briefly, No. 1; from Piggly Wiggly and the AAU basketball tournament to the Final Four and the NBA; and from striped socks to four Super Bowls.

Why, Zach, we've even got wireless communication with both coasts and one-way streets. When I started, it was still in the days we typed our stories in the press box, and then held a finished page up behind us and yelled, "Western Union!" and a guy came by and took it. We could blame errors on Western Union in those days. Not now, not with our own little laptop computers.

It's still the best life there is, Zach. Think about it, when you get older. You get in free to things people pay thousands to attend. I've sat on a moonlit beach in Miami, the night before the Orange Bowl, been stranded hitchhiking in the Balkans in a blizzard, trying to talk to a Yugoslavian cop who had no English while I had no Yugoslavian. I've been to every Super Bowl and the Masters and the Olympics and World Series and Kentucky Derby and watched the Scots fry themselves at Troon in a sunbaked British Open.

It's the best life there is, Zach. And we get paid for it to boot. My mom was right. I don't know what I'll be when I grow up.

Happy birthday, Zach.

Me? I think I'll pass. Again.

Love, Grandpa

June 2, 1991, *Denver Post*
NICE GUYS, BUMS FILL **30** YEARS

It was just past 5 o'clock of a warm Bay Area afternoon, and I had just come back to my seat in the football press box at Candlestick Park. It was almost game time.

Suddenly, it felt as though someone had shoved the press box. Someone had. The coffee sloshed out of my cup and the box swing-swayed to the east, out and out and out. I was sure it wasn't coming back.

Earthquake. It proved to be 7.2 on the Richter Scale. A big 'un, but not THE big 'un Californians still anticipate. It was enough for we auslanders. I didn't go back for Games Three and Four of the 1989 World Series between the Oakland A's and the San Francisco Giants.

The subject comes up this morning because last night was my 30th anniversary as a newspaperman in this town, and I started thinking about all the places, all the people, all the scores. Earthquakes tend to rank high.

Thirty years ago, a Saturday, Memorial weekend, I walked up the stairs at the *Rocky Mountain News* and Bob Collins, who had hired me, said, "Sit here. We can talk while I make up." Understand. Make up means designing the way the page lays out for the next day. Collins was a sweet/tough newsguy from the University of Iowa who taught me much and became a dear friend and mentor.

One of the things I learned, too late, was to never "sit here." Because that was the chair next to the phone, the phone rang all the time and for the next four years, I led the *Rocky* staff in taking box scores, holes-in-one, Lakeside Speedway results and softball line scores from City Park.

Collins is retired to Florida now. I'm still keeping score.

I started this piece by sitting on the floor in my office at home, going through envelope after envelope of old clippings, old columns. I was going to be scientific.

The hell with that. Newspapering ain't brain surgery. It's people, and what they do. And, on my side of the business, whether they win or lose and what that does to them.

So these are the unconnected Confessions of a Lifer, the little images that linger, like earthquakes, no notes, just mental free fall through 30 years.

I remember Jack Nicklaus in the interview room at Augusta five years ago. He had just won his sixth Masters. Guys 46 weren't supposed to do that. One by one, writers on deadline and then his mother and his wife and finally his sons filtered away. And Jack still sat there, talking to anyone who would listen. He knew it would be his final time, on a Sunday afternoon as the light faded, to sit as the Masters champion. I finally had to leave, too.

I have always wondered whether Nicklaus stayed on to talk to the man who came in with a broom to sweep up.

Or the frosty morning at the foot of Yugoslavia's Mt. Bjelasnica in 1984 and watching the little raspberry-colored blur come over the lip of the final wall and drop down into history—Bill Johnson was the first American to win an Olympic men's downhill gold and the Austrians couldn't stand it. All week, while they went home to avoid distractions, he had taunted them. "Top three?" he asked once. "I think I'm in the Top One." "Nose picker," the Austrians snorted in disdain. He who picks last ...

There was the night at The Broadmoor in 1969. The DU Pioneers had just won the NCAA hockey championship, and were celebrating in an upstairs suite. Then a tall guy came to the door and just leaned there, kind of wistful, watching the party. It was Ken Dryden, the Cornell goalie in a 4-3 loss. He came in and shook hands and finally wandered away. To me, he has always epitomized the gracious loser. No Detroit Piston need apply.

Where did the Ken Drydens of sports go? You look at 1-900-Canseco, at "I'm the greatest" Henderson, Laimbeer, Bosworth, Ben Johnson, and you wonder if there are any survivors, any real class. Or maybe it was always rare.

I remember Mile High Stadium—then called Bears Stadium—a third full for a Broncos game in the early 1960s. And I remember the afternoon the Broncos beat Oakland for the 1977 AFC title, and Red Miller reached down to shake a fan's hand.

The fan stole his watch.

We stood on the tar paper roof of Detroit Stadium the night the Tigers got into the World Series for the first time in 16 years, and watched waves of fans tip over a bus and trash two taxis. "Don't go out there unless you can see the Press Bus right next to the gate," a cop warned. Next to him, a young teenage girl asked me breathlessly, "Were you in the dressing room? Did you touch someone?"

Denver has gone from fast pitch softball at City Park to awaiting its final christening as a major-league baseball town while I've tried to remember always to include a verb and a noun in every sentence and to get the score correct. There have been a lot of awfully nice people and a few bums along the way. It's a percentage I'm sure isn't too different in any job.

TV has changed the business dramatically, sometimes for the good. It has forced us to emphasize the "Why?" and the "How?" more than the "What?" But it also has distorted almost everything it touches. I hope I'm still working when some athletic director or commissioner has the guts to say, "Here's our game. Here's the time. YOU adjust, we aren't."

There was Kirk Gibson's home run that froze the A's in the World Series, and Bill Buckner's error that killed the Red Sox, and watching the city before and after four Super Bowl losses, and Big Jane marching to the front of the press conference when Doug Moe was fired, and sweetly asking Peter Bynoe, "Do we come here to pick up the check or do you mail it?"

And the look on Mary Decker's face when Zola Budd bounced her out of history in Los Angeles in '84 and ... But that's a good way to end it. Unfinished.

December 8, 1991, *Denver Post*

50-YEAR MEMORIES OF PEARL HARBOR DAY

Sauerkraut. That's how I remember Sunday morning, Dec. 7, 1941.

It's not the classic memory, of course.

Our family had gone to early mass at St. Patrick's in Iowa City. Maybe I even served. Then we went to Sunday dinner at my Aunt Margaret's house. She always cooked sauerkraut, and the house was filled with its basic German smell when somebody called and told us to turn on the radio. It was one of those tabletop models with a rounded top and cloth over the speaker.

"... Japanese planes have bombed the American Pacific Fleet at Pearl Harbor ..."

Nobody knew where Pearl Harbor was. Hawaii, somebody thought. Hawaii? Isn't that way out past California? Our world was changing, and we couldn't even identify the spot where it began. The more learned columnists who work at real-life subjects have dissected that day. I just remember the smell of sauerkraut, and wondering whether Pearl Harbor was close enough we should be worried.

I was 11 at the time. I remember having been horrified at news stories of the Nazis forcing Jews to drink vast amounts of castor oil. Even a little bit was enough to horrify an 11-year-old. Then there were the bulletins the previous June that Germany had invaded Russia. We started looking at newspaper maps with big arrows on them, showing cities we had never heard of.

I had already started dabbling at drawing and sketching, and I had notebooks filled with pictures of Spitfires and Heinkels and Messerschmitts. The Germans were always on fire. Now I would add Zeroes and Mustangs and B-17s.

We had no idea of the drastic upheavals ahead for the world that cloudy Sunday morning. We just knew it was bad. Ours was a sports family. My dad coached, and my uncle coached, and we lived in Iowa City, where the University of Iowa dominated an 11-year-old's dreams. I watched Nile Kinnick star for the Hawkeyes, and then one day not long after the war started, I heard he had been killed in the Pacific.

My father had "adopted" a farm kid from outside Iowa City so he could play for St. Patrick's. We got word in 1942 that he had died on Guadalcanal. There were similar messages arriving all over the country by then, and sports was no longer the dinner table topic.

The 1942 Rose Bowl game was moved to Durham, N.C., because officials feared such a concentration of fans might be too tempting a target for shelling by some Japanese sub just off the California coast. President Roosevelt asked major-league baseball to keep going as long as it could. It would help morale, he reasoned. John Steadman, a good friend and a columnist for the Baltimore *Evening Sun,* has researched many of the changes that Sunday morning made in American sports.

The major leagues trained in the north that next spring. Travel was a military priority. It's why the Brooklyn Dodgers went to West Point, and the Washington Senators slogged through the spring rains and cold in Maryland, and the Chicago Cubs trained in French Lick, Ind., the future home of Larry Bird.

The war didn't exactly remove egos from the men who rose to command various stateside facilities. It became a matter of pride. Paul Brown assembled one of the great teams of any time at Great Lakes Naval Training Station. Don Faurot, meanwhile, began tinkering with something called the Split T right there in Iowa City, where he coached the powerful Iowa Hawkeyes. We would go over across the river and up the hill and watch them practice.

Steadman recounts two great National Football League mergers. In 1943, the Pittsburgh Steelers and the Philadelphia Eagles merged to become the Steagles. The next year, the Steelers and Cardinals joined forces as the Carpitts. Steadman is much too good a newsman to be wrong about this.

Sports pages shrank and casualty lists grew. We all knew the good guys were in service somewhere, Ted Williams flying fighters, Joe Louis staging two heavyweight championship fights with all proceeds going to charity. He was making $21 a month, and those fights earned $111,082. You wonder what Don King would think of that.

Near the end of the war, our family had moved to Columbia, Mo. Two blocks south of our house was the old University of Missouri faculty golf course. It had been commandeered and made into a prisoner of war camp for Germans and Italians. The Italians formed a choir, and Sunday's 9 a.m. mass became a civic event. There were only 94 Catholic families in Columbia at that time. Fewer than half could get into that high mass sung by those superb voices. The rest were Protestants, mesmerized by Italian tenors singing the "Ave Maria."

We waited. We knew the box scores we read, the games being played, shouldn't really count. St. Louis' Browns were using a guy with one arm. But we no longer lived or died on the morning box scores. There were far more important things going on. High schools replaced colleges as the focal point, and then it was all over.

For some reason, I was back in Iowa City the day the Japanese surrendered. It had begun there with sauerkraut. It ended with horns and whistles and strangers kissing in the street. Downtown, they rang the bell they used to reserve only for Saturday afternoons when the Hawkeyes won. It made a lovely sound.

⚜   ⚜   ⚜

CHAPTER TWO

FOOTBALL

He [Dick] took this team [Denver Broncos] in the mid-'60s, when they were about to leave town, and he wrote about them, nurtured them, drew fan support for them, made the folks in the city understand that to be a big-league town you had to support the team and they did. They expanded the stadium ... look at the Broncos now. Tell me he didn't have something to do with making them such a fan powerhouse in the NFL.

You've got to believe in it when it starts to happen. And he made it happen. People listened to him.

—Will McDonough, NFL columnist for the *Boston Globe* and analyst for CBS Sports

Dick had a great influence on our success, and where we are today. Dick was as influential as anyone inside the club, and that's very unusual. Players and coaches may come, but his influence was overwhelming. What he said, so often, was 100 percent correct. He was not an organization man, but when he made a point, it was right. I seldom disagreed with what he said, positive or negative. ... He really wrote from the heart.

—Pat Bowlen, Denver Broncos owner

I never had a cross word with Dick because I knew he was a classy guy with a job to do. I didn't always agree with what he wrote and I'm sure he didn't always agree with what play I called. I was really touched by him and his family. The things that were important to me, I found out were really important to him, too.

—Dan Reeves, former Denver Broncos head coach, now head coach of the New York Giants, who co-authored his autobiography with Dick

I remember him from the time I got to Denver, as always being fair— the fairest sportswriter in this town. He didn't mince words—he called a spade a spade—but he did it from a standpoint of knowledge.

—Haven Moses, former Broncos wide receiver, now an executive with Coors Brewing Co.

Although Dick liked all sports, he wrote about football most. It was his beat at the *Denver Post* for more than 10 years, from 1966 to 1977. (The Broncos' first season was 1960.) In those years, the *Rocky Mountain News* and the *Denver Post* each assigned one reporter to the team full-time. (Others would fill in on game day to write sidebars or columns.) In fact Chet Nelson, sports editor of the *News,* also covered the Broncos. The sports staffs at both papers were much smaller than today's, and the team was pretty bad, so why waste more manpower?

Denverites took to professional football with gusto. Years when the team's won-loss record was terrible, fans turned out on Sunday afternoons anyway. In those early years, they were grateful for any win—never mind a trip to a playoff game or the Super Bowl.

But covering them was demanding. Dick was expected to have at least one story in the paper every day. As a family we didn't have weekends together from training camp in late July or early August until after Christmas. But the children understood what their dad was doing and were proud of him. He would talk about the games and players with them and make all of us feel a part of his work. How could we complain? He loved his job.

After Dick's assignment at the *Post* changed from beat reporter to columnist in 1977, the Broncos continued to be a major sports subject. They were often the biggest story during the late summer and fall. It was fun to watch the team that had gotten no respect across the country go to four Super Bowls. I remember Dick wondering in the '60s and '70s if Denver fans would be as gracious winners as they were losers. He thought not.

But that first year on the Bronco beat, 1966, was unique. It was his first major assignment, a baptism by fire. During his four years at the *News,* he had been mostly a desk man, and had covered perhaps a dozen games of any description. Most were in Denver; one was a Colorado State University game at Fort Collins.

During his first year at the *Post,* Dick had covered recreation sports and done some desk work. So when he was offered the Broncos, he was a bit apprehensive. He worried about having enough experience to do justice to a professional team. It's a good thing he didn't know what would happen to the Broncos during his first season covering them. After that year he didn't worry about his reportorial skills. But he never quit worrying about the quality of his writing. He often said, "You're only as good as your last column."

There are more football stories in this book than other sports stories because Dick wrote more of them.

October 3, 1966, *Denver Post*
FANS BUST BUTTONS IN BRONCO WIN

"Jeez," a Houston sportswriter exclaimed from the press box as he watched in awe as Denver fans went delirious with joy.

"You'd think they had just clinched the championship." They had, in a way.

Because only a title will touch off a more emotional response than did Denver's dramatic 40-38 win—that's spelled W-I-N for those who forget—over Houston Sunday afternoon.

The roar started even before Gary Kroner's winning 46-yard field goal reached the south uprights with 27 seconds remaining. It grew to a crescendo as the official signaled the kick was good and Kroner jumped for glee with both arms upraised. Then it just rolled over and over Bears Stadium for a good two minutes as fans refused to leave and just stood to pay standing ovation.

This game had a little of their tribute with a rousing everything—even a rainbow dipping out of dark rain clouds to the east for fans who like to mix a bit of symbolism with their football.

Just a month ago, this same Houston team had humiliated Denver as few pro clubs have ever been humiliated, limiting the Broncos to just 26 total yards offense and no first downs.

Sunday, the Broncos more than paid up the mortgage on their reputation. And it wasn't a case of the Oilers being that much worse than they were a month ago. Denver is that much improved.

It was like watching two sluggers swing roundhouse rights as Denver and Houston lashed each other with long scoring passes. There was a 100-yard kickoff return by Denver's Goldie Sellers, field goals, fumbles, interceptions and finally, a back-to-the-wall goal-line stand by Denver that left a crowd of 27,203 wrung out and hoarse. ...

January 1, 1967, *Denver Post*
IT WAS "WOULD YOU BELIEVE?" SEASON FOR BRONCOS

Trying to condense the 1966 Denver Bronco season into one newspaper story is like—well, it's like, uh—lemme see now, there must be some comparison. Probably not, though. There's just no comparing the season just ended with any ever played in professional football.

Be honest now. When you were fighting the crabgrass back in July, did you really think the Broncos would spend the next five months thusly:

—With a revolt by its two veteran quarterbacks before training camp barely began?

—Or that the club would wind up looking at 11 quarterback candidates before the season ended, then have the original No. 1, John McCormick, come up with possibly his most courageous performance as he shook off an early interception and fired for three touchdowns and 328 yards in the season finale against a stacked defense in Buffalo?

—Or, for that matter, that by season's end the club would be on its third general manager and third head coach?

—That it would start the season with an historic and humiliating loss to Houston, going without a first down? And then come back to avenge that with a 40-38 victory on a field goal in the closing moments, then help determine the Eastern Division race by knocking off Boston in the "Mud Bowl"—again on a last-second score?

—That Cookie Gilchrist would refuse to report, be placed on the reserve list and eventually be dealt to Miami?

—That Denver would become the first AFL team to lose to Miami? (Well, we'll concede THAT might have entered your preseason figuring.)

—That, desperate for help, the club finally coaxed all-league tackle Eldon Danenhauer out of retirement—only to have him break his arm the second time he practiced? Or that Bob McCullough would discover a nerve condition that forced his retirement, and thus wipe out the entire right side of the offensive line before Denver played a game?

—That Mac Speedie would quit as head coach after the second game?

—That owner Gerald Phipps would take Jim Burris' place as general manager after six games? Then announce hiring Lou Saban to a 10-year contract for a reported $50,000 annually two days before the final game?

—That pro football's second-leading pass receiver, Lionel Taylor, would finish the year with just 35 catches?

—That last year's second-best offense in the league—hurt by the loss of Gilchrist, Danenhauer and McCullough—would wind up last, and that defense, next to last in the league a year ago, would wind up as a strong point?

—That it would include such other things as the Negro players' protests over alleged inequities in such things as Player of the Week awards, or that touted rookie tackle Larry Cox would be hurt in a motorbike accident in training camp, be lost half the season, then wind up as a starter when Ray Jacobs was hurt? Or that there would be such incidents as Wendell Hayes plowing his car into a tree after picking up Abner Haynes from the hospital the morning after a game?

—Or that middle linebacker Arch Matsos, stung by a demotion and angry over alleged mistreatment, would walk off the practice field and later be traded to San Diego in a deal that carried a season's worth of incredulity all by itself? Consider: Denver gives up Hewritt Dixon to Oakland in exchange for Matsos. Then the Broncs swap their No. 8 draft choice for rights to 38-year-old Tobin Rote, later released when aging muscles couldn't produce his performances of earlier years. Then Matsos is swapped to San Diego—and the Rote draft choice is wiped out. Net loss—one ballplayer.

—Or that Gilchrist would graciously—yes sir or madam, that's the exact word—agree to draw the winning ticket for the Cadillac Denver still owned as a residue from Gilchrist's contract?

Don't go away yet, we're just getting started.

Consider what the games themselves produced. Things such as:

—San Diego quarterback John Hadl catching one of his own passes and throwing it again when his original attempt was batted back.

—Bob Scarpitto, the daring gambler from Notre Dame, going 63 yards for a touchdown from punt formation while an unwitting San Diego player actually convoyed him partway.

—Gary Kroner's 46-yard field goal with 27 seconds left that beat Houston in the return game at Denver, or Al Denson's still unbelievable "rebound" catch of Max Choboian's pass to give Denver that 17-10 win at Boston in the final two seconds.

—Two kickoff returns for 100-yard touchdowns on successive weeks, the first by Goldie Sellers against Boston and the next against Kansas City by Nemiah Wilson.

—Four times throwing back Houston after the Oilers had first and goal at the one.

—An even dozen fumbles, six by each team in the rain at Boston.

—John Bramlett racing 72 yards with a blocked field goal to usher Denver past San Diego.

—The pass, interception, lateral, run, fumble, recovery, fumble and second recovery—all on the same play against Miami.

—The belligerence of the south stands following the 52-10 loss to Kansas City, or that fan who raced out and "captured" an Oakland Raider banner.

—The prominence of onside kicks, with Kansas City booting them twice in the closing minutes here, then Denver opening with one in a go-for-broke effort at Buffalo, and tacking on three more for a total of four in the game.

—Gene Mingo's attempted field goal from the 9-yard line hitting the left upright and bouncing harmlessly away, while Mike Eischeid suffered the same fate a week later when his 43-yard attempt at Oakland hit the crossbar and bounced back into the playing field.

There were other moments to report too. There was, for instance, the stunned embarrassment following Houston, with Mickey Slaughter staring sightlessly at a patch of sunlight on the floor of the air terminal as he waited for the plane next morning, or Speedie buying a toy skunk in the gift shop with a rueful smile.

Or there was the night before the Boston game when the wind and rain lashed the hotel room above the Charles River and Defensive Coach Marv Matuszak explained his side of the Matsos incident. And it is time—past time—to pay a reported debt and say the coaches were right in replacing Matsos as middle linebacker, Denver's defense was among the best in the league from the Boston game on.

Even the elements contributed. There was, of course, the rain and wind in Boston. Rain, snow and plunging temperatures greeted Denver in the Buffalo finale. And at San Diego, fog shrouded the airport just before takeoff time, grounding the Broncos for an extra night.

And, finally, there was the yeoman job Ray Malavasi did in not only regrouping the ball club but forging it into a respectable competitor.

Such a year produces victims. Malavasi and staff are among them. Surprisingly,

Don Smith, widely acknowledged as one of the best publicists in the league, also was a casualty as Saban moved to install his own organization.

Most amazing of all after such a season is the fact it ended, not on a burlesque theme of comedy and despair and ridicule, but on an optimistic note that, finally, things may have turned upward.

So, confess, neighbor and south standers, it was quite a year. There'll probably— hopefully—never be another like it.

❧   ❧   ❧

Floyd Little was Denver's first big star. He was the Broncos' top draft choice in 1967 and was the first number one to sign with the club. He played nine years, retiring after the 1975 season. He rushed for a total of 6,323 yards.

August 13, 1968, *Denver Post*
LITTLE SHUNS GRID REGIMEN

There are two things Denver Bronco halfback Floyd Little doesn't do before a game. One is sleep much. The other is eat much.

But dream?

Ah, that's an entirely different story, one that might give opposing coaches nightmares.

But let Floyd Little tell it, laughing as he recounts his pregame emotional buildup, but meaning every word.

"Do I sleep well the night before a game? No. There's no way. I may doze a little between 2 and 5 a.m., but every time I go to sleep, I find myself playing the game over in my dreams.

"And my opening dream is always the same. I return the kickoff all the way."

Always?

"It never fails. It even started a couple of days early for the Cincinnati game. I dreamed on Thursday. The guy tore my jersey off, but I still went all the way."

It's enough to put a blissful expression on the face of Head Coach Lou Saban.

Little's performance, although brief, didn't include any all-the-way kickoff returns as Denver beat Cincinnati 15-13, but it did cause smiles all around. Running with what would probably shape up as Denver's No. 1 unit in a first-quarter appearance, Little slashed through Bengal defenses for a five-yard average, gaining 30 yards on six carries, and made a 12-yard catch on a pass to keep a Denver drive going.

He showed power, speed—and perhaps more important as an indication of maturity in his second year as a pro—finesse at finding the right openings.

It was an active evening, the kind Little likes. "If I'm inactive, I lose weight. I often only eat one meal a day. I don't like to eat. I've always done that. If I stopped playing football tomorrow, I'd go down to 170 pounds (he weighs close to 200). I've got to play football and work to keep my weight up."

The one-meal-a-day schedule doesn't quite hold for football season, though he still eats far less than most gridders. A recent lunch session is a good example. While others heaped their plates from an excellent buffet, Little settled for a stuffed hot dog and cold drink.

Then a waitress came by and all but forced some ice cream on him.

"They take care of me," he grinned.

With Denver in a two-a-day workout schedule, and the first starting at 9:30 a.m., Little won't eat breakfast. A light lunch follows the morning workout. "By supper I'm too tired to eat much. Then I get hungry about 9 o'clock at night, but by then I'm in bed."

The schedule and menu, however, seem to make him thrive. Even not eating—anything—on game day. "I can't go that steak [pregame meal], even after the game. Sunday nights I'll maybe have a hamburger. I'm still too excited. But I'm hungry as hell on Mondays."

All this is not to say Little comes into any game gaunt and with circles under his eyes. Following much the same regimen, he became the first three-time All-American since Doak Walker, and showed steady progress as a pro last year. ...

October 27, 1968, *Denver Post*

BRISCOE USED TO HANDICAPS

In a world inhabited by white Gullivers, Marlin Briscoe is a black Lilliputian.

At 5-foot-10 and 178 pounds, he is regarded almost unanimously as too small to be a pro quarterback.

"Nobody looks through a man," the first black quarterback to start a major-league pro game retorts. "You don't look through his arms, either. You look between them, through the creases. So do quarterbacks 6-2 or 6-3. Steve [Tensi] is 6-5 and he can look over them."

Briscoe has been "looking through the creases" at obstacles all his life. His mother moved to Omaha with him and his sister, Beverly, now 21, when he was 4.

They have lived since in a project there. Briscoe used his modest bonus money to move his mother out of the project last summer. He also gave her his Volkswagen so she could get to her job as a cook at Omaha University with greater ease.

While he waited to begin his first season as a professional, he attended school in the mornings, then worked at three jobs the rest of the day that let him average just over five hours' sleep a night.

One was lugging 150-pound carcasses of beef in an Omaha packing house two or three nights a week from midnight to 7 a.m. "I thought I needed it to keep in shape."

When he could he was in a neighborhood park at 6 a.m. those late spring and summer days a few months back, running three miles a day and throwing footballs—he had two of them—endlessly at a tree for accuracy.

He is fully aware of his historic role in breaking the color line that has kept Negroes from the quarterback role in professional football. But he appreciates the fact Bronco coach Lou Saban has never referred to it. "I like that," he says, preferring to either make or not make it as an athlete, not some racial bellwether.

That doesn't mean he doesn't feel the extra weight, the eyes watching and people wondering, "Will he make it?"

Since his parents were divorced when he was a youngster, he grew up without a father until Al Caniglia, his coach at Omaha, became his confidant in late high school and college years. It was Caniglia, as an old friend, whom Briscoe called the night after Saban, at practice, told him, "Briscoe up. You're starting this week. Get yourself ready."

Briscoe's mouth went dry. It took him the rest of that Tuesday to accept the idea his chance had come and to shake the attack of nerves the news brought.

His starting debut, against Cincinnati, was neither distinguished nor disastrous. Three of the six times he inherited the ball he found his club pinned deep in its territory, once on the 8, again on the 13, areas where Saban said later the other club always comes harder.

Briscoe had no drop-back passes in his repertoire that day. And he was not allowed to call an audible. Both factors hampered him. Saban later said the restrictions were imposed to reduce the margin for error and keep Briscoe doing the things he does best. And Saban was pleased with the job he did. "He was under pressure and didn't crack. He didn't make any mistakes, no fumbles, no interceptions."

But even in the wake of a three-touchdown pass performance in a cause already long lost against San Diego, Briscoe's future as a pro quarterback is still an unresolved one as far as those close to the game are concerned. ...

Briscoe, for his part, shrugs. He has heard he couldn't do this or that for years. He was told he was too short to be a basketball player. He wound up an all-city performer with a 22-point average at South Omaha High.

He was told he couldn't play football. He wound up in the annual high school Shrine game, the choice as a starting quarterback of a coach who had his own all-stater sitting on the bench, watching. Briscoe piloted his underdog team to a 19-6 upset of an opponent with an All-State backfield that included one prep All-American.

At Omaha U., he finished a glittering career lauded as the greatest quarterback that school ever produced. ...

But his long-range potential is still to be proven. He has shown promise. He cannot, however, do anything about his size. And there is considerable difference between promise and fulfillment of that promise. It is extremely unfair to increase pressure by expecting too much at this point.

The question would seem to be whether he can find the creases to this latest obstacle.

November 2, 1970, *Denver Post*

PAIN GOES WITH GLORY

Somebody else buttons the collar. You can't raise your hands high enough because the ribs ache too much. Your tie drops to the floor, and it's a major project to pick it up.

A Band-aid covers the stitches over your eye. On the plane home, you can't eat. You're too exhausted. And you can't sleep. Same reason.

So you just sit there and listen to the rush of the little air vent overhead and keep your eyes closed and let the plane conversation drift over you, and you feel where the New Orleans tackle planted his helmet on one play, and that spot on the ribs where the Atlanta linebacker got you the week before, and the hand you had padded but that is throbbing now even with the pain pills dulling it some.

And the worst of it is you know it will be worse in the morning.

It will wake you when you roll in your sleep. And, if you're a veteran lineman with a lot of seasons behind you, it can be so bad your wife will have to get out of her side of the bed and come around and lift your legs out because, on Mondays until later in the morning, you can't do it yourself. Sometimes, then, you figure this is a helluva way to make a living. And you are sure of it later in the week, sitting on the training table with the little film of sweat beginning to break out just under your hairline as the doctor leaves two needles sticking up out of the skin on your shoulder while he changes syringes to inject cortisone and relieve the inflammation.

Or you sit in the fog outside the terminal in San Diego one night when the plane can't take off, your leg straight out in front of you and the crutches leaning against the low wall you're sitting on, and because you've already played a half dozen years, you know this one could end it.

It can be worse if you're not a starter, because then, by the time you're back, they may have found somebody better or just as good and you no longer figure. That kind of hurt can be even more painful—like a quarterback has when he can't let his kids go to the game and hear what they yell at him, or when the kids come home from kindergarten and ask, "Daddy, you're not really a bum, are you?" Or the awful lost moment of a cornerback at the instant he knows he's been had for a touchdown and everybody else knows it, too.

Or you come into the terminal after a losing flight home and look for your wife and spot her standing white-faced between two fans carrying signs telling you to get lost. Or maybe it's gotten so bad your wife doesn't come to the airport anymore. And at the home stadium you can hear what they yell at you but you just stare ahead and trot quickly into the dressing room.

The glamour is all there. The adulation, the good money, the travel, the feeling of hearing the fans count down the final seconds on a winning afternoon when you know all that week was worth it. But the needles are there too, the frustration, the humiliation of the actual incidents above.

They've happened to someone over the past few years, but they won't show up in any Monday statistics. ...

☙   ☙   ☙

Lou Saban resigned as head coach with four games left in the 1971 season. John Ralston was hired to replace him in early 1972. For four or five years, Ralston took the team to Pomona, California, for six weeks of training camp. Of course, the writers went along.

RALSTON STRICT ON SCHEDULES

John Ralston is big on schedules. Very big. Figures such as 3:13 to 3:27 show up on his daily practice list, and 3:13 and 3:27 it is, by God. Or by Ralston.

On the road, 4:20, 10 p.m. and 11 a.m. are big numbers. The first is when Ralston likes to arrive in a city. The second is the time for the ice cream social on Saturday night. And the third is departure time from the hotel to the stadium.

Unlike the Lou Saban regime, Ralston times his road trips, not for a consistent departure, but for a consistent arrival. Saban always left at noon. Always. It made no difference whether the club flew east and lost two hours or west and gained one. It was noon. And off tackle.

Ralston, instead, times arrival. Flying east to Cincinnati Saturday, for instance, the club left at noon and touched down at 4:15. Going to San Diego two weeks ago, they left at 3 p.m. By Ralston's figuring, arriving somewhere between 4 and 4:30 gives his club just enough time to get to the hotel, get through the routine jam at elevators, find their rooms and get unpacked before the rest of the Saturday routine.

Ralston doesn't want the players to have too much idle time. The late afternoon arrival, a half-hour bus ride to the hotel and settling in gives them just enough time for a leisurely dinner. Yet they still can get back in time for Ralston's 1972 command performance, the Ice Cream Social.

C'mon now. No snickering. Just because, mmf, mmf, you get those, hee hee, mental pictures of a 260-pounder nibbling at a chocolate sundae, and you keep getting other images of Joe Namath and his system of relaxing the night before a game.

There's method to the marble fudge. First, it's not just ice cream. There are sandwiches, cold cuts, soft drinks, other goodies for a satisfying snack before heading for bed. And bed's the other purpose—the social gets everyone back in time to make Ralston's 11 p.m. curfew.

Saban had no curfews. Ralston does. Troops are due in their rooms and there's a bed check. Denver even has one at home on Saturday nights—Ralston puts the whole club up at a motel the night before a home game, and has the ice cream social and all.

It beats the Houston Method. Bill Peterson likes to bring movies along, and everybody attends. The night before the Denver game to open the season, they all sat there on hard straight-backed chairs in a rented ballroom at the hotel and relaxed by watching the 15-year-old film "Stalag 17."

They played like it the next afternoon, then Peterson, on the flight home, refused to let 'em have the traditional two-beer ration. He also shut off all card playing or reading. He's a hard loser, that Peterson.

Peterson so intimidated Houston, the Oilers went out and lost the next week 34-13. I haven't heard what he did on the flight home from Miami after that one, but it must have included throwing a couple of players off over the Gulf of Mexico. Last Sunday, the Oilers upset Namath and the Jets.

It was either fear of Peterson or Namath was insufficiently relaxed.

October 23, 1972, *Denver Post*
JOHNSON DROPS BOMBS ON OAKLAND

OAKLAND—The soggy turf at Oakland Coliseum didn't exactly part for him Sunday, but Charley Johnson still led Denver out of 10 years of captivity by the Oakland Raiders.

The 12-year veteran used his own right arm as the magic staff, throwing for the equivalent of nearly four football fields as he and Floyd Little ended a decade of frustration at Oakland's hands with a 30-23 victory.

Legs swathed from heels to hips to protect the healed hurts of his trade, Johnson was a precise executioner as he completed 20 of 28 attempts for 361 yards and two touchdowns.

Little, netting just 15 yards rushing, demonstrated his incredible versatility as he caught one touchdown, set up another and threw for yet a third. ...

Denver hadn't beaten Oakland anywhere since a 23-6 win here almost 10 years ago—Oct. 14, 1962. (That doesn't include an exhibition Denver victory at North Platte, Neb., in 1967.)

September 22, 1975, *Denver Post*
NFL DULLSVILLE? NOT IN 37-33 BRONCO VICTORY

So much for the dull, stereotyped monotony of NFL football.

The Denver Broncos Sunday outlasted the Kansas City Chiefs 37-33 in a game that consumed three hours and 10 minutes, 70 points, 737 yards, nine sacks, a blocked field goal, a blocked PAT, a punt on the run, a 90-yard touchdown, a 69-yard touchdown, a touchdown-off-a-fumble-off-a-statue-of-liberty, two interceptions, five fumbles, two broken helmets and everything else except a partridge in a pear tree.

"I'm speechless, Denver's Coach John Ralston said afterward.

"I'm smokin' this cigar so hard I got a hernia," a Kansas City writer gasped in the press box during the seemingly endless second-half switches in momentum.

In the end, the turning point probably arrived only when Denver's Charley Johnson fell on the ball with 10 seconds left and the Chiefs out of time-outs.

Nobody left early. At the finish, the same stadium-record 51,858 fans (there were 345 no-shows) who began the sun-washed day were there, hoarse and disbelieving and trying to remember what the score had been at halftime. ...

☙   ☙   ☙

All the Connor kids were big Floyd Little fans. When Mike was in first grade, he asked Dick to give Floyd one of his school pictures. Dick reluctantly did. Who could say no to Mike? Years later, after he retired, Little opened his wallet and showed Dick Mike's picture. Little said he raised a few eyebrows by telling questioners that the little boy was "his nephew."

Floyd Little played his last game for the Denver Broncos, or for any team, Dec. 14, 1975. Reams of copy were written about him and his career. In those

days, the Connors had two tickets to each home game. I attended all of them. The children took turns going with me. It was Sharon's turn that Sunday. At 14, she had followed Little's career since she was 5. Sharon is a big football fan. Although the day was bitterly cold and snowing, and the majority of the 37,080 fans had left, she insisted on staying until Little left the field for the last time. The Broncos won that game 25-10 against Philadelphia, but they couldn't salvage a 6-8 season.

The following best summarizes Little's style as a player and a man.

December 14, 1975, *Denver Post*
THE DAY LOU SABAN FIRED FLOYD

Floyd Little's National Football League career in Denver was almost a two-year one.

"He fired me, right there on the sideline," Little said of former coach Lou Saban's reaction to a critical Little fumble against Buffalo in 1968. Denver seemingly had won the game, only to have Little lose the ball trying to run a sweep to kill the clock. Buffalo recovered, and only a saving tackle by Little prevented a touchdown runback. Instead, the Bills settled for a field goal and apparent victory.

Then, in what Little now describes as the single play he'd most like to be remembered for, this happened:

"I came off the field after the fumble, and Lou was yelling at Fred Gehrke, 'I want him out of here! I want him out! Now! Send him in!'

"I started walking to the dressing room and got down to the 20-yard line on the south end, and thought, 'Hell, no.' Fran Lynch was in with the offense. I was at the 20 on the south side. They were huddling at the 20 on the north side.

"I ran on the field, right past the bench with Lou yelling 'No, get out, get off, you're through. Go take a shower.' I got to the huddle and told Fran to go off. He looked at the side and Lou was yelling to stay in. Poor Fran didn't know what to do, but he finally just trotted off."

Bronco fans know the rest: Little literally begged quarterback Marlin Briscoe "to throw it as far as he could. I didn't care how long it was, I'll be there and get it." He did, setting up a game-retrieving field goal by Bob Howfield.

"At the end, when it was over, I ran in the dressing room. Later, Lou was talking to you guys in the press and I walked by him and said, 'Coach, I'm sorry.'

"He looked at me and said, 'You've got one more week.' Then he smiled. 'He's beautiful,' He always said, 'My friend, as long as I've got a job, you've got a job.'"

Little's other most memorable plays include three touchdowns against Minnesota, driving San Francisco cornerback Bruce Taylor into the end zone to give Denver a go-ahead touchdown, and a long punt return against the New York Jets here that set up an upset.

"But the big one was Buffalo the day he fired me."

❧   ❧   ❧

John Ralston "resigned" after the 1976 season, even though he gave Denver its first three winning seasons, including nine wins against five losses in '76. His demise came after a player "revolt." Robert "Red" Miller was hired the next month. He would take the Broncos to the Super Bowl in his first year as head coach.

December 5, 1977, *Denver Post*
MILLER FINALLY SAYS IT: "PLAYOFFS"

They were 35,000 feet and 400 air miles from Denver when it happened.

Dumas, Texas, was sliding beneath the wing of the airliner when the Denver Broncos became champions of the American Football Conference West.

"Time has run out," the announcer said, and bedlam broke loose in the aft cabin, where players hugged, grabbed each other, shouted and tried to comprehend the fact that, after 17 years, 11 weeks and some 18-plus hours, the Denver Broncos were title winners.

It was 6:12 p.m. CST, and Denver was seven miles above the sagebrush of north Texas. Braniff had arranged to pipe the closing minutes of Oakland's game with Los Angeles over the cabin intercom, and when the Raiders' stranglehold on the AFC West ended, bedlam broke loose.

"Playoffs," Coach Red Miller shouted, uttering the word he has carefully avoided all fall. "I want to talk playoffs!"

"Champions," his team yelled back. ...

⍦   ⍦   ⍦

Red Miller was replaced as head coach by Dan Reeves in February 1981 when Edgar Kaiser Jr., a Canadian, bought the Broncos from Denverites Gerry and Allan Phipps. Miller never got back to the Super Bowl. Dick left the *Denver Post* in August 1982 for similar reasons. The paper had been sold to the Times Mirror Corporation, publishers of the *Los Angeles Times*, among others. New management at both institutions wanted their own people in key positions. Dick was also told that his "style" did not suit the new owners, who wanted a more aggressive, slashing-type columnist. He was offered the sports column at the *Rocky Mountain News*, where he remained until October 1988, when Chuck Green of the *Denver Post* lured him back.

Another Canadian, Pat Bowlen, purchased the team from Edgar Kaiser, Jr. in 1984. Bowlen kept Dan Reeves as head coach and the two took the Broncos to three Super Bowls—no Super wins—during the next nine years. Reeves was fired in December 1992 and was almost immediately hired as head coach of the New York Giants. Reeves delivered one of the eulogies at Dick's funeral on Jan. 5, 1993.

October 21, 1986, *Rocky Mountain News*
THIS WAS NOT A LOSS, IT WAS AN EMBARRASSMENT

EAST RUTHERFORD, N.J.—Look at the bright side. The second half was mercifully played to darkened sets all over the Eastern Seaboard.

And some genius once decreed a football game lasts only 60 minutes.

Anything longer would have been inhumane. Watching the Broncos the first 30 minutes last night was like one of those squirming moments at some banquet when the main speaker forgets not only his lines but the resason he's up on the podium.

We'll not even try to get into the second half, even if it housed the few respectable moments the Broncos brought east with them.

They were passless, runless, defenseless and puntless. Does that miss anything? Is there anything else down there under the debris of a 22-10 defeat that needs to be taken out and buried? Shouldn't "ill-prepared" be on the list, as well, for a team that seemed baffled the whole half by what was happening to it?

Given the time (Monday night, no World Series), the place (The Meadowlands, snuggled up against Manhattan across the Hudson) and the circumstances (6-0, the only undefeated team left, against the 5-1 Jets), it was the most humiliating half in memory.

It's the second time in the history of the franchise that a Bronco team has jumped off to a 6-0 start. The first was the launching pad to New Orleans and Super Bowl XII. But Super XII is the last time a Broncos team with this kind of national stage and stakes looked as miserably inept as the one that stumbled like August exhibition losers through the opening half and into a 22-0 deficit.

When John Elway wasn't being pursued and herded like some hapless steer, his receivers were dropping the ball, he was missing them on the run or the Jets were snuffing all the life from a running game that has averaged 159 yards the last four games.

When the Jets had the ball, they played keepaway on marches of 12, 10 and 14 plays for 5:57, 5:31 and 8:06. Denver got it so rarely it seemed baffled about what to do when it did. It's the kind of total domination 6-0 teams aren't supposed to absorb.

Mark Gastineau could tap dance and raise his fists and taunt and cheerlead. He also had to rest, exhausted from chasing Elway in the course of a night that may linger as a festering sore come playoff time. ...

At Giants Stadium last night, the Jets left laughing, and Denver left grateful that what happened could cause them no more than one blemish on a season that could still be exceptional—but never again perfect.

September 1, 1988, Rocky Mountain News

STEALING SIGNALS NOT AS EASY AS IT LOOKS

Remember "I Spy," the old adventure comedy starring Robert Culp and Bill Cosby? It's still seen on cable occasionally.

A version is coming to your friendly NFL arena this Sunday.

Spying, in fact, may become the next growth industry in the shoulder pad trade. With so many teams wigwagging both offensive and defensive signals from the sideline, there has been a parallel growth in what the spy novels call "tradecraft."

It's not new, of course. Spying is as old as plays and practice. Maybe older. It's just taking on a higher-tech gloss.

"I've tried to steal offensive signals," Denver defensive guru Joe Collier conceded earlier this summer. "That usually drives you nuts. Like the Seattle Seahawks. They have come in and filmed me. They have had a guy with a video camera aimed only at me, and they'll match it up with the defense, on film.

"In other words, they'll have 10 plays in a row, and they'll pick the first 10 plays and match up my signals with the defense they see."

He looked contentedly over the practice field. "It doesn't do any good. We've tried it, tried to get the other team's offense."

Seattle? Seahawk spies in the sky? Could it be so? On a team with human temples of moral fitness such as Brian Haircut? Try to get an edge through technology?

"We don't do it," Dan Reeves said yesterday. "We have ways to offset it but I'm not going to tell you what they are. Besides, you've still got to stop the play." Knowing the pitcher is planning a 97-mile-an-hour fastball isn't going to make a .230 hitter feel a whole lot better, in other words.

But there are times, places, spots in a game where such information would be helpful. It would be nice, for example, to know a blitz is planned, or a sweep to the left is coming, or a draw play.

Watch Collier this Sunday. He'll be the one wearing a color scheme different from any others. It allows for quick identification. Watch his actions. They are those of a man afflicted with plague, rashes, swarming insects or tight underwear. It is these arm movements that tell Karl Mecklenburg what to call. It is these on which enemy cameras focus, seeking answers.

To anyone's knowledge, only the Oilers have actually bragged about using such espionage to win a game. Back in Bum Phillips' days, when Earl Campbell was their offense, Campbell was out. The Oilers were in San Diego for a playoff game with the then high-powered Chargers.

Underdog Houston intercepted five passes, drove Dan Fouts and Don Coryell nuts and won 17-14 in 1979. Somehow, the whispers ran, they had cracked the code.

"That's the only time I've ever heard anybody actually say they did," says Collier, a veteran of 28 AFL-NFL seasons. "We've had some teams try to do it, but I don't think any have succeeded. Seattle is a team that tries. There was one other, but I can't remember which one it was. There are coaches on the other staffs that know my signals. Myrel [Moore, linebacker coach] went out to the Raiders from here. He knew my signals as good as I know them."

Collier hasn't changed some of his signals in years, but it doesn't bother him. Certainly, he agrees, other teams know them by now.

"Probably. See, there are things you can do. You watch the huddle. I have one of the coaches watch the offensive huddle. And if they've got a guy with his head up, out of the huddle, either watching me or watching his sideline, getting a relay, then you can tell if they are trying to pick them up.

"If everybody's head is down in the huddle, you know they aren't. But as soon as you see in the early part of the game that one of the players is standing up watching me, or watching one of his coaches to get a relay, then I know they are doing it."

The games within games begin. "So what I do is wait. I just wait. Pretty soon, they have to go. They have to get the play called. The clock's against them, not us. It's in our favor. They risk a delay of game. So I just wait until the guy can't watch me anymore. Then I give the signal."

And just in case, he may give two or three, only one of which is a "live" one. "You give dummy signals. If I give a front, when we go out I'll say, 'Okay, this series, the second one's live. The first one's a dummy.'"

So was the NFL advance man who visited the camp of an upcoming opponent and somehow got a glimpse of a practice. It stunned him. Time after time, the team ran a flanker reverse, and the flanker pulled up and threw a pass.

"No, no," he shouted to his coach over the phone as soon as he got back to the hotel. "They were really working on that play."

The worried coach made some calls, and finally called his advance man back.

"You bleeping idiot," he screamed. "That was defense day for them. They were stressing defense, and that flanker reverse pass? That's OUR play, you blockhead. They were getting ready for us!"

April 16, 1989, *Denver Post*

HOW TO CONDUCT A BASIC BRONCO DRAFT

I don't know about you, but I think all this stuff in the paper and on the egoblab shows misses the point. They are talking and writing on too high a level when it comes to telling the Denver Broncos how to go about conducting their drafts a week from today.

They talk foot speed, and agility, and competitive nature, and pedigrees, and drafting for position instead of need.

Based on Denver's recent drafts, I really think this is too advanced for them. I think what they really need is for someone to take them through the basics, step by step. Learn to walk before you run. That sort of thing. A refresher course in fundamentals.

I'm fully aware that draftniks are almost as bad as baseball rotisserie league fanatics. Why, the Broncos' own publicist, Jim Saccomano, used to be one of the worst. I think he's since taken the cure at Betty Ford's Clinic for Statistical Abusers. But there was a point when he and John Glover, who is the press box announcer at Broncos' games, used to team up each spring to predict the Broncos' draft.

This, you should know, was before Saccomano worked for the Broncos. He was working for the Denver Bears at that time, back when the Bears were the Bears and not some wimpy, windy, substitute nickname.

Glover would corner me on the steps of St. Anne's Church in Arvada and ask me what I thought about some obscure tackle from Florida State even before the echoes of the morning's sermon had stoped bouncing around my mind. I was still thinking of St. Augustine, and all of a sudden I would confuse things and find myself wondering what the good saint used to do in the 40-yard dash and what he could bench-press.

So, this morning, I think it is time to forget all the esoteric stuff. We'll not open any of the dozens of draft books now circulating, and fergawdsake don't listen to the radio. Just say a prayer for the braindead.

What we're going to do today is address the fundamental reason Denver has messed up. It has gone away from the basics, that's why, let itself get distracted as I used to be when Glover would break that sublime trance on Sunday mornings. (It could also be I was just waking up, but that's another story.)

Anyway, if Denver is to succeed this year, it has to stick to these goals:

—Gender. It should draft a male. I know, this will raise howls from the feminists among us, but there it is. Research has proven that males tend to come in bigger sizes, and this is a crying need out there at 5800 Logan St.

—Life. Somewhere in all its measuring and poking and evaluating, the Denver scouting staff should make absolutely certain its No. 1 draft choice has all the required vital signs. It should be alive. There have been times in the past questions have come up about this.

—Agility. We are not talking ballet here. Just simple mechanical things, like not trying to move both feet at the same time while walking. Especially in opposite directions. Good scouting staffs can often spot this skill, and Dan Reeves should insist his crack cadre of scouts and the like make this a key requirement.

—Some speed. Faster than a speeding bullet is probably too much to expect, considering where Denver will choose in the opening round. But archaeologists should not be able to time the next Denver choice by the carbon-dating method, or by measuring the depth of the moss that has grown on its north side during 40-yard timing. It needn't be faster than the speed of light, just faster than Daylight Saving Time. If it starts the 40 in daylight, it should finish in daylight. The same daylight. It's these little things Denver has forgotten.

—Intelligence. Life forms come in many variations, as we all learned years ago on "Star Trek." The amoeba is a life form, but few teams with successful programs have made it the bedrock of building for the future. The ability to distinguish orange from other hues is pretty critical, though. And it should be able to tell Sunday from the other days of the week.

—Adaptability. Whatever the choice, it should be capable of fitting the role expected of it. The Broncos have occasionally strayed from this elemental fact. Say, for example, Denver drafts a defensive lineman. Many in the business think such a choice should be bigger than a breadbox, and should have arms that actually extend outward from the shoulder in order to ward off offensive linemen that would seek to block it. Or, let's say it is going to be used as a runner. There is a widely held belief on other teams that it should at least be faster than those who are chasing it. Many of them also hold to the revolutionary concept that it be as big.

The basics. That's the thing. Stick to them and you'll be okay.

Oh, one more. The draft will be held next Sunday. Somebody be sure and tell them.

ELWAY'S STREET PLAY, A THING OF BEAUTY

The whole stadium is stretched like a rubber band at the breaking point. Wind is hurling debris across the grass, fans are howling and an early winter night is already dropping the temperature.

And down on the grass, John Elway stuffs his hands under Keith Kartz' rump and glances at the defensive linemen, one in particular.

"HUT ONE!" he shouts over the din. "HUT TWO!" Then, "HUUUT THREE!" It's the "HUUUT" before the "THREE" that now makes Elway a graduate quarterback, one of the NFL's best, only a Super Bowl win away from all but certain Hall of Fame credentials.

"HUUUT THREE" and a defensive lineman lunges too soon, and Elway knows he has created that most dreaded of NFL defensive situations:

He's got himself what he calls "a street play, like you used to have when you played in the street and everything is breaking down and you run around looking for somebody."

Nobody is better at it. Elway runs, Vance Johnson or Mark Jackson or Ricky Nattiel runs deep and a huge gain soars through the wind in a no-risk situation. Elway is turning it into an art form.

Seven years ago, on a balmy San Diego Sunday afternoon, he couldn't even find the right rump. He lined up behind a very startled Tom Glassic, who murmured, "Next one, John," and the rookie quarterback sheepishly shifted one set of buns to the right.

Now, Elway is the NFL's master at drawing opponents offside in critical third down situations. It's the "free down" syndrome, the one with the flag already in the air, a defender caught in no man's land, and the football in Elway's hands. Either he completes a key pass or the Broncos get a free five yards.

"Nobody does it as well," says Chan Gailey, Denver's offensive coordinator. "They all try to copy John. Everybody is trying to copy John now." Even Gary Kubiak, Elway's backup. Kubiak caught the Washington Redskins on the same tactic at a tender point in Denver's Monday night victory.

"You don't see his head bobbing or the shoulders twitch or some of the things other quarterbacks try," says linebacker coach Mike Nolan. "It's voice inflection," Gailey confirms. "And knowing when to use it. Now, he can feel when he's got a guy leaning. He can almost feel when he's got a guy set up for it. He uses it on longer yardage when he wants to pick up half of it for sure, or maybe take a free play. Or when we've got third and four.

"It's gotten to the point where some teams now will sit on third and four."

And the pass rush is a step slow even if they don't jump offside. Gailey doesn't have ready numbers for the times Elway has completed a long pass with a yellow flag already down on the grass next to him, a reminder that no matter what happens, it will happen for Denver.

"I can't even imagine. It would be awesome. Scary. It would scare other people to know what that total is," Gailey agrees. "Even now, they sit back on their haunches. He has made some big, big plays that way."

Watch today, in the Los Angeles Coliseum. It will come, if it does, later in the game. Defenders are more primed for it by then, especially if things are close and a pass rush is needed.

"I'm always thinking about it," Elway says. "You do different things throughout the game to set people up to get them when you do need it. You might need a crucial third and four or something. You've always got that in your bag. A lot of times, I can feel a guy. I can tell when he's getting off the ball real well. They think they have my rhythm down. Then, when you get them, not only do you get five yards but all of a sudden it slows the rush down."

Gailey says Elway knows from the early part of the week whether or not a team is vulnerable. "We'll go into the week, and he'll say, 'Oh, I'll get these guys two or three times.'"

Then it's street time. Go deep. Throw hard. Laugh a lot when it works. Avoid the fireplug on the corner.

January 11, 1990, *Denver Post*

FANS CAN'T STAND ANOTHER "SUPER" LOSS

I don't know how to tell you this, Mr. Elway, but Denver right now is a city full of closets. Isn't that what you said about Broncos fans hoping you lose Sunday if winning means another Super Bowl embarrassment?

It's strange. A dozen years ago, people were naming babies Haven and Otis and Craig and Randy. They were painting their homes orange, and in hospital nurseries, newborns were being wrapped in orange and blue receiving blankets. A sort of civic euphoria gripped the whole region. Denver was going to its first Super Bowl.

Now, in closets all over the area, the mood is one of conditional dread.

Only three years ago, a young woman rode naked on a white horse on a downtown street to get a pair of tickets to the AFC championship game. (We're not making this up, understand. It's history.)

Now, they are burning incense and chanting a strange new mantra: "Don't win if ... Don't win if ... Don't win if ..."

"Enjoy it," a bemused Pittsburgh quarterback, Terry Bradshaw, said a dozen years ago in the Steelers locker room after Denver had won its first ever playoff game. "Enjoy all this. It will never be quite the same again."

A couple of hundred thousand burghers lined downtown streets for a parade—before the Broncos left for New Orleans.

"God," the nice lady from the Denver District Attorney's office was saying at the Press Club bar this week. "I hope they don't win. I don't want to go through all that again."

It's a plea being repeated in bars and offices and living rooms all over the metro area.

"Not again." But it's not the going that bothers them, you see. The going is fun. It's the coming back. They're a little tired of finding all those hopes sticking out the earholes of a badly dented helmet.

Go ahead. Go next door. Ask your neighbor: Should Denver win Sunday?

You'd get a more positive response if you asked if they wanted Rocky Flats to burn atomic waste and let the residue drift across the city.

This may be the first time in athletic history that a city wakes up rooting against its team advancing to a championship duel. The reason isn't hard to find.

It's summed up in three sets of numbers: Dallas 27, Denver 10; New York 39, Denver 20; and Washington 42, Denver 10. Three times now, Denver residents have been asked to play Linus to the Broncos' Lucy. Three times, they've revved their emotions up to a final game only to have the locals snatch success away with a humiliatingly flawed afternoon.

They've done it in exotic ways, twisting the knife. The Dallas Cowboys fumbled their first play from scrimmage in the Superdome in 1978, but recovered. A Dallas punt caromed off an unsuspecting Denver helmet. Receivers who hadn't fumbled all season double-dribbled off the carpet. For the first—and still only—time, two defenders were named co-MVPs.

In 1987, Denver built a 10-7 lead and washed up to a first down on the Giants' 1-yard line—and came away with nothing. The Giants came out in the second half and ran out of punt formation on their own side of the 50 and made the yardage. Phil Simms enjoyed a career passing day.

In 1988, Denver scored on the first play from scrimmage, added a field goal and then dropped a pass that would have stretched things to 17-0. The football world was theirs. Nothing else went right the rest of the day. The Redskins frolicked to a 35-point second quarter that may never be equalled. Doug Williams and Timmy Smith enjoyed career days.

Enough, they cry. *No mas.* And you wonder why? The family scrapbook isn't exactly packed with happy, treasured memories, is it?

"If they go to New Orleans, they better not come back if they lose," the lady from the DA's office snarled, echoing the feelings of many Denverites.

Know this: There will be no losing parades in 1990. Unless, of course, they are accompanied by tar, feathers and appropriate torchlight ceremonies.

April 25, 1990, *Denver Post*

Draft Tuesdays can be interesting

I love Tuesdays best on draft week. Oh, sure. Sundays, Dan Reeves and all the television anchor types wear coats and ties and the radio folk and the draftniks sit around with six draft books by "experts" and pooh-pooh the draft calls made by the teams which have spent a collective $65 billion trillion to compile their own books. And who have to live with them.

And the food is good. No doubt, Sunday is glamour day.

Monday, the players for some reason all sound more interesting than the ones taken on Sunday. Theoretically, Sunday's players are supposed to be better. But to listen to coaches around the league, the wonder of all wonders is that "this guy slipped all the way down here to the seventh round. Don't know. Can't tell you why. We're just glad he did."

By Monday, Reeves is in a golf shirt. TV guys don't go out to the camp on Monday. The food is passable.

Ah, but Tuesday is Revelation Day. Tuesday is when the club brings all the choices to town. "Live," as one ego-swollen TV type told a murder investigation team recently.

Tuesday is when we discover that BYU's Clay Brown, drafted second in 1981, has his arm in a cast. Nobody knew when they drafted him. The coaches walk the hallways cautiously. The scouts have an even lighter tread. Reeves' face has the look of a thunderstorm building. Tuesday is when Ted Gregory (1988) walks into the auditorium and everybody takes another look. Wasn't he, uh, supposed to be taller? Bigger? Reeves' face is taking on its thunderstorm look again.

Tuesday is fascinating. It's the day Carl Wafer (No. 2, 1974) discloses he has bad feet. It hurts to walk. You will not find him on Denver's list of everyone who ever played for the Broncos. Mr. Wafer did not play a regular season down.

All of this leads to yesterday. A Tuesday, if the calendar is correct. And to the suspicion that not all Tuesday discoveries have to be bad ones. Denver, for example, may have reversed a recent trend when it acquired Shannon Sharpe of tiny Division II Savannah (Ga.) State. He is 6-2, weighs 225, has the upper body of a linebacker, caught 40 touchdown passes in his career and has the grasping hands of an IRS agent. When Denver found him to notify him it had drafted him, he was in the weight room.

Aha, you say. Small school. Small-time. True. But he played big-time, setting the number of records a big fish in a small pond should set. And when he played good teams, like national champion Georgia Southern, he responded by catching nine passes for 202 yards and a stadium record 91-yard touchdown. "Son," bristly Georgia Southern coach Erk Russell said afterward, "I can't believe there's a better receiver in the nation."

And, when Sharpe got to the postseason all-star games, he proved he belonged. "I wanted to destroy the myth," he said yesterday at the Broncos' camp. The myth is that big guys from little schools can't make it. Sharpe was a Prop 48 victim coming out of high school, where he actually had better offers for track and basketball. But his brother, one Sterling Sharpe of Green Bay, led the NFL in receptions last year, and Shannon had idolized his older brother. So it was to be football, and Savannah State.

"I could have gone to a Division I school after my sophomore year, but I felt Savannah had taken a chance on me and I owed them something," he says. Loyalty. It's a quality that doesn't show up on draft specs. Maybe it should.

Speed? Well, maybe we're getting to the part why he lasted to the seventh round. When the combines tested him at Indianapolis, he had just come off a severe bout with the flu. "I had lost nine pounds. I ran a 4.65."

Numbers like that take on biblical proportions in NFL scouting projections, even when, as Sharpe reports, the next week he ran a series of 40-yard dashes, all of them under 4.6.

Denver hasn't had a good, big receiver since Steve Watson retired. It hasn't had a good, big burner at the spot since Al Denson and his 4.3 clockings of the 1960s. It has turned instead to what Detroit coach Mouse Davis delicately refers to as (——)ants. Little, darting, swift pass catchers. Michael Young began to break the mold a year ago.

"You run 4.3, you run it in a straight line," says Sharpe. "But across the middle, maybe you just run it 4.8. I run 4.6 the whole pattern."

And he has Watson-type hands.

He also has a chance. It's just a Tuesday hunch.

November 14, 1990, *Denver Post*

FRICTION NOT FICTION BETWEEN REEVES, ELWAY

It's time. It's past time. At 3-6 and hope of another playoff just a faint smudge on the 1990 horizon, John Elway is about to assume a different role with the Denver Broncos.

He is, he said in an exclusive interview this week, going to assume the burden of talking to Dan Reeves on the players' behalf.

"I think I'm going to have to express my opinions as from the player level. I'm going to have to go to Dan. And I'm going to have to go ... they may not like what I have to say. But I'm going to give it to them and they can take it for what it is worth.

"I think, for what I want to do and where I want us to go, we've got to make some things happen.

"We've got to get the attitude changed. Dan's got to hear it from the players' level."

The long-rumored friction between Reeves and Elway is not fiction, the Denver quarterback admitted. This year, in fact, for whatever reason or combination of reasons, it has gotten worse.

"This year has been the worst. We hardly talk to each other unless it's game time."

That's inexcusable. Here are two proud, gifted, intelligent men. They are almost unhealthily competitive, and that's part of the problem. Liking each other has never been a requirement between a head coach and his quarterback. Chuck Noll and Terry Bradshaw never traded Christmas cards. But each cashed four Super Bowl championship checks. Bernie Kosar and Marty Schottenheimer weren't bosom pals. But only Denver—and Elway and Reeves—kept them from two Super Bowls.

So if Elway going to Reeves somehow results in an air-clearing confrontation, good. What's to lose, at this point?

Leadership is one of the most glaring lacks on the 1990 Broncos. Elway has never been a vocal type. Nobody else has assumed that role. He leads by performance, a la 17 late-game comebacks to victory in his career. Defensively, the team desperately needs a Tommy

Jackson type, an emotional fire-starter, gut-turner, eye-blazer. There isn't one. When Jackson retired a few seasons back, the fire left their bellies.

Elway thinks that, too, is not an accident.

"Age has become such a big deal around here we're cutting good football players to keep youth. It ends up biting us in the rear end." He cites the 49ers, who acquired the likes of Matt Millen (Raiders), Fred Smerlas (Buffalo) and Jim Burt (Giants).

The tension between Reeves and Elway is not one-sided, the veteran quarterback acknowledges. "I know I'm not easy. It's not all his fault. I'm not easy. I'm a competitor. I feel like I've been in the league long enough to know what I feel comfortable with."

Things have unraveled with almost lightning rapidity since Denver, totally dominating, saw a victory slip away at Buffalo in a 77-second span when the Bills scored 20 points. Including that one, Denver has lost five of six games, and the losing is part of the whole scenario at the moment.

Some of the things Elway sees were there a year ago, but they were overlooked as the wins piled up and Denver went to the Super Bowl. Winning soothes, losing opens every tiny scratch into a wound.

"We need continuity," Elway said. "Hell, I've only been here eight years, and there are only five guys left on the team from then. Kenny Lanier, Dennis Smith, Karl Mecklenburg, Gary Kubiak and Sammy Winder. That's it.

"I don't care if you use the part about more friction between Dan and me," he said, after first saying he preferred it be kept off the record. "If he wants to confront me about it it's probably better anyway. Because if I don't do it now I'll do it at the end of the year, anyway.

"I've got to go in and give the views of the team. I've got to be the guy that goes and says, 'Hey, this is what's going on with the team. This is my opinion. Now, you're not going to like it, but this is my opinion.'"

Elway needs to say such things. Reeves needs to listen. He has not taken this team to three Super Bowls in four years by being a bad coach. He is one of the league's best, just as Elway is among its quarterback elite. But the two of them spending a year not communicating is not the formula for correcting Denver's calamitous slide.

Reeves always has viewed himself as a players' coach. It's a role he filled admirably as a Dallas assistant, bridging the gap between players and Tom Landry. He was shocked here in 1984 when veteran corner Louis Wright went into his office and told him his methods were about to cause him to lose the team. Elway's current feelings are no doubt going to cause an equal jolt.

But they need to be heard.

"To me," says Elway, "I don't think we're spending enough time getting other people in here, working on depth. The real dominant teams win Super Bowls. That's the only way you win a championship. Flukes don't. You look at the Raiders the year they were a wild card team, but as they went through the playoffs that year they became a dominant team. They peaked at the right time.

"A great football team is one that can handle injuries. If the 49ers get hurt, do you think it affects them? They don't even lose stride. They could lose four guys and not lose stride.

"You start questioning: How many dominant players do we have here? Players who, if things don't just go our way, are we going to be able to pull things out? To be a great team, you have to do that."

Offensively, said Elway, he doesn't think they are that far off. "It's an attitude. We're waiting for things to happen. How many times Sunday did we have big plays called back? And that keeps happening and happening and happening. (Denver has lost an almost unbelievable total of 266 yards and 12 first downs to penalties this season. You can bet at least two victories are imbedded in that statistic. Similarly, all eight of Elway's interceptions have come after intermission, with Denver pressing to hold or regain a lead.)

"It's like we're not playing to our potential because we're not playing with confidence.

"You want to make big plays but now we're rushing the ball a lot better. We used to always make big plays and make things happen when we threw the ball. Now we've got a guy like Bobby Humphrey and we've got to get the ball in his hands. So that makes it tougher offensively to make those big plays because we're going to control the ball more.

"Players make big plays happen. You make them happen. And a lot of times that's my downfall because I try to make something happen and I force it. Like Sunday, that interception in the end zone. God. That was so stupid."

He shook his head. He knows what he is saying will cause waves, but feels also it is necessary at this stage. He and Reeves are so much alike competitively it is almost eerie, and you wonder if each is really aware of the fact.

"He thinks there's no one who wants to win a Super Bowl worse than he does," Elway says.

"He's wrong. I do."

August 15, 1991, *Denver Post*

"FIRSTS" MARK 31ST ANNIVERSARY

Naw, it can't be. Really?

It has been 31 summers since Dean Griffing put together a football team called the Denver Broncos, in a league called the American Football League, and promptly won the AFL's first game, 13-10, at Boston.

It's just one of their firsts.

—First to wear cast-off uniforms from the Canadian Football League.

—First to have general manager go into stands and fight fans for footballs after extra points.

—First to reduce scouting to computers (true, by the late Ray Malavasi in the early 1960s).

—First to beat an NFL team after the 1966 merger.

—First AFL team to lose four Super Bowls.

The fastest the Broncos moved all week used to be the dash off the field at the end of a game in old Bears Stadium. There was, roughly, a small tank of hot water available. First man in got the hot water. The others sat under dripping pipes, holding feet out of the puddles on the floor, wondering if this truly was life on the professional level.

They have spawned championships and all-pros and a crazy, almost religious following in the Rocky Mountain region in the past three decades. Their headquarters in Arapahoe County is now state-of-the-art, and Mile High Stadium is really a 75,000-seat testimonial to their grip on the emotions of their fans.

Nowhere else did a whole city, threatened with the loss of a franchise that had never come close to a winning season, suddenly produce hundreds of volunteers who went door to door, soliciting donations, so the stadium could be purchased from Gerald and Allan Phipps and deeded to the city. It happened here.

There hasn't been an unsold seat in the stadium since the 1969 season, and the waiting list for tickets once numbered demand for some 40,000 seats. That is slipping now. The expectation level is high. Nothing less than the playoffs satisfy fans who once prayed for nothing more flamboyant than a break-even season.

The birth of the Colorado Rockies baseball team threatens the old one-faith grip the Broncos held here. It will be interesting to see how the franchise responds after 30 years of basically free rides in the competitive market. A 5-11 season could not have come at a worse time for the Broncos.

It's funny, now, how the faithful grumble against the high priests. Dan Reeves and John Elway have brought the city more thrills, more high points, more consistently challenging football than any other pairing of coach and player in franchise history. Yet here they are, subjected to criticism the city once reserved for Griffing and any of the lengthy list of quarterback pretenders that preceded Elway.

One bad season—and it was a stinker—and they are virtual outcasts.

Another, and they could be in a time warp, reliving the dreadful early years when staffers refused to allow Broncos decals on their cars because other drivers would give them strange but unmistakable hand signals at stop signs.

Another, and nobody will be safe.

I don't think that's going to happen. I think Elway has two burning goals—a Super Bowl win and an eventual spot in the Hall of Fame at Canton. He knows the clock is ticking as he moves into his ninth season—can it really be? So does Reeves, who has been here a decade in which winning became just a prelude. He has created the atmosphere in which just winning isn't enough. Now he suffers from it.

Like Elway, he desperately needs a Super Bowl win to validate a brilliant career....

January 5, 1992, *Denver Post*

ELWAY, BRONCOS OILED FOR SUPER BOWL TRIP?

Dream on. It's real. The orange glow grows and the eerie music may get louder before it's finished. Those of squeamish Super Bowl memories should be advised.

It's possible again. Minneapolis is within reach.

You wonder, this early January morning, how 30,000 season ticket-holders felt late yesterday afternoon, watching John Elway stage Drive II and beat Houston 26-24.

They didn't buy those playoff tickets, those 30,000 of little faith, when they were offered back in early December. Strangers sat in their Sunday pews, instead.

And the 30,000 who failed to pick up the playoff option missed perhaps the best game in Mile High Stadium history.

For 57 minutes, Warren Moon and his Houston Oilers staged a textbook demonstration of the run and shoot offense.

Moon was magnificent. The Oilers were as close to unstoppable as a team gets.

Then, just over two minutes left, it was John Elway's turn. Houston's only punt of the game was dead on the Denver 2. The Broncos trailed 24-23. They had used up all their time-outs. Memories of the 1987 title game in Cleveland flooded back, yellowed with age but still sharp.

Keith Bishop stands in the huddle, in the end zone, and looks around. "We've got 'em just where we want 'em," he snarls.

Some 98 yards and change later, Mark Jackson tumbles into the opposite end zone, Denver forges a tie and wins its way to its second Super Bowl in overtime.

Yesterday, in two wildly unforgettable minutes, Elway negated everything Moon and the Oilers had done, and propelled Denver into next week's AFC championship game. ...

If this sounds too dramatic, too improbable for a team that was 5-11 a year ago, just wait.

It gets better, more unlikely, more storybook.

Twice on that last march, Elway faced fourth down on his own side of the 50. Once he ran for a first down.

It was the second one—fourth and 10, from his own 35—that separates Elway from all the rest.

He ducked a rush, moved up, caught a cornerback unwisely looking at him instead of Vance Johnson and hit Johnson for 44 yards to the Houston 21.

One play later, David Treadwell floated a 28-yard field goal just inside the right upright, and it was Denver 26, Houston 24.

"I'm sure some of us thought it was hopeless," receiver Michael Young said of the winning drive.

"But once we got in the huddle and looked in [Elway's] eyes, you knew we were going to make it," he continues.

"He truly is one of the greatest quarterbacks of all time. No matter what happens the rest of my life, I'll remember this."

... Until Treadwell's winner, Denver was never ahead on the breezy sunny afternoon. ...

For connoisseurs, it was the ultimate taste test, Moon going one way, Elway taking his troops the other in a game-long duel.

It was classic, two heavyweights at the peak of their skills, and when it ended, the 75,301 wouldn't leave.

They stood and cheered, and Elway ran to the west side and tossed the football to a fan. It was all he could think to do. He didn't even know the guy. But somewhere, a fan has a souvenir of a game that will grow in the telling, just as Drive I has. That one, remember, didn't actually win a game. It tied one, forced overtime.

This one, scratched out of torn turf and a clock that stood still, and engineered by one of the game's great improvisers, was even more improbable. It was the 19th time in nine Denver seasons that Elway has taken the final drive of the game and won. ...

And, at the end, having just painted another masterpiece, all he could think to do was to run over and toss the ball to a fan.

It was Elway's 20th completion of the day.

January 6, 1992, *Denver Post*

IN ANY TIME ZONE, ELWAY'S INCREDIBLE

There were still thousands of fans in Mile High Stadium Saturday night when John Allen's phone rang in Bear Valley.

It was a friend, Gary Jones. He wanted to gush over the Denver Broncos' 26-24 win over Houston.

Nothing new there. Gushing is in season in the mountain country after Saturday's thriller.

"But this was from England, from Brackley, a little town near Oxford. My friend's name is Gary Jones. He's an air controller, and he said he had just finished watching the game live on BBC.

"'Well, what time is it there?' I asked.

"'Oh, it's half midnight,'" his friend replied.

John Elway and the Denver Broncos, once more, are men for all time zones. The place where Elway seems to have the most trouble getting his due is his own time zone.

Can we end that now? Was Saturday's classic enough to at least compromise: If Elway hasn't yet won a Super Bowl, he has done every other thing possible—and impossible—and more than any other quarterback except Joe Montana?

John Elway, with the ball, and two minutes left, is his own art form. Let the wind blow, the grass be ripped and torn, the snow begin to sting the face, darkness settle over the stadium, receivers slip, blocking break down, crowd shrieking and Elway is in his element.

He enters another realm, a place mortal quarterbacks never imagine. It's the place we all dream of as kids, throwing the winning pass as the clock dies. For most, it remains a dream. For Elway, it's the very substance of his career.

... He has constructed two of the great closing drives in playoff history. But he hasn't won a Super Bowl. [Houston quarterback Warren] Moon has never been to one.

Elway has taken his team to its fourth AFC title game in nine years and is one victory away from going to his fourth Super Bowl. Dan Marino has been to one.

Yet, critics look at the quarterback ratings, not the won-loss column. They don't stare long enough at those 19 come-from-behind wins in nine seasons....

Elway had let the season trickle down to three fourth downs and somehow converted each of them. His 44-yard strike to Vance Johnson looked more like some wing-shot duck than one of Moon's tight spirals.

But it got there, on fourth and 10, in the last minute.

There should be a place in the quarterback ratings for such numbers.

September 11, 1992, *Denver Post*

What transplanted Californians need to know

I read not long ago that Colorado issued 17,000 driver's licenses to people who have abandoned the California dream. Thousands of others are coming in from Texas and other states.

It occurred to me they are in for a culture shock. It would be a little like moving to Lincoln, Nebr., in late August. You are expected to adopt a new religion even if you are an atheist.

To help with this transition, today's epistle concerns survival techniques in Broncoland.

I have two daughters: One attended the Raider game with her husband, Michael, and they left early. They should have known better, but they did. Years of listening to Bob Martin and Larry Zimmer were ignored. They knew better, but they left anyway.

"We were down by McNichols Arena on the way to the car when this roar went up and I knew what happened," Sharon said. "It was Elway again."

Ten miles northwest in Arvada, our older daughter, Kathy, was watching the game alone with her six-month-old puppy, Molly. When Winston Moss shoved Elway beneath some metal stands, she leaped out of her chair, screaming, pointing and—in the interest of full and accurate reporting—cursing.

Molly allegedly has not been near the TV room since. You must understand these reactions are part of your life for the next five months. People smile on Mondays when the Broncos win. They honk viciously and cut each other off in traffic when they lose. Police can document the fact there are more fights in the stands when the Broncos are behind. There is a watchful stupor that falls over the city from 2 until 5 every Sunday afternoon—no phone calls—lower water use, even the grocery stores report reduced traffic. Hospital nurses report a dramatic drop in patient call lights being flashed—until halftime or the end of the game.

"Then, everybody wants a pain pill," a nurse at University Hospital told me recently.

So, that's what you've come to. Even if you're never going to be Broncos fans, there are a few things that will help in social situations. At parties, you can always be regarded as one of the cognoscenti by asking your table companions, "Do you think they'll ever resolve this Reeves-Elway thing?"

If you're going to a sports bar, take a designated driver. He or she must not drink, of course, but that's not the primary qualification. The DD must be numb sportswise, no feelings or reactions over point spreads, Fantasy Football totals or John Elway's interceptions/touchdown ratio.

If they were to test this individual, the DD would flatline on any emotional graph regarding sports. This way they won't use the automobile as a weapon on the way home if the Broncos lose. This doesn't happen often. But the way the Broncos play, it often makes it seem they lose even when they win. Last year, they won 12 regular season games and 10 were by a touchdown or less. A steady hand at the wheel is needed on late Sunday afternoons.

Several dozen DDs from last year are reportedly undergoing intensive long-term therapy and are unavailable for the '92 season.

Do not schedule any social function on Sunday afternoon from Sept. 1 to at least the end of December. Hostesses often wait until a Bronco schedule comes out to determine how they'll spend their fall weekends. A helpful hint here. Serve anything that requires cutting tools before kickoff. You don't want anything sharp lying around from halftime on. Halftime is for fruit and cheese. If they throw it, at least it doesn't impale you.

Do not mention Dallas—ever—for any reason. ... And never wear black T-shirts with "Just win baby" stenciled on them.

You should be aware this whole thing is highly contagious and there is no known cure. I actually know of a couple who taped, and kept, and occasionally still watch the Broncos' loss to San Francisco in the Super Bowl. They are undergoing deep therapy at family rates.

If you really must waste your weekend on something other than sports, there is always a mountain drive to view our one fall color, gold.

Or you could drive to Estes Park and listen to the elk bugle. Believe me, at 4 o'clock on a Sunday afternoon they don't care what the Broncos are doing.

Or you could walk in the park, admire the fall flowers, taste winter on the wind, fly a kite with your child.

Just be safely off the street by 5 if they lose.

❦   ❦   ❦

CHAPTER THREE

SUPER BOWLS
AND OTHER BIG GAMES

To the Editor:

Just wanted to drop a note to let you know how much the presence of Dick Connor was missed at the Super Bowl [XXVII]. Dick and I had gone back many years, and he was one of the people I most respected in the business.

In this era of "authors," as some of us call them, Dick was the rare exception, a truly fine writer who also cared about the content of his work. Dick wasn't there just to crack jokes. He hunted and searched and often uncovered the truth. More importantly, he was never afraid to write it.

To many of us, he was the ultimate professional, and as I prowled the endless press conferences in L.A., I couldn't help but miss his smiling face and dry humor. When you were not quite sure about an angle or a story line, you could always turn to Dick for an honest opinion. If he thought it was OK, it usually would work.

Writers, especially sportswriters, don't trust many people in that regard. But Dick Connor could always be trusted. He was more than just a terrific columnist. He was a terrific newspaperman. And a good friend.

Our business won't be the same without him.

—Steve Bisheff, columnist, *Orange County Register,*
printed in *Denver Post* **Feb. 14, 1993**

LOS ANGELES—... A final aside: There are now 11 sportswriters who have attended each Super Bowl, two of whom have covered all 27 games for the *Star-Ledger.*

There were 12 until New Year's Eve (actually Dec. 30), when one of the world's nicest men, Dick Connor of the *Denver Post,* succumbed to cancer after waging a battle that not only inspired his friends but caused the American Cancer Society chapter in Denver to ask him to deliver speeches to others similarly affected.

Going out there on the field and playing a professional football game takes courage and fearlessness, but not nearly as much of either as Dick Connor showed when he found out what his future held for him three years ago and decided to continue working, continue smiling and continue to tell anyone who asked that he was one of the world's luckiest people to have had such a fine family, career and circle of friends.

Dallas won Super Bowl XXVII. That's nice.

Dick Connor wasn't there to see it. That's terrible.

—Dave Klein, columnist,
Newark Star Ledger, **Feb. 2, 1993**

As you know, we noted Dick's long association with the NFL at Super Bowl XXVII in Los Angeles through a message on the videoboard, as reproduced below Dick's picture.

The NFL lost a true friend, one who will be long remembered.

—**Paul Tagliabue, commissioner, National Football League, personal letter, Apr. 13, 1993**

... The NFL paid tribute to Dick on several occasions during the Super Bowl week, including flashing his picture and a brief message about him on the video screen at the Rose Bowl. Another 100,000 learned what type of man he was.

—**Jack Clary, former columnist, Stow, Mass., personal letter, Feb. 7, 1993**

❧   ❧   ❧

Dick covered the first 26 Super Bowls. At the 27th, less than a month after he died, fans observed a moment of silence in his honor when his photo and the following inscription were flashed on the screen at the Rose Bowl: "The NFL lost a dear friend in December when longtime *Rocky Mountain News* & *Denver Post* columnist Dick Connor passed away. He covered every Super Bowl during his distinguished career."

Dick saw the Super Bowl evolve from a rather insignificant football game between the powerful NFL champions and the upstart wannabes of the AFL. A ticket to the third Super Bowl cost $12. The last couple of years, tickets have gone for $175. Programs for the first few Bowls were $1. Official programs for Super Bowl XXVI cost $10.

The first Super Bowl was played in January 1967, following Dick's rookie year as a professional football writer. Some writers speculated that it would never catch on. Dick was not among them. He loved the game, applauded the enthusiasm of the fans and regretted the corporate hype.

The Super Bowl attracts everyone. The children and I teased Dick over the years about his "Mafia" connection. One year a local sports figure, who shall remain nameless, called Dick before the game and asked if he could get Super Bowl tickets for his friend in New Jersey. Dick said he'd try, but the friend would have to pay face value for the tickets because he wouldn't and couldn't get them free.

No problem. One of the friend's "associates" would be in contact with Dick at the Super Bowl—just have the tickets available. A very large man with a very deep voice dressed in flashy clothes came to pick them up at Dick's hotel room for someone named Vinny. How much did Dick want for his trouble?

Nothing. Just the price of the tickets. Surprised, the associate paid for the tickets and left. Another reporter heard about the transaction and chided Dick for not accepting something for his trouble. No way.

For about eight to 10 years, Dick would get a call in mid-December from either Vinny himself or his Denver friend to arrange for that year's Super Bowl tickets. Dick never knew Vinny's last name—and didn't want to. Finally the calls stopped. Dick wondered what became of his New Jersey Super Bowl fan.

The most exciting Super Bowl was, of course, Denver's first appearance in Super XII. Never mind that the Broncos lost. It was great. There would be three more trips by the Broncos to the Super Bowl, but unfortunately no Super wins.

Perhaps Father John McCormick, pastor of the Shrine of St. Anne Catholic Church in Arvada, was right when he said at Dick's funeral, "Now Dick knows why the Broncos never won the Super Bowl." I wondered that day what Dan Reeves, Red Miller, Pat Bowlen, Joe Collier, Stan Jones and other coaches and former players who were there thought. If nothing else, it evoked a hearty laugh and broke the tension.

SUPER BOWL I

January 16, 1967, *Denver Post*

GREEN BAY PACKERS 35, KANSAS CITY CHIEFS 10

LOS ANGELES—A shirt-sleeved Vince Lombardi clutched the game ball and managed to avoid the question for nearly five minutes in the steaming dressing room made even hotter by hordes of newsmen and glaring television lights.

Finally he said it.

"They're a good football team. But they don't compare with the top National Football League teams. There. That's what you've been wanting me to say, isn't it?" he asked with what passes for a smile for Lombardi.

His Green Bay Packers had just methodically, mercilessly, convincingly whipped the Kansas City Chiefs 35-10 in the historic first Super Bowl, matching champions of the two professional leagues.

A crowd of 63,036—30,000 less than capacity—had witnessed the destruction of the AFL hopes that the junior circuit could, in one game, achieve equality with the proud NFL.

For 30 minutes, it appeared Kansas City had a chance, with the Chiefs striking through an often spectatorlike Green Bay defense to trail only 14-10 at the half.

But even then the seeds had been sown and were growing. Bart Starr, the Packers' Mr. Super Starr, had demonstrated the pattern—third down precision that has destroyed NFL teams—was beginning to destroy the Chiefs. And when Willy Wood stepped in front of Fred Arbanas, swiped a pass on the Green Bay 45, then dashed 50 yards to the Chiefs 5 early in the third quarter, Green Bay's time had come. ...

SUPER BOWL I: SIDEBAR

January 16, 1967, *Denver Post*

LOS ANGELES—It was like watching businessmen heading for the commuter train at 5 p.m. In fact, businessmen might show more action than did the Green Bay Packers as they filed through a cordon of newsmen, past television lights and into their dressing room under the sunwashed Los Angeles Coliseum Sunday afternoon.

They had just won the first AFL-NFL World Championship title. But except for a reserved yelp or two, and a look of gleaming satisfaction showing through the sweat on the face of Jim Taylor, you might have thought they were coming in from a workout.

No joy or celebration. No champagne pouring over coaches' heads. They were satisfied. They were champs. Questions had been silenced. And that was enough for the Packers. ...

SUPER BOWL II

January 14, 1968, *Denver Post*

GREEN BAY PACKERS 33, OAKLAND RAIDERS 14

MIAMI, Fla.—It was late in the third quarter in Miami's Orange Bowl Sunday afternoon, and for all intents and purposes the second annual Super Bowl had been decided some time earlier, say in 1959 when Vince Lombardi moved to Green Bay.

But the Green Bay Packers were poised for a field goal attempt by Don Chandler from the Oakland 31-yard line. Chandler's kick wasn't well hit, and it sailed goalward, flat and not end-over-end. It struck the crossbar and skidded over for three points.

With only 15 minutes and two seconds of playing time left, Green Bay had an insurmountable 26-7 lead and a firm grip on bushels of greenbacks.

An AFL writer watched the kick carom over. He shook his head.

"They really ARE the chosen people," he muttered.

Not many in the sellout Orange Bowl crowd of 75,546 were willing to argue the point late Sunday afternoon after the Packers had seized on Oakland errors and methodically ground out a 33-14 victory in breezy, 68-degree weather. ...

SUPER BOWL III

January 13, 1969, *Denver Post*

NEW YORK JETS 16, BALTIMORE COLTS 7

MIAMI BEACH, Fla.—The New York Jets reign supreme in the world of professional football this Super Monday, following Super Sunday No. 3. But it's a strange, schizophrenic kind of world.

For all those NFL followers, it's a nightmarish one. Some guy in long sideburns and white football shoes keeps flashing a psychedelic light spelling out Jets 16, Colts 7. Loud, harsh music sounds. There are groans. Some weeping and gnashing of teeth.

For delirious AFL fans, wandering wide-eyed into the inner temple for the first time, the hair shirts are coming off in favor of bell-bottom trousers and double-breasted jackets—and llama rugs.

And all this because the New York Jets did what they are capable of doing and Baltimore didn't before 75,377 unbelieving fans in the Orange Bowl here Sunday.

Even the skies cooperated. When monarchs die, the sun shouldn't shine. It didn't.

Joe Namath and Matt Snell and New York's offensive line and entire defense made Baltimore look like the 97-pound weakling on the beach. The Colts cooperated admirably by scooping sand in their own faces with a fumble leading to one of three Jim Turner field goals for the winners.

An NFL writer said it best. With New York ahead 13-0 in the final quarter and Baltimore going nowhere, he turned to a neighbor and sighed:

"Oh God, we've got to live with this for a whole year."

... So it's wait until next year—only this time the NFL will do the waiting.

SUPER BOWL IV

January 12, 1970, *Denver Post*

KANSAS CITY CHIEFS 23, MINNESOTA VIKINGS 7

NEW ORLEANS—Last year Baltimore. This year Minnesota. Next?

The Purple People Eaters looked Kansas City right in the "I" here Sunday and came away hypnotized.

With Len Dawson superb, the Chiefs took two hours and 40 minutes to convince the professional football world that not only are they the deserving world champions, but that quite possibly Oakland, like Penn State, is no worse than 1-A.

There was an occasional hint of this from the Chiefs' dressing room beneath Tulane Stadium here Sunday in the wake of the Chiefs' 23-7 Super Bowl conquest of the Minnesota Vikings. Oakland beat K.C. in two of three 1969 games in the AFL. ...

SUPER BOWL V

January 18, 1971, *Denver Post*

BALTIMORE COLTS 16, DALLAS COWBOYS 13

MIAMI—What's it like with 80,000 people and 60 million television viewers watching, the score tied and you, a 23-year-old rookie who can earn 40 teammates an extra $7,500 each a minute and a half from now?

"I had a dream a week ago Saturday," rookie Baltimore placekicker Jim O'Brien said Sunday afternoon in the Orange Bowl. "It was after the club got down here and I dreamed the game would be won by a long field goal. But I couldn't tell who kicked it, me or Mike Clark of Dallas. I couldn't see the Super Bowls number and the dream was in black and white so I didn't know which uniform it was. It was a long kick and I told people about it. But I said I'll have to wait until Sunday to see who won."

He got his chance in the Super Bowl. With 59 seconds left, Mike Curtis intercepted a Dallas pass and ran it back to the 28-yard line. O'Brien began to pace behind the Baltimore bench, accompanied by veteran Jim Orr, who talked to him quietly, while Baltimore ran two plays to move the ball to dead center of the field and use the clock.

... "I knew if I got it, it would be one of my best kicks all year," O'Brien said. "It started right but came back to the middle."

He leaped high and looked for approval toward the bench. He got it, even from veteran tackle Billy Ray Smith, who was playing his last game after 13 seasons. Smith had threatened to cut O'Brien's long black hair if Baltimore won.

"They're not cutting my hair now. They try to rattle me in practice, just like the Cowboys did. Who? Billy Ray, who else! Billy Ray is my adversary. My protagonist. No, my antagonist."

Except to Dallas. For Dallas, since 4:47 p.m. Sunday, he's an antagonist.

SUPER BOWL VI

January 17, 1972, *Denver Post*

DALLAS COWBOYS 24, MIAMI DOLPHINS 3

NEW ORLEANS—Onetime Wyoming star Jim Kiick, water beads from the shower still clinging to his shoulders, pulled on a sport shirt, as somebody asked if he still liked being compared to the movie character Butch Cassidy.

"Butch and Sundance died. We're still alive. We've got to feel it for six months," Kiick, Miami Dolphin halfback, said.

Dallas, which has felt it for six years, now can relax.

Sunday, the Dallas team that had earned the derisive nickname of next year's champions demolished Miami's Dolphins in every phase of the game for a 24-3 Super Bowl win that ended the annual frustrations for coach Tom Landry's powerful winners. ...

SUPER BOWL VII

January 15, 1973, *Denver Post*

MIAMI DOLPHINS 14, WASHINGTON REDSKINS 7

LOS ANGELES—It's Miami 17, the rest of the football world zero Monday after Coach Don Shula's maligned no-names, just seven years from the cradle, won it all.

A year from the time Dallas' Tom Landry said he couldn't recall the names of any Dolphin linemen, the Miami defensive line choked Washington into submission and ended an unprecedented perfect year with a 14-7 victory over Washington in Super Bowl VII. It was Miami's 17th victory without a loss.

It's never been done before, and not even the Dolphins themselves believe it will be done again—although they apparently aren't sure. ...

SUPER BOWL VIII

January 14, 1974, *Denver Post*

MIAMI DOLPHINS 24, MINNESOTA VIKINGS 7

HOUSTON—The Rice Stadium lights, turned on two hours before game time, were still burning overhead as the fog thickened a little toward nightfall Sunday.

Don Shula stood just outside the stadium. He was sipping a beer, tieless, wearing a tan raincoat and enjoying the banter with a small group of writers as he waited for the Miami team bus to fill.

Was it sweeter in 1974?

"Yes, because it's back-to-back wins now and that's harder. It's not my job to say that we're one of the best teams that ever played," he said in answer to a question, but still leaving listeners with little doubt how he might feel personally. "Look, this team has done some things the last couple of years that all you have to do is add them up."

Item: Win 17, lose zero, win the Super Bowl.

Item: Win 15, lose two, win the Super Bowl again.

"We had to be a better team this year to repeat. Since we did repeat, it proves we're better." ...

SUPER BOWL IX: PREGAME
January 12, 1975, *Denver Post*

NEW ORLEANS—He sat there with a dead cigar and a live audience, and the look on his face told you the moment was worth the 42-year wait.

On the floor above, Chuck Noll was about to hold his final press conference of Super Bowl IX week—yet nobody was leaving a ring four-deep around Art Rooney's table in the press lounge.

"Chuck Noll. He's a nice man," Rooney rasped, enjoying it hugely. He was upstaging his own coach and knew it, and not even Noll would mind when he found out.

If there ever is a poll to determine the most popular owner in the NFL, the only race will be for second. Rooney, 72, has long since retired first place.

Rooney at last has a winner, and there can't be a soul anywhere who begrudges him that. "When you've lost for as long as we did, you begin to wonder if you're ever going to win," he was saying Friday.

He kept rolling the unlit cigar with a soggy end. He held an old-fashioned cap in the other hand. He wore a rumpled brown suit and peered through thick glasses from beneath a shock of white hair.

Everyone remotely connected with the Steelers knows him by one name—the Chief.

He bought an NFL franchise for $2,500 in the depression years, and struggled to keep it alive while he and his wife, Kathleen, raised five boys in "The Ward," a district not far from where Rooney's dad owned a saloon.

"There were days right after the war when you played an NFL game and refused to go out for the second half unless they paid you your guarantee," he said.

"The team guarantee was $2,500 in those days. You traveled by bus." He signed Colorado's Whizzer White for $15,000. "That was for 1938. I think it was $15,800 because it included pay for preseason. He was the first $15,000 player in the league. Most of them were getting $100 or $150 a game."

Today, Rooney still lives in the same three-story Victorian house "a five-minute walk from the stadium. If the lights go on down there, I walk over."

"... Coach Noll's press conference has begun in the grand ballroom on the third floor ..." the pressroom PA man intoned. Rooney waved his cigar. Nobody left. He savored the moment. Give him a dollar Havana, a fistful of winning horse tickets and a sports bull session, and heaven can wait. All day Friday they poured into the Steeler quarters at the Fontainebleau Hotel. "We flew down, I think it's 180 office workers and their families and kids from Pittsburgh. And there's the 34 grandchildren, and Tim [Rooney] is bringing in a bunch from Yonkers, and ..."

"... Coach Noll's press conference ..."

Rooney wouldn't go into his team's dressing rooms in Oakland two weeks ago after they beat Oakland to qualify for the Super Bowl and give Rooney his first big title in 42 years. "This is their day," he said, standing in the corridor outside.

He hadn't said a word about a horrible officiating mistake that cost his team a touchdown before halftime. Asked about it later, he shrugged. "We all got to watch it on instant replay. He just had one quick glance."

"... We'd like to ask the writers ..." Rain began to beat against the windows on the far side of the room.

"I know the story is I bought the Steelers with money I won at the race track that day," Rooney continued. "I already owned a football team. We had been playing semipro a long time. I just paid $2,500 to get them into the NFL."

Rooney is a legendary horseplayer who still yearns for the old handbook days. In 1936, over a weekend, he won 16 of 18 races at two tracks. Some say it amounted to a million. Nobody but Rooney knows for sure, and he never has said.

But Buck Crouse, an old-time fighter who was with him on the hot streak, said on the ride home, "Here we were with all the money in the world and he stopped for an ice cream soda."

"I never bet a short horse. Two-to-one? Those aren't odds. The horse can't read the numbers on his back."

"... Gentlemen, the press conference ..."

A few stirred, reluctantly. Rooney sat on. The end of his cigar grew pulpier. The wind strengthened and drove the Friday morning rain harder against the window.

For two hours Rooney sat, through interview after interview, enjoying, inhaling the scene.

It had been thousands of losses coming.

SUPER BOWL IX

January 13, 1975, *Denver Post*
PITTSBURGH STEELERS 16, MINNESOTA VIKINGS 6

NEW ORLEANS—There was one frightful moment for Art Rooney in New Orleans this past weekend. It came Saturday afternoon at Fairgrounds Race Track, when the 73-year-old owner of the Pittsburgh Steelers was asked to present the trophy to the winner of the Super Bowl stakes.

"When they brought the horse into the circle, I noticed it was wearing Viking colors," Rooney said late Sunday afternoon from behind a massive cigar.

It needn't have. The horse didn't have to run into Pittsburgh's defense. Minnesota did—but couldn't.

The Steelers, despite losing a lineman and two linebackers during the game, held Minnesota to a Super Bowl–low 17 yards rushing, left the Vikings nothing but a futile passing game and captured the NFL championship with a 16-6 triumph in Super Bowl IX at Tulane Stadium. ...

SUPER BOWL X

January 19, 1976, *Denver Post*

PITTSBURGH STEELERS 21, DALLAS COWBOYS 17

MIAMI—There were 80,187 shivering, windblown fans in the Orange Bowl Sunday as Pittsburgh was pushed to the final play before subduing Dallas 21-17 in Super Bowl X.

Cinderella wasn't one of the onlookers.

"I kept thinking about Minnesota," said Steeler linebacker Andy Russell while recounting the hectic closing seconds of the finest Super Bowl of them all Sunday. Dallas, given a reprieve by a late Roger Staubach touchdown pass and an unorthodox strategic call by Pittsburgh's Chuck Noll, had stormed back from a 21-10 deficit to one final play from the Steeler 38 with three seconds left.

Under similar circumstances in Minnesota three weeks ago, the Cowboys' Staubach threw 50 yards to Drew Pearson for the winning score that helped bring the young Cowboys to Miami this week. Now, while Steeler fans chanted "defense" from their side of the packed stadium, the Cowboys' chances rested on one last Staubach heave into the end zone that everyone knew was coming.

"I kept thinking, They can't do it two times," the 34-year-old Russell said afterward, a shake of the head emphasizing the memory. "Cinderella isn't going to be here today. She was left in Minnesota."

Like thousands of other Steeler and Cowboy fans who couldn't get tickets, Cinderella must, indeed, still be barefoot somewhere in the Minnesota snow. Staubach's desperation heave curled down into the northwest corner, was batted high, and picked off by Glen Edwards, who ran it out to the 30 as the game ended. ...

SUPER BOWL XI

January 10, 1977, *Denver Post*

OAKLAND RAIDERS 32, MINNESOTA VIKINGS 14

PASADENA—Quickie quiz: Who's buried in Grant's tomb?

Quickie answer: Super Bowl IV, Super Bowl VIII, Super Bowl IX and, now, Super Bowl XI.

Bud Grant and the Minnesota Vikings set two records 60 playing minutes apart here Sunday. They became the first team ever to play in the NFL's postseason extravaganza four times, and then became the first to lose all four.

Oakland, with the ghosts of Super Bowl II returning bigger than life, destroyed the Vikings 32-14. It could have been worse. ...

AFC PLAYOFF
December 25, 1977, *Denver Post*
DENVER BRONCOS 34, PITTSBURGH STEELERS 21

MILE HIGH STADIUM—Paul Howard was in no mood for apologies. Neither was his head coach, Red Miller.

"Hey, I'll go into any bar with the redhead," Denver Bronco center Mike Montler laughed in the joy of the dressing room late Saturday after Denver's 34-21 playoff victory over the Steelers.

"His temper is a sense of fair play and if he feels somebody is going to extremes that verges on the dirty, then he's going to take care of his ballclub."

Miller had to be restrained at halftime as he ran on the field following an incident in which Pittsburgh's Joe Greene swung a vicious right into Howard's midsection, dropping the Bronco guard for several minutes. Greene, who twice before in previous games with Pittsburgh, has kicked Howard, once splitting his scrotum, wasn't even repentant at the finish.

... When he got the Denver job last February, one of the things Miller had said then was he would like to turn Denver "into the Pittsburgh of the West."

No more. He lifted the game ball. His club had just stopped the Pittsburgh of the East.

"And this has to be the sweetest victory I've ever experienced in my life," said Montler's favorite redhead.

AFC CHAMPIONSHIP
January 2, 1978, *Denver Post*
DENVER BRONCOS 20, OAKLAND RAIDERS 17

MILE HIGH STADIUM—The first thing we're going to have to do is get the language straight.

Carefully now, like the first sip of wine, try it.

Super Bowl.

Fine. Now gulp. There's more. All you want. For the next two weeks, that's all you'll hear or read or see, and maybe near Jan. 14 you'll be gagging on it. By Jan. 14 you'll be hung over on the stuff.

But now, it's time to savor, and enjoy, and let yourself get a little giddy. Eighteen years on the temperance wagon are long enough. Pour it down.

... The Denver Broncos, the clown princes of the old AFL, the court jesters, had seized control of the kingdom and toppled the king himself. ...

SUPER BOWL XII

January 16, 1978, *Denver Post*

DALLAS COWBOYS 27, DENVER BRONCOS 10

NEW ORLEANS—They were sitting on the three buses drawn up outside their hotel Sunday afternoon, waiting for the police escort to take them to the Superdome.

Fran Polsfoot leaned across the aisle to tap Andy Maurer: "Where's Mickey's big hand?" he asked.

"When it gets to Mickey's nose, it's time to move," said the veteran tackle, smiling.

The buses got to Super Bowl XII on time, but Denver's offense never got to Mickey's nose Sunday. It stayed hung up on second and third and long, and here came Harvey Martin and Randy White and there went the football and Denver's hopes of ending a brilliant season with its biggest win of all.

You don't play second-and-nine with Dallas, or with Oakland, or Pittsburgh, or Baltimore or any of the other good ones. The 27-10 final count on the Superdome's orange scoreboard is mute and absolute testimony to what happens when you try.

There were no sour grapes.

... "There's no use crying on anybody's shoulders," said defensive end Barney Chavous. "We lost. But we have the coaches and ability to correct that."

"Buses, five minutes," somebody yelled.

The big hand never reached Mickey's nose, but it came closer than anybody ever dreamed it would. Happy New Year.

SUPER BOWL XIII

January 22, 1979, *Denver Post*

PITTSBURGH STEELERS 35, DALLAS COWBOYS 31

MIAMI—Terry Bradshaw leaned against a concrete pillar, spitting tobacco juice into a paper Coca-Cola cup, and talked triumph.

Jackie Smith sat surrounded, his 14-year-old son on the outskirts of the crowd, and discussed personal disaster.

America demanded heroes and goats, victors and victims, and it got both—plus probably the best Super Bowl game yet in Pittsburgh's 35-31 bombfest over Dallas in the muggy, carnivallike Orange Bowl Sunday evening.

Bradshaw, who has been accused of being one of the world's dumbest celebrities, proved himself a master of his trade as he replaced the legendary Bart Starr by halftime in Super Bowl passing records, and had the yellow towel–waving Steeler hordes chanting "Brad-shaw, Brad-shaw" in the second half.

Smith, meanwhile, was feeling all of his 38 years.

With the score Pittsburgh 21, Dallas 14, in the third quarter, Smith had lined up on a new spot, filtered out of the Dallas formation and was all alone into the Pittsburgh end zone.

... "I was wide open and I missed it." That was Smith, still in full uniform, in front of his locker, with his son watching from the fringes. Son, like father, is a tight end. Hopefully, he'll never have to face a moment like his dad did Sunday. ...

SUPER BOWL XIV

January 21, 1980, *Denver Post*

PITTSBURGH STEELERS 31, LOS ANGELES RAMS 19

PASADENA, Calif.—The spread. All week, the point spread for Super Bowl XIV was a major conversational topic as the Los Angeles Rams downgraded it and the Pittsburgh Steelers ignored it.

Sunday, as it turned out, the Steelers beat the Rams, the spread, football history and anything else in their way in a game that began under bright sunny skies and ended in darkness, and the only numbers that counted to Eddie Brown were six and five.

... The Rams had just picked off another Bradshaw pass, stopping a drive. Their fans, some of whom booed them earlier, were making almost as much noise as the raucous Steeler followers. And, although unable to move the ball at the start of the fourth, they had gotten a soaring, 56-yard punt from Ken Clark, then a stiff defensive stand that left the Steelers exactly where Los Angeles wanted them, facing another third-and-nine at their own 28.

"I thought we had six [defensive] backs in," Brown was saying afterward, his voice barely audible. "With six backs, I help on the outside." But with five backs, he goes to the deep middle. The Rams, with Brown apparently unaware, had switched.

It left Rod Perry desperately trying to get back inside to cover John Stallworth, who was racing uncovered down the middle toward the south end where the Rams themselves had dashed to just a couple of minutes earlier.

Perry didn't quite make it. Bradshaw's pass curled into Stallworth's waiting fingers at the L.A. 32. Perry's desperate lunge just missed, and the Steelers led for good, 24-19. The play covered 73 yards. Los Angeles never regained the lead. ...

SUPER BOWL XV

January 26, 1981, *Denver Post*

OAKLAND RAIDERS 27, PHILADELPHIA EAGLES 10

NEW ORLEANS—It should have been scripted.

"Cue the Romans. Trumpets and dancing girls. Chariots and marching legions."

"Mr. Davis? Are you ready for the escort to take you down?"

Al Davis turned. "Hell," he said, "There are seven minutes left."

The owner of the Oakland Raiders was wearing, not a toga, but light gray slacks, a white shirt with black piping and—stitched over the left breast in white silk thread—the words "The Oakland Raiders." He sat in the press box for Super Bowl XV. "I want to stay where the action is," he told an NFL type who suggested he sit in the owners' box reserved for his use. Davis always sits in the press box. Always. Everywhere. Just as he always goes on the field before the games and stands on the enemy 40 and watches them warm up.

Al Davis. He carries a set of weights on the road to stay in condition. He collects the discards of the NFL and turns them into the most valuable players of the Super Bowl. He infuriates his fellow owners, drives them screaming up the corporate wall. And, quietly, much more quietly, he sends money for a player who is on hard times, attends a funeral the rest of the league forgets, brings a cancer specialist to the bedside of an ailing writer and offers to provide around-the-clock nursing. None of that makes the papers.

In between, for the better part of two decades, while Dallas became something called "America's Team," Oakland became what its captain, Gene Upshaw, called the NFL's "Halfway House." It also became the most successful franchise anywhere over that stretch.

So maybe Davis earned his little moment of drama early Sunday evening, when—by plan, by accident, you have your choice—he made Pete Rozelle wait a few minutes in the Raider dressing room to present the Lombardi Trophy that symbolizes the best there is in the NFL that year.

The league adopted a Romanesque posture years ago, figuring the use of Roman numerals gave the game a little class. So if Al adopted an imperial posture Sunday, nobody should get mad.

He waited upstairs. And when he finally arrived in the Raiders' cramped and eager rooms, it was like watching a hero of the Imperial Rome regally come up the Apian Way, his troops lining the path, cheering, while he strode past, right fist raised and clenched. It was precisely what 27 other owners didn't want to happen—and were secretly certain would. Davis and his Oakland Raiders won the Super Bowl from Philadelphia 27-10. It was never close. ...

SUPER BOWL XVI

January 25, 1982, *Denver Post*

SAN FRANCISCO 49ERS 26, CINCINNATI BENGALS 21

PONTIAC, Mich.—In a game nobody thought they would ever reach, and on a day when one of their buses almost didn't reach it, the San Francisco 49ers outlasted their own history, football tradition and the Cincinnati Bengals to win Super Bowl XVI 26-21.

With three rookies in their secondary, a baby-faced quarterback only a few semesters out of Notre Dame, with 20 players new to the roster and no winning tradition, they jumped to a Super Bowl record 20-0 halftime lead, then grimly held out in the third quarter until regaining momentum.

Just three years ago, the 49ers were 2-14 and one of the worst teams in football. Sunday night, they rode off on team buses to a victory celebration, and the only question is whether Joe Montana ever got his tape back.

"I was listening to it before the Dallas game," said Montana, voted the game's most valuable player. "It's by Kenny Loggins and it's called, 'This Is It.' I thought it was, uh, fitting."

So, marooned in traffic for almost a half hour on the way to the game, he turned up the volume. Teammates liked it. So he put it on again when they finally reached the Silverdome "20 minutes before we were supposed to be on the field."

Then he looked around the 49ers locker room. "I've gotta get that tape back."

With the nervous Bengals blowing an early scoring chance, then yielding a total of four turnovers that resulted in 20 San Francisco points, the 49ers led from the outset. ...

SUPER BOWL XVII

January 31, 1983, *Rocky Mountain News*

WASHINGTON REDSKINS 27, MIAMI DOLPHINS 17

PASADENA—It was the simplest of questions. For Miami, it was the most obvious yet painful answer.

"What happened in the second half?"

"Nothing."

They had gone to the halftime rest leading 17-10. In the whole second half, it was literally day into night. The late sun climbed up the neighboring San Gabriel Mountains and faded. So did the Dolphins' hopes for a third Super Bowl championship under Don Shula. They got just two first downs. They managed only 34 yards. They died and there was no life support system, none of the big plays they had managed the first half.

There was a relentless quality to the way the question kept coming up all over a Miami Dolphin dressing room early Sunday evening.

It pounded at them, much as John Riggins had done from daylight into early dusk in the gorgeous Rose Bowl setting.

"I don't know," David Woodley was saying. His locker was just inside the door. Outside, the throb of the Washington Redskins' fight song could be both heard and felt, a mocking, pounding kind of counterpoint to the subdued mood inside.

... "I don't know," Woodley was saying to the 10th wave. Or the 12th or 20th. Many of his teammates had already showered and left to find escape in the dark buses. He was still in full uniform.

"... We couldn't come up with a big play in the second half. We couldn't complete a pass and we couldn't run the ball. We couldn't do anything."

Outside a huge full moon was climbing over the east rim of the Rose Bowl.

The scoreboard was still lit.

Washington 27, Miami 17.

It was the only answer that counted.

SUPER BOWL XVIII

January 23, 1984, *Rocky Mountain News*

LOS ANGELES RAIDERS 38, WASHINGTON REDSKINS 9

TAMPA, Fla.—There was nothing subtle about the way the Los Angeles Raiders wore the laurel wreath in Florida's cool early evening here Sunday.

They had just demolished the season's most consistent team, Washington, by a Super Bowl record 38-9 margin. Then they gloated. They do not go modestly into that gentle night that ends the NFL season.

They swagger and strut and search for the proper density of spotlight, the right pitch of the trumpet. If America permitted what the Romans once gave in tribute to its heroes, Davis and the Raiders would ride in chariots down Wilshire Boulevard. No team in sports history has ever adopted a more appropriate symbol than the Raiders' thinly disguised skull and crossbones.

Like their owner and creator, Al Davis, they are sore winners.

They are brash and brassy and swaggering and obnoxious and strutting and taunting.

And they are marvelous.

They are what Dizzy Dean once defined. "Ifn' you kin do it, it ain't braggin'," Diz said once. They do it.

They do it so often and so wondrously well it seemed almost fitting this week to drive about this Florida city where pirates once refitted in the bay, and see all the billboards proclaiming their "Commitment to excellence."

No other team in football would dare erect such monuments to itself—before the game.

"We're not interested in what other teams do," Davis snapped triumphantly. He had stood, looking away, visually refusing to acknowledge the presence of NFL commissioner Pete Rozelle on the winners' platform. Rozelle was there to present the Lombardi Trophy, symbol of victory in the NFL.

Davis glanced only briefly at Rozelle as they exchanged a limp handshake that had the warmth of a northern winter.

Then he seized the moment to praise Tom Flores as one of the best coaches ever, and his 1983 team as the finest ever for the Raiders and maybe the best ever, period.

Humility is not a treasured quality in a Raider scheme. ...

SUPER BOWL XIX

January 21, 1985, *Rocky Mountain News*

SAN FRANCISCO 38, MIAMI 16

STANFORD, Calif.—You did not need the scoreboard in Sunday's foggy night to determine the winner of Super XIX.

You had only to look at the uniforms of the two quarterbacks.

See Dan Marino there, walking head down into the Dolphins' quarters with center Dwight Stephenson? He took a lot of Stanford Stadium grass in with him staining the white Miami jersey.

"I'll talk after I shower," he murmurs to writers about his locker.

In the interview tent, Joe Montana stands in a uniform almost as spotless as when he walked out of the dressing room four hours earlier.

There is a small stain on the right hip. But unlike Marino's future cleaning job, this one is a happy memento, deposited there in the south end zone when Montana dove for San Francisco's third touchdown.

"No team has ever come back to win after trailing by more than seven points in the Super Bowl," the league statistician proclaimed when Montana's score made it 21-10.

That scoring wall is still intact.

... When Montana ran Sunday, it was for effect, for first downs or to create a passing situation he quickly turned into more yards. When Marino ran, it was like someone being chased in an alley. ...

SUPER BOWL XX

January 27, 1986, *Rocky Mountain News*

CHICAGO BEARS 46, NEW ENGLAND PATRIOTS 10

NEW ORLEANS—The celebration has ended.

Super Bowl XX is finished.

So are modesty, humility and the old virtues of dedicated allegiance to such things as the training table and curfews.

If winning the Super Bowl sets trends, we are in for swaggering bravado, Big Macs (with fries and double cheese) and Bourbon Street at 2:30 a.m. instead of bed checks.

We are also due for 27 teams trying to imitate the Chicago Bears' guerrilla defense, headbands, threatened holdouts and 300-pound halfbacks. A generation of high schoolers will line up to buy headbands and wraparound sunshades this morning.

Then they'll probably head for the pool hall and skip geometry.

"I would describe this as one of the best seasons in history," said Jim McMahon, the spiritual guru of this band of athletic iconoclasts.

Modesty? "We were going for 60. We just ran out of time," said McMahon. None of that "we beat a great team today" stuff for him.

Humility? "We fumbled or they might not have scored. And we punted two or three times. We didn't want to have to punt at all."

Empathy for a fallen foe? "I saw the same thing in [Tony Eason's] eyes that I saw in the second game: confusion. 'I hope we're not in for another one of those.'" That was linebacker Mike Singletary. Eason vanished early, 0-for-6 passing, not even a first down to show for it.

All week leading up to this record-shattering 46-10 demolition by the Bears, the Patriots had been quiet. Now we know why. ...

They were so bad they erased almost all the negative records the Denver Broncos had left after XII here in 1978. Nothing worked. They couldn't run. They couldn't pass. They couldn't even get the officials to enforce the rules.

... Are the Bears really that good?

New England learned the answer yesterday in a game in which the Pats had negative yardage the first quarter, no first downs until just before the half, and Eason and Steve Grogan spent the game looking like conventioneers trying to lurch back to a New York hotel through the wee hours and the muggers. ...

They proved clean living and discreet silence may be obsolete, that Gatorade doesn't equal Jack Daniel's, that quiet efficiency is good only when applied to accounting firms.

The Bears said they would dominate and they did.

... The Bears shattered everything yesterday, records and custom and decorum and the Patriots. ...

AFC PLAYOFF

January 5, 1987, *Rocky Mountain News*

DENVER BRONCOS 22, NEW ENGLAND PATRIOTS 17

MILE HIGH STADIUM—"Click!" the game plan went.

"Click-thud."

Throw deep. Run. Run. Throw deep again.

"They have such great people back there. They are what we call 'cluers,' guys that read your eyes.

"If we could run 'em off, get them to thinking about the deep ball, it would open some things underneath for us," John Elway said.

Click!

It isn't called by that name, but the Denver Broncos played Russian Roulette with the New England Patriots secondary yesterday.

Throw deep, get Vance Johnson or Mark Jackson streaking somewhere past the 40-yard boundary, out where Denver really hasn't explored that often in one game this season.

Load the weapon. Spin the chamber. Throw deep. Click! Never mind the misses. It only takes one.

Unofficially, it took 11 deep attempts before they found the loaded chamber.

It settled into Vance Johnson's chest as he fell across the south end zone as the third quarter ended, and Denver now advances to the AFC championship in Cleveland next week.

Click ... Bam! Cleveland.

Denver 22, New England 17. ...

AFC CHAMPIONSHIP

January 12, 1987, *Rocky Mountain News*

DENVER BRONCOS 23, CLEVELAND BROWNS 20

CLEVELAND—The wind was blowing in out of the open end, off Lake Erie, straight into Denver's faces, a gusting, arctic reminder that this was a foreign place.

The crowd was already celebrating. The Cleveland Browns were in the Super Bowl. The score said so: Cleveland 20, Denver 13. Denver was pinned against its goal.

Up in the old stadium next to the lake, fans were thrusting gloved fists into the frosty air, barking, laughing, hugging each other, screaming their joy and anticipation. In the paper that morning, there were 17 different ads for Super Bowl trips.

There were five minutes, 32 seconds left, and the Denver Broncos were inside their own 2, a step and a half from total disaster.

Cleveland's Brian Brennan had snatched an underthrown Bernie Kosar pass away from Dennis Smith and dashed into the end zone for what looked like the first Cleveland title since 1964.

"Woof!" they screamed. "Super Bowl!" By then, the end zone Denver faced was so littered with dog bones it crunched underfoot.

National Football League officials had already taken the Lamar Hunt Trophy to the Browns' locker room. Ahmad Rashad had moved into the Browns' quarters to interview the winners for NBC. Marv Albert, in charge of the losers, was standing on the Denver dugout steps.

Standing in the Denver huddle in the end zone, guard Keith Bishop looked upfield, and then around at that hostile scene, and then at tackle Dave Studdard.

"We got 'em just where we want 'em," Bishop drawled in that lazy Texas twang.

"We giggled," Studdard said at the memory. "I about fell over," said guard Mark Cooper.

"We worked our way down to the dog bones," center Bill Bryan said. "They were out of 'em by then."

Ninety-eight yards and only five minutes from extinction, these mud-caked giants were bent over, giggling at themselves and their plight.

Cleveland, with a seven-point lead, was about to become one of pro football's historic victims. "I never felt, even at the 1-foot line, we were gonna lose," said Studdard.

In the Denver huddle in its own end zone, one of the great drives in NFL playoff history was being launched on a stale joke and some gallows humor.

Five minutes later, 98 yards and 15 plays upfield from where taunting Browns fans had been tossing the dog bones at the Broncos in pregame warmups, John Elway sent a laser beam that Mark Jackson skimmed off the surface, and the most memorable march in Denver history had earned the Broncos a 20-20 deadlock and overtime.

Rich Karlis' 33-yard game-winner 5:48 into overtime was almost foreordained.

... Sammy Winder slashed for the first third-down conversion. It began. On third-and-18 at midfield, Elway found Mark Jackson for 20. On third-and-one at the five, he found him again for history.

... "I didn't see the catch," Elway admitted.

It wasn't necessary. Some 80,000 stunned Cleveland zanies did, and a national television audience did, and Bishop and his friends did.

So did NBC and the NFL. Quickly, the trophy, Albert and Rashad changed places, hurrying past each other as the Broncos drove for Karlis' winner.

With that magnificent march, they hammered their way into history and into their second Super Bowl in 10 years and they did it in a way that would make John Houseman proud: They earned it. ...

They belong.

... Exit laughing. They had just giggled all the way from their 2 to Pasadena.

SUPER BOWL XXI

January 26, 1987, *Rocky Mountain News*

NEW YORK GIANTS 39, DENVER BRONCOS 20

PASADENA—He was off in a corner, in front of the blue drapery with the No. 7 hanging from it.

The New York Giants were up a few stairs, to his right already explaining how they had won Super Bowl XXI, when league security people began ushering John Elway through the mob in front of his podium.

He was wearing a white terrycloth robe, and the muscle folks kept pushing people aside, creating a moving aisle.

He looked like a heavyweight boxer being escorted to the ring. Under the circumstances, there was something appropriate about that image. But it wouldn't fit a Rocky Balboa script. Rocky always wins.

Elway didn't. The New York Giants simply took over with a magnificent second half at the Rose Bowl, and won 39-20, and while Denver may argue it should have been closer, the Broncos did nothing the last 30 minutes to make it anything except what it was, a brilliant declaration by the Giants that they are the best team in football.

Elway became the Denver offense, and against the best defense in the league, it wasn't enough.

He ran for a score. He threw for a score. He had at least three other scoring chances abort down near the New York Giants' goal line. He ran left and threw 54 yards back down to the right, and a whole nation sucked in its breath. And it produced nothing.

He had first-and-goal at the Giants' 1, at a time Denver could have broken out to a 17-7 lead and who knows what else, and got nothing.

And gradually, all the things that have troubled the Broncos at times this season began to coalesce on the floor of this giant stadium, and nothing football's new golden boy could do would reverse it. ...

AFC PLAYOFF

January 11, 1988, *Rocky Mountain News*

DENVER BRONCOS 34, HOUSTON OILERS 10

MILE HIGH STADIUM—So much for conventional wisdom.

It dictates that coaches go ultraconservative in the playoffs, that they spend the week leading up to these events ripping whole chapters out of the playbook, reducing a thousand meeting hours since spring to two or three simple little things a man can master in the noise and the frost and the snow and the wind.

September high-tech becomes January Neanderthal. Run. Block. Don't fumble. And don't-for-gawd's-sake-take-chances.

Translated to sartorial terms, playoff teams would appear in lace-up brogans, two belts and a reinforced set of suspenders.

So why was Steve Sewell standing next to his locker in yesterday's early evening, his eyebrows reaching toward the top of the room?

"No, I never expected to be used that much," the number one draft choice from Oklahoma admitted. He was making his first appearance since a broken jaw side-lined him some two months ago.

"We put some stuff back in the game plan, but I didn't realize they were actually going to call them."

There was, oh, the halfback pass, the one he couldn't get away. There was the one where he lined up at tight end, with center Larry Lee at fullback and Sammy Winder diving over the middle. On that one, Sewell came within a fingernail of a touchdown.

There was the direct snap from center, with John Elway acting the part of a confused man, standing, waving his arms at the sideline. That one netted about four yards on two tries.

But it may have triggered a fatal response by Houston's Jerry Glanville after Denver used a direct snap to Sewell on its third play.

There was, it seemed, a release of all the pent-up plays Dan Reeves hasn't been able to call since first Gerald Willhite and then Sewell went out with injuries.

It's as if Reeves had been keeping a secret list, and he began checking it off one by one as his team routed Houston 34-10 to advance to next week's AFC Championship against Cleveland. ...

AFC CHAMPIONSHIP

January 18, 1988, *Rocky Mountain News*

DENVER BRONCOS 38, CLEVELAND BROWNS 33

MILE HIGH STADIUM—Once again, the Denver Broncos proved the El-way is still the best way. Barely.

Once again, the Cleveland Browns proved they still don't believe it.

And what began on the 2 next to Lake Erie a year ago, ended on the 2 in Denver yesterday, and if you want to talk about The Drive this time, you'll have to make it plural. And totally bipartisan.

Denver's 38-33 triumph over the Browns in the AFC Championship game was filled with nothing but drives, some of them 13 plays, some just three, seven of them packed into a second-half track meet threatening mass whiplash for 76,197 witnesses.

The only things missing in the second half yesterday were stops and boredom.

Oh. And Jeremiah Castille. The free agent cornerback from Tampa Bay dressed hurriedly and fled the dressing room yesterday after the biggest play of his professional life.

"No comment," he said. "After the Super Bowl."

No comment? After he preserved the win for the Broncos by stripping Earnest Byner of the ball at the Denver 2 just as Byner was about to create a 38-all deadlock and yet another AFC title game overtime between these two clubs?

... Remove the 2 from the field and Cleveland, not Denver, would be heading for its second straight Super Bowl, the first team to do so since the Pittsburgh Steelers at the end of the 1970s.

Denver started its 98-yard march there a year ago. Byner's bobble ended the Cleveland dreams there yesterday.

And somehow, at the end, there was a curiously subdued atmosphere under the south stands.

"Numb," Dan Reeves said. "We know what the Super Bowl is all about," said owner Pat Bowlen. "It's not 'Alice in Wonderland' this year."

Is there something mystical about Mile High? defensive coordinator Joe Collier was asked. Something that decrees the Broncos will somehow come up with a big play?

"It came a little late this time," he sighed of Castille's dramatic play with 1:05 left. ...

Is there any better way to decide a championship than the script the Browns and Broncos have perfected the past two seasons?

Big games rarely live up to the adjective. This one overwhelmed it. They couldn't even get it decided in the closing seconds when Elway slid a yard too early, thinking he already had a clinching first down.

It forced a safety, a Denver free kick, and left eight ticks on the electronic scoreboard high over the south stands.

Eight? Enough. Enough for Bernie Kosar who completed 26 of 41 passes, for 356 yards, three touchdowns and a second half fit for instant enshrinement at Canton. ...

This was a game they should record and use for those moments when the Super Bowl dies, as it does annually at some point. ...

SUPER BOWL XXII

February 1, 1988, *Rocky Mountain News*

WASHINGTON REDSKINS 42, DENVER BRONCOS 10

SAN DIEGO—Let's get something clarified right at the outset here.

Wasn't it Washington's Doug Williams who woke up with the abscessed tooth on Saturday?

So, how come then it was the Denver Broncos who got the root canal?

Why was it Joe Gibbs and not Dan Reeves who lingered and lingered and lingered in a smiling aftermath in the interview room? Why did Pete Rozelle give the Lombardi Trophy to Jack Kent Cooke and not Pat Bowlen?

Why was it Williams, not John Elway, who walked off with his helmet thrust triumphantly into the soft San Diego night?

Why did it remind so much of 19 Super Bowls ago, when Joe Namath trotted off the floor of the Orange Bowl, his right index finger thrust up, signaling the end and the beginning of eras?

The Jets' win marked the emergence of the AFL. Williams' triumph ends the next-to-last racial barrier in the NFL. Now, Williams can just be a successful quarterback, a Super Bowl winner, and not a standard-bearer.

And Denver has to live its off-season remembering.

... "Attention press. That was the earliest score in Super Bowl history."

John Elway, on Denver's first scrimmage play, had found Ricky Nattiel for a 56-yard touchdown, and the Broncos led.

All the zanies were in ecstasy, all the orange-clad idolators who had followed this team for so long. ...

"Attention press. The whole Washington defense has just switched to longer cleats."

Denver had driven its second possession to a 24-yard Rich Karlis field goal and a 10-0 lead, and was driving again.

"Attention press. The 80-yard touchdown pass from Doug Williams to Ricky Sanders ties a Super Bowl record set by Jim Plunkett to Kenny King in Super Bowl XV."

There would be no more "Attention press" to commemorate Broncos' successes. "Attention press," was finished for Denver. ...

By halftime, it had gone past mere embarrassment and into some uglier realm. There were no chants, no orange pennants being waved, no Broncos fans dancing in the aisles.

They sat glumly, arms folded, watching the halftime show. It had taken two hours to get to the 88 pianos and the Rockettes. It had taken Washington only five minutes and 47 seconds of total playing time to generate five touchdowns, 356 yards and leave Denver staring at itself and wondering. ...

That was as bad as a Super Bowl team has looked, that second-quarter collapse. Elway couldn't start a drive. Joe Collier's forces couldn't stop one.

It's the second time Denver has led and died, and been dismantled. ...

All the shortcomings and injury factors they've managed to disguise and overcome in the season were there yesterday. Plus one more.

Elway, the man who took them to San Diego, couldn't take them the extra few feet down the concrete corridor to the interview rooms reserved for winners. ...

SUPER BOWL XXIII: PREGAME

January 22, 1989, *Denver Post*

MIAMI—Relax, Denver. It's someone else's turn. Ski. Linger over a late lunch. Go for a walk. Wash the car. Take a nap.

But don't worry. This time, some other city has to take the blame.

The 1989 Super Bowl onus belongs elsewhere for a change, and not a Denverite will miss the burden.

If attendance at the stock show is up—and it is—and the Nuggets, even in a slump, are showing an increase, and the lift lines seem longer an hour to the west, it's understandable.

When you woke this morning, that was not a Chinook howling past your window. It was a sigh of civic relief.

Denver's Broncos are not in the Super Bowl. May we join hands and observe a moment of silent thanksgiving? We deserve it. No city should have to undergo the back-to-back pillaging Denver has endured in Pasadena and San Diego, or XXI and XXII by the Rozellian Calendar. ...

The Super Bowl is to Denver as Lucy is to Charlie Brown. ...

Serenity has settled over the Mile High City. Three o'clock isn't a dreaded appointment with fate. This time, it's just midafternoon. ...

Let some other burg practice civic humility for a change. After XXI and XXII, Denver has raised it to an art form.

So enjoy, Denver. For a change, this loss is not on you.

SUPER BOWL XXIII

January 23, 1989, *Denver Post*

SAN FRANCISCO 49ERS 20, CINCINNATI BENGALS 16

MIAMI—He stood in his bare feet, wrists still taped, holding his 19-month-old daughter, Jaqui. She kept reaching wet fingers for the microphone, and Jerry Rice kept trying to gently brush them away.

The microphone under Joe Robbie Stadium didn't work. It was the only part of Jerry Rice's game that failed on Super Sunday XXIII.

Never, not even in Green Bay's dynastic era nor Pittsburgh's domination of the late 1970s, has one single man done more in one single game than Jerry Rice did for San Francisco and to Cincinnati Sunday.

... Sunday, Rice and Joe Montana were Star Wars, laser technology to take into a new century, on a scarred football field here in America's tropics.

If a great game must produce great moments and great performances, Super Bowl XXIII qualified by the finish of San Francisco's 20-16 victory. From a soporific start, it escalated into high drama by the end, Montana driving his team to a historic third win in this decade with Rice his magic wand. ...

AFC PLAYOFF

January 8, 1990, *Denver Post*

DENVER BRONCOS 24, PITTSBURGH STEELERS 23

MILE HIGH STADIUM—Only an art lover could find true beauty in the Denver Broncos offense.

Forget realism. Search for meaning. There's a disconnected kind of form to it, like trying to find the theme in a Salvador Dali oil.

There. Can't you see the face? And there's an eye. There see? An eye. Let's look for a chin now. It's in there somewhere. It must be. They win, don't they?

Yesterday, for the 16th time in John Elway's career, he drove his team from behind to a win in the final minutes. From a first half when his unit seemed to get the ball only every other decade, the Broncos extracted a 24-23 thriller that puts them into their third AFC title game in four years.

Something has to be working.

And the way they won, the timing, the high drama after low comedy, is now as much a part of Denver as orange jerseys or Elway's arm or Dan Reeves' sideline wardrobe.

Don't ask Elway to explain how a team that has been hammered for three hours suddenly rallies itself. For one thing, he's reluctant to identify the key element—himself.

Is it possible he's more focused then?

"It's a little more wide open, maybe," he thinks, trying to explain what happens when the clock is nearly gone.

... Judging only on style points for the whole afternoon would put them on vacation by this point. It's a team that hangs on, then lets the shot clock tick to near zero before escaping.

... With 2:27 left, Elway had brought his team from behind to win again.

"I just tried to make something happen," Elway said. "I didn't actually try to make it as dramatic as it was."

But drama and Elway have been inseparable. Even his near disasters come in spectacular form. He ran 32 yards late in the third quarter and cartwheeled into a one-point landing—on his helmet.

It had a stadium anxious, wondering. ...

Why the fourth-quarter success? Reeves has another theory. "I guess it means we haven't played very well for three quarters," he said.

Sometimes there's that, too.

AFC CHAMPIONSHIP

January 15, 1990, *Denver Post*

DENVER 37, CLEVELAND 21

MILE HIGH STADIUM—Theey're baack. And now they're even taking victory laps. They laughed and waved and trotted about Mile High Stadium, and the next time you get a glimpse at them, they'll be indoors in Nawlins.

For the third time in four years, the fourth since they started this frustrating little odyssey back in 1978, the Denver Broncos are going to the Super Bowl.

They have dominated their division and their conference over that stretch, winning more conference titles, more games, more home games.

But there always has been that catsup stain on the front of those postseason tuxedoes.

Since XII, as the NFL likes to tell time, Denver has not been able to win when it gets to the Roman-numeral stages. It hasn't even looked good.

But it gets there, and who is to say there isn't one more improbable finish to this most improbable of seasons? ...

SUPER BOWL XXIV: PREGAME

January 28, 1990, *Denver Post*

NEW ORLEANS—Memories.

Some of them good.

New Orleans is both the best and worst place for a Super Bowl. It's best because no other venue offers the concentrated excitement of Bourbon Street and the French Quarter. If you're in town for the game, you go there.

It's a magnet. In California, in Miami, fans are so dispersed that the real big-game feeling arrives only when you get to the stadium on Sunday.

Not New Orleans. It's there all week, building. We'll get back to that.

Worst. Because only Miami Beach does a better more professional job of gouging. Both cities have been threatened with removal of the game (they actually did pull it from Miami for a while) because of this civic hobby.

New Orleans has what amounts to Velcro menus, adjustable by the day, the hour or the meal.

"Where you heading?" the cabbie asked me once a few years back. I was going out to a basketball game or something. I can't remember now. I just remember his response when I gave him the address.

"They got a game there? Well, don't pay attention to the meter, then. If there's an event, it's higher."

But if your wallet and patience can stand it, the intimacy of a New Orleans Super Bowl makes up for all the rest. It's the best food, best atmosphere, most fun of any. ...

Some folks remember Super Bowls for their scores, I don't, especially after three sterile trips with the locals to New Orleans, Pasadena and San Diego. No, I remember them for vignettes.

New Orleans especially. It seems to produce the bizarre, the unusual, the dramatic.

There was IV, for instance, the final game pitting champions of the old AFL and NFL before they merged. Minnesota was heavily favored, with Joe Kapp the very persona of the macho quarterback. Kansas City had a quarterback, Len Dawson, who was built more like a soccer player. And he was being accused by a Detroit district attorney of being a major figure in a gambling probe.

So this cloud hung over Dawson, who roomed with Johnnie Robinson, a great free safety. Robinson had cracked ribs the previous week against Oakland. All night, he moaned and tossed and turned and moaned, and Dawson stared at the ceiling, wondering what would come next from Detroit. It was a lively room.

On Sunday, they went out and dominated the fearsome Vikings. But, before the game, organizers had these two hot-air balloons. The Vikings mascot, that guy in a Viking suit, climbed into one. A guy dressed as an Indian chief got in the other.

The Vikings balloon never quite got airborne. It bounced and clattered across the Tulane Stadium turf and crashed into a crowd of southern belles gathered in one corner. The balloon set one girl's gown ablaze.

And all week, the temperature was so cold, the fountain in front of the Chiefs' hotel froze.

New Orleans is where the Steelers began their fearsome drive through the league in the 1970s. And I remember outside the Olde Absinthe House at about 1 o'clock one morning, two Steelers fans started a hurdling contest over police barriers. One hooked a toe and took a face divot out of Bourbon Street.

I remember going to the Steelers' Mass that Saturday night. And for some reason unknown to me, I wound up as one of the readers. I'm claiming no cause and effect here, understand, but the Broncos have never asked me to read at THEIR pregame Mass, and. ...

New Orleans is where Cookie Gilchrist and Abner Haynes boycotted the 1964 AFL All-Star Game and had it moved to Houston because of prejudice.

Oh. And it's where former Broncos general manager Fred Gehrke ordered 50 sets of vertical striped socks made up and put in each locker before the 1978 Super Bowl against the Cowboys.

As it turned out, they should have worn them.

SUPER BOWL XXIV

January 29, 1990, *Denver Post*

SAN FRANCISCO 49ERS 55, DENVER BRONCOS 10

NEW ORLEANS—Forget, for the moment, last night's final score. (Try. To help, I'm not even going to mention it. You'll have to remember or look it up on your own. Meanwhile, gulp another aspirin.)

Measure Denver's fourth Super Bowl humiliation in another way. Oh, yes. There are several. Gauge it by the announcements that kept breaking over the public-address system in the Superdome.

"Attention media," the litany would go as it got worse and worse. Or better and better. This is an equal-opportunity column.

"Joe Montana's last completion has tied a Super Bowl record set by Terry Bradshaw."

And then things would go along, John Elway would throw another interception, or a receiver would drop a ball, or Jerry Rice or somebody would run another uncontested deep post route, and there would be that voice again:

"Attention media, the 49ers' six touchdowns tie a record set by Washington's Redskins in Super Bowl XXII against the Denver Broncos."

It was followed quickly by yet another.

"Attention media, Joe Montana's five touchdown passes break the record shared by Terry Bradshaw in Super Bowl XV and Doug Williams in Super Bowl XXII."

One by one, all the old giants' swords were broken on the anvil of one of the great games in championship history. Roger Staubach, Terry Bradshaw, even one-day giants such as Phil Simms and Doug Williams were banished to the old shadows.

... You can spot the trend, I'm sure. By then, even 49ers fans were starting to ease their way into the soft New Orleans night, heading for dinner or a drink. Broncos fans had those goals firmly reversed.

... "Attention media, the 55-10 score is the worst championship defeat since San Diego beat New England 51-10 for the 1963 AFL championship."

Still, as bad as you feel this morning, consider this: You could be a Cleveland fan and know your team lost to these same Broncos. Again.

SUPER BOWL XXV: PREGAME

January 27, 1991, *Denver Post*

TAMPA, Fla.—He stood there on Jan. 15, 1967, that gap plainly visible between his front teeth. His Green Bay Packers were gathered around him, about to go on the field to play in the first Super Bowl against Kansas City.

In the other tunnel at the Los Angeles Coliseum, the Chiefs were grim-faced, tense. Defensive tackle Buck Buchanan was so emotionally peaked he was crying.

But as I watched Vince Lombardi through field glasses, he was telling a story. Suddenly, the whole Green Bay team broke out in laughter as it trotted out.

"I don't know," former Green Bay great Jerry Kramer was saying here last week. He was voted to the Super Bowl's 25th Anniversary All–Star team.

"Vince was a master at that sort of thing, but I can't remember what he said that day. He had a wonderful ability to judge the emotional level of the team. He could give us something inspirational, a dramatic pep talk, or he could say, "Anybody know why Belgians are so strong?" Belgians are the ethnic group in Wisconsin that catches all the grief.

"We'd wonder, 'What the hell is he talking about?' And finally, we'd say no, why? "'Because they all raise dumbbells.'"

"It sounds stupid, but we were so tight, getting ready to play the Bears for a divisional championship when he told that joke, it seemed to loosen everybody all at once."

As with most of what Lombardi did, it worked.

It's why the trophy given to the winning team tonight is called the Lombardi Trophy, emblematic of excellence. Lombardi drew excellence from those around him.

The Super Bowl, born out of the merger of the old American and National Football leagues, has grown into America's great midwinter pageant. The nation stops, pauses, shoves back in its recliner chairs. ...

SUPER BOWL XXV

January 28, 1991, *Denver Post*
New York Giants 20, Buffalo Bills 19

TAMPA, Fla.—On a soft Florida night when they worried about getting to play at all, the NFL finally gave us a Super Bowl to match its pretentious title.

They flooded us with drama.

They stretched nerves with suspense.

This one—for the first time—came down to the final play. It came down to one yard, and one point.

The war-tense world was even treated to a two-minute drill by Buffalo's gritty Bills that actually meant something. Counting Joe Montana's winning surge against Cincinnati two years ago, it's just the third one in the 25-year history of this traditionally one-sided game.

There were two insoluble problems for Buffalo and the AFC—too few minutes and too few footballs. The New York Giants hogged both. Those final two minutes represented almost the Bills' whole ration for the fourth quarter.

By the time Buffalo got its last chance, it rushed upfield and into field-goal range—and failed by a yard.

... This time, we got Scott Norwood's 47-yard field goal try climbing into the lights with eight seconds left and then sliding a yard to the wrong side of the right upright. The New York Giants had won their second Super Bowl 20-19. The Bills had lost their first try.

... The Bills played with passion, and precision, with muscle and flair, and all the things a Super Bowl team would like to bring to the year's final game.

The only thing they could never get enough of was the football.

In a game that had a thousand dancers, a dozen floats, inflated Disney characters, army helicopters hovering nearby in case of terrorism and the hundreds of doves the NFL seems to like so much, there was one glaring lack:

For every minute the Bills had possession, the Giants had it two. ...

And as the Giants did in strangling the San Francisco 49ers a week ago, they simply kept the ball so long Kelly and his no-huddle offense were left as spectators.

Until the final play, they still had a chance to win. It may not have been the prettiest, but it was the best Super Bowl yet.

AFC CHAMPIONSHIP
January 13, 1992, *Denver Post*
BUFFALO BILLS 10, DENVER BRONCOS 7

ORCHARD PARK, N.Y.—The Age of Miracles limped into history here yesterday, but Denver's gimpy exit left many former critics wanting more, not less.

Strange, isn't it? The team only its mothers wanted in the Super Bowl is now covered with new respect.

It got better and better as the season wore on, and eventually took itself into a place nobody forecast—January.

Then, 40 yards short, it ran out of miracles. The team that experts insisted didn't belong proved it was every bit as good as its 12-4 record, but one play shy of a possible fifth Super Bowl, thrillingly, agonizingly close.

There was no climactic late dash against the clock—although for seconds after Steve Atwater recovered an onside kick with less than two minutes left, another miracle seemed imminent.

Denver lost to Buffalo 10-7 in a defensive classic, and nothing is going to change that bottom line. The high-powered Bills never scored a touchdown against Wade Phillips' brilliantly executed defense. For big stretches, the Bills couldn't even manage a first down.

No matter. A John Elway screen pass was batted, intercepted and returned for a score, and Scott Norwood, the goat of Super Bowl XXV, drilled a late field goal that proved the difference.

Maybe, in the dark night, that redemptive kick will help Denver's Steve Sewell. Or ease things for David Treadwell. Or even soothe Elway, who had to watch the last quarter hobbled on the sideline with a deep thigh bruise, then nearly fainted at his postgame press conference.

Maybe. But not probably. This was a game in which Denver outplayed the defending AFC champions on their own field. It squeezed Jim Kelly and Co. to a paltry 58 yards the first half and 213 for the game. It left the Bills talking to each other, confused.

It moved the ball itself but kept running into Cornelius Bennett or Bruce Smith or Darryl Talley at all the wrong moments.

And all the while, the game scoreless, there was this tantalizing chance that Denver, not heavily favored Buffalo, would be advancing to the Super Bowl.

Then, when Gary Kubiak replaced Elway and drove Denver to a score, and Atwater recovered the ensuing onside kick, it looked like last week's win over Houston was on the replay screen.

It was then that Sewell took a first down pass seven yards to the Bills' 44—and was stripped of the football by Kirby Jackson with 1:28 left.

... Kubiak, who has spent nine years in Elway's shadow, who is retiring to coach, outpassed both Elway and Buffalo's Jim Kelly in his final outing. ...

But it wasn't enough. ...

SUPER BOWL XXVI
January 26, 1992, *Denver Post*
WASHINGTON REDSKINS 37, BUFFALO BILLS 24

MINNEAPOLIS—Note to desk. Get out old columns about Denver–New York Giants, Denver-Washington, Denver–San Francisco.

Change names. Any place you see word "Denver," please put in word "Buffalo." Substitute Jim Kelly for John Elway. (Elway won't object, believe me.) Put in Mark Rypien for, oh, Phil Simms. Insert Thurman Thomas for any number of Denver runners from the past.

It even sounded similar when it ended. "They made the big plays. We dropped a few passes," Buffalo's Marv Levy said, sounding like a modern echo of Dan Reeves five years ago, or four, or two.

Statistics will stand almost as is. Big ones for Washington, little bitty anemic ones for Buffalo. Oh, and make the score Washington 37-24. That doesn't begin to describe how this game went, but it's all we have to work with on the scoreboard.

That's it. Otherwise, all the columns from Denver's 1987, 1988 and 1990 Super Bowl blowouts will do nicely, thanks.

Denver has set standards for ineptitude in this game, but Buffalo became the new leader in the clubhouse in the first half in the Metrodome last night. Ignore those late scores they managed. It was like trying to put a good face on missing the mortgage payment.

This was as ugly as anything the Broncos ever did in the NFL's final game. Kelly was intercepted four times, tying Craig Morton from XII. (Morton, like Elway, may mail a thank-you to Kelly.) The Bills didn't score the first half.

Buffalo couldn't even get its star runner and player of the year on the field for the first series.

Thurman Thomas, the guy who pouted about lack of attention this week, couldn't find his helmet.

All those game-plan hours, all the time watching tape, all the thought, and your top runner can't find his headgear, and you wind up punting on your first series of downs. "It didn't hurt us one iota," Buffalo's Marv Levy insisted afterward. But it should be noted Thomas' replacement gained one yard, ran the wrong way on the next play and Kelly was sacked on the third. It's not the ideal scenario for starting your biggest game of the year.

Meanwhile, Mark Rypien, the guy Joe Gibbs wasn't sure about as late as summer, the guy he talked to Denver about replacing with Elway, shreds the Bills with an almost perfect game and winds up the Super Bowl MVP.

So, while Gibbs stood on one platform, his quarterback was about three first downs away on another one, both explaining Washington's third Super Bowl triumph. It was like explaining a 10-on-one street mugging.

"Put 25 seconds back on the clock," the officials insisted at the end, Gibbs, already being escorted off, had to go back to the sideline.

So the game that couldn't start on time—they rekicked because an official wasn't set for the opening boot—couldn't even end when it should.

If ever a game didn't deserve 25 more ticks of the clock, this was it.

Washington was everything it has been all season. Buffalo wasn't even a shadow of whatever team it was that cruised through the AFC.

And in a game and week that is an exercise in excess, they exceeded themselves. The Bills twice helped Washington with penalties on scoring drives. They fumbled six times, dropped passes, ran the wrong routes and continued the offensive malaise that began in their 10-7 victory over Denver in the AFC title game.

It could have been much worse. Washington had an early touchdown taken away on instant replay. The Redskins got to the 2, 11 and 17 and came out with just three points before Rypien and Co. finally adjusted the fine-tuning.

"Yeah, I was worried," Gibbs said. "We were very concerned. We'd been right at the top of the league in scoring when we got down there. It was very uncharacteristic of us."

It was the last hint of hope for the Bills. Fighting off all that potential disaster, they managed only three first downs before Washington led 17-0 at intermission.

Thomas, the man who would be king (if he could find his helmet), was three yards for six tries. Kelly had two passes intercepted. The Bills had eight yards on the ground.

Even Denver had done better.

It's almost the worst thing that can be said about the Bills last night.

CHAPTER FOUR

GOLF

✤ ✤ ✤

Late in life, Dick reintroduced himself to golf, a game he had abandoned three decades before. It was not easy. "Just once," he groaned, "I'd like to get this dad-blamed ball airborne with a driver."

... As a writer, Connor was in a class by himself. He brought style and dignity to the sportswriting profession he called a privilege, not a job. He chose his words caringly, words that created incomparable finger paintings on paper. He was not a comic, frivolous or filled with himself. Ridicule was the weaponry of others. ...

"But anyone who mistakes me for a golfer has just arrived from Mars," Connor said.

—Kaye Kessler, retired sports columnist,
***Columbus Citizen Journal,* and first publicist for**
International Golf Tournament, Castle Pines, Colo.

✤ ✤ ✤

One of Dick's all-time favorite assignments was covering the Masters Golf Tournament in Augusta, Ga., every spring. It was such a contrast from professional football or even college sports that it rejuvenated him. If it was spring, it must be Masters time.

He gave up playing golf in his 30s because he didn't play it well, nor did he have the time then to develop his game. Rather than embarrass himself, he hung up his clubs.

What helped him decide to quit golf was when TV sports caster Starr Yelland announced Dick's score on his show. It was the worst in some charity tournament. Dick liked to be good at what he did, and he liked to win.

During the last two summers of his life, he took up the game again, primarily at the urging of his longtime friend, Kaye Kessler, who assured him he could get better at it, and that it didn't matter that much if he wasn't a scratch golfer.

But whether or not he played the game, he loved to cover golf. He wrote in the Apr. 12, 1991, *Denver Post,* "If I had to take just one event to cover each year, go on some sort of professional diet, my choice would be Augusta in April. There is nothing else quite like it in sports."

April 10, 1981, *Denver Post*

IT'S EASY TO SEE WHY MASTERS ISN'T JUST ANOTHER TOURNEY

AUGUSTA, Ga.—Was ol' Greg pumped?

"I didn't think so. I normally hit a 5-iron 180 to 185 yards."

But, he's never come to the 18th hole at Augusta National Golf Club. Not while a very official-looking man in appropriate jacket and tie informed the huge gallery that "appearing in the Masters championship for the first time, from Australia, leading through 17 holes at 4-under-par, Greg Norman."

The official sounded like the ring announcer at Madison Square Garden. Norman promptly swung like Rocky Marciano, and smashed that 5-iron 205 yards, uphill, was short chipping back, missed a 25-footer that slid on past by six and finally ran that in. So, Greg Norman woke up Friday morning in a four-way tie for the lead in the 45th Masters.

He also woke up realizing this isn't just another golf tournament, and that Augusta isn't just another golf club.

"The galleries aren't too large in Europe," said this 26-year-old from Australia's east coast. He earned $250,000 on the international circuit last year, but virtually is unknown to American fans. Until Thursday. "I had chills driving up here this morning," he admitted, although he went to the first tee determined to "play it like a practice round."

That's like dropping by St. Peter's just to see if they have the doors open or bingo scheduled. Golf writers like to picture Augusta National as the Sistine Chapel of the sport, and in April with the azaleas spilling down the manicured hillsides and framing holes with picturesque names like "Flowering Crabapple" and "Pink Dog-wood" and "Camelia," there can be few more gorgeous spots anywhere.

In our business, there are a certain few events you want to cover, to attend, just because of what they are, or represent. The Masters—and Augusta—always have been on that list for me. Thursday, ol' Greg and I finally made it.

If he got chills coming up Magnolia Lane to the front of the clubhouse, so did I. Even though the first Masters was less than a half century back, this whole place has an almost antebellum presence to it. It is old. Old buildings,. but new white paint. Old waiters, but a new Mercedes pulling up the drive in front. "Second Floor, Gentlemen Only," the sign cautions. It is fixed to the wall, across the hallway from the engraved portraits of all past Masters champions.

A Masters badge will bring $500 from a scalper, but the threat of arrest doesn't mean as much as the fact the committee probably would lift your name from the ticket list. A gold badge admits you to the clubhouse, to the locker room ...

Down the hall, another trophy case. This one is some 20 feet long, and the recessed lighting reflects on a line of clubs previous winners have donated. A 5-wood from Ray Floyd (1976), a 1-iron from Arnold Palmer (1958, the first of his four wins here), a 4-wood from Ben Hogan (1951), a 1-iron from Jack Nicklaus' 1963 win.

"Theah's the man," a lady next to the 18th green had said earlier, pointing back to the south. "Who" her companion asked. "Mistah Pah-mah. Look how tan he is."

If you're going to compare Augusta in April to an outdoor cathedral, then Palmer is the pope emeritus. He is in his 27th Masters and it doesn't matter what he is shooting. He strides through corridors of human devotion here, smiling, waving, arm up as if he's bestowing a benediction on the faithful. This is his country. ...

<hr>

April 13, 1984, *Rocky Mountain News*

TREVINO MAKES THE MOST OF HIS FAST START

AUGUSTA, Ga.—The new Lee Trevino, reluctant dragon of Masters history, woke up Friday in second place, only a shot off the lead of a tournament he has spent years panning and avoiding.

He's sorry he didn't do this earlier.

Was he shaken, he was asked, when he bogied a couple of holes on the back nine?

"Sir," Trevino shot back, "I've been hit by lightning. I've been whupped. I've had two marriages. I don't get shaken by nothin'."

And from now on, here in the rollng garden that is Augusta, he doesn't plan to let anything shake him again.

This is the place, remember, that Trevino twice actually refused to visit when invited. He had once been angered when the haughty Masters cautioned Chi Chi

Rodriguez' wife about a daring dress. He didn't like the course. He thought the whole atmosphere too snooty.

Thursday, it was different, sort of.

"Am I in the right seat?" he asked in the interview room.

He had just finished a round that began with three straight birdies and ended with him at 68, one behind Ben Crenshaw and 4 under par.

Trevino had prepared for the golf world's most august tournament by playing three nine-hole rounds in California a week ago, traveling all day Monday, staying in his room Tuesday "because it was too cold here," and playing the front nine Wednesday.

"Then I went out and watched them milk cows last night," he said of a friend's local dairy farm.

It was a day of quips and serious answers, mixed about as he mixed seven birdies and three bogies in Thursday's almost perfect weather conditions.

Item: Is the 68 his best round here?

"Yes. It is. And I am very excited about it because I think the first round in any golf tournament is the most important one. It gets you set. You know you have some shots you can lean on."

Yes. He's happy with his putting. "If I keep going like this, I wear a 42 short," he said, a deadpan reference to the green jacket awarded the winner. "Any questions? But I'll take a 46 long."

Serious again. "I'm still not in love with [Augusta]," he said. "But it's an important golf tournament and means a lot to win it. Yes, I do regret not having come at times [twice]."

His new wife, he said, talked him out of the idea he was over the hill, too old to be good anymore. So did pro Jackie Burke, who cautioned him this week, "Those clubs don't know how old you are."

As for not coming, he elaborated. "I regret the years. Definitely. You think about those things. I guess you grow up, you would say. Even though I was 29 or 30 years old when I did it, but I had not been in professional golf that long. I don't like [the Masters]."

But the pride intruded. He doesn't want to go down in history as never having won this tournament. "I would be remembered not for what I did but for not having won the Masters."

He has not given in totally here.

"I just came to play because I am playing very well. That's the only reason. I think the feelings—I've got to be truthful—my feelings are exactly the same."

And the course?

"I've always been able to play the course," said the man who has said in the past his game was not suited for Augusta National's sprawling spaces.

"I think I've been my own worst enemy. I've been telling myself that I wasn't able to. Then if a problem comes up you use it as an excuse. It was strictly a copout and I take the full blame for it."

"It won't happen this week," he said. "I can take bogey five times in a row and I won't blow up."

And when did he decide this?

"When I married that mean woman," he said of his second wife.

And her name?

"Claudia. Same as my ex-wife. I didn't have to buy any new towels or sheets. We can use the same checkbooks and everything."

Exit Trevino, the new Trevino—but the old one, as well.

"How the hell do I get out of here," he asked, and an official motioned toward a door.

"No," Trevino said, smiling. "That's the back way. I've been going the back way all my life."

April 15, 1984, *Rocky Mountain News*

FAIR GOLDEN BELL RUINS ROUNDS

AUGUSTA, Ga.—Like a siren from Greek mythology, she lured them with gentle songs and lovely promises.

Golden Bell, she's called. Every hole at Augusta National has a name as well as a number, and Golden Bell rests in splendor between White Dogwood and Azalea, nestled into the deepest corner of this onetime orchard, waiting for the unwary.

Saturday, she waited and tempted, showing her most benign face—then grabbed the leaders in the 1984 Masters by the throat in the gloaming while lightning played and thunder rolled over the Georgia hills.

"This is the toughest par three in the world," Gary Player says of the 12th hole, as Golden Bell's alias goes.

Tom Kite, who left her Saturday almost with a fist raised against the gods, says, "There is no way of playing the hole."

Craig Stadler abandoned her furiously on Friday by whirling and throwing his ball into Rae's Creek that runs in front. Saturday, mild-mannered Ben Crenshaw, Gentle Ben, hurled his golf ball into the woods. Each had bogied.

There is something about 12 that seems to bring out the worst in men—and women. Fans come every year, the same fans, to this same historic spot, like disaster-seekers who like to sit in the corner at Indianapolis.

They perch on three-legged stools or sprawl on blankets and wait for the bones to begin to show.

They are rarely disappointed.

Saturday was no exception.

All through the day, as Nature ran from heat to hail to ground mist and back to another thunderstorm, Golden Bell waited for the leaders.

Friday, she was the hardest on the course, giving up only six birdies and 50 pars, while charging 10 double bogeys and 22 bogeys. And Stadler's golf ball.

Saturday, not a ball was hit into the water in front. The winds were calm, club selection relatively easy.

This is the hole, remember, where Tom Weiskopf earned undying fame. It was not for being good enough to finish second four times. It was for taking 13 strokes to escape Golden Bell in 1980. He lifted five straight into the creek, watching in growing astonishment.

Jack Nicklaus hit "the most humiliating shot in my life" here in 1964 when he shanked his drive and almost decapitated Bobby Jones in a golf cart to the side of the green.

Nothing has changed. They come careening off the front side, hopeful, eager, and stare down the long nave of No. 10, knowing what's ahead. Herbert Warren Wind of the *New Yorker* named the stretch from 11 through 13 Amen Corner. It's appropriate. It is the Omega of hope, it's finish in many cases.

In Kite's, perhaps? Or Mark Lye's?

Neither knows.

"I have all night to practice that putt," Lye said early Saturday evening of the 20- or 21-footer he faces on No. 12 at 8 a.m. Sunday. All night to practice, or worry.

Kite has the same period to wonder about his sand shot. There was a period Saturday, the lightning and thunder flashing and crashing, when he called over some officials to the tee box.

Somebody asked if he was worried about playing the hole under the conditions.

"I never want to play that hole," he said honestly. "That hole is so scarey and so tough you don't want to pull the club out of your bag because you know there are 13 others in there that might be the right one."

Weiskopf is proof sometimes none are the right one.

No, said Kite. What he did not want to do at 8 a.m. was hit a few practice balls, then be whisked out to have to start the final day at the Masters facing Golden Bell from the tee.

Nightmares are pleasant compared to that.

Actually, windless through much of Saturday, it played only 134 yards to the hole instead of the 155 listed. The pin was cut far left, even more enticing if anything, and most of the field went at it. When the rains came, they left the area behind the green heavy with runoff even after it was squeegeed. Crenshaw had to hit out of that, contributing to his problem. Golden Bell was beginning to frown.

If the wind comes up, as it does, the hole is a frightening thing, since at one point Saturday when the storm was nearing, the flag first blew to the left, then the right—as Weiskopf stood on the tee and watched.

Then it died, and he parred the hole.

Billy Casper has said, only half in jest, that he's hit everything from "a 9-iron to a 2-iron off that thing."

"Always wait until the flag on the 12th pin is limp," Ken Venturi once observed.

The only thing that could be prettier for Lye and Kite Sunday would be to discover a flood during the night had washed Golden Bell into golfing history. She's already a golfing legend.

April 16, 1984, *Rocky Mountain News*

CRENSHAW FULFILLS HIS PROMISE

AUGUSTA, Ga.—Destiny and Ben Crenshaw finally got into hand-shaking proximity with each other Sunday.

They've been edging cautiously toward it for a decade, ever since the young Texan joined the PGA Tour and won his first start, the 1973 San Antonio Open. Immediately, the golf world began to anoint him as the next Jack Nicklaus or Arnold Palmer.

But it has taken a decade just to become the first Ben Crenshaw everybody waited for, and when he sat in the press interview building after the 48th Masters ended in Sunday's twilight, wearing the champion's green coat, he looked almost shaken at his new status.

His voice kept catching. His responses at times were halting. There were moments he seemed to be listening to himself, almost bemused. He was a man still trying to get used to the thought he had broken the pattern.

He was no longer the Harold Stassen of the green grass set, the man who always runs but never wins.

He had won the big one. THE big one, and it had still not penetrated to the marrow. That will come later.

But The Thing is gone, that dark question mark hanging over his career. It is banished from the psyche of this likeable man who became so frustrated a couple of years ago, he left the tour to look at himself. No matter what he did, there was always the "Yeah, but—."

He won. He won here, where any pro would sacrifice family and soul for a green jacket and what it implies. He won coming from behind, on a day when nobody seemed to want it for a while, and then nobody could stop him when he moved.

It was a day on which, quite literally, any of almost a dozen golfers might have won. Crenshaw did. It must be doubly satisfying.

This was a cavalry charge, with no bugles. The soft Georgia afternoon remained strangely quiet for much of the final round, rousing itself from slumber only when Crenshaw began to surge and leaders Tom Kite and Mark Lye fell off the pace as all three made the turn onto the back nine.

"When I saw that ball go in at 10, I said maybe, well maybe this was my day," Crenshaw said. It was a putt that carried over three time zones and a small mountain range. Or 60 feet. Whichever comes first.

It was not only what it did *for* Crenshaw but what it did *to* Tom Kite, at that point his nearest challenger, that made this almost Crenshaw's umbilical cord into a new and better life as a pro.

"We saw his putt go in on 10 and it was like lights out," said Mark Lye, who began the day as the leader and played well only to fade with the rest.

"Tom, you could see it virtually hurt him," he said of playing partner Tom Kite, who promptly bogied. As the leaders after Saturday's rain delay was finished early Sunday, they went off last, right behind Crenshaw and Nick Faldo. So they were standing back up the hill, watching Crenshaw's putt erase hope.

It may have been a factor a couple of holes later as well when Kite, knowing he had to do something, triple bogied on the 12, the Golden Bell that has been such a factor so often.

Kite had been 9 under and Crenshaw 10 under when they made the turn. Kite's bogey and Crenshaw's splendid birdie created a three-stroke crater for the rest of the day.

Kite's tee shot on 12 went into the water. Crenshaw saw it, and immediately went into a defensive game. At that point, his biggest threat was himself and his history, and he conquered both.

By the time Crenshaw came up 18, and reached in the hole to pull out his final putt, there was less elation than relief.

This is a man who finished second in the 1975 U.S. Open, the 1979 British Open and twice here (1976 and tied with Kite for runners-up a year ago). He lost a playoff to David Graham for the 1981 PGA. Always, that close, but not quite.

Yet he has won 10 tournaments, earned $1.8 million, including $108,000 for surviving Sunday's pressure.

But Sunday was not money. It was more important than that for Crenshaw, who almost thought himself off the tour in 1982 out of sheer frustration.

"Coming up 18, for some reason I started thinking about high school golf. I don't know why. I started thinking of all the help I have had, the people who have talked to me. I won this tournament for my friends. I am so happy to have so many of them."

Kite, a Texas prep rival who now is "as close to Ben as we've ever been," says the reason Crenshaw is liked is simple.

"He's just a nice guy. Nice guys are liked and jerks are not."

Ben Crenshaw, nice guy, golf's champion-in-waiting, is waiting no longer. The green jacket confirms it.

⁂   ⁂   ⁂

The following is one of the entries that won first place for personal column in the Colorado Press Association contest in 1986. Traditionally, three columns or articles are entered in each category.

April 14, 1986, *Rocky Mountain News*

THE SOUND YOU HEARD WAS THE MAKING OF LEGEND

AUGUSTA, Ga.—I will remember Jack Nicklaus and what he did, and what it meant to a 46-year-old man who hadn't won a major tournament in six years.

I will remember the poignant moment he hugged his son, Jackie, who caddied for him, when his final little putt fell and he began his vigil to see if it would be enough.

I will remember the tensions as Greg Norman, a half-hour behind Nicklaus, got ready for his second shot on No. 18, with the whole state of Georgia ringing the long uphill finishing hole, many of them silently rooting for the disaster that occurred. Would they have attacked with Rebel yells had he birdied instead of bogeyed?

Most of all, I will remember the sound when I think of the 50th Masters Golf Tournament. It became a physical thing as the Georgia afternoon wore on, the drama grew and history and the shadows began to envelop Augusta National. At one time or another, five men led or shared the lead, generating four eagles and 36 birdies among them, each accompanied by a new roar.

Nobody was exempt. The noise and emotion caught all of them. Nicklaus, he said later, had tears in his eyes four times on this sun-drenched afternoon.

The 50th Masters was a triumph of golf artistry and tension and composure and high theater. And over it all was that steady drumbeat.

The sound was part of this one as much as the players that created it.

Nicklaus had to back away twice on the ninth tee, first when Tom Kite eagled, then when Seve Ballesteros followed with one of his own.

That launched it, that pair of eagles on an afternoon grown almost sleepy up to that point as it basked under a warm sun and relatively undramatic golf from the leaders. It was sedate enough that you could hear crows cawing to each other in the top branches of the pines. Until then. That's when it began, at 3:27 p.m. EDT. That's when the first explosive decibels came surging through the pine trees.

But it was nothing compared to what would come.

Kite couldn't hear his caddie as they were walking away from the 13th hole. Greg Norman heard one roar and misinterpreted, thinking Ballesteros had eagled the 15th. It was Nicklaus. They were caught in an azalea-bordered sound chamber, and nobody will forget it.

The roar that greeted a near hole-in-one by Nicklaus on the par-3 16th floated back up the hill to Ballesteros, and the Spaniard plopped his next shot into the water fronting 15.

The next roar was the unkindest. They cheered Ballesteros' misfortune. It confused Nicklaus, who was its beneficiary, the reason for it, really. In a place that prides itself on tradition and golf etiquette, they booed a shot that helped change the tournament.

It was classless, a misguided example of nationalism, of what the afternoon and the developing scenario were doing to everyone on the course.

"It was a funny sound. I backed off my tee shot on 17. It wasn't the sound of a cheer and yet it *was* the sound of a cheer. It said something happened."

It had. Nicklaus had eagled 15, birdied 16 and gone to 8 under par. He had come out of the week and his own slumping career to challenge. Ballesteros, leading until then, had fallen back to meet him.

All week, the foreign stars had dominated this uniquely American classic.

The galleries were polite, enthusiastic, receptive. But something was missing. The noise, said old-timers, was not the same as when Palmer and Nicklaus prowled these manicured paths in their prime.

Even Tom Watson joked about it, imitating the various crowd sounds when an eagle or birdie putt dropped.

It wasn't the same.

Until midafternoon yesterday. Until the numbers began to appear, until eagles by Tom Kite and Ballesteros playing together on No. 8, and until Jack Nicklaus' name abruptly went up on the leader board at 3:56 p.m.

At that point, he was the only American with a chance. But he was not any American.

It was Jack Nicklaus. It was Augusta. It was Sunday afternoon, a time and a place that used to belong to him, and a man most of us had written off was in the hunt again. Jack Nicklaus was back in late afternoon in a tournament he had won five times, and the silence was ended.

"A roar went up. Then another roar. Then another roar and another and another," Norman said later. They did not stop after that. It was constant, a rolling, pulsating thing associated more with knockout flurries at a heavyweight fight than some gentlemen's game waged on green grass in the sunlight.

"It made Winged Foot [where Norman challenged for a U.S. Open title] more like playing through a graveyard," Norman said. "The atmosphere, the emotion on this golf course are so much greater than any other."

And Jack, well, he owns this place, basically.

He owns golf, basically. But it had been six years, since the U.S. Open and PGA in 1980, since he had collected any major dividends. "I can't remember the last time I broke 70," he had said a bit wistfully on Saturday.

Yesterday morning, with Nicklaus four shots off the lead, a son had called, asking what it would take. "A 66 to tie, a 65 to win ought to do it," Nicklaus replied.

He shot 65. He did it against a leader board packed with four former champions, all locked with him into the sweep of an afternoon that will be remembered as special even in a place that merely tolerates the exceptional.

Augusta National has a new classic to discuss this morning.

Once its collective hearing is restored and those frightened crows can be coaxed back to the course.

<hr>

July 22, 1989, *Denver Post*

ODDS ARE YOU CAN BET ON THIS OPEN

TROON, Scotland—Pete Rose and his friends would love this tournament. Augusta National and A. Bartlett Giamatti would view it in some horror.

They not only allow betting, it's all but encouraged. Daily odds are posted on the press-room bulletin board—on official release forms used for interviews and other announcements. Players talk openly of betting on themselves or others.

Tom Watson said Thursday, "I got myself odds of 40-1 to win."

If you can solve the picturesque, twisting, two-lane motorway, if you drive remembering that left is right and right is wrong, it's easy to put a few quid on Watson or Nick Faldo. Or you can buy one that no American will finish in the top five.

They have commercialized the tournament beyond any American promoter's wildest hope—and not tarnished it in the least.

The approach to the course looks like some updated version of a medieval fair, with acres of huge tents. All it lacks are two knights on horseback and some ladies-in-waiting—all wearing sponsors' labels in prominent spots for all to see.

There is a blocks-long exhibition tent to one side of the course. It is jammed with concessionaires—golf equipment, sweaters, slacks, shoes, rain suits.

They hawk it shamelessly. Outside the course, row after row of other tents and push carts—almost a mile of them—offer food and souvenirs and catered services to all the corporate swells. Even individual golfers are sponsored—by a woolen mill, by an investment company, by a sportswear firm. Payne Stewart was wearing his Oakland Raider colors yesterday, part of his arrangement with NFL Properties. In this setting, it looked natural.

In 1985, one Simon Bishop tied for 16th while representing Biggs Beefburgers— at Sandwich. But unlike the big American tournaments that sell out completely to those who can afford high-priced "season" packages, The Open is truly that for the average fan.

Walk up to the gate. Slide 11 pounds (roughly $18) through the cage. You're in. No impossible waiting list, no "sold out" signs. "Composite" tickets are available, but nobody is turned away, and there is no such thing as putting ticket rights in a will, as happens at Augusta. The little guy is more prominent here than at any other major. It's homier, less haughty, more ... well, open.

"They are more restrained, more knowledgeable," said Lee Trevino of the galleries. "Golf in America is beginning to sound more like a football game."

Scots have a tendency to applaud only the exceptional, not the routine. But they also remember. Arnold Palmer was saluted like a reigning monarch at the end of an opening 82 Thursday.

The Open. They don't add the national adjective here. It's simply The Open. "The oldest and most important of the four major championships," as they modestly proclaim in the official program.

When Jack Nicklaus came to this same course in 1962 as the new champion of the U.S. Open, he found himself listed for a 4:45 p.m. tee time. "I was paired as 'Jack Nicklaus and marker,'" he said this week.

Rotated over several courses, the British Open is played this year here on the western coast some 30 miles below Glasgow. Five miles south, Robert Burns was born, and his Brig a Doon still spans the River Doon in Ayr, founded by the Romans.

Troon is the snout of land jutting into the Firth of Clyde. It's a derivation of the Cymric (Welsh) word "trone" which means nose.

Just south, Prestwick airport sends huge jets roaring out over the course like LaGuardia spawns them over Shea Stadium in New York.

Some bunkers on Royal Troon are so deep there are wooden ladders. In World War II, it was taken over by the Royal Navy, and the Army used the adjacent beach for practice landings to get ready for Normandy. They conducted hand-grenade practice next to the sixth tee.

But they never quit playing golf, even if it required a few new rules.

"In competitions," the special wartime rules read, "during gunfire or while bombs are falling, players may take cover without penalty for ceasing to play.

"A player whose stroke is affected by the simultaneous explosion of a bomb or shell, or by machine-gun fire, may play another ball from the same place."

There was a small catch, however. He also would have to penalize himself one stroke.

July 24, 1989, *Denver Post*

An American leaves Aussies down and out

TROON, Scotland—Should we start with Greg Norman, everyman's victim, the guy who now has lost four majors literally with the final shot?

Yesterday, he set a course record with 64, ran off six straight birdies to start—and wound up chopping out of a bunker, out of bounds and out of any lingering hope.

He had 11 birdies in 22 holes and even that wasn't good enough to give him his second British Open title.

Or how about poor Wayne Grady? The guy almost defines the meaning of the word "journeyman." He's 32, has played all over the world, won four times in more than a dozen years, leads this tournament for two days and 15 holes and appears to have it locked. Then he bogeys the 17th hole twice in the same hour, once in regulation, the last in the playoff.

And they tie.

For second. At the end, while Mark Calcavecchia was accepting the trophy, the two losers sat glumly, running fingers over little silver serving dishes they got as runners-up, and tried to explain what happened.

Neither finished, officially. They were told on the first tee it would be that way. The playoff was to determine a winner, not second and third.

And it did, on the fourth hole of the playoff at Royal Troon, in the 118th British Open, where a 29-year-old American stayed around long enough to end Europe's grip on the tall, silver trophy.

And Calcavecchia is your new British Open champion only because his wife is still expecting.

Luckily, he stayed around long enough to play yesterday. "My wife is expecting at any moment. If I had gotten a phone call last night, as important as this tournament is, it's still just a golf tournament.

"I'd have gotten on a plane and gone home today."

Norman and Grady won't take much consolation in what might have been. It was Grady's first big moment in the international sun, and he was almost good enough to make the most of it.

For Norman, the scene is getting sickeningly familiar.

In 1984, he lost the U.S. Open to Fuzzy Zoeller in an 18-hole playoff. In 1986, he lost the Masters to Jack Nicklaus and the U.S. Open to Ray Floyd.

At the PGA in Toledo, Ohio, Bob Tway chipped out of a bunker to beat him. The next spring, in Augusta, Ga., Larry Mize holed out from 140 feet in sudden death at the Masters and Norman was left to stand and wonder.

"Do you think destiny might owe you one?" a polite inquisitor with a British accent asked yesterday.

Norman glared.

"Bleep!" he said, not smiling. "He owes me about four, I think."

It was a strange, dramatic, marvelous windup to a tournament nobody expected.

Winning it became almost an obsession to the 34-member American contingent, one of the biggest ever.

"I did think about that. I sure did," said Calcavecchia. "I saw Payne Stewart and Fred Couples when I came into the scorer's tent after my round, and they said, 'Man, if there's a playoff, do it.'

"I felt I had to for our tour, and for America or whatever."

It sounds a bit like patriotic mush, it didn't in the setting next to the Firth of Clyde, and with a huge audience of Scotsmen applauding outside. Here, the rivalry between the American tour and the rest of the world is deeply felt.

"I used to wonder how those guys ever stood the pressure in a playoff," said Calcavecchia. "That was before I joined the tour. I would get nervous just watching them on TV."

Yesterday, he didn't know until just before it started that the Royal and Ancient adopted a four-hole aggregate format five years ago, and that it wasn't sudden death.

If it had been, Norman would have won with a birdie on the first extra hole, a fact that must torment the Australian even more in view of his history.

Strangely, neither Norman nor Grady even thought of Calcavecchia as a challenger until they heard of his birdie on 18 to pull even at minus 13. "Greg was the only one I was thinking about," Grady admitted.

They were staging their own little version of "The Empire Strikes Back," two Aussies about to duel for the British title. But Grady's stumble on 17 with Norman watching in the clubhouse pried the whole finish open again.

"I had such a beautiful 4-iron on 18, man, I was just watching it the whole way. It was so pure, in midair, I almost didn't care where it ended up. It's the best I ever hit," said Calcavecchia of the next to last shot that set up his winning putt.

"I marked the ball, and saw Greg's troubles, and knew, 'Man, I can three-putt from six feet and win the British Open.'"

He still has two putts coming.

August 11, 1990, *Denver Post*

VICKERS' LEGACY: THE INTERNATIONAL

CASTLE PINES—A gentle morning breeze stirs the awning shading the long patio on the second level of the clubhouse. Sprinklers hiss over the manicured green carpets stretching into the distance. The day's thunderstorm is still hours away, just some puffy clouds hanging over the Front Range to the west.

Jack Vickers sits with his back to all this splendor.

Five years ago, he was caught up in the frenzy of launching a new and dramatically different golf tournament, The International. The pros weren't sure. Their comfort levels were set on stroke play, cumulative scoring, leader boards on which red was good and black was bad. CBS wasn't certain. How televise an event that didn't build gradually to some convenient climax on the 18th hole? This one could be ended in sensational fashion on No. 17. The galleries didn't know: Do you follow somebody, or do you find a hole that promises an eagle—say the aforementioned 17th—and stake squatter's rights for the day?

Through it all, Vickers wore the tight smile of a man who knew he was right. He just had to prove it. It's been Jack Vickers' signature smile through a life in which he has spent as much time swimming against the current as taking time to enjoy its soothing flow.

And now, on a hot July morning, he has to admit something.

It's not far from what he envisioned. Not there yet, understand. He would never concede that.

"I feel real good about it. I'm really pleased with the way it has progressed. We've had a lot of fun doing it, and had some controversy. That's all part of it. That's all been a contributing factor in helping put the tournament on the map.

"And I sure as heck think it's on the map, now."

CBS has learned how to cover it, describe it. The galleries are knowledgeable, the pros have learned how to play it and the tournament Vickers envisioned on the course Jack Nicklaus created is now a solid late summer fixture following the PGA Tournament.

But, to be honest, not much that Vickers envisions and sets out to create doesn't wind up this way.

"I think it's nice to be a dreamer, in a lot of ways. It's more important, though, that you get the dreaming into reality. I've always gotten more of a kick out of planning new things and watching them come together than I have sitting in the office 12 hours a day counting the beans."

Real estate, oil, the family enterprises, a hockey team, a basketball team—some have gone well, some not so well. Beans can go both ways. But a Vickers venture has always been daring, demanding.

Castle Pines itself was the result of a solitary drive south from Denver, along a canyon, and instant recognition that here in a blend of canyon and pine and achingly beautiful vistas of the mountains a man could dream himself a special kind of golf course.

The difference is that Vickers then set out and did it.

A legacy, maybe?

"Oh, I suppose so. At least the golf club. That's my pet, my love; the course, the club, the tournament. I'm spending probably 90 percent of my time on that anymore. All my business things I've got pretty well set up with managers. It moves along. My real interest at my age now is the club, the fellowship at the club, and the tournament, the kick I get out of that, the associations with the players, the PGA people and so on. It's fun. I really enjoy it."

He nursed and coaxed and cursed and sweated it into reality, and now it's about to celebrate its fifth birthday.

"I'm never one to say I'm going to retire, but I will say I'm slowing my engine down," Vickers concedes. "I've got a lot of good people now, I'm delegating more to them. I keep abreast of what is going on through them.

"I'm trying to get to the point where I'm not worrying about as many things."

Not every man can do it on a course he created.

THINKING ABOUT GOLF LESSON CAN BE DANGEROUS

I stood there frozen. That's embarrassing, but true. My whole system was locked up like some computer with a virus. Nothing was working.

The view was spectacular, the west end of the Vail Valley spread out before me, a warm sun burned my neck, little white carts were toting golfers along a fairway far below. It was perfect, idyllic, what every man dreams about on vacation.

Except my thumbs were numb. My legs were mush. Nothing in the whole world, not even a sudden grizzly attack out of the gulch behind us, was going to make me move.

I was thinking. That's the problem. I was trying to remember to rotate my hips 45 degrees and my shoulders 90 degrees and cock my wrists and not grip too tightly and shift the weight from my left side to my right side and then shift it back and not overswing and don't try to kill it, meanwhile keeping the target aligned and staying perfectly relaxed. And while I stood there, poised, the very picture of the perfect golf swing forming in my posture, I had made this horrible discovery:

Not one single bone, not one muscle, not one synapse or ganglia or whatever else, was hooked up. They were all just loose in there, independent, humming along, doing their own little things, ignoring all the signals I was trying to send mentally. "You wanna swing, buddy? Swing. Just don't ask for our help."

After nearly 20 years, I was taking a golf lesson. I had given up golf and cigarettes at about the same time in the early 1970s. I don't miss the cigarettes. But I have always envied the flat bellies I follow in my line of work, the young, lithe athletes whose drives always go 280 yards, straight. ...

So, after all that time, I had come back. Sort of. Will Lampley, who is old enough to know better, had insisted he could find usable timber in the wreckage. So I had gone to his Swing Dynamics Institute at Vail and Singletree. It was like taking an ancient touring car to a Mercedes garage.

And now here I was, standing over a range ball, body cocked, perfectly aligned, coiled as if for CBS' cameras or a PGA Tour highlight film. And it wouldn't work.

And I got to wondering, since I couldn't move and had nothing else to do, what it would be like if every human being tried to walk as if he or she were taking golf lessons.

"All right, now. The essential thing, the most important, is balance. You don't want to get the torso out too far over the feet, or the feet too far in front. Heel and toe. Nice and easy. Don't overstride ... noo, noo, that's too far, back just a little ... there, better ... right hand and left foot out at the same time ..."

We would be a nation of scab faces, that's what. Band-Aids and plastic surgery would be the national industry.

I would be standing outside the *Denver Post*, late for yet another baseball press conference, and my body would not work. Do I swing my arm on the SAME side as my foot, or the other side? Where should my hand have reached in its arc as I am shifting weight from the heel across to the ball of my foot and ... whap!

Face down on the concrete.

Think about thinking about walking. Go ahead. We have time. Your body will no longer move. Are you swinging your hand back far enough? Out too far? Is it on the right line, so your shoulders don't sway and you don't look like the motor is somehow out of synch?

"Look at that poor man, dear. He's either drunk or taking walking lessons. His lips are moving. Lessons. He's thinking, the poor thing. Whoops! Face down again."

I was not a star pupil at Will Lampley's classy class. I noticed, toward the end, the instructors would pause by one pupil, or another. "Great," they would say. "You're getting it." And then they would, well, sort of scurry past my station, mumbling, "Work at it."

I'm not even sure they noticed the morning I stood frozen over the ball from 9 a.m. to lunch, trying to remember everything.

I would give the damn game up again. Forever.

Except, we went out and played in the afternoon. And every once in a while, I would produce an actual shot right out of Lampley's class, one that went somewhere, often in the right direction. And then came the moment.

I hit the world's most perfect 5-wood. It went out rising, straight and true and vanished in the distant light, too far away over the curvature of the earth to even imagine where it came to rest.

I was back. It was a classic flat-belly shot, a career 5-wood. I had just this one tiny problem. Now, I could no longer walk.

April 13, 1992, *Denver Post*

WINNER FULFILLS FLOYD'S BELIEFS

AUGUSTA, Ga.—He stood on the 12th tee at Augusta National late on a Sunday afternoon and the world and his past almost overwhelmed Fred Couples. ...

"It's the most nervous I've ever been," he said later, the green jacket of the 56th Masters Championship draped casually across the counter in front of him.

Nobody asked about 1989 and the Ryder Cup, when the European captain told one of his members to "just get the ball up there. Couples will choke." We should have asked. Did it flash through memory, just for a nanosecond?

"Choke" is an ugly word, the harshest in sports. But the fact is, Couples did not make a makeable putt and the United States lost.

"He blamed himself for that, but I told him it was a team game, and that missing that putt would make him a better golfer. He might not believe me then, but, someday, he would," U.S. captain Raymond Floyd said.

Last fall at Kiawah Island, S.C., Couples was the key figure as the U.S. captured the Ryder Cup.

And yesterday, staring out at 155 yards of green turf and blue-green water fronting the 12th, Couples plunked his tee shot into the bank, where it rolled tantalizingly back for about a yard—and stopped.

Nobody of long memory here could recall a ball hit where Couples hit it stopping short of the water. It's almost a cliff. Gravity demands it roll into the briny deep.

"I don't know how it stayed up," Couples admitted. "It was the biggest break of my life. I'm not sure what would have happened if it had gone in like everybody else's."

Maybe we'd all be saluting Floyd for being the oldest (49) man ever to win a green coat.

Or maybe we'd be toasting Corey Pavin for his first major title.

Or maybe it would have given life to someone else and that wouldn't be an All-American trio on top of the final leaderboard this morning.

"But that's how you win," Floyd said later of his friend and pupil, the 32-year-old he convinced two years ago could make himself a great golfer.

"You need breaks. Everything you do in a 72-hole golf tournament isn't perfect. You need breaks."

Couples, the No. 1–ranked player in the world, the man needing only a Masters jacket to somehow validate a greatness already evident, got that break on No. 12.

"It was just a perfect lie," he said. "It wasn't a hard shot. But I saw people walking up to the ball and I didn't want anybody near it."

So, his right foot just inches from the artificially green water of Rae's Creek, he chipped to within two feet, saved par and fled up the hill to the 13th tee.

"I just knew, once I got by that hole, I was going to win."

He got by, and he won, and if Floyd is to be believed, this may just be the first of many visits to the interview room on Sunday night at the Masters.

"Fred's got the game to win this tournament as many times as a Nicklaus or Palmer," Floyd said.

Couples, Floyd said, has now elevated himself and his game to that elite level. Floyd had waited in one of the cottages near the 18th green to watch Couples finish, then walked up and hugged him at the end. Early in the week, he had said that if he couldn't win it, he hoped Couples would. Couples shouldn't need a sport coat to confirm his status. But even Floyd conceded, "You are not going to see too many Hall of Famers who don't win a major."

... Yesterday's 2-under-par 70 was his 134th round under par in the past year. He has had just three rounds over par this year.

Yet the green jacket somehow drapes him with a new stature those starkly brilliant numbers don't. Does it bother him that the world wouldn't put "great" in front of his name before?

"I couldn't care less," Masters champion Couples said.

Now, he doesn't have to even if he privately once believed them.

✤   ✤   ✤

CHAPTER FIVE

BASEBALL

✦   ✦   ✦

Every morning was a sunrise serenade. Dick Connor wrote like Glenn Miller played. On his computer keyboard he composed sweet, smooth, stylish songs. ...

Dick Connor's permanent legacy to life are his symphonies of sport. ...

Dick spent decades trying to bring major–league baseball to Denver, partially because he wanted to write about the team, but, more so, because he wanted his and other's grandkids to be able to watch the big leagues.

... Dick felt that sports—from the Denver Nuggets to the Regis High basketball team—helped make Denver a good, well-rounded place to live.

—Woody Paige, sports columnist, *Denver Post*

✦   ✦   ✦

Dick covered his first World Series in about 1977, the year he became a columnist. He enjoyed the Bears, Denver's AAA team, both as a reporter and as a spectator when he took the children and grandchildren to games.

He hated the name "Zephyrs," which the Bears became when the team was sold. He vowed never to use that name in his column—and he didn't.

He always hoped Denver would get a major-league ballclub. He believed that Denver fans would support baseball. If the response to the Rockies' first two seasons is any indication, he was right.

He saw the major-league franchise awarded to Denver, visited and wrote about the training facility in Tucson and covered the team's first Class-A game in Bend, Ore., but didn't live to see the Rockies' opener in 1993. He would have loved it.

December 15, 1977, *Denver Post*

"SANDLOT PLAYER" DAVIS BELTS
MAJOR-LEAGUE HOMER FOR DENVER

Major-league baseball came to Denver shortly before 2 p.m. Wednesday.

Marvin Davis may never be the same.

"Is it proper to describe you as a billionaire?" the female reporter asked in the subway-at-rush-hour crush of people jammed into Davis' office on the 11th floor of the downtown Metro bank building.

He looked at her and smiled, and you weren't certain he meant it.

"I haven't looked lately," he said, waving at some papers on his desk. "I don't know."

They came to hear Davis announce at a 4 p.m. press conference that he has reached terms with Oakland A's owner Charles O. Finley to buy the A's and move them to Denver in 1978. ...

January 24, 1978, *Denver Post*

NOW, OR WHENEVER, THERE'S A BUYER

Save your baseball money, boys, Marvin Davis will rise again.

If there is any one thing to come from the past month and a half of baseball talk in Denver, it's the single fact that the Mile High City now has a bona fide, identified, qualified owner whenever the grand old sport gets around to settling a franchise here.

Marvin Davis is ready to own a major-league baseball team.

Two months ago, as Broncomania neared terminal stages, any talk of putting a major-league baseball franchise into Denver was in the vague, down-the-road language you use when you talk of things like going to Europe or sailing to Tahiti. Maybe someday.

There were no catalysts, and this includes the mayor and governor and their wistful journey to the baseball meetings.

That was nice, but the baseball moguls were looking for something more, like a man with the money and the interest. Denver couldn't produce one of those.

Then abruptly, over a span of a dozen days, Davis emerged, dickered and agreed with Charlie Finley, and it appeared that Mile High Stadium would have gone from the old city dump it once was to the home of Denver's latest major-league endeavor.

It was a gaudy kind of Christmas season—the Denver Broncos headed for the Super Bowl, and a major-league baseball franchise coming in the spring. What more could you ask, except for more snow in the mountains?

Enter Finley's enemies, the long-standing feuds between Oakland and San Francisco, and Davis' unwillingness to wait forever for somebody to make a decision. Add baseball's virtually total lack of any kind of mediation.

Bowie Kuhn, as expected, did too little too late, there were appropriate tsk-tsks from other quarters and now both the San Francisco Giants and Finley's Oakland A's can resume their plunges toward bankruptcy and failure in an area that can support just one of them.

But, while it may take longer than first appeared, Denver has emerged as the next franchise target. It may be a case of which league gets here first. Or gets to Marvin Davis first, to be more accurate. ...

April 1982, *Denver Post*

REGGIE'S BACK IN OLD FORM

NEW YORK—There was never a doubt, not from the moment it left his bat and lifted through the smoke and mists and headed toward the upper deck above the 353-foot mark in right field.

As he used to do on those frozen October nights with a World Series game hanging in the balance, he stood a moment, watched, then lifted his arms in a gesture of triumph and joy and began his trot, like some Roman general being feted for a victory.

Reggie was back. Reggie Jackson, hitting a paltry .173, all singles, nursing a strained calf muscle, still trying to get used to the palms of Anaheim instead of the canyons of Manhattan, had saved his first home run of 1982 for his first game back in Yankee Stadium as an enemy.

It was cold, it was rainy, it was vintage Jackson, and it was marvelous.

Off it went into that smoky, drizzling evening, giving the Angels a 3-1 lead, and Jackson another reason to be known as one of baseball's most dramatic personalities.

This was his stage, a stadium filled with fans who had braved the weather to watch his return, and he rewarded them.

Just how much they appreciated it was obvious. They demanded a bow, got him to the top of the dugout steps, then began an obscene chant directed at Yankees owner George Steinbrenner, whose contract squabbles with Jackson have made Jackson a Manhattan martyr as well as a California Angel.

He had upstaged the NFL draft, the managerial debut of Gene Michael, even the weather. ...

"You want to introduce me?" he asked an Angels official during a pregame press conference. He then led the laughter. ...

Jackson does everything with a flair. He even made a production of selecting a bat, taking out one, examining it, putting it back, taking another. It lasted two or three minutes, while a half moon of some 50 writers and cameramen watched in fascination. Finally satisfied, he trotted out to the night's first ovation in right field.

... "I would have loved to end my career here," he said with feeling. "I would have loved wearing No. 44 and ending up in Yankee Stadium. But it wasn't meant to be."

Neither is it meant that someday his profile will adorn one of the plaques of Yankee greats fixed to the wall in center field, beyond the 430-foot mark on the fence. Those plaques are not for the enemy, even those wearing an Angels cap. ...

"Reg-gie! Reg-gie!" they chanted as he circled the bases.

"This is like a World Series out here tonight," Yankees coach Joe Altobelli had said before the game, walking past a batting cage lined with writers. "We have a World Series–size press tonight."

And they got a World Series–size performance from Mr. October, who may have misplaced his calendar but certainly not his place in Yankees history.

March 23, 1984, *Rocky Mountain News*

HOPE STILL ALIVE FOR THE CUBS

MESA, Ariz.—When the white men came to this desert valley, they found a network of ancient canals.

"Who built them?" they asked.

"Ho Ho Kams," the Indians replied. "Those Who Have Gone."

Never has a spring training site been more perfectly named for the team it houses. "Those Who Have Gone" and "YOUR Chicago Cubs," as they are introduced to sunbaked crowds, are as beautifully matched as desert and heat.

"Ho Ho Kam Park," the sign proudly states. "Winter Home Chicago Cubs." The Cubs worship their ancestors, even as they fail to replace them.

Every February, they come south to prepare new recipes. Every April, they head north and starve again. But by September, their legions are grumbling and grousing and making sarcastic references to ancestry and biology, even as they steadfastly plan next March's trip to Ho Ho Kam and a renewal of faith.

The Cubs are not a team. They are a cult, one, it can be suggested, as self-deluding as that led by Mr. Jones.

He, at least, hinted at immortality. The Cubs merely promise a pennant.

You don't know the way to Ho Ho Kam, the city stadium with a hedge running around the outfield that resembles Wrigley Field's ivy? Don't fret. Simply wait a moment, and watch. When an Illinois license plate goes past, fall in behind and follow. They flock toward Ho Ho Kam and the 1 p.m. exhibition game start like great bleached pilgrims freed from the winter up north, descending on the temple where all will be made right.

"Soo-va-neers! Getcha Cub soo-va-neers right here!" He has the belly of a man who enjoys the sacramental beverage that gave it to him. He has the voice of a man who must spend the summers outside Wrigley Field.

They obediently buy pennants and caps and batting helmets and T-shirts, like faithful stocking up on holy water as they approach Lourdes.

"There!" the terminally obese lady shrieks, pointing. She is radiant in pink shorts, a lime-green top and a fresh sunburn. "It's him! Harry!"

It is, indeed, Harry Caray, beginning his 41st year as a broadcaster, third as a Cub high priest.

Ho Ho Kam. The Cubs and their true believers are nothing if not traditionalists. They worship the past, Those Who Have Gone, and hope. ...

October 6, 1984, *Rocky Mountain News*
TIGERS END 16 YEARS OF FRUSTRATION WITH WIN

DETROIT—Maybe, by now, by the time you pick your morning paper from the drive, there is room to walk again on Michigan and Trumbull outside Tiger Stadium.

At 11:30 p.m. EDT Friday, movement was restricted to what you could do with your elbows to protect your ribs.

We stood, about half a dozen of us, on the tar-paper roof of the stadium looking down.

"Look," said the usher in the orange windbreaker.

We looked. A bus, the big kind, was being rocked back and forth, teetering, dangerously close to going over on its side.

The din was continuous, rising, punctuated by blasts from the horns of automobiles locked helpless and motionless in the gathering mob. A couple of firecrackers went off.

They had waited since 1968 for this moment, 16 years and a depression in the auto industry and layoffs and whatever else you want to attribute to the economy and the end of the Vietnam War and grim civic luck.

Now their Tigers were heading back to the World Series.

And the most curious fact of all on this frenzied, emotional night is that the men who are going there, the Tigers, were less wild than those who will cheer them when they get there.

... From day one, from the opening 8-1 win at Minnesota to Friday night's 1-0 clincher in the October frost, they were never out of first place.

Never. It's gorgeous testimony to what the right talent and managing can accomplish, and the Tigers, Friday, seemed more inclined to savor it than to celebrate it ...

June 22, 1989, *Denver Post*
ROSE EPITOMIZES SPORTS TRAGEDY

So, they found a smoking betting slip?
With his fingerprints all over it?

And it indicates he bet on the Reds.

To win.

That last won't earn him a pardon, I'm afraid.

It's the one missing link, and unless someone has performed a rather remarkable bit of forgery, to the point of installing Pete Rose's fingerprints on a slip that shows he did, indeed, do the thing he has denied, we are witnessing what can only be described as an American sports tragedy.

I mean that in the old, classical sense, the one that requires a king be dethroned, that he do it himself, that his hand is the one that creates the downfall. King Lear was a tragedy, a Shakespearean masterpiece.

King Pete is another. But it's not a masterpiece. It's a damn shame.

Peter Edward Rose, b. Apr. 14, 1941, Cincinnati, Ohio, his entry in the *Baseball Encyclopedia* begins on page 1409. You might as well go ahead and close the entry: Career ended June 21, 1989. If the data leaked to the *New York Times* are accurate, Pete Rose's career in major-league baseball is finished.

Does anyone else see a certain calendar irony here?

Here, on the first day of a new summer, Pete Rose, the ultimate Boy of Summer, has left his fingerprints all over an otherwise brilliant career.

It's hard to separate the man from the boy from the player from the player-manager from the manager from the adult who never quite grew up or understood that rules are for everyone. He belly flopped his way into our hearts as fans, mesmerized us with that hair-flopping dash, the all-out playing style, and then he leaves himself vulnerable like this.

Charlie Hustle they used to call him. What will they call him now?

Baseball commissioner A. Bartlett Giamatti has a 225-page report that Rose is desperately battling to contain or refute. "I never," he finally said this week, after weeks of nondenial.

Others gamble, some say. George Steinbrenner gambles. Ty Cobb gambled. Doug Moe gambles.

(But if Rose defenders see no difference in betting horses, dogs and betting on a team you manage, it's their problem. Beyond, there is this rule in the baseball kingdom. It's simple, understood by all the inhabitants—if you gamble on this game, you're gone. Rose knew this. Now, if the story is true, he's been caught.)

I keep seeing Pete Rose in two places.

The first was a cool October night in Philadelphia in 1983 when the Phils benched him at home, with his son in the dugout next to him. Pete Rose, benched, in a World Series. I kept watching him through the field glasses, almost ignoring the game on the field. He kept sitting on the top step of the dugout, his son a few feet away. And his son kept peeking at Pete, and Pete kept staring out with his field-level view of a game he never thought would do this to him.

Benched, in a World Series game, before a home crowd in Philadelphia.

After, he set a record—for him—getting to his locker. We waited, and waited, and waited, and he finally showed, and it was obvious he didn't understand, didn't want to understand, and would never understand.

Next night, he played again. But there will always be that long tableau, Pete Rose, sitting on the dugout steps, watching a World Series game while his son watched him. Neither could believe it.

The second memory was a year later, in Florida, early in spring training. The club was gone, driving somewhere for an exhibition game, and Rose had come into the clubhouse. Will Grimsley of Associated Press and I got Rose at his locker, and for an hour and a half, sat and talked baseball and hitting and Ty Cobb and what it would mean to catch him and how Rose's injury—I can't remember now what it was—was coming along, and how soon he'd be ready.

He caught Cobb, of course. It's there, on p. 1409 of the *Baseball Encyclopedia*, under hits: 4,256 in 24 years of swinging a rounded piece of hardwood at a slick white ball and driving it safely into empty parts of the ballpark more often than any man in history.

I'd rather remember Rose those two ways than as that stark story that came over the news wires last night. Betting slips found. FBI. Fingerprints. Commissioner has irrefutable evidence.

He never grew up, I suspect. He was the consummate Boy of Summer, the butterfly who never dreams of winter, never suspects the temperature can drop and frost can form and food get scarce. He could—and would, as he did that spring morning in Florida—stand by his locker or the batting cage or sit in a dugout and talk baseball and hitting and other players for hours. Don't bother to look up the figures—they'll be accurate.

Pete Rose gives you a batting number, it's for real.

Apparently, if he gives you another number, it, too, is for real.

Even though this whole thing sounds like a plant from the commissioner's office, something to counteract the attempt by Rose's lawyers to get the upcoming gambling hearing transferred to a court, it also sounds as if there are tendrils of smoke rising from the betting slip.

They've got something, obviously, and it's devastating.

If Rose is found to have bet on his team, he's finished forever in baseball, and to be honest, I'm not sure which will miss the other more. He was what every player should be—and no player should ever be. Stretching the irony, so was Cobb.

Say it isn't so, Pete? Why? If last night's stories are accurate, it's a little late for denials. Just bid farewell to the king. Tragedies end that way.

❦   ❦   ❦

On Oct. 17, 1989, Dick was in the press box at Candlestick Park awaiting the start of the third game of the 1989 World Series between the San Francisco Giants and the Oakland A's when an earthquake struck at 5:04 p.m. and temporarily stopped the "Bay" series.

I got a call from our daughter, Kathy, about half an hour later. She had heard the news on the radio and was worried about Dick. I told her that since game time was probably about 5:30 or 6 p.m. San Francisco time, and he always arrived at a game at least two hours early, he was no doubt at the ballpark and not on the highways, where most of the damage was occurring.

About four hours later, I got a call from Gary Yunt at the *Denver Post*. He said Dick was on another line dictating a story on the quake. I knew that if Dick could get to an operating telephone, he'd call in his story first, and then let us know he was all right. His stories on the earthquake were printed in the front section of the paper, not in the sports section.

October 18, 1989, *Denver Post*

FEW LIGHTS GLOW ACROSS DARK CITY

SAN FRANCISCO—Downtown San Francisco is an eerie blend of darkness punctuated by people walking around with candles and flashlights.

It's 9 o'clock, four hours after the earthquake and one of America's great party towns is dark.

People are huddled on curbs, there are long lines outside several liquor stores on my walk here and there is almost a festive mood.

The quake struck at Candlestick Park just as the capacity crowd of more than 60,000 had filed in. It shook the press box on top of the west side like a puppy wagging a blanket.

We swayed east, then back to the west, and all the while there was a little shuddering undertone. I first knew something was wrong when coffee sloshed out of a fresh cup all over my score pad.

Curiously, when the tremor stopped, the crowd cheered.

To the credit of the crowd there was no panic. Many just sat talking excitedly among themselves, but those in the upper tiers quickly began filing out. When the aftershock rolled through some 20 minutes later, most of the upper deck was empty.

I worked my way down the stairs to the field. There was a gorgeous pastel sunset that was sort of incongruous with what had happened. People were very patient on the stairs. There was no shoving, no pushing.

By then the Oakland A's players had begun to take their families from field-level boxes and walk them to an exit in deep right field.

Many left the ballpark still fully dressed for the game, including spikes.

Giants manager Roger Craig drove off in his pickup with his grandchildren. He, too, had his game uniform and spikes on.

Thousands stood outside milling around.

"We don't know what we are going to do." Oakland coach Rene Lachemann said. "We're gonna get on the bus and try to decide.

"We were sitting in the dugout and when everybody ran out, I thought they were looking for skydivers."

He said as far as he was concerned he didn't care if the Oakland bus went all the way to Los Angeles before it crossed over [the San Andreas Fault].

Eventually they rerouted themselves around the south end of the Bay and back up the east side to Oakland.

A sign on the wall leading to the field referred to drinking. "Please drive carefully, the Giants want you back."

There's a real question whether the Series can be continued here. There are reports of huge cracks on the upper decks and an escalator being knocked off by a foot [at Candlestick].

There was no official announcement that the game was called off because the PA system was silenced when the quake came through.

People with portable radios were telling others what was going on around the city, such as part of the upper span of the Bay Bridge collapsing on the lower span.

Outside the stadium a guy in the parking lot was trying to buy ticket stubs.

While we drove in from the stadium, the two-way radio on the bus kept talking about looters on Third Street, and we were coming in on Third Street. I saw no signs of it, just some broken glass and lots of people sitting on curbs in the dark just watching people drive back and forth.

At one bar, an enterprising soul had parked his tow truck in the front door to give the place interior lights.

As we went deeper into San Francisco, the bus driver said to get off the bus quickly and get into the St. Francis Hotel because there had been some looting in that area.

During my eight-block walk to the hotel, I saw no signs of looting.

There is no electricity. People at the Raphael House, a shelter for the homeless, are working by candlelight as are the people at the St. Francis. People in rooms on the upper floors of the hotel can't get to them because there is no power for elevators.

The hotel is filled with British tourists—all trying to call home. Outside, there is nothing but fire trucks and police cars going by.

October 19, 1989, *Denver Post*
STARK NIGHT YIELDS TO SUN'S RAYS OF HOPE

SAN FRANCISCO—It is the morning after. It is filled with sunshine and confusion.

There is no electricity, and it's amazing what that simple lack can do to a sophisticated lady such as this. All the tall buildings depend on sleek elevators to whisk people to upper floors. Now upper floors are ghost towns, their former residents lounging or stretched out on the floor in the lobby. The elevators run on electricity.

Business is at a standstill. There are almost no phones, no restaurants, no lights, no power. San Francisco awoke a badly bruised civic orphan yesterday.

But neither is there any huge display of destruction downtown. There is across the Bay, where I-880 collapsed, and there were devastating fires in the Marina district Tuesday night.

Downtown is just canyons of tall buildings with no lights or phones and no streetlights on the corners, and with sidewalks roped off in places where plaster and brick were shaken loose somewhere up above.

But that's it. Destruction, the real and tragic devastation of 5:04 p.m. Oct. 17, 1989, is elsewhere. There is no "big picture."

San Francisco this bright, warm morning after the earthquake is just trying to get back to normal. Power is being restored, block by block, after they check for gas-line ruptures.

I slept fully clothed Tuesday night, shoes on, on top of the bed. And then I learned in the morning that I had slept right through an aftershock registering 5.2 on the Richter scale.

My hotel is patronized by tour groups from Great Britain. Many of them slept in the lobby Tuesday night, refusing to go back upstairs. A porter with a flashlight guided me up seven flights to my room. I could feel the plaster underfoot.

Yesterday morning, I got up with light and found the lobby jammed with Brits, waiting for a tour bus to take them to Los Angeles.

On a nearby rooftop, a man in an undershirt is walking around, looking, peering down the sides of the building, checking. There are men on rooftops and in basements all over town. Little knots of people were just walking in the early light, looking, inspecting.

I heard a droning sound and looked up. It was the Goodyear blimp, chronicler of big events, gliding slowly overhead, its side silvery in the dawn light. Somehow, the blimp seemed to fit.

I saw a couple sipping coffee from Styrofoam cups. "Where did you find coffee?" "That hotel," they said, pointing to the Beresford on Sutter Street. It didn't matter if you were registered. Just walk through the candlelit dining room and get a cup.

It was like that. People helped each other. There was a sense of relief, of camaraderie, of compassion. Coffee? Please. Take a cup. We're all friends this morning.

A store, no lights, was peddling bottled water, juices and doughnuts. I bought a small pack of doughnuts, and stood on a corner, balancing coffee and doughnuts on top of a news box, breakfast al fresco, post-earthquake style.

A newsboy was on the next corner, actually shouting "Extra! Extra!" With no power, few had TV. It was like an old movie. The paper was back as the source of news. There were lines of people waiting to buy one and read the stories under the headline, "Hundreds Dead in Huge Quake."

At the swank Westin St. Francis, the lobby was gloomily lit by candles and faint illumination from an overworked generator. It was eerie.

"Where were you?" was the dominant question in the semidarkness. Nobody asked "When what?"

At the foot of Market Street, the flagpole atop the Ferry Building is cantered crazily some 40 degrees to the south. I Magnin, across the street from the commissioner's press conference, has some 20 plate glass windows shattered or cracked.

Upstairs at the St. Francis, in a huge ballroom lit only by half a dozen candelabra flanking the podium, baseball commissioner Fay Vincent did his sport rather proud, I thought. Baseball, he said, was just a tiny portion of this thing. It would wait to see what, if anything, it should do, where it fit.

Outside, John McGrath and I began the mile walk back to our hotel.

"I'd kill for breakfast," I said. John nodded. He hadn't eaten anything at the ballpark the night before. He, too, had been escorted up the seven flights in the pitch dark.

Next to our hotel, the Sutter Street Bar and Grill was open. Miraculous!

"We only have eggs or sandwiches," the lady said. Perfect. In a city famed for its international cuisine, simple eggs and sandwiches never sounded so good.

Upstairs, up those seven flights, I opened the door. The maid had been there. Sirens kept rushing past in the street below. A reeling city was struggling to come back to life. But the bed was made. It was a start.

October 19, 1989, *Denver Post*

CLASSIC MISTAKE: DECISION TO PLAY SERIES IS WRONG

SAN FRANCISCO—Don't play it.

Let it go. Tilt the appropriate finger toward 86 years of tradition and let the 1989 World Series come quietly to rest beside some earthquake asterisk in the record book.

There is no way the so-called Fall Classic should be resumed under the circumstances.

Too many have died, too much has been wrecked in terms of property, lives, business, futures. There is no excuse to gloss it over with now meaningless games.

Yesterday morning, baseball seemed almost inclined to do the decent thing. But by late afternoon, another motive had entered the process.

They will try to play next week, right here. It is absolutely wrong.

This is not a time for baseball to play games and I really don't care if they continued to stage it during World War II. It had a different impact.

This is too close, too personal. The NCAA should not have staged the 1981 finals the night Ronald Reagan was shot. The Olympics should not have resumed when the Israelis were killed in Munich in 1972.

There are simply certain times when life is larger than games, and this is one.

Never mind moving, or delaying. It simply should not be played. There is a macabre, selfish quality to any argument in its favor.

The NFL disgraced itself by its business-as-usual attitude the Sunday following President Kennedy's assassination in 1963.

It's a blotch the NFL will never erase. Some of its more thoughtful leaders still cringe when reminded. Baseball has no business duplicating it.

Now baseball thinks that by waiting a week, everything will be OK. Bullfeathers.

"We made the decision not to play tonight," baseball commissioner Fay Vincent said yesterday morning. He spoke in a setting that looked like some Transylvanian castle.

Banks of candelabra flanked him, their flames making shadows come and go on his face. He was tieless. It could have been some occult ceremony. In a way, it was.

He was eloquent in his understated way. The man said the proper things, the correct things, the needed things.

"There has been a substantial tragedy in this community, and baseball is not a major priority," he said.

He spent the day getting engineering data from both Candlestick Park and Oakland's stadium where the first two games were played.

"We want to be very sensitive, as you would want us to be." Jose Canseco's hitless streak and the Giants' 0-2 start and whether or not Bay Area people care all ended as issues at 5:04 p.m. Tuesday when a violent earthquake devastated this region.

More than 270 people are known to be dead. Damage is in the billions. Hundreds of thousands have been without power and light and phones and water, and many are homeless.

Hits and runs and cheering on some autumn night are totally out of place. And if they have to move it a thousand miles to finish it, why bother? In God's name what is the compulsion to require three or four or five more games?

"People need something to take their minds off this," baseball is saying to justify its action.

Hogwash. There is no justification. It is wrong, wrong, wrong, wrong. They are still extricating bodies from the freeway that collapsed not far from the Oakland stadium.

Can't they see the shocking contradiction? While crews working by torchlight tug human remains from smashed autos just a few miles down the road, baseball feels obligated to decide its champion under huge floodlights on national TV. Oakland will practice today while rescue crews burrow into concrete four miles away.

Wrong. Wrong, wrong, wrong.

But they will play.

And they deserve the scorn that act will bring them.

Six million people will be able to tell you where they were at 5:04 p.m. Tuesday. That, not a World Series, is the only score that counts. It's as simple as ABC.

<hr>

October 20, 1989, *Denver Post*

TURN OUT THE LIGHTS ON THIS BASEBALL SEASON

SAN FRANCISCO—Something was wrong. I wasn't certain what as I came out of a deep sleep, but something.

Light. That's it. The room was lighted. The lamp on the stand next to the bed was on again. It was 5:30 a.m. yesterday, and power had come back to the Carlton Hotel.

The lights had been off since 5:04 p.m. Tuesday when the earth quaked. I had tested the lamp each time I returned, and evidently left it in the "on" position the last time.

When power came back the lamp went on and it woke me.

Little by little, that vignette is being duplicated all over the Bay Area. Power is restored to a city block. Another business reopens. Exhausted—and heroic, there's no other word—disaster crews work on.

There is no way to chronicle the thousands of little incidents people have helped each other in the past 60 some hours.

It's one reason I find the decision to continue the 1989 World Series almost nauseous. Why? There are too many other ways to use the energies, the manpower, required to stage even one game.

We are seeing the human race at its most noble and most venal.

It is a season begging for its own end, not a fake continuation "to help the healing process," or because "we need something to distract us."

... Call it 2-0 A's, put an asterisk beside it and get on to spring training. ...

What of television contracts? Player shares? Those parts of the country without this tragic personal stake who want diversion, entertainment? What of all the bets, for heaven's sake?

None of them matter. It's time to end 1989 baseball. Now. Rescheduling it for 5:35 p.m. starts—prime time in that darling of network television, the Eastern Seaboard—should indicate where some of the pressure has come from.

If baseball at its purest, most traditional, is the only consideration, why not at least make them day games?

Give fans a chance if the lights go out again.

The 1989 World Series has outlived its usefulness, its purpose. Let it go and get on with the world.

⚜   ⚜   ⚜

Dick's opinion was not a popular one. The Series did resume and Oakland won easily in four games.

December 6, 1989, *Denver Post*

Don't call us, we'll call Baseball

I have an idea:

Don't call us, Major League Baseball. We'll call you.

When we think the time is right. When we determine you have finally gotten your own house in order, thrown out the loonies, looked at free agency for what it is—utter fiscal insanity. There is nothing free about agency.

The winter meetings are under way now, and, finally, you seem actually serious about adding two teams to the National League. We'll pause for very muted applause, since we've all heard that refrain before.

You—or rather, your former emperor, Peter Ueberroth—issued a list of demands a few years ago. Any city not meeting them was not going to be considered on any expansion plan, Peter the Great decreed.

Solid ownership was one demand. Does that mean the owner should have been convicted of a felony, as one of baseball's present owners once was? Or does it mean we should search and find some zillionaire nuts enough to spend $60 to $70 million to buy an expansion team the other owners will gleefully use like a city dump, discarding all their used-up players in a draft to stock it?

Build a stadium dedicated solely to baseball, Peter the Great continued.

No more multiple use. You want a team, you build a stadium. Yet the fact is there are only a half dozen or so parks in the majors where baseball doesn't share with some other sport.

Actually, this is one dictum I agree with (not the exclusivity, the priority). The two best places in the world to watch a baseball game as it was meant to be watched are Fenway Park in Boston and Wrigley Field in Chicago. Some would add Dodger Stadium and Royals Stadium, but they don't have the same atmosphere. Fenway. Wrigley. End of list. The crowd is in close, the parks are set in the middle of residential neighborhoods, the game is centered where it began, among the fans.

Denver, should it kiss enough rings and genuflect to enough owners and thus qualify for a franchise, has the chance to do it correctly right from the start. Baseball pays for itself. Build a Denver stadium along the South Platte, next to a relocated Elitch's, across from Mile High and McNichols, tie in a refurbished riverfront a la San Antonio with shops and walks and restaurants, hook it up with the convention center and 16th Street Mall and we have an exciting reason to go downtown. Or to stay there after work.

Toronto did this. It has worked for generations in Boston and Chicago. There is no other possible site in the Denver metro area that remotely offers the same possibilities. But I digress.

If Denver is to invest that kind of tax money, it should make some demands of its own. First, and last for right now, restructure the way baseball stocks a new team. Make it meaningful. Make it such that the new team has a chance to be competitive in less than a decade. Expose all but a dozen players on a team's entire roster to the expansion draft. Let the new teams have a choice of legitimate players who can help them win earlier and, thus, be attractive enough to fill the stadium and pay off the bonds.

When the American League expanded in 1977, it protected 14 players off each major league roster. Reducing that by at least two would expose that many more major leaguers and create more competitive expansion clubs. Seattle, one of the teams added the year Denver first went to the Super Bowl, has still not had a winning season.

Some of that was club stupidity. Toronto was smarter, going for younger players, betting on the come rather than going for a quick box office fix with marquee names that could no longer handle a curve ball.

"I'm not interested in putting out two teams that lose 100 games," National League boss Bill White said recently. Good. Listen, please. The man's correct. It does nobody any good, even the established clubs. Toronto lost 104 games its first season. Seattle lost 97.

So let us know, baseball. When you've got it fixed, we'll call you. Until then, work on it.

March 17, 1991, *Denver Post*
NEEDED: HARD CASH, NOT MORE BLUE SUITS

If the money is as plentiful as the blue suits, Denver is a lock for major-league baseball.

They were everywhere Friday. The blue suits, that is. Over the years, I have arrived at a rough ratio—it takes four blue suits in the back of the room for each principal on the dais at a major press conference or corporate announcement. I've never been certain what the blue suits do except look important and carry real leather briefcases.

The occasion was a press conference in a downtown bank room, where Coors announced it was contributing "in excess" of $30 million to the quest for a major-league team in Denver. I don't know what "in excess" means. And I don't know what form(s) it will take.

I just know that, for that 40 minutes or so with the cameras grinding, Coors' name was printed eight times in easy camera range up front, where Peter Coors signed a letter of agreement witnessed by lead owner John Antonucci and Steve Ehrhart, who will be president if Denver gets a team. "Coors Field" will be the official name of the stadium at 20th and Blake St. ...

... Denver—the extended Denver, the six-county area that will be the core of any future baseball franchise—has done everything baseball required. It has formed a tax district, passed a bond issue, identified a stadium site, even volunteered to buy 20,000 season tickets and sent in more than $1 million in earnest money to prove it.

Baseball, meanwhile, keeps changing its own rules. That "baseball only" stadium requirement suddenly became a Robbie Stadium in Miami that was hurriedly ripped up to show it could be used for baseball. That requirement for a broad-based ownership group with heavy local flavor vanished just as quickly, depending on who was wining and dining.

Now, a Florida senator is greedily talking of not one, not two, but three franchises, while, unless I've missed it, Sen. Tim Wirth has become suddenly mute.

Ownership and politics, not the more fundamental areas of fan support and a stadium, are the present battleground. Denver has a future stadium promised, a present one far more suitable for baseball than Joe Robbie Stadium and 20,000 season tickets on order.

What it doesn't have is a granitelike ownership combine. Most of Antonucci's top-level associates are, like him, from out of town. A Coors presence helps, but would help much more if it was as a general partner. And it would be an absolute clincher if Coors, not Antonucci, was the leading partner. ... Denver knows little more of Antonucci than does major-league baseball.

"It has been our goal to reach $120 million in equity," says Antonucci. "We are close to $100 million now." Baseball experts figure the eventual start-up costs, including the $95 million extortion fee for the franchise, could reach $150 million.

Fans—voters—have guaranteed a stadium, and a big season-ticket base. They have done their part.

Coors has acted as a responsible corporate citizen even if a few of us had hoped for a much more dramatic role.

Hard cash, not the number of blue suits in the back of a big room, are what the greedy barons of baseball are going to be inspecting here on their visit Mar. 26.

May 11, 1991, *Denver Post*

WHO SAID DENVER'S WEATHER BAD FOR BASEBALL?

I once caught pneumonia sitting in right field to cover the Toronto Blue Jays in an American League Championship Series game in October. True story. Year and attending physician furnished on request.

And I was in the football auxiliary press box when The Pretty Big One But Not the Really, Really Big One hit the San Francisco area before Game 3 of the 1989 World Series.

I also froze at a Mets game, and got drenched at one in Baltimore and rained out at another Mets game in Shea and once, at 12:30 a.m. of a dark, stormy night, couldn't get a cab to come into the Yankee Stadium lot to pick me up, and couldn't get the guard to take me out to find one. Neither felt sufficiently armed and I refused a combat pay bonus.

Now, tell me again about how terrible it is going to be to play in Mile High Stadium—or Coors Field after 1995—on one of our patented 70-degree summer evenings, high clouds lit by a full moon, a soft breeze blowing and not a mosquito in sight or hearing.

You'll read elsewhere about the survey the *Denver Post* has conducted among National League players and managers on where they think the two expansion teams should be located and where they would like to play.

My franchise this morning is concentrated on misconceptions.

I offer as our first witness the charming, smiling, ever-affable Will Clark of San Francisco. "I think baseball should be outside in the heat and humidity, not in the cold," said Will the Thrill. And where would he like to play? In Tampa–St. Pete. In the dome.

Thanks, Will. We'll ask your opinion again when you drive one over the south stands. The intriguing one from that club is by Jeff Brantley. "If I was a hitter, I'd be loving to play in Denver," he says. "Could you imagine Kevin Mitchell in Denver? It could get ugly. He could hit 100 home runs there. ..."

But weather and altitude seem to be the big objections.

So, with that in mind, we asked the local baseball team if it has kept a list of rainouts. It has. We submit it as People's Exhibit A:

This year, so far, there have been two postponements. One could have been played. But the team already has been stopped three times on the road, in areas where the so-called major-league teams play without weather interference. A year ago, the locals were stopped once, Apr. 10, by cold. Four of their road games were rained out.

It was two games here in 1989, three on the road and four-three in 1988.

More to the point, the huge bulk of Denver postponements come in April and early May. From June on, the record is almost spotless. There have been five rainouts in the summer months since 1983.

Five. Read my lips, National League owners, and put away your umbrellas. Five. Outdoors. Under God's sky, with no bugs, no humidity and very little mercy on the pitchers.

This is one view of Denver I think is accurate. "From a logistics standpoint, Denver makes a lot of sense," said one San Diego pitcher not identified by name. "But from a pitching standpoint the thing that would scare me is the altitude. The ball would just fly out of there." Breaking balls don't break as sharply here, and there is no question the ball carries as nowhere else.

I can't blame a pitcher for shuddering. "No way do I want Denver to get it," says Houston right-hander Xavier Hernandez. "I pitched there, and it's a nightmare." It should be noted that Mr. Hernandez has managed to find nightmares at lower altitude and in thicker air, as well. He is currently 0-2 with a 4.08 earned run average, all at or near sea level. But hitters should be standing in the airplane aisle, salivating as they refine their swing on the way into town.

Easterners look at the nightly weather map and see the blob over the mountains and say, "Ooops, Denver's getting snow again." Even those who land at Stapleton and take the two-hour ride to Vail never seem to get it through their skulls that the environment in the mountains is totally different from the semiarid one here at the edge of the Great Plains.

And nobody understands how fast it can change. Take last week. An overnight storm dumped several inches of snow on Denver. Then, as happens more than 300 days a year, the sun came out. By late afternoon the snow was gone, the playing field at Mile High was clear and dry and they played a game that night.

Weather my occluded front.

July 7, 1991, *Denver Post*
BASEBALL FOR DENVER, AT LAST

It was one of those feel good days. There were big, fluffy clouds against a Colorado blue sky and you could watch the heat shimmer off the downtown streets.

"Play two!" Ernie Banks would have hollered.

It was a day for sloshing 30-sunscreen over your body and tipping your new Colorado Rockies cap so the bill shaded your face and leaning back to watch your Colorado Rockies play, say, the Los Angeles Dodgers.

Two years, sports fans. Two years from yesterday. After 30 years, it's just two years. Actually, it is more like a year and a half, but why quibble on such a warm day?

"It's just like the second game of a doubleheader when the first game went 15 innings—and you won 'em both," said Charlie Metro, the former major-league manager.

Yesterday, they made it legal. No more promises. No more American League Kings Xs. This one counted. It took five minutes by conference phone, and when it was over, it was unanimous. Denver and Miami are in.

"I would like to tell you, officially, that as of 10:40 a.m. Mountain Standard—Daylight?—time, you have become officially a member of the National League ..." NL president Bill White said in an upstairs ballroom at the downtown Hyatt. Maybe he said something else, too. It was drowned in cheering and applause. We'll pardon the uncertainty about our time zone. Nobody in New York has ever gotten it straight. And the double "officially" just served to underscore the momentous if anticlimactic morning.

Denver is officially officially a major-league baseball town, and now we have the logos and T-shirts and caps to prove it. John Antonucci and the Colorado Baseball Partnership protected the logo and the name better than the United States has protected plans for the Stealth Bomber. It was the only real drama left for the late morning press assembly.

Would it be Denver or Colorado? It's Colorado. And it's Rockies, and to be honest, I prefer Denver but I don't care that much, as long as it's here. The logo is nice. You'll like it.

"The Colorado Rockies symbolize strength, power, majesty, stability, endurance, coldness and beauty," Antonucci said in explaining the name choice. Funny. I've been looking at them for 42 years and never thought of all those things. But if they can just find some pitching and a few good young hitters, I promise I'll try.

The suits were there, nice navy blue ones with just the faintest pin stripe, set off by power ties. Dark suits and power ties before lunch are sure signs it's big stuff. And there was the governor, and the new mayor, and the ownership group, and all the people like Roger Kinney and Larry Varnell who have worked so hard to make the dream come true.

And in back, discreetly hemmed in by velvet ropes, were several dozen fans who had wandered in to watch history on a hot July morning. Or maybe they just wanted the air conditioning.

For Varnell, who helped head up the Baseball Commission that got the stadium issue passed, it was the end of a 17-year quest. "I started back in 1974 when Jim Burris [who then headed up the Denver Bears], and Rex Jennings [head of the chamber] and I went to the major-league baseball meetings in New Orleans.

"We took along a model of Mile High Stadium. Marvin Davis had told me, 'You find us a team and I'll write the check.'"

They were all there yesterday, including Burris, who has not gotten enough credit for the groundwork he laid with the minor-league team.

No, that's not quite right. John Dikeou was missing, and that's too bad. It would have been difficult for the Denver realtor and owner of the minor-league team, the little man who had this passion to one day own the major-league club when it arrived. Being there, watching somebody else at the podium, would have hurt too much.

It's doubtful Dikeou could have mustered the huge support systems that came together last fall and made it all work, eventually. It's more likely Denver would have been among those like Buffalo and Washington and Orlando, patted on the head, "Nice try," maybe next time.

Instead, we had a big ballroom and TV lights and all those dark suits, and we had White saying it was officially official and Antonucci glowing like a proud papa. We had Mayor Wellington Webb saying he and the governor expected a World Series in a couple of years, and the governor admitting to "real shivers" at various points in the chase.

We had baseball. After 100 years in the minors, we finally made it. Play two. Hell, play three.

<hr>

March 3, 1992, *Denver Post*

HAPPY CAMPERS ON BOTH SIDES

TUCSON—It rained here yesterday.

That fact is notable because, as storm drains flooded and little lakes grew in the streets, the Colorado Rockies announced they are going to hold training camp in Tucson for at least the next five years. One of the reasons they chose Tucson was the nice weather.

It was a cooperative civic love-in. While Rockies chief John Antonucci promised to bring lots of high-spending Rockies fans south in the spring, Tucson promised to send some of its high rollers north in the summer to watch major-league baseball.

Both sides seemed happy. ...

Colorado gets all revenue streams in connection with spring practices and games. Tucson gets Colorado visitors and their cash.

Roughly, that's the deal without putting too fine an edge on details. ...

The Rockies, as part of the deal, are getting a completely refurbished Hi Corbett Field facility—an increase from 7,900 to 10,000 seats, a 10,000-square-foot clubhouse, some new practice facilities and other things. ...

March 11, 1992, *Denver Post*
GNP: GROSS NATIONAL PASTIME

Note to baseball:

That's a tunnel you see at the end of the light ahead.

It's got a darkened freight train in it, no engineer, throttle tied down, and it's coming straight at you.

One of man's lovelier inventions is about to go the way of savings and loans, and banks, and maybe insurance companies, too. The unthinkable becomes commonplace.

Baseball, at its present pace, will price itself out of business.

TV won't pay. TV has its own problems. Radio is not the solution. That's like an aspirin to treat one of the big-time diseases. And you and I? Sorry. I love the game, but there are limits.

The only people who don't seem to understand that simple statement are baseball owners.

This subject comes up because I was in Mesa, Ariz., a week ago, standing in a fenced lot outside the Chicago Cubs' cinder block bunker of a building that serves as their winter headquarters. And Ryne Sandberg drove up in his new, shiny, red Carrera, and the chairman of the *Chicago Tribune,* the conglomerate that owns the Cubs, was waiting for him.

That's right. Stanton Cook was inside the blockhouse, having flown in from Chicago on the company jet.

This rainy Sunday, the Cubs and the aforementioned Mr. Sandberg did not do business. Oh, he practiced, and they negotiated, but nobody signed. That came the next day, before massed cameras and pencils and notepads, the way these things are done now.

And the aforementioned Mr. Sandberg was flanked by his wife, Cindy. I wrote down what he said. I wanted to be sure to remember it. He said he was happy with his new $31 million contract because it meant security for him and for his family, and that, really, was all he was ever after.

I thought about that. The contract equates out to about $7 million a year.

Do you have any idea how secure I could feel for just ONE of those years? Sandberg, everybody agrees, is one of the truly nice guys in the business. Deserves it.

Deserves $7 million? Well, I suppose he does. See, I don't begrudge the Ryne Sandbergs of sports. Or the John Elways. Or the Michael Jordans. They are superstars. They earn their keep, whatever modest total that might come to.

What I fume over, and what I see as the ruination of sports, are the mediocrities who are so overpaid it's laughable.

Just three Octobers ago, Minnesota's Kirby Puckett became the first $3 million man in baseball. Right now, there are 70 major-league baseball players who make $3 million or more. More than a third of the major-leaguers make at least $1 million for throwing and running and laughing and spitting and scratching themselves. And the total grows daily.

There is a rampant insanity in sports, particularly baseball. The NFL has something called sharing the wealth. Whatever teams make in certain categories—national television, for instance—is tossed in the common pot. Everybody shares. It allows the teams in smaller markets, such as Denver, Green Bay, Kansas City, Phoenix, to operate on a footing equal to the Chicagos, the New Yorks, the Los Angeleses.

The National Basketball Association., with the enlightened help of its players association, installed a salary cap. It is based on gross income, and what it does, if I understand it properly, is keep teams from destroying themselves financially with outlandish salaries.

Now comes baseball. This year, according to one estimate, the average salary in the big leagues—the average salary—will be more than $1 million. And the chairman of the board jumps dutifully on the company Lear and zooms from Chicago to Phoenix to make sure his prized second baseman doesn't get away, and, somehow, he comes out of it sounding like it was a really good deal that he could pay him that much.

So what happens? What happens is that Kirby Puckett will want more. Or the next guy will want more. I'm not sure there is a ceiling on security. I don't know just how expensive security is these days. Is there a point where a bloke with a .296 lifetime average can quit thinking about food stamps?

The Oakland A's are now straining under a $39 million payroll, and some people in Arizona think the new expansion teams could have payrolls of $25 million. I don't. I don't think the Rockies think in those terms. Maybe $20 million, if it's their money.

No matter. The basic point is baseball, with no governor on its greed, no willingness to share, no ability to devise a workable plan, is heading for disaster. And all they can do is scream for somebody to protect them from themselves.

June 7, 1992, *Denver Post*

MORE THAN 500 TRY FOR DREAM SEASON

It was a field of dreams only for a few soggy moments in the early morning yesterday. Just while the clouds cleared and the sun came out and the long grass dried enough to snatch at a young man's baseball cleats and his dream and slow him for the 60-yard dash.

Then, it was just the University of Denver baseball field, and for the huge percentage of nearly 500 would-be baseball players, it was as close as they'll ever get to the major leagues.

It was the Colorado Rockies' tryout camp, and it was a numbers game beyond anyone's dreams.

"We didn't know what to expect," general manager Bob Gebhard admitted. He and his staff sat around on Friday night, finishing last-minute plans, and then they all guessed how many would show up the next morning.

"Guesses ranged from about 160 to 600 or so," Gebhard said at noon yesterday. They went past 500, all shapes, sizes, strengths. "I've hit to about 30 kids and none of them has made the throw to first," scouting director Pat Daugherty said at one point.

A few balls bouncing through the infield, a few throws to first, a 60-yard dash, and they are left to hear Gebhard at noon read off a painfully short list of those invited to stay on for the afternoon. Dream ended. Reality restored.

"Those whose numbers I've read off, sit tight," Gebhard said. "For the rest, we thank you for coming, and drive carefully on the way home."

Even the Rockies admit trying to evaluate 500 players on a June morning is all but impossible, but they did as good a job as possible under the circumstances. Everybody got a taste, if not a meal.

It wasn't as unscientific as it sounds, even given the almost impossible logistics. Even the untrained eye could pick out dozens and dozens who had no business being there. They couldn't move. They couldn't throw. Balls caromed off dugouts and unwary players and even a fan or two.

"If you wanted to be tough, with 90 percent of these kids you could watch them try to field and throw one ball and yell, 'Next guy!'" Daugherty observed. But the Rockies weren't tough. Everybody got some chance, even if it might not have been a morning of personal inspection.

"We want to welcome all of you," Daugherty had told them at home plate as the throng gathered about, each carrying his workout bag, maybe a favorite bat or an extra pair of cleats. "A lot of you have traveled a long way and some didn't get much sleep last night. And I know you've been to other camps and you were all overlooked," he quipped.

It was by the numbers all morning. "Okay, 175 up, 176, 177, 178 on deck," somebody would yell. A few pitches, a few ground balls, a few throws to first and go sit and wait. And if your number wasn't read off later by Gebhard or Daugherty, thanks for coming.

"Some of you are going to go home disappointed and rightfully so," Daugherty had said at the start. And some of them did. "I hope that kid's parents didn't miss breakfast to get him here this morning," Daugherty said at one point, watching a skinny kid bounce the ball twice on the throw from short to first. "But I'll tell you what: 40 years from now, he can tell his grandkids he tried out for the Rockies and got screwed."

"It's tough," Gebhard admitted. "You sit around and sit around, then have to jump up and catch five balls." And your dream of a future in the major league is over. You will not be one of the Boys of Summer, and you had better hurry home and get on the softball team before it fills up, too.

Tryout camps are not all failures. Frank White came out of one and spent 17 years in the majors. So it's possible. But for yesterday's collection wearing T-shirts and sweatshirts from every high school and college and junior college in the Western Hemisphere, it was mostly those nervous moments waiting to field a few grounders, and then sitting, waiting in vain to hear their number called out shortly before noon.

"The amazing thing—and God bless 'em, I guess that's what makes this a great country—is that every one of those kids deep down in their heart they think they've got a chance. One of the other beautiful things is that in a lot of cases they go away happy just having been here. A lot of them go away mad that you screwed them. 'They didn't give me a chance. I got four balls and Daugherty hit a ball to me that took a bad hop. The field was rough.'"

Work, Gebhard told them. Get stronger. Come back next year.

Meanwhile, in the dugout, a half dozen of the Rockies' newly signed rookies had gathered to watch. They would work later in the day.

"What time is practice tomorrow for the players—our real players?" an aide called out.

The field was rough. It was a short dream.

June 17, 1992, *Denver Post*

IT WAS A NIGHT FOR BASEBALL AND APPLE PIE

BEND, Ore.—It wasn't the World Series (although it was cold enough to qualify).

Historically, it was just a blip on baseball's Richter scale.

It was just Colorado starter Mark Thompson striking out the first hitter he—and the whole franchise—faced as a professional and shortstop Jason Bates scoring Colorado's first run.

Most of all, it was Will Scalzetti's grand-slam home run in the eighth inning that will mark Colorado's first game ever and a 6-4 victory over Boise.

And it was the Colorado Rockies taking their first tentative baby steps toward next year's official National League debut.

It didn't have to be anything more. What it was was baseball—and Americana—at its grassroots best.

There were speeches. There was a guitar band just inside the main entrance to greet early arrivals. They served hamburgers, baked beans and potato salad on a small deck down the left-field line while the barbecue smoke was tugged away from the field by a steady mountain breeze. ...

This was Bend, big time, and for one night, it didn't have to be Yankee Stadium with October bunting draped over the upper deck.

But don't mistake last night for anything resembling Class A short-season baseball. Last night was show biz. The real, honest-to-goodness Class A season starts tonight when the Rockies and the Boise Hawks, a California Angels affiliate, play game two. No balloons. No speeches. No more celebrity status. The long bus rides now begin. ...

July 18, 1992, *Denver Post*

WOMEN'S LEAGUE AHEAD OF ITS TIME

She still has the combative instinct of the athlete she once was.

"Tell Fred Leo," Pepper Davis said, "that he owes me $25. He fined me that much for arguing with an umpire and I want it back."

All the while, she kept signing—programs, baseballs, hats. The line stretched for at least a block on the roof of the San Diego Convention Center, where FanFest was in progress as part of the 1992 All-Star Baseball Game.

The table of gray-haired women was easily the most popular single stop in the elaborate display of baseball memories that included many from Cooperstown itself.

Pepper Davis was a key figure in the All-American Girls Professional Baseball League (AAGPBL) which is featured in the current movie, "A League of Their Own." She is retired and lives in Van Nuys, Calif. She helped advise movie makers on the production, and was also the one who wrote the song that became the league's theme.

Leo is a retired Denver broadcaster who served as commissioner of the AAGPBL from 1947 to 1952. "We still keep a directory of former players," Leo was saying recently, "and they hold an annual reunion."

The movie is No. 1 on the charts this summer, having displaced "Batman II," in sales, but Leo wouldn't put it with "Field of Dreams." "It was fictionalized to the point it does very little justice to what those girls who played in that league really accomplished."

Phil Wrigley and Branch Rickey founded the league as a hedge against wartime manpower shortages, and it began play in 1943 and stayed in business into 1954. "It finally died because we ran out of sources of players," says Leo. "Remember, colleges and high schools didn't have girls' softball in those years. If that league was to reopen, there would be a whole new source of players these days."

Pepper Davis thinks it's feasible. "From the interest we're seeing," she said at FanFest, "with the right ownership, sure, I think another league like ours would work." At that point, she and the other women were on their third day of 10 a.m.–3 p.m. behind the table, signing as fast as they could with no breaks.

"We started with softball and gradually moved to strict baseball," says Leo of the league's shift toward the traditional game the men played. The original four teams grew to eight—the Rockford Peaches, Peoria Redwings, Muskegon Lassies, Grand Rapids Chicks, South Bend Blue Sox, Ft. Wayne Daisies, Racine Belles and Kenosha Comets.

"We outdrew the men's minor-league team in Fort Wayne," Pepper recalls. "Totally."

She played from 1944 to 1953. "I would have been in on the first year but they didn't scout California that year, so I got married and then started to play the second season. That's when I wrote the song."

After she retired from the AAGPBL, she tried softball again "but it wasn't the same after that."

They were good. "We had a girl named Dorothy Kamenssheck who played for Rockford. She was so good at first base you couldn't believe. A minor-league club in Florida offered her a contract. We had Connie Mack come up to Kenosha one night. Connie watched the game from the dugout. In the seventh inning they said 'We better get back to Chicago.' The A's were playing there.

"Connie said, 'I'm not leaving until I've seen the whole game.' He couldn't believe what he was seeing."

Marty Marion (St. Louis Cardinals) "saw a shortstop we had by the name of

Dottie Schroeder. She could field as well as any man you've ever seen."

Leo stirs his coffee. "This thing was 40 years ahead of its time. We ran out of players. The league held their contracts, and we would assign new girls by position after spring training. We paid as much as $125 a week. They started at $75. Every team had a chaperone, most of them former nurses.

"She had to approve any dates."

But when the war ended, gasoline became plentiful again, television began to make inroads on the American entertainment scene and the league's future became grim.

"You could start that league again in towns of that same size," Leo believes. "We ran professional men's baseball out of Peoria. They had a team. They couldn't compete with us."

The movie? Good entertainment, fair history. If there is one basic criticism, it's that Tom Hanks, who plays the Rockford manager, never learned to spit. He keeps dribbling it all over his chin. I have a year-and-a-half-old grandson who does better. I imagine some of the original members of the AAGPBL could have done better, too.

August 20, 1992, *Denver Post*

LAST HOORAH FOR MINOR-LEAGUE TEAM

The field still shows lines from Friday night's Phoenix-Denver exhibition football game, and maybe there's something sadly fitting in that.

The Denver Bears—they aren't called that anymore, except in this space—will play their way out of nearly 100 years of Denver history at Mile High Stadium Tuesday night.

I think, for that night, Mayor Webb should rename Mile High Stadium, give it back its real name, Bears Stadium. Let us have one last fling with our past before we confront the future with a major-league label and major-league pretensions.

I went out early Friday, long before the football game, just to sit and look and remember. For some, like the *Post*'s Frank Haraway, memories go back before dirt. For me, they go back only to the cool, wonderful summer of 1949, when our family moved to Denver from Columbia, Mo.

"The first thing we do," my dad said, "is go out some night and watch the Bears."

"Who?"

"It's a minor-league team, Class A. They've just built a new stadium, and it's the best thing in town." He was right. We became regulars, watching the Bears play Colorado Springs and Pueblo and sitting there on insect-free, balmy Colorado evenings before we had a downtown skyline and not giving a damn if it was major- or minor-league. It was baseball. It was summer. It was perfect.

They built dreams on an old city dump, and as I sat there Friday night, I remembered the ballpark when it was simply one story, built down a hill to the field. There were no south stands, no soaring east or west stands, just room for maybe 18,000 people and you didn't even have I-25 beyond the left-field fence.

I'm told the outfielders could smell some of the detritus that oozed up from the dump on hot day games, and I know there was an uneven drop in the northeast corner beyond the third baseline. The imperfections just made it more endearing. ...

Baseball filtered some of its best through this ballpark, both with the Bears and as visitors. It extended even to field bosses and GMs. Billy Martin got his managerial start here. Bob Howsam, one of the great builders, laid the foundation both for major-league ball and for the Broncos.

So did the Phippses, Gerald and Allan, still the measuring stick for responsible local ownership.

I envy today's kids. They will grow up with a major-league team to watch, heroes still learning to walk at the moment, styles and records yet to be developed. Those of us who grew up with the Bears are left with long-distance memories all too often. Just when we would become attached to a player, he would be recalled.

It will be a long while, I suspect, before I become as genuinely excited as I was that summer of 1980 with Tim Raines and Tim Wallach and Randy Bass and Co. It was a team that left you leaning forward in your bleacher seat, and I would settle for that club, too, next year.

The Bears—and their miserably named successors—have always deserved better than they got in the way of local support. We have been a city in love with a major-league label for decades, and it has hurt.

We have watched them grow from old Merchants Park to Bears Stadium to Mile High, from Class A to AAA, flannels to doubleknits, and become at times the top minor-league franchise in the nation.

John Dikeou deserves a pat for keeping the lifeline open, and for enduring some undeserved criticism over the years. He made a horrible mistake at the outset when he listened to Tal Smith and renamed the Bears, rupturing those decades of tradition and familiarity. But he persevered.

Now? The Rockies own swagger rights now, but if they are smart, they will study why the Bears worked so well for so long. Like Dikeou, they made a huge mistake in naming themselves, but that's done.

Keep the fireworks. Keep the Businessman's Special on Wednesday noon. Keep some thread, however thin, to link this team and this franchise and this city with its past.

It is too good to bury with the garbage beneath the stadium.

✤　　　✤　　　✤

CHAPTER SIX

BASKETBALL

✦   ✦   ✦

Dick and I go back a long way. He was here in Denver when I got here in 1975, and I always found him to be a very professional writer. He was kind of from the old school, where he had a great ability to communicate. When he needed to be tough he was, but every column he wrote wasn't negative and biting. He was able to use his communication skills to communicate with the reader.

—Dan Issel, head coach, Denver Nuggets Professional Basketball Team, and former NBA player

✦   ✦   ✦

♦ ♦ ♦

Dick loved basketball. He grew up in Iowa and Missouri. Basketball in the 1940s in the Midwest was an all-consuming passion. His father and uncle coached basketball at the two parochial high schools in Iowa City. The rivalry was intense.

Dick was on the winning Hickman High School basketball team, an experience he remembered with great fondness. As a columnist, he covered professional basketball periodically and always, if possible, made it to the college Final Four tournament. That may have been his second favorite national event.

May 27, 1977, *Denver Post*

NUGGETS WEAR HAPPY FACES, AGAIN

Feet up, chair tilted back, a wall full of plaques behind the desk in the earth-tone office, Carl Scheer mulled the question.

"This time a year ago? Let's see. The merger was June 17. Four weeks before that, we were beginning to formulate plans for the funeral."

The ABA was terminal. "We had lost to New York in the playoffs in early May and by this point all my energies were exerted toward whether or not the league would survive."

By late May, it was almost a CIA scenario. Scheer, San Antonio's Angelo Drossos, Dave DeBusschere and NBA commissioner Larry O'Brien were registering under assumed names in New York hotels, hoping against hope some formula could be worked out. Merger seemed far off.

"I didn't have a code name," Scheer recalls. "I think I used John Smith." The incongruity of it struck him and he smiled. "Not very imaginative." If he hadn't brought luggage they probably wouldn't have let him past the lobby.

The times called for imagination. The ABA was on its deathbed and everyone knew it. Franchises were dying. By May, it looked like the fort in Beau Geste, with all the bodies propped in the parapets hoping the enemy would mistake them for live ones. The NBA wasn't fooled.

"We were in a doomsday kind of atmosphere. You know how it is when you get a phone call at two in the morning? You know it is never going to be pleasant news. That's the kind of telexes we would get from the league office: 'Emergency meeting at Kennedy Airport,' or somewhere. It was a crisis mood."

O'Brien, the consummate politician, kept at it. He wanted merger, in some form. Denver, Indiana, the New York Nets and San Antonio finally proved to be that form— but only after the NBA extracted terms that still work against their newest members. Scheer was a major figure in constructing those terms, adopting the philosophy of the 96-year-old who, asked how he felt, answered: "Considering the alternative, not too bad."

Extinction was the alternative. The terms eventually included such items as no television money for four years, a $3.2 million initiation fee, $3 million of it up front and an ABA team agreement to soak up any indemnification to other, dying ABA clubs.

Scheer still remembers the first meeting with the NBA group in the Plaza Hotel in New York. "Bill Alverson then was president of the Milwaukee Bucks and was chairman of the NBA board of governors. O'Brien got up and said, 'Bill, why don't you start.' Bill got up. Obviously, he had a game plan. And he said, 'As far as I am concerned, I wouldn't meet with you SOBs. You have cost my franchise millions. Don't talk to me about what is good for basketball. What's good for my franchise and the NBA is good for me.'" Scheer smiles at the memory. "Even Larry O'Brien sank into his chair a little at that start."

From such an acorn, merger grew. ...

October 31, 1984, *Rocky Mountain News*
BORYLA GIVES NUGGETS A LUNCH-BUCKET IMAGE

The anniversary date will pass unnoticed except by trick-or-treaters.

But the Denver Nuggets fortunes began to follow a decidedly different path precisely one year ago today.

That's when Vince Boryla and Red McCombs began mutual heavy breathing.

If it is not sacrilegious to talk of things other than Orange at this sacred season, the results of that momentous first meeting are still being felt.

The Carl Scheer administration was still in power, but it was a reign that already had limited horizons. Both sides knew it. Scheer had saved and stabilized and preserved the game here, but neither he nor McCombs, the new owner, were comfortable with each other. Something was going to happen.

"I had my first meeting with Red on Halloween Day a year ago," Boryla was recalling over breakfast coffee late last week. His team was about to launch its 1984–85 season. Already, as distinctive as the Romanesque nose he wears, the Nuggets had taken on a Boryla look.

"He called me a couple of days before that and said, 'I'm coming into town. I'd like to visit with you.' So I met him at the airport. He started talking."

They met for two hours. Boryla estimates McCombs talked about an hour and 55 minutes of that.

McCombs, the master salesman, was dealing with Boryla, the master deal maker. It's too bad history did not have a tape recorder handy, just for the enrichment of future generations of students.

Eventually, some months and meetings later, one millionaire convinced the other millionaire he needed the job not for the money but for the challenge. "You're the right man, at the right time."

And last week, his team about to tip it off, Boryla admitted it was almost more of a challenge than he wanted.

"The first couple months were bleepin' horrible," he says, in the earthy adjectives that mark his conversation. "My whole body chemistry changed. Gettin' up. I couldn't sleep. And if I did, I'd wake up at 3 in the morning. There wasn't a bleepin' day that went by that I didn't say to myself three or four times a day, 'What the bleep am I doing this for?'"

What the bleep, indeed. He was doing it because he loved it. He was doing it because his knees wouldn't let him play racquetball anymore and there was no outlet for the competitive juices that still flowed. And he was doing it because, many suspect, he might turn out to be as good at it as anybody ever has.

At 57, he didn't need the job. He's made his, several times, several ways. He has nothing to prove. And that, says this 57-year-old from East Chicago, is the whole point.

"I've got an advantage. I'm not playing scared. I don't need the bleepin' job. You can't hire a better guy than me, my type of guy." This ain't bragging. He's right. He's done everything you can do in basketball, from playing to running a team. Nothing he does has to be based on someone else's feelings, or some indefinable pressure, or a worry about whether Red McCombs will agree. "I've got carte blanche." And if Red doesn't like it, Red can have the job back.

Which means, one suspects, that Red is going to love it, and that the job will be done the way both Red and Boryla like. Already, there is massive change.

It took Boryla precisely one month to trade away Kiki Vandeweghe, whom many had identified as one of the untouchables.

"When I took over, on May 7, on a scale of 1 to 10 which I use an awful lot, I think we had a club that ranked about a three," Boryla was saying as another patty of sausage disappeared. "I think we're at a six or seven now."

For that one player, Boryla's bold dealing with Portland landed three starters, a draft choice that became a rookie with talent (Willie White) and a No. 1 for next year.

They also landed a new look, a new style and a new franchise birthmark. The Scheer era was over. The Boryla era had begun.

"I feel good about this club," he says now. "If somebody had bleepin' told me in May that I'd feel the way I do about this club today, I'd have bleepin' sent the guy to Pueblo. Whether it turns out that way or not, I feel very, very good about this club. I'm not making any predictions, but my feelings are excellent."

Scheer had taken over a sagging, desperate franchise, glamourized it, built it, nursed it, even brought it into the NBA, but never had the wherewithal to do everything he wanted. McCombs had then bought it, but the two, as noted, had never seemed to establish a rapport.

"We're in a transitional stage now," Boryla says, "a tremendously transitional stage. A phrase that maybe covers it is let's say we're changing over from a tinsel, glamour group to a hardworking lunch-bucket group."

Boryla loves that concept. It reeks of sweat and grime and the work ethic and aching muscles and maybe thumping away on somebody else once in a while. The flashy stuff is for other guys.

"I like hard-ass basketball because hard-ass basketball carries you through a lot of valleys. The valleys don't become so deep.

"I consider myself very uncluttered mentally. I am an uncluttered business person, too. I don't worry about things that are bleep things to worry about. Those things will take care of themselves. Like tickets. If we win, play well, those will take care of themselves. I am a very pragmatic person. I have been all my life. I came from a blacksmith area, a steelsmith area. That's my basic philosophy. Even in business. You know, some guys talk about the sky when they talk deals. I talk about the gutter—have I covered my tail nine ways? Is it a good deal? The rest takes care of itself.

"I tell everybody I'm in a bleepin' hurry. I ain't got no five-year plan. My bleepin' plan is month to month. I'm in a hurry."

You bleepin' got that? When Vince Boryla goes trick or treating, it's for keeps.

October 27, 1987, *Rocky Mountain News*

BORYLA RESIGNS AS FOREMAN OF LUNCH-BUCKET BRIGADE

Vince Boryla is gone as foreman of the Denver Nuggets lunch-bucket bunch.

Retired is the polite word used on the press release.

Fed up might be closer. Or shoved. The closest would be a combination of those two, I suspect, and yesterday afternoon's press conference announcing Boryla's departure as president and general manager of the Nuggets—and appointment of Pete Babcock as his successor—was notable for one major absence—Boryla's.

If a man goes agreeably and pleasantly into that good night, wouldn't he at least like to sum up the career he is discarding? Everybody was there yesterday except Boryla.

It spoke volumes.

"What was that great phrase I heard Doug [Moe] say about me on the radio?" Boryla said one day a few years ago. 'When you talk to Vince, you don't talk about the weather.'"

Boryla would not have talked about the weather, or made public relations nice talk yesterday. So he didn't go. He and Shlenker have an agreement. It covers 10 years, and retains him as that most elusive of humans, a consultant.

Maybe it also ensures he will leave his phone off the hook for the present.

"I'm a meat-and-potatoes talker and thinker and everything else," Boryla had said on a September morning in 1984. He was explaining the blockbuster trade for Kiki Vandeweghe that acquired Wayne Cooper, Calvin Natt and Fat Lever plus a draft pick. It cast the Nuggets in a completely new mode, a tougher, no-nonsense one that reflected Vince himself.

"My lunch-bucket brigade," he delighted in calling them. Meat and potatoes. Those things fit in a lunch bucket. Sushi and nouvelle cuisine don't. There is a strong temptation to draw that comparison, that Boryla dealt in staples and the new Nuggets are drifting toward those little piles of steamed vegetables with a dab of some sauced-up meat in the middle of the plate.

Whatever way you want to accept yesterday's event, the fact is they are now going to have to prove they are better, or even as good, without him than they were when he occupied that bunkerlike office deep inside McNichols.

The Nuggets lost their profane, intelligent toughness yesterday. It will be up to Babcock and to owner Sidney Shlenker to prove they can compensate for what they will miss in Boryla's day-to-day presence.

That there was a team left for Shlenker to buy is due at least in part to what Boryla accomplished, what he threw out and what he kept and what he fashioned after taking over in May 1984.

I don't know how good Babcock can be. There is a vast difference between being an effective No. 2 and a competent No. 1, and he now gets the chance to prove he can make that transition. The point is, Boryla had nothing left to prove. There were no doubts of his abilities.

Denver was on the verge of coming apart three and a half years ago. Vince, hired by then-owner Red McCombs, put it back together, hammered it into place and restored it to playoff respectability.

He relished the job after a decade out of the business. He has been part of basketball—and it has been part of him—for half a century. He played it and coached it successfully at the highest levels as a collegiate All-American and as a top pro.

He ran the New York Knicks, and years later, after assembling a fortune in various endeavors, he turned the Utah Stars into a model franchise before the old ABA died.

The second smartest thing McCombs did in pro basketball was hiring Boryla to put Denver back in shape. (The smartest was selling the whole package to Shlenker, but that's another story for another time.)

McCombs gave Boryla full authority. "Run it," he said. Boryla did—all the way to a 52-30 Midwest Division championship and the Western Conference finals that first year. A year later, Shlenker bought the team, and the seeds of yesterday's divorce were probably sown then.

Shlenker was not an absentee owner. He wanted a hands-on role. Vince had been not only No. 1, but No. 2 and 3, as well. Two strong-willed men were at work on each other, and Boryla's authority began to erode. ...

Boryla can curse like a longshoreman. He is abrasive, and tough and opinionated and, on occasions, a soft and gentle man who has died a little through his wife, Cappie's, prolonged illness. He is also a multimillionaire who possesses that most enviable quality—he can tell the boss to go to hell when he feels like it.

For any number of reasons, including the intrusion of a whole new high-tech philosophy and marketing emphasis Boryla disdained, I think that is ultimately what happened.

They talked sky. He talked gutter. They might eventually get to the same spot, but the difference was too great.

He didn't want to put up with the bullfeathers anymore. What's more to the point, he didn't have to.

It is Sidney's team, and he has every right to cast it in whatever image he wishes. If he and Boryla could not make their relationship work, fine. Many of us wondered it lasted as long as it did.

It is Babcock's chore now to redirect the Nuggets. If he's half as successful as the man he replaced, he will have earned the respect Boryla carried away yesterday for himself.

What is obvious, however, is that the Nuggets won't be quite the same again. The lid has been slammed on the lunch bucket.

April 17, 1989, *Denver Post*
T. R. DUNN WINS GAMES AT HIS END OF THE COURT

Time out. The Denver Nuggets were just over a quarter into one of the year's key games at McNichols Arena this past Wednesday evening. Things were, well, unsettled.

"Take Worthy," Doug Moe ordered as T. R. Dunn stripped off his warm-ups and started toward the scorer's desk.

At the other end, Pat Riley stood in the midst of his Mercedes Benz lineup and glanced down court.

"Don't worry about Dunn shooting," he told his assembled millionaires. Concentrate, instead, on sagging inside against Danny Schayes and Blair Rasmussen and Alex English. Don't worry about Dunn with the ball.

What we had, in that divided moment, was the whole crux of Theodore Roosevelt Dunn's career and his special place in the world of professional basketball. "Take Worthy." "Don't worry."

What happened? Denver, trailing 45-40 against the world champions, sent Dunn into the right corner. L.A. sagged. Dunn hit a 15-footer off the baseline. Next trip, Dunn went left, again uncovered. Two from the corner. Next trip, left side baseline, two more.

In three successive possessions, Dunn buried three uncontested shots, Denver regained the lead at 46-45 and never trailed again. Worthy, who had scored six points before Dunn arrived, was in and out of the lineup and did not score again in the half.

"Take Worthy." Take Aguirre. Take Jordan. Take Bird. Take the hot hand and ice it. Take a marquee figure and make him a mere human. Take the guy making a million dollars and a million points and a million headlines, and reduce him from godlike status to frustrated mortality. That is what Dunn has done as well as anybody in the NBA for a decade. Frustration is his stock in trade. Three straight from the baseline are a bonus.

Yet here is this quiet Alabaman, built like the prototype strong safety, working always in the shadows of the scorers, and if it weren't for him, a strong argument can be made the Nuggets would not have enjoyed the success they have in the 1980s.

"He does for us at one end what Alex English does for us at the other," Doug Moe was saying the day after Denver's 120-106 victory over the Lakers. "He is just a rock defensively like Alex is a rock offensively."

Only a few months ago, the stories were circulating as fact. T. R. Dunn was gone, cut or traded, banished to make way for an Otis Smith, or Mo Martin, or somebody. Funny. None of the stories quoted Doug Moe on the subject.

"You never heard me say that," he said firmly this week. "We kept T. R. because he wins games for you." What could be simpler, more fundamental? You keep T. R. Dunn because you would lose without him.

"He didn't have a good year last year, but we didn't have a good team," Moe continues. Denver needed Darrell Walker's scoring, instead, even if Walker was not the overall player Dunn can be with a good team around him.

"He can shut people down," Moe says simply. "He can win games. If you don't have enough scoring, then you are forced to play other people who are not as good. When you heard all those stories, that wasn't me. They wanted new blood, revamping. But I knew if we were going to be good, T. R. was going to be one of the reasons."

There is a clipping in the Nuggets' files, one from Dunn's rookie year with Portland in 1977–78. "There seemingly is no spot for T. R. Dunn with the Blazers," the story begins. The NBA is soaring ballet, double figure scoring, throat-tightening slams. It isn't a quiet, determined—Moe calls it "driven"—kid from Birmingham who can accept a nonstarting role after years as a starter and still come out and "take Worthy" and fog the great man's protective glasses.

"Every player that comes into the league envisions himself as a scorer," Dunn concedes. "But you have to do something to make an impact as a rookie, to get noticed." For Dunn, with Jack Ramsey watching approvingly, that something was defense.

Dallas' Rolando Blackman, asked to list the best defensive guards, names Dennis Johnson and T. R. Dunn. Jordan, asked to name the five best defenders he's faced, has Dunn on that list. "He wins games for you," Moe repeats.

Can there be a better reason to keep a man on any roster? Dunn is 10th on the NBA's all-time leader list for steals. Typically, a reporter had to inform him when it happened.

Dunn, the man who wins games, is now being rumored as one of the Nuggets who will be left exposed to the upcoming expansion draft. Don't take bets on it. "All you can do is block it out," says Dunn. Block it out. Do what he has always done—win games. The rest will take care of itself. Someday, certainly, it will end. Then, he's thinking of a coaching career. Someday.

Meanwhile, take Worthy. Take the world. And shoot when you're open.

June 4, 1989, *Denver Post*

MICHAEL JORDAN AND HIS MAY MAGIC MISSED

Bring up the house lights. Drop the curtain. Let the music fade and let's all go next door for a late espresso and talk about it.

Oh, yes. I'm intrigued by a rematch of Detroit and Los Angeles, with all the created hype, the good guys–bad guys story line, the three-peat element, the who-is-wearing-the-most-expensive-suit sidebar, the kissy-kissy, lotusland vs. Godzilla, finesse vs. thuggery.

Jack Nicholson vs. Lee Iacocca would be nice, and there will be a certain nostalgic quality to Kareem Abdul Jabbar's unflattering exit from the spotlight.

It has a lot going for it, this June matchup for the NBA championship.

It just doesn't have Michael Jordan and his May Magic, and so it isn't what it might have been.

No doubt, the right team won. It was bigger and better and deeper and by far tougher and it deserved to win. It's just that the right guy lost, as well, and some of the visceral excitement he brought to our lives the past month disappeared into the calendar with him.

Did you see Friday night's finale as Detroit ousted Air Chicago?

The part where Jordan, right baseline, sweeps toward the hoop, apparently intent on a reverse layup with the right hand, only to find a huge Detroit paw in the way at the last moment. So, afloat in his natural element, he flipped the ball from right hand to left and then, soft as a baby's breath, kissed it in off the glass with a little wrist flick.

Right there, that move, that magnificent ballet in the sky, Jordan showed why he is the most exciting man who has ever played the game. Pity he has to play it almost alone. When Bill Laimbeer's elbow sent Scotty Pippen to the hospital for the night, it sent any lingering Chicago hopes with it.

What it proved was that even someone as distinctive, as great as is Jordan can't do it alone. But he came close.

I know, it's dangerous to get caught up in the best-worst-least-most-highest-lowest-fastest-slowest syndrome that seems to seize all of us at times, but I honestly don't remember a player who has done what Jordan has. I covered Elgin Baylor in his prime, the Big O, Wilt Chamberlain, Jerry West. I have watched Larry Bird in person and on the tube since I covered his duel with Magic Johnson in Salt Lake City for the NCAA title in 1979.

And nobody touches Jordan for sheer dramatic impact on a night.

He took a sub-.500 team and dragged it onto the national stage and kept it there until almost 4,000 playing minutes since November began to tell and there was nobody else in the Chicago lineup to pick up the slack.

I'm going to enjoy watching Magic with his earthborne talents, the sleight-of-hand passes, the no-look assists, the long bounce passes through two or three startled defenders. It will be fun to see whether Detroit's grinding defense can slow the Lakers, or whether the Pistons' penchant for falling behind early will prove fatal against a much more lethal team.

The whole white hat–black hat scenario that marks this series is the stuff of good theater.

But it ain't like watching Jordan every time he comes down the floor, waiting, expecting—something. What? A 360 tomahawk stuff off the free throw line? A behind the head jam, tongue stuck out like a kid in intense concentration, and the wild joyous look as he heads up the floor afterward?

Have we seen his like before?

It says here we haven't. ...

<hr>

December 20, 1989, *Denver Post*

A CHRISTMAS CAROL—NUGGETS STYLE

"Bah!" Doug Moe says.

Or, more precisely, "Bah Bleep."

"Humbug!" Alex English retorts.

And Tiny Tim, in his $30 seat just behind Gucci Row at courtside, shakes his head.

"What're they yelling at each other?" he asks his father, just back from climbing the stairs to buy a $40 hot dog and a $10 coke for the little urchin.

"Alex doesn't like to be yelled at," his father explains. "And that's the only conversational tone Doug Moe ever uses."

"But, don't all coaches yell?" the waif asks.

"Not as, um, creatively," his father answers. "That's why we're sitting over here, across the floor. You're too young to sit behind the bench."

"But hasn't he ever yelled at Alex before?"

"Sure. Lots of times. But Alex was scoring 30 points a game in those days and he'd just come off the floor and towel off his face and ignore Doug. Now, he's not scoring like that, and it hurts, and when he comes off and gets yelled at, it hurts more."

Tiny Tim watches. Alex shoots. And misses. And shoots. And hits. And the man he is guarding drives past him and scores. And Moe yells.

It's the misses that make the difference, his father explains. Alex used to go out night after night, and he'd score 35, or 25, or 29, or 27, and he'd have five or six assists, something that everybody ignored. Alex is also a great passer. But he is not what basketball types call physical.

"He's a misplaced poet who plays basketball," his dad explains. "He shoots this stylish, floating little jumper like nobody else in the league, and he's been shooting it so long and so well he's going to wind up in the Hall of Fame. It's not as spectacular as some of the stuff Michael Jordan does, but it's just as distinctive, just as much a signature shot. Only the great ones have that. They even used him for a movie: 'Amazing Grace and Chuck.' Alex was Amazing Grace. He had this amazing shot, but somehow, he had lost it."

"Like now," Tiny Tim said.

"Like now."

"Well," Tim said, swallowing the last of the cold dog, "who's right?"

His father watched Alex miss. He watched Moe swear.

"Neither one," his father said. It used to be, Alex English could carry the other Nuggets on nights when he was the only one they could count on to score at critical times.

It used to be Alex English was never on the bench at the end of a game. "That's what they call 'crunch time,'" Tim's dad explained. "That's when you want your best guys on the floor. Now, Alex is sitting during crunch time. Doug Moe even said once a month ago or so that he forgot about him and that's why he didn't put him back in."

"How can you forget about Alex English?" Tim asked.

"That's one of the things Alex is upset about," his dad said.

"But I was sitting over behind the Nuggets bench one night when Alex missed about three shots and his man drove past him, and a rebound came off and bounced off Alex out of bounds and the other team got it. Doug swore and swore and sent somebody in for Alex. And when Alex came past him to the bench, Doug said, 'Dammit, Alex, I can't leave you in there when you do that.'"

"Well, that doesn't sound too bad," Tim said.

"It wasn't. But I think Alex was already upset at himself right then. He knew he hadn't played too well. And sometimes, it's better not to say anything. But that's not Doug's nature."

They watched a while longer. Sometimes Alex scored. Sometimes he missed. Sometimes Moe swore. Sometimes he didn't.

"If you had to keep just one, which one would you keep?" Tiny asked.

"Good question," his father answered. "Good question. Moe, I suppose. Nobody likes to get old. Alex is. It's hard. And Doug isn't making it easier."

"God bless them, every one," Tim said. "Except their agents."

February 3, 1990, *Denver Post*
Following Nuggets' front office like reading Russian novel

Stay with me now. It's complicated. It will take time. It's a little like tracing the patronymics in a Russian novel, but you'll need the family tree outline to understand what comes later.

Once upon a time, long ago, Pete Babcock became president and GM of the Denver Nuggets.

Okay so far?

Then, last July 10, Bertram Lee and Peter Bynoe announced they had purchased the Denver Nuggets, and that Dave Checketts henceforth and forever was the new president of the Denver Nuggets. Babcock was to become vice president in charge of basketball operations.

He held that post until Oct. 10, when the aforementioned Lee-Bynoe, with help from previously unmentioned Robert Wussler, officially bought the team they had officially announced they had bought three months earlier. But now, they also announced that Dave Checketts of Salt Lake was going home, had quit and Babcock was back as president and GM.

Go ahead. Jot down a name or two just to help you remember. It helps.

So, from Oct. 10 to Nov. 2, Babcock was back as what he had been before, once upon a time. Aha. But on Nov. 2, it was announced that a Messr. Jon Spoelstra was now and forever the new president and GM of the Denver Nuggets, and that Babcock would now be vice president in charge of basketball operations.

"I feel as though I have joined the president-of-the-month club," Spoelstra said at his baptismal press conference. He laughed. The press laughed. Nice line. Appropriate. Babcock did not laugh.

(We'll pause here, while you quickly run down the above paragraphs, refreshing your memory as to who was what when.)

Yesterday, there they sat, dark suits, muted ties, shoes shined, garb totally appropriate for funerals, press conferences or power lunches.

Pete Babcock, who has spent the past three months in what he calls a state of limbo, unhappy, uncertain, unseen, took his place next to Bynoe, who was at the podium. Spoelstra took his place at the far end of the table. For those of us who like to read Kremlin walls at the May Day parade, assigning power levels based on how close to the middle a man stands, it was not a good sign for Mr. Spoelstra.

"Personal reasons," he said of the ensuing revelation that he, like Mr. Checketts, is no longer president etc. of the Denver Nuggets. Now and forever was getting shorter.

Babcock is back as GM. Bynoe is boss.

"There is no president," said Bynoe.

What we've got here is government by chaos. It's become the Nuggets' natural front office state. Nobody knows who's in charge. Or why. Maybe, now, finally, they will.

"We are going to try to establish stability," said Bynoe, who has had five chief executives in seven months if you count Babcock twice and Bynoe now. "We are going to try to establish continuity," said the man whose underlings have taken to putting their names up on office doors using Velcro so they can be quickly stripped away. There are rumors the man who prints executive stationery has since retired to his own island, laughing hysterically.

And how, Bynoe was asked, does he think the public perceives the Denver Nuggets?

"As an organization in turmoil," Bynoe said. "Too many changes."

He is trying to stop them. He would love, he said, to "get off the front pages with organizational news" and leave it to the exploits of his basketball team.

It's vital he do exactly that. They've become a national joke with all the front office bumper pool, the uncertainty, the signing of Blair Rasmussen to a megamillion contract that Bynoe and Lee say they didn't even know about.

We've heard all this before. It's time for deeds, not press conferences to announce another new layer of titles. ...

March 21, 1990, *Denver Post*

NCAA TIME IS BEST OF ALL THE "NOWS"

"What's your favorite sport?" they ask after the little breakfast or lunch talk.

"This one," I say.

"Well, I mean, what's your favorite season?"

"Now."

The trouble is, I really do mean just that. Except, maybe, right now is a little better than most of the other nows. Right now is the best of the nows.

Now. March. Basketball. Tournament time. Hope and despair and triumph all in the same night, the same big arena. All those tear streaks running through all those little cat's paws and initials painted on cheeks. All those TV shots of brimming eyes, staring at reality, still not quite believing what they are seeing, while across the floor, insanity reigns.

It's Oklahoma's Jackie Jones in warm-up jersey and crimson sweatpants, wandering the halls of the Erwin Center Saturday night, while the periodic roars of the crowd from the Arkansas-Dayton game penetrated the long concrete tunnel.

I had walked over to the game behind several Oklahoma students, listening to them talk, anticipate, wonder where they would stay in Dallas for the regionals this week.

North Carolina simplified the decision, and maybe Jones was staring at that. He had been screened so he couldn't quite get to the Tar Heels' Rick Fox in time. Fox had come along the baseline and then sifted into the low post just enough to shoot past Jones and score.

The clock showed :01. "King Rice inbounds to Hubert Davis on the left side of the court, swings it over to Fox, who goes right, along the baseline, into lane, nails the three-foot bank shot. Crowd goes nuts."

That's the official play-by-play description of the end of all those Oklahoma dreams. It would fit, with changes, for Montbello's exit, for Littleton's demise, for the way Colorado finally succumbed to the Sooners in the Big Eight tournament. It fits March. So did the clump of delirious Carolinians at midcourt.

"Crowd goes nuts."

So does, "cheerleaders weep."

So does the vacant look in Jones' eyes as he walked the tunnel past the North Carolina room where TV cameras and dozens of writers still camped. It was supposed to be the Oklahoma quarters that served as the magnet. Was he walking the tunnel, replaying that final few seconds, wondering what he might have done differently?

Will we get the same empty-eyed view from Loyola Marymount this weekend in Oakland? Or will Tark Arslanian look even more like a sad-eyed bloodhound than normal? Is North Carolina's surprising late run to end in Dallas against Arkansas? Will all those little black footprints on cheerleaders' cheeks begin to run while the hall fills with "Sooooie!" screams?

This is the best time. Winter ends. Spring arrives. I've been darting back and forth between the seasons for two weeks now—escaping the blizzard to find spring in Kansas City at the Big Eight tournament, winter back in Denver. Home two days, then spring in Texas and back to snow and fog Sunday morning. Now back to spring in New Orleans.

And I remember too many years ago, senior year, Hickman High, Columbia, Mo. No divisions in those years. Big schools, little schools, they all qualified for the same tournament.

We made state, and caravaned to Springfield, Mo., in one of those chilling spring rains on a grim, cold day. I don't remember who we played, just that we lost. We had strutted about town in our shiny gold warm-up jackets in one final burst of misplaced confidence, then went out that night and got our heads handed to us. But when we got back to Columbia a couple days later, the rain was gone.

Spring had slipped gloriously into town in our absence. Trees, shrubs, flowers, everything had exploded. The city smelled of new grass and blossoms.

Losing didn't mean as much.

It was the best time again. Still is.

BUBBLES AND TEARS MARK MOE'S EXIT

Champagne and teary smiles—there are worse ways to go.

Doug Moe sipped one and fought back the other, and his wife, Big Jane, saved the day. ,

"What I want to know," she asked a hastily assembled press conference at McNichols yesterday, "is whether they mail the check or whether we come by and pick it up."

Doug Moe was fired yesterday, ending a 10-year association with the Denver Nuggets. It also ended a bloody personnel summer and continued a bizarre sequence of front office maneuvers that have marked the franchise for a year.

For all the high-sounding reasons like "they have got to have their own identity," they trashed one of the league's top coaches.

If Paul Westhead is indeed the replacement, they at least can stay with the same pell-mell style Moe used and to which he drafted this past summer.

"He deserved it after what he did to Alex," the talk show denizens crowed yesterday, thus proving they can compare apples and oranges and discover a prune.

English and Moe are both men who deserved better fates. Moe's stubbornness and English's inability to recognize his own failing talents created the script with a lousy ending. But neither "deserved" it. English would never have become one of the league's top all-time scorers except for Moe's system. Moe would not have won as he did without English. But I think that was just a convenient excuse, if indeed it was a factor in yesterday's front office hatchet job. Watching English depart and now Moe is like watching a long marriage dissolve and never really being able to isolate why.

Now, this troubled franchise is paying ex-presidents Vince Boryla and Pete Babcock and Jon Spoelstra, and ex-coach Moe, and we are left to wonder if the NBA will be forced to institute a front office salary cap as it did for players? They may have more going out to nonworking execs than to players.

I sat yesterday and couldn't tell who was most uncomfortable, GM Bernie Bickerstaff, who already had Westhead in the wings, or Moe, who was somehow left in the untenable position of having to announce his own firing, but never quite used that exact word.

After fighting it for a year, he'll be better off away from it all for a while. The question is whether Denver will be.

Moe broke down and had to back away from the podium. That's when Big Jane called from the back, "Is it time for the champagne?" Promptly on her own cue, she marched to the front and poured a glass for herself and her husband, and asked the classic question: How do they pick up the $2 million the club owes her husband for the next three years?

"I have a bottle of Dom Perignon at home in the refrigerator. We'll open that later," she said as she watched Moe work his way through postpress-conference questions. "Sidney Shlenker gave it to us when we signed the contract.

"The one this morning Chopper [trainer-traveling secretary Bob Travaglini] had

in the training room. I think it's left over from one of the division championships."
So there are wet circles on the bar today from that tale of two bottles. Champagne
for a new contract, champagne from an old title and now champagne for the end of
a long, splendid, profane, tumultuous, successful, uncertain era.

Make no mistake: From this point on, the Nuggets are a different team, a different organization. Alex English is gone. Fat Lever is gone. Danny Schayes is gone.
Doug Moe and Moe-ball is gone. It has rookies in key spots and a new coach to be
named momentarily. All vestiges of the old Nuggets left with Moe yesterday.

This was to be a year of dramatic change anyway. It became increasingly evident
Moe was not going to fit. The betting was they would let him lose into December or
January and then fire him.

Yesterday's timing, like its strange format, was the weird element. Why now, at
this point? Why not last summer? This is a team that has lost the knack for doing
things right. Maybe Bickerstaff can restore some of that, but only if they cut off all
the phone calls to the east and leave him alone.

"It's funny," Jane recalled. "When they fired Doug in San Antonio 10 years ago,
Angelo Drossos did it by phone. Two of the boys were about to go out to play a
tournament game, and Doug turned to me and mouthed, 'I've been fired.' He didn't
want to bother the boys with it just then.

"I had some champagne and I turned while he was still on the phone and
opened the door to the refrigerator and got out a bottle and opened it right then
and there."

This one tastes a little flat. Moe, an emotional man and an emotional coach,
couldn't stem the tears when he tried to announce he was gone. He turned to
longtime friend and Nuggets' exec Carl Scheer. "I told you," he said.

Where was Peter Bynoe, the resident owner? He should have been there instead
of saddling Bickerstaff with the distasteful chore. Where was the invisible string-
puller Bob Wussler, who never liked Moe and who, I believe, is doing everything
he can to engineer things so this club can eventually be yanked away from Denver
and placed elsewhere?

Moe and Bickerstaff and Scheer handled the thing with as much taste and class
as the occasion permitted. Strangely, nobody actually used the word fired.

"He was fired," Jane said flatly.

Bynoe and Bertram Lee, Moe said, "are my friends." Note, he did not also say
Wussler, that eastern carpetbagger/controlling owner who will ruin this franchise
yet.

Sip quickly, Douglas, before the bubbly goes flat. And cash the check promptly.

May 10, 1992, *Denver Post*

ISSEL CROWNED BEFORE THE CORONATION

Funny, isn't it? We've all seen men, regimes, governments toppled by the press.
(See Richard Nixon. See Watergate.)

The most amazing part of this past week has been to watch a man crowned by the media, scarcely quoted but immediately lionized and all but installed before he is even interviewed.

From the columns to the talk shows to the blow-dried pronouncements on the 10 p.m. sportscasts, Dan Issel has been named the newest Denver Nuggets coach.

Did he ever formally apply? Or did Bernie Bickerstaff float a balloon and then watch it grow beyond anyone's expectations, maybe even Issel's? I can remember conversations in the latter stages of Issel's playing career when he flat said he did not want to coach in the NBA. Certainly a man can change his mind, and four years on the fringes may have done just that for The Horse.

A question I would want answered if I were Bickerstaff is just how committed Issel is. Coaching is both an addiction and a dedication. It is at once one of the most rewarding and one of the most frustrating things a man can do. A coach is in the middle—management on one side, demanding wins to fill seats to swell the bottom line, and often balky players on the other. Plus there is the press and its demands.

Doug Moe somehow steered safely among these shoals and made it work. He was a player's coach, although not a rookie player's coach. He was basically the same, win or lose. He was successful, he had a distinctive style and a flair and eventually he also developed health problems.

Can Issel duplicate all this (health excluded)? He has an acerbic wit. It worked in the locker room, on a player level, because he could then go out and have a 30-point night and back it up. Sarcasm is not a good teaching tool. And, if Issel takes the job, teaching is going to be one of his principal chores. He would inherit a team as young and fragile as those spring flowers beginning to show in the garden.

Encouragement, not sarcasm, will have to be one of his strengths.

So will patience. Do we have a measure of that in this man who quit as the fourth-leading scorer of all time? Can he grit his teeth and stay silent when that is needed? We have no measure of Issel in some of these areas.

I'm not one who thinks experience is the essential ingredient for a man to take on a head coaching post in the NBA. Too many have come in and succeeded with only minimally better credentials. Issel, after all, spent 15 years answering 5 a.m. wake-up calls, fidgeting in airports, trudging down hallways in foreign arenas and establishing himself as one of the best to play the game.

He knows the NBA. He knows basketball. He knows when to substitute, when to call for a time-out. The questions hanging over him are from the less tangible areas—how will he be at handling people, at teaching, at maintaining his and his team's equilibrium during the bad times that are still ahead?

We don't know. But we don't know those things, either, about some of the assistant coaches Bickerstaff has interviewed since firing Paul Westhead. Look at Westhead himself. He won a championship with the Lakers, but was the subject of a palace revolt by his players. He coached the Bulls. But his Denver tenure was star-crossed from the beginning.

Did experience help Westhead?

Denver certainly would be better off gambling on Issel and what might be than hiring one of those failed coaches who turn expert on the television circuit. Better Issel than any of those retreads.

I went back to an interview with Bickerstaff about Christmastime in 1990. He was still settling in, searching, analyzing.

"You have to have a plan and you adhere to it. Don't let surrounding pressures influence you. Then you can say you did it your way." It's the Sinatra approach. "It's like the tortoise," he continued, switching metaphors. "If you never stick your neck out you never advance."

Maybe Denver should be searching for a turtle that sings like Sinatra and make it the new team mascot. But the point is, Bickerstaff is not afraid to take a chance, to gamble. Issel, for all his local popularity and for all his playing experience, would be a gamble.

The fact Bickerstaff seems to have already worked to provide support in the person of Charlotte vice president Gene Littles hints strongly that Issel is his man. The fact that Issel, the czar of tourism for the commonwealth of Kentucky, watched the Derby from Arapahoe Park would hint he is more than passably interested in the Denver job.

He is available. He has been successful at virtually everything he has tried, and he comes equipped with instant acceptability on the part of the local fans and media. He is intelligent, knows the game and its personnel and won't have to spend a second learning about Denver.

Why Issel?

Why not?

✤   ✤   ✤

CHAPTER SEVEN

COLLEGE SPORTS

❀   ❀   ❀

I tell you what Dick Connor meant to me. He tolerated the sports cliches and stereotypes that other people snickered at. He allowed us to fulfill a posture a football coach takes. Every time a football coach talks to the media, you need to understand he's also talking to his team. There's no way of getting around that, because kids read what you say.

The thing I appreciated in Dick Connor besides his obvious talent was he tolerated us. When you're in this business for a while and you see [writers] who are smug and intolerant, you appreciate the ones who have keener insight. He was the old vet, but he didn't act old. He was part of what was happening now. That's worth something to me.

—**Bill McCartney, head football coach,**
University of Colorado Buffaloes

❀   ❀   ❀

Dick never felt that covering college sports was a lesser assignment—lesser than covering professional sports.

He couldn't always spend as much time as he would have liked writing about college teams in Colorado and Wyoming, but when he did, he reveled in it. He liked the whole ambiance and would arrive at Fort Collins or Boulder, or Laramie or the Air Force Academy, hours before kickoff or tipoff. He wanted to soak up the flavor of the day, watch the college kids on the field and in the press box and feel their excitement before a big game. He even liked press day—the day at the start of each season when the press was invited on campus to meet the players and coaches.

The first column in this chapter was one of the trio that took first place for best general column in the Colorado Press Association contest in 1986. It's a college story, but not a Colorado story.

November 27, 1985, *Rocky Mountain News*

FAUST HAD EVERYTHING NOTRE DAME WANTED— EXCEPT A WINNING RECORD

"The legend of an epic hour
A child I dreamed—and dream it still"
—G. K. Chesterton

There will be no epic hours for Gerry Faust. The dream died, frozen far short of whatever goal it had assumed in the mind of this gentle, immensely likeable man who wore his college coaching career as he did his clothes—wrinkled and ill-fitting.

He quit Tuesday as football coach at Notre Dame.

He is rooted, now, in the legend of the place. But the words future generations will read about him are not the ones he sought. Not for Faust the historic halo of a Rockne, the majestic aura of a Leahy, the still active reputation of a Parseghian.

They will remember Faust as a loser.

It's an unfair and distorted epithet for a man whose life and record point in such differing directions. He was, in every way but one, a person to emulate, to follow, to look up to.

Faust's strength was living. His weakness in this case was making a living. Because of where he practiced that living, and what the place demands of its principals, his dream could not survive his talents. One consumed the other, and the Gerry Faust Era will not be remembered kindly there on the Indiana farmlands where the Grotto and Touchdown Jesus and Cartier Field and the Golden Dome are as much of American football lore as, well, as pigskin itself.

It is not a football factory that demands perfection. But it is a place of success and image and even a touch of legend, and Faust didn't live up to it and would not let that tarnish the place. So he woke up Tuesday morning and resigned, one game from the finish of his five-year contract.

He is a nice, raspy-voiced, Christian man who didn't do the job. He is everything the university wanted in a coach but one. It was the most important one. He failed where he had to succeed most, on that 54-year-old football field Rockne's success built.

Whether Faust was pushed or jumped voluntarily really doesn't matter. The end result was destined from the moment he was hired out of Cincinnati, where his legendary record at Moeller High had earned him national acclaim.

It is a sad day, but not a surprising one. Faust, in five years, lost more games than any Notre Dame coach in history.

The students were already chanting his professional obituary a year ago when Air Force went into South Bend and beat the Irish for the third straight time. "Goodbye, Gerry, Goodbye, Gerry, Goodbye Gerry, We're Glad to See You Go," they sang in the cruel manner of youth and others who have nothing on the line. It had assumed the status of a sort of Gregorian chant at some pagan athletic ritual.

Down in the stands in front of the press box, a relative moved into the little group around Faust's wife and put a comforting arm around his daughter, who had managed to sit stiff-lipped through much of the gray, dismal afternoon until that moment.

When the chant began, the dam broke and she sobbed.

Afterward, moving up the tunnel to the dressing rooms, Faust spotted a son standing dejected to one side and detoured to give him a reassuring hug. "It's all right," Faust said, smiling. "It's all right." Faust, unlike those vocal executioners outside, was never one to misplace his priorities.

It was the dreams that went wrong.

"I think one good year, with a major bowl at the end of it. I think from then on it would roll. Eight-and-three and the Sugar Bowl or Fiesta or something like that."

He had offered that cure for himself and his program during an interview on the Thursday before that Air Force game a year ago. He was wearing his coaching sweats, little strands of grass falling on the blue carpet as he sank into a chair only to bounce up when some new thought struck. He was never still.

"There have been times when I've been down in the dumps. But never to the point of quitting," he said. Then he added, "The thing that bothers me most, and this is the tough thing to cope with, is how other people feel."

Two days later, the chanters told him.

Asked how he would like to be remembered, he had said, with a laugh, "As the one who lasted longest." He had launched his Notre Dame career with a 27-9 win over LSU and a giddy Irish staffer had bubbled afterward: "We may never lose another game." He lost his final home game, last Saturday, to LSU, a strange alpha and omega requiem to a career.

For Gerry Faust, there was never a question—the glass was always half-full, and it contained nothing but the elixir of the gods. He did not sip. He gulped.

He was honest and candid and thoughtful and friendly.

It would have been perfect had he just, somehow, managed to combine that with winning.

February 17, 1989, *Denver Post*

STRANGE CELEBRATION FOLLOWS HISTORIC VICTORY

It was the strangest victory celebration on record.

In the first place, the best team had to play the preliminary game. In the second, when they had captured the school's first conference basketball title in 20 years, they weren't allowed to cut down the nets. And please get off the floor quickly so the men can lose.

Finally, when the final horn sounded and the hugging and laughing and high-fiving at midcourt had ceased, they all filed dutifully into an anteroom outside their dressing quarters—and each of them sat in a chair facing a blackboard like students awaiting the arrival of the professor.

Oh, she showed up, a little rumpled from all the hugging, bemused as they were that they had actually done it, a little confused, as they were, as to what comes next.

The University of Colorado, after all, is not used to celebrating such historic events. It hasn't worked out the intricacies of mugging for a camera or dousing each other with diet soda or screaming "Hi Mom" greetings from the bench.

The CU Lady Buffs are champions. They just were having this problem Wednesday evening trying to figure out what you're supposed to do. They loved the championship T-shirts the school had all at the ready, and they had already changed the standings on a board next to the door. Now, it showed CU's Big Eight record as 11-0.

It's a mark Tom Miller and his Laddy Buffs can only fantasize over. What they dream of, Ceal Barry and the Lady Buffs now have. "We've contended for the last three years. Now we've won. Now, we have a program," this diminutive Caesar was saying at the end.

Now, they have. It took her just two losing years to begin to forge it. It has taken four more to put them on top. And now, they are just three games from that Nirvana of any team, an undefeated conference campaign.

So she can be pardoned if she diplomatically dodges answering when asked how it feels to have to play at 5 p.m., when a cheerleader is spotted hurrying down the hill from a late class to just make it for tipoff, or a band member gets there just before the National Anthem.

CU finances, she says, make it necessary to play doubleheaders, rent the CU Events Center at the lowest possible cost. And the Lady Buffs, instead of going center stage as befits the No. 15 team in the land and the No. 1 team in the Big Eight, play when the rest of the world is hurrying home for dinner.

Nowhere else in the conference do the women's teams play as many prelims. But that will change. That definitely should change. Since beating second-ranked LSU back in January, the Lady Buffs are drawing as many fans as the Laddy Buffs. And they are winning more than once a month. Their title-clinching 87-71 win over Kansas State Wednesday was their 14th in a row since a 72-67 loss to Ohio State Dec. 28.

They are the best team—either gender—on the Front Range, and by far the least known. "Yeah," Barry acknowledges. "We've got three conference games left, Oklahoma, Nebraska and Kansas, the bottom three teams. We need to beat them to keep our ranking." If they can finish in the top 16, they would get a first-round bye and a second-round home date in the NCAA tournament.

"We don't dare lose. We're not a name team. People don't vote for us. We don't get a lot of exposure in the East." Truth is, they don't get what they should here, either.

There is a number fixed in black ink in the upper left corner of the board: "CU 31-3" it reads. That would mean a national championship. "My assistant put it up there before the season," she explains. "Only 10 more to go. It looked pretty bleak when we were 7 and 3." That came with the Ohio State loss, their third in four games. They have not lost since.

One of eight children, Barry likes to describe herself as a people person. Tactician, disciplinarian, easy rider? "A combination, I think. I think I read people pretty well."

A guard at Kentucky as an undergraduate, she has spent 10 of her 34 years as a head coach, the past six at Boulder, where she replaced the popular Sox Walseth—and paid a price.

"People didn't like me when I first came here. I was an unknown, from the Midwest. We lost [she was 16-40 her first two years]. I was tough on the kids. Players quit. They didn't know me. I'm shy sometimes, I don't go out to people. They misread that."

No more. Ceal Barry and the Buffs are now, officially, irrevocably, champions. They just haven't quite got the hang of it.

❦   ❦   ❦

Sal Aunese, starting quarterback for the Colorado University Buffaloes, died in September 1989 of stomach cancer. His battle with the disease and his death profoundly affected the team. They dedicated the season to their teammate. They ended the 1989 football season with an 11-0 record and were tied with Notre Dame as the No. 1–ranked team in the nation. However, they lost to the Irish on New Year's Day in the Orange Bowl.

<hr>

September 23, 1989, *Denver Post*

SAL AUNESE SUCCUMBS TO CANCER

Ah, Sal, I'm sorry. For us.

It was such a valiant struggle, and one that was so blatantly unwinnable from the start. And you still fought it. We're the losers—and the winners. We lose because we can't watch you demonstrate the human spirit at its best any longer, and we win because of what you leave us as a model.

But it doesn't make it nicer, easier, more understandable.

I have never had an easy time of it, accepting the death of a young person. I may grieve for a parent, a friend, a peer. There is nostalgia involved, a sense of loss, of a sudden vacuum. But there is also a certain completeness to it, when the pain subsides. A sense of a life completed, work done, finished, a legacy left.

The worst of war is the loss of so much that is young, unused, wasted promise, of potential destroyed rather than fulfilled. How many Shakespeares, Rembrandts, Beethovens were obliterated on the Somme, at Gettysburg, along the Rhine or in some unpronounceable Vietnamese hamlet? Was the cure for cancer, the one that took you, left unborn in the mind of some kid wasted on a frozen hill in Korea?

How much of Sal Aunese was unused? Most. That's the saddest part, the hardest part.

You inspired your University of Colorado teammates, and your coaches, and friends, and a vast public that watched and hoped even as it knew there wasn't any. President Bush wired you. Former President Reagan called. You touched a nation as you never could as a quarterback. But the part that's most difficult is to wonder what would have happened otherwise? What would you have become, contributed, added to society?

I remember, age 5, standing in the funeral home car, between my parents, looking out the back window as the road curved and cut off the view of the canopy over my sister's grave. She was 4. I didn't understand it then. I'm not sure I do now. I just know, every once in a while, I wonder what it would have been like, had she lived.

The least fulfilling part of this job is that, too often, we see athletes on Saturday, or Sunday, names and numbers on their backs, age, weight and height in the program. That's it. We measure them in yards, or tackles, or passes thrown or caught. And we miss them totally as people.

I'm sorry I missed you. A few hurried conversations in a dressing room after a game are a lousy way to know someone. I remember being in the end zone at Iowa City last September for what was probably your best moment as the CU quarterback. You drove the Buffs 85 yards on a saunalike Iowa afternoon and you beat the 20th-ranked Hawkeyes.

This would have been your third season as the CU starter. Nobody else has managed that since Bernie McCall from 1964–66. Somehow, it would have been fitting. You had to sit out your freshman year, a Proposition 48 victim. Then, just when you won the job, you were benched again for an off-field incident.

A guy in your dorm screamed invectives at you from the safety of a third-floor window. Only he fled when you raced up after him. If your self-control snapped, that was your fault. Mine would have, too. I'm just sorry you missed the guy.

But you came back last year, and beat Iowa, and nearly beat Oklahoma and Nebraska, and took your team to the Freedom Bowl. You always came back.

You were even determined at one point after you were diagnosed this spring to be back in time for the start of fall practice. Instead you sat upstairs, in the Flatirons Club, and it was obvious the effect your presence had on your team. Anytime a player did anything, his first, instinctive reaction was to point upstairs, to you. This is yours, Sal, they said.

You were determined to make it to Nov. 4, to the Nebraska game, to watch your Buffs win the Big Eight outright, your goal since you arrived.

"Sal" was the word they have worn sewn on their jersey sleeves this year. I think it's imprinted indelibly on their souls now. Sorry, Sal. For us.

RITES FOR AUNESE EMBODY SAMOAN TRADITION

BOULDER—His brothers and cousins wore white shirts and black ties and black, knee-length skirts. Bare feet completed the costume as Sal Aunese's relatives bade farewell to their Samoan warrior yesterday.

An enormous red lei was draped over the coffin, and a tanga, a grasslike blanket, was placed over its foot. If the old ceremony was different 200 years ago in the South Pacific, this is what has come down, endured into its American version on a crystalline early fall day next to mountains his ancestors would never have imagined.

Those far-off islands were his ancestral home, and Oceanside, Calif., is where he was born, but Boulder had become Aunese's chosen spot in the last few years. There was something fitting about yesterday, his teammates red-eyed in seats below the stage, his coach subdued, his chosen friends bonded as they may never be again.

His relatives sang the traditional peace song, and three of them then sang a personal song, a special one, also traditional when a male dies. The family stood on the stage, and Aunese's 5-month-old son, Timothy, kept reaching for one of the flowers on the shiny dark wood casket.

The University of Colorado athletic program suffered through one of its worst moments and celebrated one of its finest simultaneously yesterday.

CU officially said goodbye to Aunese, its 21-year-old starting quarterback who died Saturday night after a six-month battle with stomach cancer.

Hundreds packed Macky Auditorium on the CU campus. They came in business suits or in shorts, wearing backpacks, hurrying in from class. They heard the governor and the university president and chancellor and its athletic director and two of Aunese's teammates talk of his legacy here. And they heard CU coach Bill McCartney salute them all for the love they gave, and received.

With Aunese's closed casket at one side of the stage, and his family around it as they had surrounded him through his ordeal, the hall echoed with the sounds of weeping, and snuffling, and blowing noses and throats being constantly cleared.

After, there was much hugging, including McCartney spotting Ed Reinhardt in the lobby and hurrying over to hug him, as well. Reinhardt was a CU tight end who suffered paralysis in a game five years ago. The story of his fight back, and his family's support, is, like Aunese's, the stuff of movies. Or, as teammate Michael Jones put it, legend.

Aunese may be impossible to dismiss. His impact as a person, a leader, a battler may go far past any he might have had merely as a football player. "Pass on Sal's legend," CU co-captain Jones told Aunese's fellow Samoan teammates Okland Salavea and Tamasi Amituanai. Aunese helped recruit Salavea, and they both helped persuade Amituanai. "Down through the ages," said Jones, "Let it live. He'll live longer than anyone in this room."

He was a 21-year-old with a huge heart and a permanent smile and a diseased body that finally surrendered. "I've said it before, Sal didn't lose his battle with cancer," CU senior receiver Jeff Campbell said. "Sal won his battle with cancer."

Certainly, his battle has left indelible marks on his team and his coaches. Five years ago, Reinhardt's struggle brought out the best in those around him, and Aunese's long fight through the spring and summer has had a similar, galvanizing effect.

"I don't know how to handle it," McCartney admitted later. This, like the Reinhardt accident, is new to him and to his team. The sun-dappled shade outside the auditorium and the students hurrying away to afternoon classes seemed to ease the intense emotions inside. There was a sense of routine returning.

"He did the one thing every football player wants to do," McCartney had said inside, relieving the atmosphere at one point. "He was a starter on this football team and never went through spring drills."

That in itself should put the young Samoan warrior in the land of legends.

November 23, 1989, Denver Post

CU COACH DEFIES EXPLANATION

I have come to a Thanksgiving Day conclusion regarding Colorado's Bill McCartney:

It is far easier to simply accept the man than it is to explain him.

He is what he appears to be—a deeply religious football coach and very committed and good at both. It doesn't have to get too much more complicated, but for some reason, it does.

We sat last Tuesday in a small deli across the street from KCNC-TV where he had taped his show. He ordered hot water. Period. He had brought his own tea bag. "Herbal," he explained. "And please make the water real hot. Hot, hot, hot."

The waitress gushed. She put a Styrofoam cup of water in the microwave. Hot, hot, hot. She volunteered to babysit for McCartney's grandson.

"It's been eventful," he begins, smiling at his own understatement. Seven years ago, he was hired off the Michigan staff. Five years ago, he was glumly staring at a 1-10 record at Thanksgiving. Two years ago, he was that close to taking the head coaching job at SMU.

This morning? He's on the verge of playing for a national championship, has conquered Nebraska and Oklahoma and Washington and Texas and Illinois and as much other nonfootball adversity as one man should ever have to encounter.

And he's smiling, relaxed, at peace. "I don't know why controversy seems to follow me, but it does," he admits. The reason is easy. He is a man of strong, unshakable convictions. Not all are popular. It doesn't bother him. "There are certain things you have to take a stand on. If you don't, your life won't have counted."

The CU administration shuddered collectively when he agreed to be the featured speaker for an antiabortion group that has had chronic confrontations with the law. An assembly hall of mourners gasped when he publicly conceded what had been privately understood, that his daughter had given birth to a son fathered by McCartney's late quarterback, Sal Aunese.

His testament to his daughter was touching and heartfelt and deeply moving, but he acknowledges, "My daughter, because of the position I'm in, she is subjected to national scrutiny."

The McCartneys and their daughter are raising the infant in their home. Conviction.

He has known he would coach since he was "that high," he says as the waitress arrives with the cup of water. "Here you are, love, hot, just the way you asked."

McCartney nods his thanks. As always, he was up at 5 a.m., read the Bible, made entries in his daily logs of life and spiritual insight, went to the office by 7. In season, he won't get home until 10:20. "Just when the sports come on. It times up just right. Then I zonk out."

It's Bill McCartney. Accept him. He is one of the nation's best coaches, and there is nothing remotely artificial or contrived about him. He believes that his fate is in God's hands, that he is doing what he is supposed to be doing, and that his 1989 team "has a special anointing of the Lord over us."

He could be right. There is no other team in the land with quite the mix of muscle and aura of destiny. Since Aunese's death, the word "obsessed" has fit its whole dedication to winning.

When it is suggested to McCartney that logic dictates Notre Dame should win the Orange Bowl New Year's night because it has greater experience in such things, McCartney smiles. "Go with your heart on this one," he replies.

He arrived as a coach, he says, just a year ago. Former CU coach and athletic director Eddie Crowder urged him to take off the headset on Saturday, let his assistants take larger roles while he stepped back and took an overview.

"It was hard, because I had to swallow my pride. You want to do it all. I had to take a more subordinate role. So I took the headsets off for the Oklahoma game and haven't put them back on since. It was a turning point for us."

Conviction. It's Bill McCartney, coach and Christian. Don't even try to separate the two.

January 2, 1990, *Denver Post*

A FAIRY TALE, MINUS THE HAPPY ENDING

MIAMI—Sometimes, no matter how vivid, how real, mere dreams aren't enough. And "once upon a time" doesn't always end with a happy conclusion.

So forget that raised index finger. File it for future reference. It won't be required exercise for the next few months.

Pack it carefully, however. The suspicion lingers that this won't be Colorado's lone visit to these American tropics in the next few seasons, or its last stare-down with a chance to use that finger and scream, "We're No. 1."

But that won't help the CU seniors, such as John Perak and Jeff Campbell.

"Easy for you to say," Perak chokingly told a teammate who had tried to comfort him amid the emotional debris of the CU locker room last night.

"You get to put that uniform on again."

Perak's teammate studied the wet concrete underfoot. There was no response.

They had carried the dream for months, almost made it real. It's the almost that hurt most.

There was no repairing the psychic damage of a storybook year that came up to the very brink—and stopped in midsentence. Colorado manufactured every chance it needed to put the game beyond reach in the first half—and failed.

Then the Irish took charge. This was the year CU could match Notre Dame ghost for ghost. It just couldn't find scoring combinations to make the dreams reality.

Notre Dame 21, Colorado 6, national championship, zero.

They had spotted the Irish their famous fight song, matched it with Ralphie's opening gallop, knelt and pointed skyward in Sal Aunese's memory and then gone out and done everything short of winning it all in the first 30 minutes.

Eric Bieniemy fumbled in the open field at the 19. Ken Culbertson missed a field goal after CU drove to the 5. And the offense failed to score after Bieniemy's squirming run put them in business with first-and-goal at the 1.

The gods of football don't look kindly on such profligate waste.

Miami's Hurricanes will win the title the Buffs squandered. Miami did to Notre Dame what the Buffs threatened to do all through the pregnant first half.

It finished the job. CU never could.

"Once upon a time," fairy tales begin. "Once upon a time." And they always end happily.

Colorado had the beginning, it set the plot, the characters were in place, the suspense was there, the drama intact. It just lacked the ending it planned to a season that finished 11-1, and a yard from 12-0.

It carried the dream to the Notre Dame goal in the first half. Who knows? Did Bieniemy dent the stripe on first and goal? NBC's cameras said yes.

The Atlantic Coast Conference officials said no.

It's as close as CU ever has come to a national championship. Had the Buffs scored, the way they were dominating, they could have pried the game open.

"We let it slip away," Campbell said. On fourth down, after Bieniemy's first-down frustration, Campbell was supposed to pass out of a fake field-goal formation.

But none of the three possible receivers ever got into the end zone. Campbell's desperation try to run it in on his own was smothered by the Irish's Troy Ridgley.

"I told him, 'Forget it, man. We'll get another chance. We're kicking their butts,'" quarterback Darian Hagan said when he grabbed his tailback after Bieniemy's early fumble at the 19.

All year, 11 times, they have made good on second chances.

Notre Dame played an almost errorless game, the kind Colorado had envisioned. And at the finish, the Irish played keep-away, driving to their last score the way champions should.

"When you get two tough teams, something's gotta happen," said senior line-backer Michael Jones, a captain. "Something did."

"I'm not depressed," said fullback Erich Kissick. "It's been a fabulous experience here. We just lost the damn game. But I made some great friends. We won the Big Eight. We played in the Orange Bowl, and played for the national championship.

"Now I'm going to be a salesman."

"It hurts worse than it looks," Campbell said through tears, voice catching. "I should look at the positive things, I suppose, but it's hard to find them right now."

He will. They'll surface. He'll remember. Once upon a time.

October 8, 1990, *Denver Post*

FIFTH-DOWN CONTROVERSY WON'T CHANGE WHO WON

No, I would not necessarily have wanted to be in the Big Eight offices yesterday afternoon. Or in the Missouri coaching offices. Or even in the Colorado coaching offices.

Oh, it would have been interesting to watch the squirming, the rationalizing, the desperate searches for a way to make a wrong a right. But I would have missed the good stuff, the real anguish.

Where I would really have liked to be yesterday afternoon was any place in the state of Nebraska.

I would just like to sit and listen. Just listen.

And they'd be right.

The rules say four downs. Colorado used five to beat Missouri at the gun Saturday. The crazy part, the unbelievable part, the still unexplainable part, is that nobody on either coaching staff was seen to be trying to warn anybody. They didn't know. The official working the down marker didn't know. The scoreboard operator didn't know.

CU's team didn't, or didn't act as if it did, and neither did Missouri's.

Can't anybody count around here anymore? The NCAA brags about its "scholar-athletes," but here were roughly 150 S-As on a hot Missouri afternoon and not one could count to five.

Plus you have two coaching staffs whose whole role in life is to go to endless meetings from dawn until just before midnight, plotting the minutest "what if?" scenarios. What if it's third and three and they line up like this, what do we do? They chart every play, down, distance, defense, result.

And yet nobody knew CU had already used up its quota and was still a yard shy of the Missouri goal line.

Nothing is going to change. Understand that. The Big Eight isn't going to change the result despite Missouri athletic director Dick Tamburo's demand yesterday that the game result be reversed. It won't happen. The Big Eight said a "complete review" will be made. That should be easy: "One ... two ... three ... four ... five." But a league spokesman also said he doubted the commissioner had the power to change the outcome. There is no known mechanism that would permit it.

CU "won." It went to the finish to tie Tennessee, and lost at the finish at Illinois and needed Eric Bieniemy's did-he-or-didn't-he? dive on fourth down to defeat Stanford.

Whatever you may think of the Buffs, they are not boring. And one of the worst parts of what happened at the finish Saturday is that it totally obscures a majestic drive generaled by a young quarterback making his first big college start, and by a team that is finally playing up to itself. CU is a legitimate Top 10 team even if its math skills are a tad limited.

Dave Nelson, secretary and editor of the NCAA rules book, says that the rule "says the team that has the biggest score at the end of the game is the winning team. Once the referee says the game is over, that's it."

Could it be simpler? Colorado, on an illegal fifth down, beat Missouri 32-30 and is 4-1-1 for the year and 1-0 in the Big Eight. It will stand.

It's not a regular thing, but in the swirling chaos of a football sideline in the closing moments, anything is possible, even losing track of a down. In the NFL opening weekend, both Dan Reeves and the Raiders' Art Shell called plays based on the wrong down.

In 1968, the Chicago Bears beat the Los Angeles Rams 17-16 with the aid of a fifth-down play in the third quarter. Norm Schacter, the referee, and his entire crew were suspended for one week. But the game stood.

Bill McCartney yesterday acknowledged that, yes, there were five downs. The overnight damage control line was that CU deserved the win anyway because the field was unplayable.

Sorry. It was and that's one thing the league can do something about. But that was a totally unrelated item. CU isn't going to do the decent thing, anymore than Nebraska or Oklahoma—or Missouri—would. And the Big Eight isn't, either. Missouri has justice on its side. CU has money, a potential Jan. 1 bowl date somewhere that feeds the whole conference.

This is a game, and a result, that will live in infamy, to paraphrase an old presidential classic. But, tainted or not, CU swallowed it and let the grease run down past the smiles.

November 7, 1990, *Denver Post*

BUFFS HAVE ADDED INGREDIENT—TOUGHNESS

"Football is great. You get to kick, bite, sweat, spit, fight, win and afterward hug a blonde."—Kyle Rappold, Colorado nose tackle, 1987.

I hated it when Rappold graduated. It was like losing a treasured old notebook or list of private telephone numbers. Rappold was a quote for all occasions.

His name flitted through the swinging memory doors not long ago, right after Colorado beat Missouri. I kept wondering, what would Rappold have said of all the fuss over the fifth down? And what would he have given to be able to play on a team that beat both Nebraska and Oklahoma, back to back, in consecutive years?

Going through a rather detached autumn that gives me a chance to sit back and take the long view, I have come to a conclusion:

This year's Buffs would have beaten last year's Notre Damers and won the national title. This year's CU team is not as good—McCartney prefers the word "smooth," "not as smooth"—as his 11-1 team of a year ago. But it has an ingredient that team lacked.

It is tougher.

It has been forged in so many fires that it has that quality McCartney still feels was the difference in the Orange Bowl, and the reason his Buffs didn't win.

From the moment George Hemingway had a long touchdown run negated against Tennessee, this is a team that has faced one obstacle after another. It led at Illinois, and lost. It lost its quarterback for a game, its star runner for the Tennessee game, and it had to absorb unbelievable trash over the fifth down at Missouri.

(One side comment on that: CU didn't create that down, the officials did. CU created the situation that made it special because the Buffs, under backup quarterback Charles Johnson, had just driven 88 yards in the final minutes. And the whole point is, when they got the chance, they made the most of it.)

... A year ago, they were one of the great stories in college football. But they surprised people, maybe including themselves, by winning. They were rarely tested. This year, they were marked from the start, a target, last year's deposed No. 1. There would be no surprises in one of the nation's toughest schedules.

And when they stumbled out to a 1-1-1 start, we all nodded. "One-year wonders," we murmured.

Wrong. At halftime of the Orange Bowl, McCartney says two things happened. His team, he feels, "had squandered some opportunities and we really had a kind of semi-letdown. Notre Dame, I think, went in and said, 'Enough is enough.' They were toughened and seasoned and used to that. And they just responded. And we, there was something missing."

The fourth quarter at Lincoln proved how far this year's Buffs have advanced on the toughness scale. It began, McCartney thinks, in the fourth quarter at Austin, Tex. "Our offensive line ran out on the field and pounded on the defense during the change. We as coaches talked about that a couple days later, trying to isolate what happened. There was a determination there that was special."

It was a signal, McCartney says. "The fourth quarter at Nebraska demonstrated that the mental toughness we needed a year ago and didn't have has developed out of all the things that have happened to us this year. That's the difference."

Give McCartney credit. He has not let them quit on themselves, despite enough crossroads that the season looks like a tic-tac-toe board. He's in the midst of his best job as a coach.

And if they get to halftime in the Orange Bowl this year with the national title in reach, I like this team's chances better than a year ago. Toughness is the difference.

<hr>

January 2, 1991, *Denver Post*

THE COACH CAN VOTE WITH HEART IN TODAY'S POLL

MIAMI—A year ago, Bill McCartney voted for Miami as the nation's No. 1 college football team.

This time, he'll get to vote with his heart—if he can locate it lodged up there in his throat where Notre Dame's Raghib Ismail left it with seconds left.

His Colorado Buffaloes are the national champions even if all the losers may demand a recount.

"You look at what Colorado has done the entire year, the teams we have beaten, we deserve to be No. 1," he said a little after midnight in the Orange Bowl last night.

He's right. His team entered the game ranked No. 1. They still are, and should be. No apologies are needed. ...

Colorado 10, Notre Dame 9, finesse and artistry and perfection zero.

It was not a game the NCAA will enshrine on the ceiling of its version of the Sistine Chapel.

It doesn't matter. It doesn't have to be. Not every championship has to be clinched with soaring passes and dazzling runs. Grime and grunting and will-power still count.

This was a game earned by mud and grass stains and bloody noses and sheer determination. "The whole second half was a gut check," said wide receiver Mike Pritchard, who played with a broken hand.

Colorado intercepted the Irish's Rick Mirer three times and pounced on two Notre Dame fumbles and still managed just one touchdown from that whole shambles.

It spent the whole, endless evening getting scrape marks from pressing its back to a wall.

It lost its starting quarterback, Darian Hagan, on the Buffs' final play of the first half. It lost half its devastating linebacker tandem, Kanavis McGhee, for the entire second half. It never entirely solved the ravages of Notre Dame nose guard Chris Zorich, who was the defensive MVP with 10 tackles and a sack.

It doesn't matter. Nothing does this morning except that raised index finger and statewide laryngitis. Charles S. Johnson, the engineer of CU's infamous Fifth-Down win over Missouri, came on in relief of Hagan and was voted the game's MVP. Paul Rose replaced McGhee and produced key tackles and a sack. Colorado made one of sports' old cliches a reality—it found a way.

Johnson was one. Rose was one. Deon Figures, suspended a year ago, snuffed Notre Dame's final drive with an interception. George Hemingway, sent home in disgrace before last year's game, produced 78 yards running that included a 20-yarder.

The manner of the win, coupled with impressive triumphs by No. 2 Georgia Tech and No. 4 Miami, may lead to the closest final ballot in years.

But the Buffs will be the 1990 champions, and should be. The night was decided on toughness, the element McCartney admitted was absent a year ago when, under identical circumstances, Notre Dame dominated the second half and won 21-6.

"We played totally different this year," Pritchard said. "They got a first down on our 5-yard line to start the second half and didn't score," he said of CU's key defensive stop, forcing a field goal and a 9-3 deficit instead of a 13-3 Notre Dame lead.

It's the gospel McCartney has preached steadily for a month—that the 1990 season forged a tougher mentality in a team that, next to Notre Dame, played the nation's toughest schedule.

"Georgia Tech, I'm sorry," Pritchard said, grinning. "We got the national championship. You're No. 2. Maybe next year."

Outside, as the CU band was playing itself lipless, Buffs followers refused to leave.

"Last year, we let one slip away," safety Tim James said. "It sat there on us all summer."

And last night, when Ismail raced 91 yards with CU's final punt, it was James who sat calmly back upfield, enjoying the bedlam. "I was tired. And I knew it was coming back. I was the guy who got clipped. I was sitting next to the yellow flag."

It came with 35 seconds left, leaving the Notre Dame side in delirium and CU's faithful in shock until they, too, saw the flag and exhaled.

"It wasn't a pretty victory. It was an ugly victory, but as Al Davis says, 'We just won,'" Eric Bieniemy said.

It was all they had to do in the ugliest, most beautiful game CU has ever played.

March 24, 1991, *Denver Post*

"TINY" GRANT QUITS AS CSU BASKETBALL COACH

FORT COLLINS—The question was simple enough. The answer was an indictment of college basketball.

Question—Playing by the rules, could a school such as Colorado State University ever hope to win a national championship?

Answer—(After Boyd "Tiny" Grant thought a moment): No.

How many CSUs are there in the NCAA's Division I? Most, sad to say. Maybe only a couple dozen schools can ever even hope—not plan, hope—to win an NCAA championship. Fewer still can actually plan on it. The rest are fodder, good only to fill out the 64-team bracket and to provide television time leading up to the inevitable.

The North Carolinas, Dukes, Indianas, a Big East representative, a handful of others will be annual visitors to the Sweet 16 and the Final Four. All the others are pretenders, self-deceivers. They can't play straight and ever expect to be there.

The Tar Heels, Blue Devils and a few of the elites have built-in advantages too great to overcome. They don't have to cheat. As somebody once said of Notre Dame recruiting, they don't recruit, they select.

But, back to Grant. He sat in a sun-washed corner office on the second floor of Moby Gym this past Friday, a couple of days after announcing he was getting out of college coaching. There isn't enough time left over to live, he said simply. It really is that simple. Don't look for hidden motives, subtle shadings.

Grant doesn't deal in those. He worked on the railroad under his dad's tutelage for 90 cents an hour to pay incidental expenses while getting a degree from CSU. Grant is bluntly honest, with a shrewd mind masked by his down-home style.

He had just come from watching his son play high school baseball. That's why he's quitting at age 57. There was too little time for that when he had to recruit. "I missed too many Thanksgivings, too many Christmases, too many birthdays." And college basketball is going to miss him far more than he is going to miss college basketball. He is what the game desperately needs to keep. He has played by the rules, recruited by the rules, won by the rules. It wasn't enough. That simple "No" is a terrible admission.

If he didn't cheat, he had no chance of ever going to the Final Four, where this year's best teams meet in Indianapolis this coming week. Cheat, or lose. Grant did neither. A lot of other coaches are like Grant. They can win, play straight, but it isn't quite enough.

Either you have such a built-in program it overwhelms all obstacles, or you have to see where you cut corners, compromise.

Grant surveyed a pile of letters on his desk. "The NCAA has to find a way to protect those that don't [cheat]," he mused. Instead, it puts a program on probation, and two years later, using the talent that caused the probation, that program goes to that year's version of Indianapolis. Kentucky, which can't play on TV because of probation, nevertheless has its coach, Rick Pitino, doing commentaries for ESPN and writing a column for *The Sporting News*. And the coach that got them on probation, Eddie Sutton, had his Oklahoma State team in the NCAA Sweet 16.

Go figure.

And the honest coaches such as Grant sit in sunny offices and contemplate the future of their profession. Grant can take the long view now, the elder statesman's perspective. "I don't know how I've ever viewed myself as a coach. I guess down deep I've always felt like I gotta work harder, I gotta do more, I gotta give more, get more out of this." Like his father always cautioned, be sure you give a dollar's worth of work for a dollar's worth of pay. Grant has.

He has done it his way, and been successful at it. But he has never taken a team to the NCAA's ultimate weekend. "That doesn't mean I never dreamt of it." They all do. Then sunlight streams through the window, the dream ends and it's another day.

And there is something wistfully sad about a coach who does things honestly, correctly, superbly even, all the time knowing that it won't be enough.

He's right. The NCAA, in addition to punishing its cheaters, must find a way to reward the honest coach, the honest program. When Grant, who fits every criterion one could want in a coach, says an NCAA title is beyond him, something is terribly wrong.

<hr>

May 10, 1991, *Denver Post*

DIAL 1-900 FOR LOST COLLEGE DIGNITY

I forget where I was headed one recent Saturday, but I had tuned in the Mutual Broadcasting System and the day's Notre Dame game. For someone who grew up in Iowa, and used to seclude himself in the attic on hazy autumn afternoons to listen to Irish broadcasts, it was a continuing act of faith.

You listened to Notre Dame on Saturday. You went to Mass on Sunday morning. All was right with the world. You sprawled on the attic floor, watching dust motes in the sunlight coming through the window, and waited for another Notre Dame triumph. The next day, you gave thanks.

"And don't forget the new 1-900 number," the announcer was saying. "Hear Lou Holtz and his assessment of the upcoming opponent, the latest injury data ..."

What? A 1-900 number?

Somewhere later that same day, I was watching the Notre Dame telecast, when what to my wondering eyes did appear but a Notre Dame commercial, this one pitching goods from the Notre Dame gift shop. It looked like one of those endless shill jobs on Ted Turner's network late at night, where they repeat the phone number every 15 seconds and you finally buy a peel-all vegetable dicer just to get the sound out of your mind.

Was Rockne twisting uncomfortably in that all but unmarked grave near the big tree in South Bend? Was Frank Leahy having a raised eyebrow attack wherever it was he was? What would George Gipp think? For that matter, what did Father [Theodore] Hesburgh think, not that there is anybody left on the Notre Dame hierarchy who would listen to this wise and thoughtful man.

A 1-900 number?

Notre Dame has become the college equivalent of Jose Canseco, hawking itself like some common two-bit athlete—of whatever gender or persuasion. I have this theory that the Irish have become something much, much worse, but we'll hold that for a few paragraphs.

When Hesburgh was president, he talked some Southeastern Conference schools out of setting up their own TV network. "One for all, all for one," was his honorable pitch. Then he retired, and Gene Corrigan moved on in 1987.

Suddenly, under the guidance of new AD Dick Rosenthal, Notre Dame became the Ted Turner of college athletics. Sell, sell, sell.

It shocked the football world when, with no warning, it announced its own $35 million pact with NBC. One for all? All for one? As long as the one is Notre Dame, cheer, cheer.

Their impact on the 1992 bowl picture was almost unholy until Tennessee upset them last week. But the reverberations are still being felt as those sanctimonious, hypocritical bowl officials—and college athletic directors—scramble to assure a place in the sun on New Year's Day. Understand, Notre Dame is not alone in its newfound greed. It's just more prominent, and so far more successful.

You can find a growing body of coaches and athletic directors who are fearful that the NBC contract puts the already powerful Irish so far out of reach in the recruiting war that the whole battle is for distant second place.

And their undue influence on the upcoming bowl season is enough to make even a nonplayoff viewer begin to think maybe a true playoff system to determine a champion is the only sane way left to go. I've opposed it. I've always thought you emerged with 17 or 18 champions, and there was nothing wrong with that. Ending the bowl system would end the delights Colorado State University enjoyed a year ago at the Freedom Bowl.

But even the bowls violated their own decrees this year, shuttling about from school to school like conventioneers on East Colfax on Saturday night. The shorter the skirt, the more they rolled down the car window.

The Fiesta, Cotton, Sugar and Orange have formed a consortium that—by their claim—can eventually help produce a true national champion. Pardon while we all choke a bit. If it does not include the Big 10 and Pac 10, it ain't valid. They even agreed, did all these bowls, to fine miscreants $250,000 if any of them actually signed bowl teams before this Sunday.

Pardon again while we lapse into unconsciousness while laughing. If there's a bowl that doesn't have its opponents already locked right now, it's only because, in cases such as the Orange, two Big Eight teams still have a chance.

"I see, particularly this year, more positioning and more deals in the back room," says Wyoming athletic director Paul Roach. His Pokes are not in the bowl picture this year. Besides, he tells the truth even when it hurts.

It's a travesty. "This year, you see more scrambling and more group dealing than ever before," says Roach.

Colleges and the bowls have lost all dignity. There is an ancient word that sums them up.

It rhymes with more. Just dial 1-900 for details.

<hr>

May 11, 1991, *Denver Post*

NO AGENTS WAITING FOR THESE SCHOLAR-ATHLETES

The story you are about to read is true. No names have been changed. They might even furnish valid Social Security numbers on demand.

It is the story of two college basketball players who enrolled in school, stayed there all five years, are graduating with high honors from the stiffest academic environment you can imagine and were never arrested.

True, hard as that may be to believe in this age when grade point averages often are confused with case numbers.

They even contend they had fun doing it even if they didn't leave practice and climb into BMWs or Mercedes or Rolls Royces, and neither has even met an agent, let alone signed with one.

Somehow, I think they'll survive despite such obvious holes in their collegiate experience.

Meet Hank Prey of Lakewood and Dan McKeon of Rampart High School in Colorado Springs. Today, when Colorado School of Mines holds its annual commencement, Prey and McKeon graduate with distinction (3.5 GPA or better) in mechanical engineering. The Colorado Council of Engineers certificate of merit is given to just three graduating seniors. McKeon (3.89) and Prey (3.72) are two of the three.

What's more, when the 1990–91 GTE/CoSIDA Academic All-America team was announced recently, two-fifths of that prestigious national quintet were, you guessed it, McKeon and Prey.

For five years, they have ridden Mines vans on 13-hour safaris to the edge of Mexico, across mountain passes, scarfed up more McDonald's than any self-respecting Dookie would ever allow into his hallowed system and just hoped the heater worked in whatever cut-rate motel they managed to book for the night.

I just thought, in an age when we measure athletes too often by the parole record and detox centers visited, you might like to know there is a side of collegiate athletics that actually works.

"When we stayed at Motel 6, that was a big night," Prey says of Mines', um, frugal travel budget. "We got four dollars for breakfast, five for lunch, six for dinner. That was the food allowance. At the start of a trip, we might blow some of it on a big dinner. By the end, we'd be down to two meals."

Yet they persevered and won two conference titles and gave Mines some of its finest basketball moments even as the coach, Jim Darden, was recuperating from major heart problems.

"Coach Darden only counts wins," says Hank. "This year we were 4-0." There were 19 other, uncounted results.

This is not a tome against big-time athletics, understand. I was at the Orange Bowl and watched Colorado's joy at winning a national championship, and at Indianapolis and watched Bobby Hurley leap in Christian Laettner's arms at the finish. I just wonder if they really had more fun.

"We never flew," says Prey. "We had 12 guys—big guys, basketball size, in a van."

"I was the smallest," says the 6-1 McKeon. When they ventured south across the mountain passes and into the desert, the trip could take 13 hours. When they went to a holiday tournament in Missouri one time, it was 18 hours. "I have no regrets at all," McKeon says, while quickly adding he is also realistic enough to know he wasn't going to walk on and win a spot at CU or Duke. "But when you sat in the back of that van hour after hour, sometimes you wondered.

"If we got a motel with two beds and a heater that worked, we were happy. I remember we got one once where there was no heat. I wore my sweats to bed and froze."

And there was the time a year ago, heading across Wolf Creek Pass toward Durango and a game with Fort Lewis, where the van hit some ice just as a semi crested the hill and zoomed down. It totaled the van, but the ice saved them, letting the van slide instead of being crushed. Nobody was hurt.

"Three guys hitchhiked on into Durango. The rest of us waited until Adams State sent another van that took us on. We had just played Adams State."

Waiting, they built a fire beside the highway. You wonder how many roadside fires Hurley and Laettner ever shared on a mountain night. "With us, driving on the interstate was a big deal. Usually, it was a two-lane road," McKeon says.

So today, it's over, officially. "I better call Coors back and tell them I'm taking that job," Prey had said late this week during the interview. "They've made the offer and that's where I'm going, but I haven't told them yet. I'd hate to have them read it first."

McKeon is heading for California, and a job with Mobil.

In their careers, by the Darden Count, they won 53 games. There were 60 other games. There were no bad times.

September 14, 1992, *Denver Post*

VEE BAR RANCH, SATURDAYS A PERFECT COMBO

LARAMIE—There are two major differences between college and pro football. One is obvious, the talent and money level.

The other is that it is infinitely more fun getting there for a college game.

There isn't much nostalgia about wheeling off I-25 into one of Mile High Stadium's parking lots. Nor does it do much for the soul to plow through New Jersey to Giants Stadium on a Sunday afternoon. And if you can find anything uplifting about a Raiders game in Los Angeles Memorial Coliseum, I would suggest immediate therapy.

The pro playing level will be higher, the game faster, the passion just as intense.

But there is no way to compare it to the Plains of West Point on a lightly foggy Saturday morning with the Corps marching up to Michie Stadium for the game. And it doesn't come close to a snowy atmosphere at South Bend before a game with Air Force.

No self-respecting Washington Huskies fan would ever confuse a mundane Sunday trip to the Kingdome for a Seahawks game with a traditional Saturday boat ride to Husky Stadium.

I haven't been to some of the more glamorous athletic spas in the South, so I can't compare, but I have my own list of football venues that I anticipate more for the getting there and the ambiance, than for the game itself.

I'm writing this from one of them.

It is the Vee Bar Ranch, about 20 miles west of Laramie on the road to the Snowy Range. It's a former stagecoach stop that is on the National Register. Duane and Susan Harm have turned it into the perfect place to spend a golden Friday afternoon and totally ignore the Broncos, the Rockies, court trials, spoiled athletes and a sports world I sometimes think has gone mad.

The Little Laramie River flows about two first downs beyond the kitchen door. Today, I'll go watch Air Force and Wyoming. But I'll probably spend some time with mental images from the ranch.

I never have that problem in Cleveland.

Notre Dame and West Point are two other places that leave mental images. I've only been to West Point once. There are ghosts there and no way to escape them, especially if you go in the chapel early Saturday morning and stand quietly looking at the battle flags and shadows overhead. It's like Air Force Academy. Both are special places for special missions.

But West Point also has one of the great tailgate traditions and the tempting aroma of hamburgers on the grill permeates the place. Notre Dame succeeds in turning a weekend football game into something of a solemn high mass.

I was there once during Gerry Faust's reign. It was one of those bleak, blustery Friday nights with snow on the wind. The band marched around like a pied piper. The students fell in behind and they all trooped over to the gym.

My glasses smoked over the moment I stepped inside. No matter. It was something you had to hear and feel, not see. Gerry Faust would have been coach of the year on Friday night. He would have been undefeated if he could have played all his games with Indiana snow outside and Notre Dame kids hanging from the basketball standard.

There was one problem. The next day Air Force beat him again and he was booed off the field.

Colorado schools really don't have any of these traditions. Air Force comes closest with the flyover and the cadet march-on. They also have a pretty good tailgate atmosphere. Colorado wastes its band, using it only to serenade special guests for the president, instead of a much wider mission on game day.

Notre Dame's band, for example, plays a concert on the steps of the Golden Dome and everyone on campus can enjoy it. Not just a few presidential nabobs. CSU's stadium is so far from campus I'm not sure what they can do to turn it into an asset.

Keep Three Rivers Stadium. Enjoy Candlestick. Take the Astrodome and put a convention in it. I'll take West Point. I'll take South Bend. I'll take the Vee Bar Ranch and Wyoming on a perfect autumn afternoon.

✤   ✤   ✤

CHAPTER EIGHT

HIGH SCHOOL SPORTS AND LITTLE LEAGUE

... I think he taught a lot of us how to write, just by reading him every day. The thing I'll always remember about him was the bigger the event, the smaller was his focus. Like I remember when the Broncos beat Oakland in Mile High Stadium for the AFC championship. I think there was some guy in the top row who just sat there for several hours after the game and wouldn't leave the stadium. So Dick wrote about him and it just perfectly captured the moment. I'm sure everybody else in the press box was gagging, while he was over there making it real small.

And the smaller the event, the bigger he would go. Like a high school state championship, he could make it sound like they'd just won the World Series or something. I also remember him always keeping his notebook behind his back, and I'd be thinking, "This guy is not going to get the quotes. What's he doing?" What he was doing was listening, of course; and if somebody said something that knocked him out, he'd write it down. What that taught me was, hey, you're the writer, and we're paying you to tell us what you think and what you think is probably more lyrical and more insightful than what some naked, 280-pound guy has to say in the locker room. Another lesson he taught me was that it's OK to step outside the rules and look around a little bit ... like the night John Elway came to town and the rest of us were all told to stay in the media room, and he went out and got Edgar Kaiser introducing Elway to [Dan] Reeves while the rest of us sat there, too scared to move because we might miss something.

—**Rick Reilly, writer for** *Sports Illustrated,*
National Sportswriter of the Year

❦   ❦   ❦

Dick attended as many of our kids' games as he could—soccer, football, base-ball, swim meets. If he was in town and not on an assignment, he was there.

He didn't like it when parents yelled at their own children or others' during games. It made him very uncomfortable. But I remember he would often pace outside the outfield at the boys' baseball games because he would get so caught up in the action, he was afraid he would embarrass himself or them. He figured it was safer to be out of earshot.

June 1, 1981, *Denver Post*

SADLY, I NEVER CALLED PAT PANEK

In everybody's life, there are some things you should have done. And didn't. Pat Panek is one for me.

"What're you doing?" It was Clyde Cushion. He grew up in Iowa and played and worked there, and then at the *Denver Post* before retiring a few years back. His health has been so-so, and it was good to see him in the department again last February.

When he worked here, we had a running thing: He coached winning Bronco games, and I was responsible for explaining losing ones over coffee the next day. I also was in charge of firing coaches that didn't satisfy him.

I dreaded Mondays. He was merciless.

So it was nice to see him that cold February morning. It had been a while. We talked, and it quickly became clear he was not here for a seminar on the relative merits or demerits of Edgar Kaiser or Dan Reeves or Red Miller.

"I want you to do a story on Pat Panek."

"Why?"

"He's going to be 80 the first of next month and he isn't doing too good. Some-body ought to do something on him right now. I'll set it up."

"Clyde, wait. I don't know him."

"Everybody knows Pat Panek."

That's not quite true, but close. I read the other day that we are being flooded by immigrants from other parts of the country, many of them young professionals who probably never heard of Pat Panek, or the fact he is the second-winningest football coach in America. Or care.

"Doesn't make any difference," Clyde insisted. When could I come out? He'd set it up. They lived near each other out in southeast Denver. Better yet. Here's his phone number. Call.

"All right. I will."

"That's a promise?"

"Yeah. I will."

"OK. Somebody ought to do something on him while it still means something to him."

High School Sports and Little League—173

We talked a bit and I had to leave to meet somebody and we left it at that. I would call. I jabbed the note with Panek's phone and address on the spike on my desk and decided I would call the next morning and set up an interview at Panek's place.

I still haven't. And now, of course, I won't. Panek was buried this morning, barely into his 80th year. And his name and phone number are still on the spike in front of me, blunt evidence, accusing, unforgiving.

Some things you mean to do, should do and never do. There was an unexpected story that broke the next morning, then some follow-ups and then a long series of road trips.

And I'd come back, glance at the spike, resolve to call tomorrow, and ... well, there was always something, it seemed. And then it was June.

"You hear?" It was early afternoon, and a friend from the backshop stopped by the desk in sports. He is a man whose children attended Machebeuf High School out in east Denver. It's where Panek coached for 11 more years after the Denver Public Schools' mandatory retirement age of 65 ended his career at East High.

"Pat Panek died. We just got his obit."

Don't look at the spike.

If you measure a man by how he is remembered, Pat Panek was an incredible individual. I've spent a lot of years in this business, and I do not know of a single coach who has seemed to inspire the kind of lasting loyalty, almost worship, that Panek could put into a kid that played for him. They never forget. You tend to remember your first girl and your first coach, but age may put pimples on one memory and clay feet on the other.

Not Panek's.

There is no telling how many lives he somehow shaped, turned, polished, pointed in the 52 years he worked the sidelines and classrooms in Nebraska and Colorado. And they all remembered. Every one. There was a huge campaign to get him into the Colorado Sports Hall of Fame a few years ago, and it was conducted by his former players who could not understand why he wasn't in it already. After listening to them, they were probably right.

He had spent more than half a century, won 328 games and a thousand lives.

He was still prowling the sideline and coaching the single wing at a time most of his contemporaries were dead. He was the Amos Alonzo Stagg of the prep set. He was what you would like your son to play for as a coach.

And he won't mind that I didn't do a column on him. He didn't need it. I did. Sorry, Clyde.

December 20, 1991, *Denver Post*

JUST DON'T SAY IT WAS A TOUGH DECISION

I lament a misspent youth as I read the sporting pages these gloomy days.
It was spent learning to spell instead of learning to hit.
What a waste.

I have five grandsons, and by spring, I plan to have every one of them, even 10-month-old Connor Richard, out in the vacant lot, swinging at everything I can muster out of a sorely used arm.

Think of it. Poor Jack Morris sobs his way to Toronto for a mere $5.8 million. That's per year. And Wally Joyner was even more lacrimose as he stood at a podium in Southern California, explaining how difficult it would be to go to Kansas City and play baseball for $4.5 million. That's per year.

"It was a tough decision, a big decision," said Morris. I wish, just once, I would be confronted with such a dilemma. "Would you like to come conjugate verbs and misuse adjectives for us for, say, $5.8 mil?" some misguided publisher would ask. "That's per year, of course." And I would squirm and cause wrinkles to appear on my forehead, and close my eyes as if in deep thought.

And I would scream "YESSSSS!" and the whole process would take one-half a nanosecond.

I thought of all this late this week as the *Denver Post* feted young Greg Jones, the linebacker from Kennedy who is this year's Gold Helmet winner and next year's star at the University of Colorado. Already, he has the poise and presence once reserved for some five-year pro veteran. He turned down Stanford, and Cal-Berkeley, and Washington, and Notre Dame. He didn't even visit the latter two, calling them and cancelling. Notre Dame immediately sent an assistant coach to Denver to woo Jones, but his decision was made.

Colorado.

And, as we sat at lunch, I mentioned I thought somewhere soon the honey pot would dry up, that this insane salary escalation was going to stop, had to stop because there was no way to pay for it.

"Well, I hope it doesn't stop right away," Jones' father, John, said with a quiet smile. If I had a son as talented as Greg, I would hope for an extension of the insanity, too.

But Greg is leaving the last bastion of innocence. It vanishes year by year from now on, until you are Jack Morris, before a microphone, tears running down your cheeks, actually believing people believe you when you say going somewhere to pitch a baseball for a fortune is "a difficult decision."

Across the table from Greg this week was his athletic director, Larry Lindauer, and his coach, Bruce Abeyta. Abeyta once coached my youngest son at Holy Family. "We actually had a bigger budget there than we do at Kennedy," Abeyta said.

"We have $15,000 budgeted for boys' sports and $7,000 for girls' sports," said Lindauer. That $22,000 has to cover all expenses for 19 sports. "A helmet costs $100. We buy 10 new ones each year, and we buy six new uniforms each year." And if they are careful, and keep filtering the new equipment into the system, none of it ever gets quite too tattered or looks too bad.

I keep thinking of the locker room at a pro level, with expensive shoes piled carelessly on the bottom, a pair for rain, a pair for turf, a pair for grass, a pair in case the barometric pressure changes between innings. "Our kids buy their own," says Abeyta.

You probably saw the story in the *Denver Post* a couple of days ago, the one saying that a third of all major-league baseball players now make $1 million a year or more. Bobby Bonilla's salary is 200 times what the average teacher makes.

Is what Bobby Bonilla does really that much more difficult, that much more valuable to the advancement of humankind, to our pleasure or our needs?

Of course not. It's just the way it is. But I think young Greg Jones should hurry. The athletic recession is coming. I expect, by the end of this decade, that the present obscene salary levels will have slackened. Television won't be pouring billions into sports, for one thing. And there is a limit to what owners can charge their fans to watch in person. We are close to it here in Denver at the moment.

So where does the money come from? Wise businessmen don't build a widget that costs $1 to make if they know they can only sell it for 50 cents. Yet baseball owners have been busily at work trying to prove otherwise for some years now.

I hope this whole process doesn't disillusion Greg. He is an honor student, an outstanding citizen, a tremendous athlete. It's not at all hard to envision All-America honors down the way, even a high pro draft berth when his years at CU are over.

I hope he gets every dime he can when that time comes.

Just do me one favor, Greg: Don't stand at a microphone and say it was a tough decision to take it.

March 15, 1992, *Denver Post*

HOTCHKISS DESERVES A PARADE, COMPLETE WITH TROMBONES

It will be the mother of all parades on Colorado's Western Slope today.

"We understand the whole town—the part that isn't here [in Denver] already—is planning to meet the team on top of McClure Pass tomorrow afternoon and drive them into town with horns honking all the way.

"And that's a long way, maybe 50 miles or so down the mountain and into town," said a Hotchkiss booster on the way to the parking lot outside the Denver Coliseum late yesterday afternoon.

So, if you are planning to turn left out of Glenwood Springs this afternoon, maybe you ought to wait until the Hotchkiss High School Bulldogs go by. You'll recognize them. They'll be the ones with indelible grins planted on faces that were still trying to register belief after their 81-77 conquest of top-ranked Denver Christian in the Boys 3A championship.

And please note that 3A denotes the size of the schools, not the size of the hearts involved.

Note, also, I didn't use the word upset. Hotchkiss didn't play like a team that didn't belong. And Christian played like a team that has been ranked No. 1 since before this long season began last November.

This was a game straight out of central casting. Small-town team from across three mountain passes drives five hours to big city. Rookie coach is in state tournament finals for first time, against a guy who has coached for 28 years, been to eight finals, won five state titles.

Winning coach has twin sons playing for him. They wreck all odds. From the opening tip, they are set on full throttle. Everybody on Denver Christian is about 6-4. Everybody for Hotchkiss seems to be 6-0.

"We knew we couldn't play half court with them," said Kenny Clay, whose dad, Coach Harold, will lead today's welcome-home parade. Kenny Clay played just this side of out of control all the long, brilliant afternoon. He was the red-clad blur dashing upcourt on a wild dribble, forcing the taller Crusaders into fouls or pulling up for a three-pointer. He finished with 15 points. His brother, Kurt, had 24. And another senior, Chase Weining, led everybody with 30.

The Three Musketeers. "We've played together since we were kids, everything, baseball, football, basketball," said Kenny. Their dad kept trying to coax them into his apple and cherry orchards, "but I'd have to get them away from a ball game somewhere to get them to work," he said.

Oh. Don't forget Cheyenne Watson. At 6-3, he was Hotchkiss' only starter over six feet. The last two state tournament games, he played one minute. "Coach had me take the jump to start the game," he explained in the delirium of the Bulldogs' quarters. It was no cameo role for Watson yesterday. He scored seven points, grabbed seven rebounds and had at least two blocked shots that don't show on the final statistics sheet. Like Wiening and the Clay boys, he was what the big-time scouts like to call "a presence" on the Coliseum floor yesterday.

"I told him he was going to start today. Our sixth man had a sprained ankle. I told him 'I need a big game from you. I'm going to start you to get you some confidence,' and he just played super."

All of this came against a Christian team that never lost its patience. It just couldn't find its shot at key moments, and it could never control Hotchkiss' torrid tempo. Christian's Bob Tamminga had the game of his life with 34 points, and it wasn't enough.

"We played with good discipline," said Christian coach Dick Katte. "I thought we played hard. It's just that they were better shooters than we were." An 8-of-16 line on three-pointers, said Katte, "is as good as you'll ever see even in the pros." In the end, it was the killer.

Every time the Crusaders threatened, a "3" shoved Hotchkiss out of reach again.

"No school the rest of the year," principal Dan Burke shouted. It was like tossing gasoline on a forest fire.

They had come to the big city, and clawed their way through all the preliminaries, and arrived at this afternoon showdown on the big, shiny court against a team the whole state had been chasing for four months.

And somewhere, maybe in the seed planted back in third grade or fourth, they had found the stuff that made it all possible on a warm March day a long way from home.

There are so many story lines in this thing it's hard to catalog them.

Team Possessed beat Team Poised. Denver Christian, understand, did not play a bad game. It looked every bit the state's AAA power. But Hotchkiss looked better. The Crusaders never lost their poise, or patience. They were down by nine and came back. They were down by 10 and came back. But each time, one of the Clay boys would drain a three, and the Bulldogs would ease back out.

"We could never get that hump basket," said Katte, who is almost a fixture at these March affairs. "And we had our chances. I feel badly we lost. I don't know of any group of kids that deserved to win more—except Hotchkiss."

It was a classy exit line. History teaches that Denver Christian will be back. It also teaches the third time was the charming one for the cross-state Bulldogs.

"We lost our first game as sophomores here," said Kurt Clay. "Then last year we won our first game and lost our second." This time, not even the top-ranked team in the state could halt their almost frantic dash to the trophy.

Somebody find Professor Harold Hill and 76 trombones. They deserve a parade.

April 2, 1992, *Denver Post*

LITTLE LEAGUE COACH HAS PRIORITIES STRAIGHT

There is this Little League where my grandson, Zach, plays in southeast Denver. It recently had a practice game, and at the end, my son, Mark, asked the coach what the final score was.

"Fun to fun," the coach replied.

I think I could like that guy.

Isn't that how sports began? Isn't it how they should still begin, even if they end with agents and seven-figure salaries and drug rehab and petulant behavior?

... I envy that Little League coach. And I envy his players. They are playing at exactly the right level—the only one left where all that matters is that it is "fun to fun."

❧   ❧   ❧

CHAPTER NINE

THE OLYMPICS

✤   ✤   ✤

Dick Connor was a great friend when I first came here in 1968 as a rookie sports information director at [the University of] Colorado. He took a lot of his own time to give me the lay of the land with this whole confusing thing called the Denver media.

In the years following both at CU and a couple Olympic Games, I became increasingly aware of just how special he was. He may be the last of the professional journalists with whom you could share a two-way association, both as a friend and a person who had journalistic responsibilities. He could do both and do them right.

—Mike Moran, director, Public Information/Media Relations, U.S. Olympic Committee

Perhaps a few of his regular readers were startled when, in the middle of a thoughtful piece, he spanked the Olympic Committee leaders for their whining and carping on the reasons the USA didn't win all the medals in the 1992 Winter Olympics.

—Bob Paul, Public Information, U.S. Olympic Committee, retired

✤   ✤   ✤

Colorado has a love/hate, on-again/off-again relationship with the Olympics.

In 1972, voters gave back the 1976 Games after they had been awarded to Colorado by the USOC in 1968. It was, and still is, the only time since 1896 that a city or state said thanks, but no thanks, to hosting the Games. Richard Lamm, then a first-time candidate for governor, walked the state to get the Games defeated on financial and environmental grounds. He also won his bid for governor and served a total of 12 years.

In 1989, Colorado again bid for the Olympics—this time for the Winter Games. Dick thought it would be a futile exercise. He was right. The Games were awarded to Nagano, Japan.

In 1988 he wrote the following in the *Rocky Mountain News*:

> Denver and Colorado have no chance. To put the whole scenario in the down-to-earth lexicon of Doug Moe, it is a "no hoper."
>
> Denver wooed and won the 1976 Winter Games. Then, right at the altar, we voted them down in a statewide election that left the IOC scrambling desperately to find some place to stage its quadrennial winter carnival.
>
> And now they are expected to listen to new love songs? ...
>
> You had to have been here, really, to appreciate the mood of the election of 1972. It was more a total renunciation of a bungled program and administration than a rejection of the Olympic idea. But try and sell that to some European nobleman. ...

The Denver dailies didn't always send writers and columnists to the Olympics. They became serious about it after the newspaper war was declared. Dick covered the 1984 Games in Yugoslavia and Los Angeles. He was still at the Rocky *Mountain News* during the 1988 Olympics in Montreal and in Seoul, Korea, but was not assigned to the Olympic Games. He was slated to attend the 1992 Summer Games in Madrid for the *Denver Post,* but he took himself off the assignment because he realized it would be too much of a physical challenge. (His cancer had been diagnosed in September 1990.)

I think he enjoyed the Winter Games in Sarajevo the most. He was a voracious reader of history, especially books about both world wars, so he found the setting especially interesting—despite a blizzard, language barriers and the communist atmosphere. He hoped we both could go there as tourists someday. Someday became never when fighting and shelling turned the areas he remembered into heaps of rubble. He wrote about that, too.

HASSLES MISSING IN SARAJEVO

SARAJEVO, Yugoslavia—"Good morning.

"It's now 7 a.m. in Frankfurt. That's London off the left side of the aircraft. The weather in Frankfurt is typical—40 degrees and raining. We should be landing there in exactly one hour."

The voice brought us awake, or at least out of the dozing numbness that passes for sleep after six hours of flying. The Pan Am 747 was crammed with military heading for Germany and newsmen heading for Sarajevo and the 1984 Winter Olympics.

It was morning below. It was 1 a.m. in New York, and 11 p.m. back in the Rockies, where my personal time clock had been set. Prolonged travel gives some people jet lag. I had the hiccups. They were going to bed in Denver and New York and they were waking up down below in the gray overcast of a European morning. And at the moment when I could see the famous city for the first time, after waiting so many years, all I could think of was finding a glass of water and holding my breath.

It wasn't the last incongruity on a three-day trek to this mountain metropolis known more for one bullet than for anything else in its 2,000-plus years.

We had been given warnings for months: List your personal equipment, carry this special Olympic identification number, be prepared for long delays when you go through Yugoslavian customs, they had said.

In Zagreb, braced for our first contact with the socialist bureaucracy, it was like leaning into a wind that failed to blow.

"No," the man in the brown uniform said, waving startled journalists through. "No need. The bus is outside."

No customs inspection. No hassle. No wind.

"Dobradosli" the first sign read. "Welcome."

"Avis" the second sign read. It was directly across from the airport entrance. "Coca-Cola" read the next, displayed prominently on a billboard next to the road into town. A crow landed in a field. It, too, looked the same in any language.

The plan had been relatively simple. Fly to New York, catch the overnight to Frankfurt, switch planes, go to Zagreb and take a train up into the mountains to this city where Gavrilo Princip assassinated Archduke Ferdinand and helped launch World War I.

It was not quite that simple. You can get here from there. But not quickly.

"There is a problem with the heating unit on the train," the guide said. "There will be a delay." There was. Three hours. While we stood on the platform, some 70 American writers, staring across a set of empty tracks, about the same number of Yugoslavian commuters were waiting for another train, staring back.

Periodically, a train would pull in, steam swirling, looking like a visual cliche of everything you've ever seen in "Dr. Zhivago" or "Reds" or the "Orient Express."

We killed time walking. More surprises. There is a startling amount of graffiti scrawled or sprayed on buildings, enough to make even a New Yorker feel at home.

The "Olympik Ekspress" finally arrived, express in name only. For the next seven hours, it sought out every platform in Bosnia. It stopped every 10 minutes at some dark, frozen station. Nobody ever seemed to get off, or on. But it stopped.

At 12:30, three hours late, we were in Sarajevo. "I am practicing now my English four years in school," our guide told us. It was vastly superior to any of the Serbo-Croatian issuing from the Berlitz dictionaries on the press bus.

Two army vans pulled up for the luggage. In Zagreb, a man in a sport jacket, tie and hat had labored alone to transfer luggage. In Sarajevo, a cordon of troops formed a human chain. They have brought in buses and translators and electricians from all over the country for the Games.

... Marshal Tito's portrait still decorates every other flagpole, and inflation and unemployment still occupy the working man's worries much more than grown men sliding down an ice chute to collect a medal.

Everything is ready. Except the trains. Let the revels begin.

February 6, 1984, *Rocky Mountain News*
WELCOME TO THE LAND (AND ERA) OF "BEEDLEBEEP"

SARAJEVO, Yugoslavia—Beedlebeep. Twenty years from now, if there is a single sound that will summon back a single image of Sarajevo in 1984, it is this.

Beedlebeep. It's the almost melodic electronic signal that comes from the walkie talkies used by the milijcia (militia) and soldiers on casual guard duty about this mountain town.

It's a soft sound, quick, lasting only a second or less. But, instantly, you know a uniform is nearby. In a land of people straining to make the Winter Olympics a success, it is a muted reminder that not everything is as newly Western as it appears. But it is just one sound in a symphony.

And the uniform is just one sight in an exotic collage that fills American senses as much as downhill times and compulsory figures and how the U.S. hockey team fares. The sights and sounds are the essence of these Olympics in this part Eastern, part Western nation of part socialism, part communism and part capitalism.

Here, then are a few:

The gray light has barely erased most of the shadows when a little girl is spotted by an American as he jogs on a road near the press complex. She is tugging on her boots. It seems early for school. He keeps running, looking as she walks a muddy lane to the road—the first streets were not paved here until 1901. Once on the road, she crouches and begins picking up glass from a bottle tossed carelessly during the night. Four days earlier, the Americans had left a land in which litter is almost a way of life. In New York, it's an art form.

There is little street crime. Perhaps it's because penalties are so severe. Maybe it's also due to the fact inflation is about 50 percent. The average semiskilled worker earns the equivalent of 50 cents per hour, and mugging simply doesn't pay.

Prices are low, but Yugoslavian shopkeepers are showing a remarkable adaptability. A good meal, with wine, in a very good restaurant, costs 1,600 dinars for two. That's about $6 each. When the Americans started to tip, a Yugoslavian newsman shook his head when asked if 15 percent is correct, as is customary in the United States. "No. Never ever even 10 percent. Five percent for exceptional services. Put 40 dinar down." He did. That was about 30 cents.

There are shops where handwoven wool sweaters can be purchased for approximately $30 U.S.

But the process can be involved. At a duty-free shop off the workroom in the press building, a simple purchase of five cigars requires first, U.S. currency. Then the shopkeeper makes out a receipt. In triplicate. With his name on it. The buyer gets one, the red-lined copy. The cigars then are placed in a plastic sack as big as a shopping bag in a supermarket. Total transaction: $2 U.S. Total time required: seven minutes Yugoslavian. Beedlebeep.

"Did you ever think you'd ever see the day," one writer asked another as they walked to rooms in the press village well past midnight, "when you were comforted by the thought you are being guarded by communist troops?"

Nearby, two of them strolled, each with a submachine gun slung over his shoulder. Beedlebeep. Writers who covered the last Olympics in Lake Placid go out of their way to contrast the Yugoslavian efficiency at running buses and operating the whole complex support operation. But it is also true that if a bus is scheduled to leave at noon, it will not leave a millisecond earlier, even if it is so loaded they are standing in the aisles.

You know you have brushed the Middle Eastern culture when you stroll through old town, that more ancient section of this ancient city, and suddenly see the muezzins standing in their pencil minarets, calling back and forth, summoning the faithful to prayer. Immediately, the courtyard below begins to fill with men. They stand and smoke and chat until another call, then take off their shoes and enter the mosques, the shoes left outside under a light rain.

Sight: In the midst of the sea of brown and black shoes is a pair of very white, very new Adidas. Sound: Next door, a Catholic church bell sounds.

If you know German, you can get by here. It is the second language. Sign language is now the official third one. When an American with nothing but English got into a cab with a driver with nothing but Serbo-Croatian and German, it went this way.

"Speak English?"

The driver shook his head and countered, "Sprechen Sie Deutsch?"

They sat silent for a moment. The American wanted to go to old town and to the Princip bridge, where the shot that launched World War I was fired. "Market" he tries. Nothing. They sat. The American rifled through a dictionary, finding the word for market and pointing to it.

"Ah!" Gears were engaged. They swept through tiny, twisting cobblestone streets, up and down hills, horn-honking around corners, and pulled proudly up to the curb next to a store with a neon sign flashing "Mini Market." It was the Sarajevo equivalent of a 7-Eleven.

More sitting. More silence. Finally, the American pretended his fingers were a pistol, and went "bang." Instantly, the driver smiled. Within three minutes they were at the bridge, where footprints have been immortalized in a paving block where Gavrilo Princip stood and became an instant folk hero in this intensely nationalistic Bosnia.

Latin is not a dead language, even here. ... The use of Roman numerals is not pretentious. The Romans were here. They conquered this land in the time of Christ. But so did the Turks and the Austrians and many others who had an army and used the Balkans as a highway.

The Yugoslavian fighters battling Nazis are still shown daily on local television. It is a land of four languages and two alphabets and magnificent people eager to make a good impression. The surgeon general's report did not reach the Balkans. Everybody smokes. Palls of the stuff hang in restaurants, in bars, in hallways, even at the rail and bus platforms where dozens wait at all hours.

There seem to be no dogs in Sarajevo. Small packs of cats roam the market area going from garbage heap to garbage heap, but there are no dogs.

Sound: A rooster that must be operating on Central Atlantic Time is serving as the wake-up call in the press village. He goes off between 3 a.m. and 3:30 a.m.

Rock singers sound the same in any language. So do amplified guitars. A Gary Cooper western was shown on local television Saturday. So were interviews with David Bowie and Wolfman Jack.

Contrast: The high-tech bobsleds up on the run, the self-important television crews, the hordes of celebrities arriving, the almost reverential way in which members of the IOC are treated and the little man in a gray coat and hat on a sidewalk Friday in the rain, shoveling a head-high pile of coal into a basement through a window. Or a girl in a smock who cleans ashtrays in the pressroom. You are getting ready to leave. She smiles and waves. "May you have successful words," she says.

Beedlebeep.

February 11, 1984, *Rocky Mountain News*
ONLY YUGOSLAV HOSPITALITY BRINGS UNITED STATES OUT OF THE COLD

SARAJEVO, Yugoslavia—We felt like aliens on a distant planet.

The monster storm that has gripped Europe was wrapping the Dinaric Alps in an especially icy embrace. Temperatures hovered just above zero. The wind made the snow seem heavier, bending limbs of towering Douglas fir trees that border Veliko Polje (Big Field) below Mount Igman. ...

This is Denver at Christmas 1982, or Thanksgiving 1983. Except they do a far better job of clearing the roads.

There was a foot of it on the ground when we woke up Friday.

"They can't possibly run the downhill today," we agreed, and headed for the bus to Veliko Polje and the men's 30-kilometer cross country, instead. If the United States had a medal in it anywhere this week, it might be here, where 26-year-old Bill Koch had a chance.

Up the mountain again, on a well-placed but narrow road, and down into the valley where communist partisans fought the Germans 40 years ago.

A milijcia guard pointed us down an even narrower road and we started walking toward a distant line of trees when a van skidded up next to us and several Yugoslavs in orange and blue coats waved us inside.

The driver had a big, square jaw and a kamikaze instinct. We went careening down the lane, horn tooting, scattering pedestrians, sliding on the turns, him cursing in Serbo-Croatian, which seems a very versatile language for that hobby.

"Hvala!" we murmured. "Thank you." The other word most of us have mastered is "pivo." Beer.

A figure in red glided past in the murk beyond the lodge.

"Anyone know what is going on? Who's leading? Where it is?"

An American team official helped. "Koch's on the course, but he's out there with a Korean, a Mongolian and I forget. Nobody's pushing or pulling him. He can't judge how he's doing. And the scoreboard is out."

There was chanting and the distant ring of a cowbell from a line of fans almost lost in the snow up a rise to the right. A cowbell? We headed up, through knee-deep snow.

What happened next has no American counterpart. We ski cross country to get somewhere and sip wine, or view scenery, or exercise. It's recreational. Scandinavian Europe skis cross country almost as a way of life. And when they put bibs on as contestants, it is deadly serious.

There was a wooden bridge arching over the course, which was outlined with little red and green flags to keep skiers on the track as it went up the five-degree slope for 300 yards and disappeared into more dark pine woods.

More than 1,000 spectators had gone over the bridge and stood with their backs to the wind, lining the track three and four deep for almost half a mile from the bridge down to a distant turn. In back of them stood 49 flagpoles, the banners of the 49 nations here at the Winter Games almost tearing away in the wind.

There was nothing haphazard about the way the crowd stood. The Russians were high on the hill, near the bridge, the big snow-frosted hats almost a caricature, two of them waving large Soviet flags when a skier from the USSR came pumping up the hill toward them.

There were no American flags. There were no American voices, in fact, amid the choruses of "Haya Haya" from the Swedes, or "Sasha Sasha" when one Soviet skier went by. The Finns and Norwegians had their own chants, but it was too far downhill and the wind tore it away, anyway.

There was near silence when Koch, his trademark black and yellow stocking cap marking him, came past under the bridge and vanished into the trees. The American fans here had gone to the hockey game Thursday night, or the pairs skating Friday, or had gone to the downhill until it was canceled. They save themselves for the glamour events. Cross country is a spectator sport only to Scandinavians and Russians.

They had come out in the storm just after dawn for the 9 a.m. start and stood there until it finished at 11:30. They had traveled 45 minutes out from town, then paid to stand in a blizzard for three hours and ring cowbells. Then, eyebrows frosted, feet numb, cheeks burned red, they had trudged back through the snow, up the road, back to the bus and the 45-minute return ride to town.

Somewhere along that frozen vigil, there was a commotion up near the bridge. Miraculously, three kids had brought a huge steel vat of hot, sweet tea. Three of us stood, watching, as they ladled it into Styrofoam cups.

One of the girls offered a cup, and we knelt in the snow and held it over the vat while the boy ladled the hot liquid. Nobody asked for a cent or a dinar.

By 11:30 it was over. The Russians were one-two. "Sasha! Sasha!" Was it a nickname? A Swede was third. "Haya! Haya!"

It was not a good day for Scandinavia. It was not a good day for Germany. It was not a good day for Koch or the USA. Koch finished 21st.

But there are at least two Americans who hope it was a great day for three kids who brought hot, sweet tea to a Balkan hillside in the snow.

February 17, 1984, *Rocky Mountain News*

JOHNSON CALLED HIS SHOT

SARAJEVO, Yugoslavia—In your face, Europe.

William D. Johnson just slam-dunked your Super Bowl, to mix sporting phrases.

He pointed to center and homered here. He was Joe Namath on the eve of the Super Bowl III. "I guarantee it," Namath said. He made good. So did Johnson. He created golden splendor in the snow for the U.S. Olympic team that desperately needed it.

"Will you finish in the top three tomorrow?" Johnson was asked Wednesday, on the eve of the men's downhill at the Olympics.

"Top three? I think I'll be in the top one."

It's the outrageous kind of thing he's been saying all week while Europe snickered and the world waited for the weather to clear and permit the race, the glamour event in any Olympics.

It's the one Europeans point for, wait for, hope for. Now it's the one an American owns.

And a sandy-haired American who looks more like a surfer came sailing over the final bump, a tiny little speck floating out of the shadows and whiteness above.

It was almost symbolic. He came flashing from those shadows and down the final slope and into the sun and history. He was Namath in ski goggles, Babe Ruth in a skin-tight racing suit with red candy stripes. He called his shot—then did it.

Bill Johnson, 23, is the first American man to win downhill at the Olympics. He did it as he said he would and the United States woke up to a new hero Thursday, albeit an unlikely one.

Here's a young man who was arrested at 16 for stealing a car for a joy ride. He was given a choice: Get your act together or go to reform school. "I haven't taken anything since," says Johnson.

He became a ski bum after high school. "If you don't do anything but ski for five years, you ought to get good," he said this week in another of his startling pronouncements. At Lake Placid four years ago, he talked his way into skiing as a forerunner, those skiers who come down the course just before the race begins. Two years ago, he was tossed off the team for not training.

Thursday, the last forerunners were still standing here, chests heaving, when Johnson made history. It was Franz Klammer, the arrogant Austrian who had dismissed Johnson's win at Wengen earlier this month as a fluke. "He's a nose-picker," Herr Klammer sniffed.

Ah, but is he?

"The great ones have confidence," said Bill Marolt, head of the U.S. ski team. Like Johnson, he was surrounded at the foot of the hill. "The good ones know they are good."

Johnson knew this hill was his almost from the moment he saw it. He staked claim to it for himself and for the United States, and nobody in the long series of weather delays did a thing to dislodge that claim. In five training runs, he was seventh, then first, second, second and first again.

The Austrians sent their team home for 48 hours, for $10,000 in a private jet, to get proper rest. The Swiss pampered their team, ensuring the right diet, sleep, a fitting setting for Permin Zurbriggen, World Cup leader.

Johnson and the only other American downhiller, David Lewis, stayed in the village and went out to watch hockey games. Thursday, Johnson took the lift up, skied a trail on top for half an hour to loosen up, stood cracking jokes and chewing tobacco, then blitzed the world just as he said he would.

He was the sixth man down the hill, slid under the Cilj (finish) banner, turned to look at the computer time and was giving interviews and raising his right forefinger aloft almost before he had his skis off.

He knew. So did the Austrian fans on one side. They had come to cheer Klammer but they stayed to toast Johnson. Theirs is the view of the connoisseur, "John-sone," they yelled across the white expanse at the bottom of the hill. "Bil-ly."

Kings and queens and maybe even ABC's Roone Arledge had whooshed to the site in helicopters, stirring up great clouds of snow and deflating two hot-air balloons near the finish line. Long ermine coats mixed with simple cloth ones and lots of down jackets, ranging in snow 10 feet deep up along the course to where the shadows started.

They had come to see if the American would live up to his words or be forced to eat them.

"If I hadn't won," he answered afterward, "I would have been real bummed."

Up on top as he said it, Johnson was chewing tobacco, signing autographs and spitting. If Olympic day did anything to Johnson, it helped. "I was nervous about 20 minutes before the race," he admitted. Then he produced the fastest run since they arrived.

He may be a free spirit, a throwback to the flower children, someone who teetered for a while on the brink of something worse in the future.

But he is no accident. He won the Europa Cup for budding World Cup racers a year ago. No American has ever done that. He won the World Cup downhill at Wengen just before coming here. No American has done that.

Now he has a gold medal draped about his neck, and no American has ever managed that, either.

"The hill was easy," a Europa television interview suggested.

"If it was so easy, why didn't they win it?" Johnson snapped. Later, he was asked what the Austrians must be thinking. He broke into a wicked grin.

"I just love sticking it to the Austrians. Not the Swiss. They are very nice. But the Austrians think they should win every race."

Thursday, after a week's delay, Bill Johnson won the race every skier in the world envies him for. Franz Klammer finished 10th.

February 18, 1984, *Rocky Mountain News*

NOTHING MORE TO PROVE

SARAJEVO, Yugoslavia—He had the look of a man who has just wrestled demons and won. But barely.

"I've never been this tired, physically or mentally," said Scott Hamilton. It was the morning after. His coach, Don Law, had his gold medal for safekeeping.

Hamilton had slept in, almost missing an appointment to go downtown and do the CBS and NBC morning shows. A CBS driver was waiting anxiously outside the athletes' village gate as Hamilton walked slowly toward it.

He's been suffering from a cold and an ear infection, and he celebrated after Thursday's performance by gulping a cold tablet.

"I couldn't take one before because of the doping process," he said. "Antihistamines are forbidden."

America has been waiting almost a quarter of a century, since David Jenkins in 1960 at Squaw Valley, to win the men's figure skating at a Winter Olympics.

Now this almost elfin young man had delivered it, but not with the explosive final bang he had planned. Twelve hours later, it still bugged him.

He has restored the sport to athleticism from its years of spangles and perfumed hair spray. He has gone out of his way to cultivate a macho image, as macho as a man whose growth had been stunted by a childhood illness can be, and who buys clothes off the boys' racks in the store.

He spends time with Bronco running back Dave Preston and linebacker Tom Jackson. They were at his going-away party for Sarajevo.

But he is first, foremost and forever a world champion, with the total dedication and single-mindedness that implies. And when he messed up a couple of portions of an otherwise more than acceptable free skating program on Thursday, it left mental marks.

"I feel goal-less now," he said, strolling along the wet pavement, nodding and waving as various athletes offered their congratulations as they spotted him.

As contradictory as it sounds, he stands out at 5-foot-3 in a village full of athletes of far greater height and weight.

"No," he told a well-wisher. "I haven't seen my dad yet this morning. We're supposed to get together this afternoon sometime." His parents were biology professors at Bowling Green, where his father still lives. His mother died of cancer. Hamilton is adopted.

"I'm exhausted," he said, resuming the walk. "All the media. God. When they picked me as the favorite, sure you know, it's something I worked for a long time. I wanted that. But at the same time it was hard to deal with once it came right down to the reality."

The reality was he just didn't skate as well as he had planned in the final night, and it rankled, even now in the daylight with a light snow sifting down.

"Things had been going so well and I think I just burned myself out here. I did skate well. But not my best."

So now he is going to the World Championships in Ottawa next month, "skate like I intended to skate here," and then retire and turn pro.

It's time. There is nothing left for him to do on the amateur level except pile up repeat championships in a sport he has dominated like no one else in its history.

The Mahre brothers, Phil and Steve, obviously stayed a year too long on the Alpine ski team. They lost their desire—and their ability to win. There is nothing sadder than watching an athlete who overstays his body and his mind. Hamilton has not reached that stage yet, but with no new worlds, he could.

Right now, he is eager to get home to Denver. "That's my refuge."

But there's another reason. He can't wait to have his own plaque installed at Colorado Ice Arena, where he trained for the gold. "They have had four Olympic champions. What can you say? I can't wait to get my sign," he said, sounding like an astrologer.

"They have a sign that says, "Colorado Ice Arena is the skating home of John Curry and Dorothy Hamill, 1976 Olympic gold medalists. Then it says, Home of Robert Cousins, 1980 Olympic gold medalist."

He broke into a laugh. "Now I get my sign." Make it a big one.

He had to go all the way to the Balkans and survive a major case of nerves to get it, but he did it. "I think I want that sign as much as the medal itself."

The actual medal, he said, "will go to the museum down in Colorado Springs. It might be able to promote skating. It will only collect dust in a safety deposit box."

The car was waiting. In minutes, his grin would be spread over early morning television screens across the United States. If it had its normal effect, a whole nation would be smiling back.

"I've done everything I can in skating," he said. "I hate to sound cocky, but it's time to move on."

For a guy with size 5-1/2 shoes, he'll leave enormous footprints to follow.

February 20, 1984, *Rocky Mountain News*
AFTER ALL, A GOOD OLYMPICS

SARAJEVO, Yugoslavia—It was, in many ways, a strange Olympics. There was too much snow, and too much wind, and it took a week and nine separate hill preparations before they ran the men's downhill.

Some of the Americans expected to win did not.

Some nobody thought would, did.

They got more fourths (six) than firsts (four), or seconds (four).

The hockey team was a bust. Bill Koch failed to place in the cross country, and Tamara McKinney was a blink out of the bronze in the women's slalom.

But Bill Johnson, the old nose-picker (as Franz Klammer dismissed him), swept down Mt. Bjelasnica to the United States' first downhill gold in history, and Denver's Scott Hamilton survived his nerves to capture the men's figure skating gold.

If some expected as many as 15 to 17 medals for the Americans, this was not a good Olympics. But perhaps we all expected too much. The fourths demonstrate how close this team was to almost living up to those expectations.

And the Mahre brothers, Phil and Steve, were almost symbolic of the whole journey to history's first Winter Games in Eastern Europe.

They broke down at their final press conference, crying in joy and relief at having made up for a season of disappointment and a Games of frustration. Their gold and silver finish came as they prepare to exit the World skiing stage.

It was a nice way to depart, and for Victor Tikhonev, perhaps now he won't hear the words anymore.

Lake Placid. His Soviet hockey team had just produced an awesomely efficient gold medal win over Czechoslovakia, 2-0. If anyone needed testimony to what losing at Lake Placid meant four years ago, they had only to watch the emotional reaction as the final seconds ticked off at Zetra arena Sunday afternoon.

The Soviets raised arms, hugged, then leapt over the boards to sweep down on their 32-year-old goaltender, Vladimir Tretiak. He had been benched in the course of the loss to the United States in 1980.

Now they mobbed him.

And when that ended, Tikhonev seized his own moment, grabbing his veteran of 14 years, hugging him, kissing him on each cheek, then playfully ruffling his hair. ...

Lake Placid and Sarajevo have been Alpha and Omega for the Soviets and Americans, euphoria and bitter disappointment on the hockey ice. ...

But the Americans have shown growth elsewhere. They now can ski with the Europeans, as they proved. They almost jumped with the Scandinavians, as Jeff Hastings proved by finishing fourth in the 90-meter Saturday, only a point away from a bronze.

If it wasn't an unqualified triumph, the U.S. visit to Yugoslavia was not the looming disaster that it looked a week ago. Johnson, Debbie Armstrong (gold for giant slalom), Hamilton and Steve Mahre saw to that.

It wasn't great. But neither was it bad.

And when the two final press conferences broke up, and fans were filing up the hill for the final ceremony, it was snowing again in Sarajevo.

July 30, 1984, *Rocky Mountain News*
PRESS CONFERENCE WAS REAL CONTEST

INGLEWOOD, Calif.—And now, for your listening pleasure, we present the ever-popular Bobby Knight.

For 40 minutes, the warlord of America's basketball hopes in the 1984 Olympic Games had watched and screamed and cussed and fumed while his awesome collection rolled mercilessly over the People's Republic of China 97-49.

It was never a contest.

The only contest came later, in the postgame press conference.

The Olympics do things their way. Every time a team or an individual gets behind a microphone, the result must be given in at least two languages, one of them French.

Knight is accustomed to finding a microphone and doing what comes naturally, talking into it.

So he entered, sat, grabbed the mike and he started.

"I thought, in the, uh ..." he began.

"Coach," a functionary interrupted. "I'll introduce you and the players."

"Get on with it," Knight murmured.

The young man proceeded to butcher Alvin Robertson's name.

"I think I could have done a better job," Knight snapped.

This is a man who, his team leading by 40 Sunday afternoon, was screaming at one of his players who failed to cover a weak side lane and allowed a Chinese rebound. This is the man who, when he got disgusted with his starting lineup in the second half, yanked the whole aggregation and never put them back as a unit.

Patrick Ewing, the Georgetown star, didn't even start. You could scarcely blame the Chinese when their team failed to turn up at the customary postmortem.

This was their first venture outside China to an Olympic basketball floor since 1948. After Sunday, and Knight's devastating welcome, they may never come again.

"Was it a relief to get the tournament under way?" a man wondered, and Knight began to answer before he was interrupted again. A young woman, acting as the French interpreter, was getting rattled by Knight's growing impatience.

He settled her. "I would defer to her for the French," he said, but stared stonily at the master of ceremonies.

"Your part I'm convinced I can handle."

By this time, the girl had forgotten the question. So Leon Wood leaned over and told her, in French.

"Leon," Knight exclaimed, leaning down the table to slap hands. "That's pretty good, kid. You learned more at Fullerton State than I thought you did."

When he told his listeners, in answer to another question, that he had chewed Robertson out for three quick first-half fouls, and then ordered him out for the second half with the command, "Get your ass out there and don't foul," the interpreter blushed.

"I can't translate that."

"Use derriere," Wood suggested.

Knight was reasonably happy with his team's performance. China obviously is not ready for this level, if any team in the current field is. Knight's team is being compared with the 1960 American one, generally regarded as the best ever.

This could be its equal, but Sunday was no test. By late in the game, Knight had his charges working on little bits and pieces as if they were at a practice.

They even left the two Chinese coaches laughing and pointing and nudging each other appreciatively as they witnessed the growing disaster on the court.

But Knight is relentless.

No, he said, no American player or coach scouted the Yugoslavian team which played just before the United States. The Yugoslavs are rated a possible threat.

"I would ask the same about the Canadians," a man asked. Knight gleefully grabbed the mike.

"Obviously, since Canada has not yet played, we did not watch the Canadian team play." Slam, and dunk.

"Can you tell us, at this point, where this team is and where it is going?"

His eyes became slits. This was a hanging curve, fat, right over the middle.

"At this point, my best answer is to say we are still at the Forum, and we are going to leave and go have supper," he said happily.

The interpreter didn't even try. The young man who interrupted early had long since been silenced.

Knight's team had won, overwhelmingly, done what he wanted, got things started. He had won the press conference that followed.

"Thank you," he said, turning to the young interpreter, smiling at her.

"Tres bien, mademoiselle."

"And au revoir."

He said that.

Any further questions?

August 9, 1984, *Rocky Mountain News*

TIME COMES FOR SADNESS, PRIDE

LONG BEACH, Calif.—Even if she looked forever, Debbie Green could not find a smile in herself. It had been almost 30 minutes since the final Chinese drive had caromed off an American hand and off into the crowd and the record books.

China, competing in its first-ever Olympic women's volleyball tournament, had defeated the United States team, which was competing in its first-ever Olympic final.

Now, they were making the awards. Debbie, 26, bent to let them drape the ribbon with the silver medal on it about her neck. She didn't have to bend far. At 5-foot-4, she is the shortest American. But, like Flo Hyman, at 6-foot-5 the tallest, she goes back to the beginning.

And that's why the smiles on some of her teammates' faces were absent on hers. She soberly accepted the bouquet of flowers each medalist receives.

Then she stood, staring, a sightless stare, while teammates chatted on either side. ...

Debbie Green was lost in her own private vacuum. Maybe, by now, the pall has lifted. I hope so. Lord, nobody on this 1984 United States Olympic team has worked harder—or longer—than those women who stood on the silver platform Tuesday night.

Nobody in our history ever has.

That's what made the moment so ineffably sad, bittersweet. There was pride in being there, joy at having come so far. But there was this smoglike feeling that draped them, too.

Since they came together as a team back in Colorado Springs in the late winter of 1978, this final game in Long Beach on a California summer night has been their goal. It was their Holy Grail, the only ultimate destination.

They reached it. That they didn't get everything is, for most, beside the point. For Debbie Green in those moments, of course, it ended a step too soon.

So that was one memory I had as I watched those ceremonies. It brought another. It was late winter of 1980. Then-President Carter had announced the boycott of the Moscow Games. But there was still a lingering hope something might happen and the United States would get to go after all.

At the Olympic Training Center in Colorado Springs, Green and three of her teammates sat at a lunch table. I can't recall the other three.

But I do remember her. I had asked about their two years of training, training so intense it would make a Marine drill sergeant proud. Arie Selinger, the one-time Israeli commando and Nazi concentration camp victim, had demanded a total dedication.

They had given it.

Now, forces beyond them had snatched away the potential fruits of all that work. Only somebody who went through it could understand the empty feeling it evoked.

"I don't have a boyfriend. I haven't been able to finish school. I spend my life in a dorm room that looks like a cell at times. I have to go buy some laundry detergent, and I think I have $34 left in my checkbook this morning," one said.

Debbie? I think so. I remember the quote. It could have been any of them. That life, and the game they finally reached, were part of the sisterhood that bound them.

Never in American amateur sports has one team been assembled so long, so intensely.

Selinger had begun putting it together as early as 1975. When the training center opened, they moved there, and the odyssey, the one with a Grecian quality to it, was under way.

Except for a two-week vacation each Christmas, they trained or played or traveled for seven years.

Ours are cellophane dynasties in Olympic team sports. We bring them together once every four years, patch talent on talent, rarely with time for a true blend, and rely on sheer ability levels to overcome team deficiencies.

Sometimes, as at Lake Placid, it works.

But it is not in the American ethos to bring a team together and keep it together with such single-minded dedication for almost a decade.

They ignite, flame, draw oohs and aahs from the American public, then the ashes are dispersed. Not this team.

It has stayed and made history.

And Tuesday night, when that decisive Chinese blast sailed beyond recall, the American women watched, turned, looked at each other, then huddled in the middle of the floor.

All night, workers had been summoned out to blot up perspiration on the floor. This time, nobody came to dry the tears.

This was a Last Hurrah. A number, maybe most, will retire now. There are hints Selinger himself may give it up.

So an era ended. Maybe that's what Debbie Green was staring at. They had come out for the victory ceremony, two by two, arms about each other's waists. It was as if, by touching, they would cling to something.

They didn't want to let go. When they did, they would lose contact with each other, and with their lives of the last seven years. A part of them would go forever.

It was not a prospect to smile about.

MARY DECKER'S DAY IS HERE

LOS ANGELES—She was too young for Munich, too hurt for Montreal, too American for Moscow.

But Mary Decker may finally have found the time and the place for herself when she lines up against the world in Friday night's 3,000-meter run. Maybe, finally, that driven quality will be satisfied, at least for a while.

Decker turned 26 a week ago.

She has spent her teens and now her young adulthood trying to outrace the world. It has created a warped kind of life, but it's one the world-class athlete in any sport endures, even seeks.

"If they do that in the final, I'll kill 'em," she said Wednesday night after women behind her in the semifinals twice nicked her heels. She means it. There is a killer quality to her nature. You don't win what she has won without it.

You don't survive what she has survived without developing it.

At 12, she started running, here, in California. By 14, she was a ranked international figure. She celebrated her 15th birthday winning a race in Africa. They wrote about her in the national magazines. A year later, her world was collapsing about her. Her parents were divorcing. She had a stress fracture and spent six weeks with her ankle in a cast. A mere 5-foot, 89-pounder at 14, she had mauled her legs with too much, too soon. They rebelled.

The pain began in her shins. She had shot into the running firmament like some kind of comet, and then vanished, trailing unfilled promise. At 16, prom time for most, she was washed up, dismissed. It was a questioning Mary Decker who submitted to an interview in her apartment in Boulder in 1978.

By then, she was 5-6, 115 pounds and back to running 90 miles a week. "This time last year I couldn't run without limping," she had said quietly. Outside a light snow fell. Inside, among the surfing posters and the plants hanging on macrame ropes, Mary Decker looked almost vulnerable.

It's a word that will draw scoffing response from most people these days. She left little but ill will behind for her year in Boulder when she ran with the Colorado track team and tried to rediscover the old talents. She has alienated a significant portion of the national press with her arrogance.

But nobody said she had to be a lady.

And that early spring noon six years ago, she was just a 19-year-old still unsure if there was a future in running.

She was looking forward to her first summer season in four years. She tugged up her jeans, displaying white scars on the front of each shin. Bilateral faciotomies on each had, finally, relieved the pain that had reduced her to tears, curses and exile.

"People thought I was a head case," she said that snowy day. "It went on so long and shinsplints aren't supposed to go on for years." She couldn't run without pain. Soon, she couldn't run at all.

"One full year, I didn't," she said. "Everyone kept saying I should rest."

That was another problem. She got advice. From everyone. She was a teenager, thrust into the fastest of lanes, with everyone telling her what to do and no real support system.

Montreal and the 1976 Games came and went, and she could only watch.

But after that 1978 campaign, Mary Decker was ready again. "I think I've got at least two good Games in me, agewise," she said. Nobody, then, could foresee the 1980 boycott.

So now, she has one good Games left, one race, one big night.

She has been married, divorced and is planning to remarry early next year. She has defied the experts and exploded back on the world scene, winning world championships at both 1,500 and 3,000 meters in 1983. She has held two world records. Since 1980, she has lost just one time, in the Olympic Trials, running the 1,500 less than 24 hours after she had won the 3,000.

Mary Decker is light-years from the uncertain young woman who looked at a Colorado snow and wondered about herself six years ago.

And now, finally, she is on an Olympic stage, with Zola Budd and Romania's Maricica Pulca there to push her, challenge her. It's almost appropriate she arrives with an aching Achilles. If something wasn't ailing, it might not be Mary Decker.

✦　　　✦　　　✦

Mary Decker did not win the 3,000-meter race. She and Zola Budd collided and Decker was too injured to continue. She said she had been fouled (elbowed). Budd insisted it was an accident. Budd won and was awarded the gold medal, amid some criticism. It was Decker's last Olympics.

August 11, 1984, *Rocky Mountain News*
Knight's team is new standard

LOS ANGELES—The score was 52-27, the United States had the ball in its forecourt and Leon Wood lost it out of bounds.

"Dammit!" shouted the tall man in the red-striped golf shirt. He kicked a towel and a metal folding chair.

I suppose Bobby Knight had to do something just to stay awake. ...

Certainly, here, the second-best team in the tournament was the one seated to Knight's left day after day as his club just outclassed the world to run its Olympic record to 77-1. The one still rankles, just as the absence of the Soviets cast a sort of listless film over this year's tourney.

They would not have won. But the thought of a Soviet team before an American audience on an Olympic floor for the first time since Munich would at least have left something of interest. Knight, the prince errant of basketball circles, was a marvel of deportment. The unofficial count in eight consecutive routs was one technical and two chairs. ...

The ceremonies following Friday's 96-45 victory were almost symbolic of the whole U.S. tradition.

They carried Hank Iba off, an American answer a dozen years later to the ignominy of Munich and his team that had to endure that one defeat. This was a pent-up reward, a dozen years in the delivery. They lifted Bobby Knight to their shoulders, a double ride, the past and the present. ...

DID LEWIS BEAT OWENS, TOO?

LOS ANGELES—The problem now is, do we compare Carl Lewis to Jesse Owens, or do we compare Jesse Owens to Carl Lewis?

Lewis swept a half-century of records aside in the late afternoon shadows here Saturday, anchoring a world-record effort in the men's 4x100 relay to finish off a historic week.

He had set out to duplicate Owens' feat of four gold medals in 1936.

He completed the job with a typical Lewis flourish, the 8.94 split on which he scorched the surface of the Coliseum. That split matched a similar number by Bob Hayes at Tokyo in 1964 as the fastest 100 meters ever in the Olympics.

This time, there was no question. No lingering raised eyebrows at his effort, or boos for lack of it. America and the Olympic crowd and Lewis got all of Lewis here Saturday, every last bit as he leaned into the electronic beam and history.

Fifty years from now, will they make an emotional movie on his life, maybe inspire some kid as Lewis himself says he was inspired by Owens?

Lewis has suffered some here this week.

But in every event, each of them a mirror of Owens' events 48 years ago, he beat Owens' time or distance.

Each of them. Owens ran the 100 in 10.3, Lewis in 9.99. Owens did the 200 in 20.7, Lewis in 20.49. Owens long jumped 26-5 1/4, Lewis 28-0 1/4 on just one jump. Owens' relay crew did 39.8. Lewis' crew set a world record of 37.83.

The numbers are there. The personalities, the times, the mood, the relative futures are so different it will forever be impossible to draw a true measure in human terms. But the numbers argue indisputably for Lewis the athlete.

Not until late did Owens capitalize on his achievements, if he ever can be said to have done so. Lewis already is capitalizing on his. Owens, to some degree, was a historic accident, a hero because of circumstance. Lewis is a millionaire.

Lewis is as programmed for his place on top of the track world as any hard-eyed young corporate executive looking for an office on the top floor. ...

We are comparing a legend 50 years in the building to a new one at its genesis. We are attempting to compare two totally different individuals. It's not fair to either.

"This is not 1936," Lewis said. "The Olympics have gone totally commercial. Everything has opened up to where it's a lot more difficult. More people are there. It's a lot more involved. I think in most cases it's a more difficult situation. I think anyone who compared the two times would agree with that."

He had to wall himself off. Even a year ago, he admitted, he himself didn't think it was possible to duplicate what Owens had done. "Jesse Owens is still the same man to me he was before. He is a legend. I'm just a person."

Legendhood takes time. Lewis has that. He's young, and maybe hasn't even peaked yet. That's frightening to contemplate.

When somebody asked what he felt had happened to his image under this microscopic examination of the past two weeks, he was direct.

"Actually, right now, I don't care." He had come, he said, to win.

"Now that it's over, the joy of my life is over. So if I made 50 cents or $50,000, I don't care. Because I have four gold medals, and that's one thing you'll never take away."

Maybe, though, in California's summer shadows, Lewis freed himself from the one thing Owens never had to face—Owens.

July 1, 1992, *Denver Post*

FOR ONCE, THE UNITED STATES HAS SENT ITS BEST

I don't know. You don't know. Certainly Cuba and Canada and Panama are clueless. So maybe we come to the only conclusion possible:

There is no way anyone in the world is going to stop Dream Team USA short of a mass hostage situation or some really bad food. They are as close to unbeatable as has existed in sports. Best ever?

Maybe ...

You only had to watch a few minutes of the game against Cuba Sunday to realize that nobody has caught up to the NBA. It was one of the greatest 40-minute exhibitions of poetry and power and dazzling brilliance I've ever seen. If I were coaching one of the teams the United States must play, I'd never let 'em look at film, and I would forbid them going to the arena to inspect their destiny in person ...

Please don't enter me among those who think the United States has sent too good a team, that we should somehow feel guilty or apologize for this interstellar group that will go to Barcelona. The rest of the world has sent its best for years. We've sent collegians, with college coaches who never smile, all handpicked from the same stable of NCAA "stars" where the coach, not the player, is the important figure.

For once, at least, we've sent our very best, and it was fun just to see what it looked like on Sunday. Pity them, as one colleague suggests? See if the Cuban baseballers pity the Americans at Mile High Stadium on Saturday. Or if the Austrian downhillers take it easy on some Yank on an unpronounceable hill at the next Winter Olympics.

Nah. Roll it up. Dazzle us with four touch passes in a row, the ball never reaching the floor until it is smashed down into the net at the finish. Thrill us with a club that has any number of notches to which it can turn, on order. Delight us with Michael Jordan passing up his shot to feed Charles Barkley, or four pros moving the ball to get Christian Laettner a layup. Guilt? Shoot treys at the finish. Why should the United States play by a different set of rules from the rest of the world?

No, all Chuck Daly has to do is make certain his math is correct, that he has five men on the floor at any given time. It doesn't matter which five. Frankly, maybe four would be enough. I am waiting for the foreign whining to begin, but we'll probably have to get that in Spain.

This team is so good even the IOC bureaucrats and the officials won't be able to defeat it. ...

❧ ❧ ❧

CHAPTER TEN

PEOPLE

✣   ✣   ✣

I never met a man who didn't like Dick Connor.

He may have been the only opinionated newspaper columnist in history who made no and had no enemies. ...

Dick could criticize a coach in such an honorable, poetic fashion that the coach would call and thank him. When Dick wrote that a team could play better, the athletes knew he was right. If Dick said it was so, it was so. ...

The NFL hierarchy despised Al Davis, the maverick owner. Almost nobody gets along with Davis, and he doesn't care much about outsiders, particularly sportswriters, who he would banish to Devil's Island. But Davis and Connor, who had nourished the AFL, respected one another.

For years Davis was kept from his deserved spot in the Pro Football Hall of Fame, but for years Connor, a member of the nominating committee, fought for Davis' inclusion. Eventually the other members listened to Connor's voice of reason, and Davis was selected in 1991. ...

With the same resolve, Dick labored and lobbied in Denver for the survival of the Golden Gloves program—because he felt it was important for the youth in the minority communities. ...

Dick wasn't a hard-drinking, chain-smoking, loud-talking, ego-worrying, king-making, mean-driving sort, like most in our trade. He was quiet, calm and loyal to his word, his family and his God.

And, on occasion, when the column had finished singing, he would light up a big, foul-smelling cigar and grin because he knew he had told the story.

—Woody Paige, sports columnist, *Denver Post*

He was very knowledgeable about sports, but what made him a good writer was his sense of history. His columns had a poetic, almost literary nature. When he criticized a player or an operation or a team, people really listened because they knew he wasn't just taking the shot of the week.

—Dusty Saunders, *Rocky Mountain News* **TV critic**

He was never a destructive writer. He never tried to tear down institutions or people. I never felt that he would go for the cheap headline or the cheap shot at someone who wasn't doing well. He just never did that. He was a square shooter.

—Gene Amole, *Rocky Mountain News* **columnist**

✣   ✣   ✣

✦   ✦   ✦

Dick genuinely liked people—most people. He didn't suffer fools gladly, but he could forgive most foibles and follies in others because he didn't think he was perfect. He did have an uncanny sixth sense about some. And he would never, never change his mind if he decided someone was truly a phony. He enjoyed meeting and getting to know the famous and powerful in sports, but he also would talk enthusiastically about people he met in airports, hotels, ballparks and at Little League games. He said his favorite columns were the "people" ones. They were the ones he remembered.

<hr>

October 27, 1974, *Denver Post*

JIM LOVED GRUMP ROLE

"May you be in heaven an hour before the devil knows you're dead."

—Old Irish saying

In Jim Graham's case, the devil probably knew right away but hid until he saw the late *Denver Post* sports columnist head the other way. After all, why try to run a nice place if some guy's gonna come in and rip it?

Graham reveled in his reputation as a full-time Scrooge, a grump, an iconoclast in a cotton-candy world of hero worship. He delighted in the art of asking blunt questions.

Remember the time Sonny Liston lost the world's heavyweight title in Maine, resting on a stool between rounds from a punch nobody was quite sure ever landed?

Afterward, reporters jammed into the dressing room, the elite of the so-called name press packed elbow to elbow. And mute. Graham, who covered big fights for the *Post,* was there and looked with disgust at his colleagues.

"All right," he snorted. "I'll ask it. Sonny, were you hit or did you take a dive?"

Three years ago one of the all-time great hitters—and reporter haters—came to Denver as manager of the Washington Senators. Ted Williams grew up in the bitter daily warfare between press and athletes in Boston.

Jim Burris, chief executive of the Denver Bears, set up an interview.

"I warned Ted that I had a onetime Boston writer coming, and it was like waving a red flag," Burris recalled this week after Graham was found dead in a hotel elevator in San Francisco, victim of a heart attack.

Williams eyed Graham warily as a few reporters filed in to meet the baseball great before the exhibition game that summer. Graham glared back.

What follows is close to a verbatim transcript of the way that meeting began.

Graham: "I used to watch you at Fenway Park. I always had the feeling that after you got your one-for-three or two-for-four for the day, you didn't really care what happened the rest of the day."

Williams: mouth agape.

Graham: "And you've got a mistake in your book. You're talking there about what you did at the plate on your first at bat with Boston. I was there that day. That's not the way it happened."

Williams: "I was there, too, and that's the way it was."

Graham: "No. It wasn't."

Williams: "The hell it wasn't, goddammit. I'll bet you."

Says Burris now, chuckling at the memory: "I knew right then that Ted was dead. Graham proved it. After that, the two of them started getting along real well. I think Ted began to appreciate that Jim knew baseball and liked it as Ted did."

They may not have parted friends, but Williams thawed enough to show Graham some of the techniques he used as one of the game's greatest hitters, and the rest of the session was almost pleasant.

When Lou Saban stepped down in 1971, Graham was in the front row at the press conference.

"Did you jump or were you pushed?" he wanted to know.

The first heart attack was last May, in the office, in the morning, and scarcely any of us were even aware of it at the time.

It ruined some of the best Graham anecdotes since he had to go on a rigid diet.

"Breakfast of champions," he'd intone, sitting at his incredibly cluttered desk and shoving enough old releases and mail aside to make room for a Coke, a package of peanut-butter crackers and a candy bar.

Once he came to the office complaining of a bad night. Since he was extremely moderate in his drinking habits, we knew that was not the problem.

"Maybe you've got the flu," somebody suggested. "It's going around."

"Yeah. I was sick all night. And it came on so fast. I felt fine early." Graham enjoyed good food. He had prepared a duckling, with a special sauce, and some wine. It was a fine, but lonely dinner. Most were for this 52-year-old bachelor.

"I was still hungry so I went over to Baskin Robbins."

There, he bought—and ate—a quart of licorice ice cream.

It's funny that these are the things you remember about a man you've worked with and traveled with for nearly a decade. He seldom interviewed so much as he challenged.

A veteran of the European war, he suffered frostbite there and detested cold. He'd arrive in midsummer, sweater on, tie clinched at the neck and shut the office windows.

Yet he loved San Francisco and Candlestick Park, where his favored Giants played. Some of that fun left when Willie Mays did, but the opera remained, as did those lovely hills and the cold Bay breeze.

He was evidently either going out for a walk or returning when the final heart seizure hit last Tuesday night or early Wednesday morning. They found him on an elevator at the Clift Hotel.

Knowing Jim he probably swore at it for being late.

SAYERS—A MAN WITH PERSPECTIVE

"... This is mine tonight. It will be Brian Piccolo's tomorrow ..."

There's still a terrible poignancy to that line, even when you hear it again years later in a darkened pub room under totally different circumstances. Gale Sayers watched it on the screen as segments of "Brian's Song" were replayed at a press luncheon last Wednesday. Occasionally, he'd turn away and take a sip of water.

"That's history," he said of the famous movie depicting his relationship with the dying Chicago Bear runner. "That was a very close relationship and a very important part of my life. I've got a lot of good memories of Brian. I prefer to recall those. Those (nodding his head toward the dead screen) were bad memories."

I've never been able to watch that movie, partly due to circumstances and partly out of choice. Along with a thousand others, I happened to attend the New York Football Writers' dinner at which Sayers was honored as the comeback athlete of the year. He had just enjoyed an outstanding season coming off massive knee surgery.

The speech was short, delivered in a clipped, rapid tempo that still characterizes the onetime kid from Omaha who did so many magic things on Big Eight and NFL fields. Sayers accepted the trophy and, as he said, dedicated it to Piccolo. There wasn't a sound in the Waldorf-Astoria ballroom that night. The normal clink of glassware and incessant coughing were totally absent. Sayers, and the moment, had captured everyone.

There were few dry eyes at the finish, either.

... "I've been out of football six years. It moves me that so many people still remember Gale Sayers. ..."

Sayers has been assistant athletic director at Kansas the past three years, spending "about 80 percent of my time" helping raise funds for the athletic program.

When the knees that had done unbelievable things across all kinds of NFL fields finally signaled enough, he was ready. "I prepared myself to quit. I had gone back, gotten my degree, become a stockbroker, involved myself in other things.

"I wish I could say that 100 percent of the players today do the same. Many feel that football is going to be their life's work, rather than a means to an end, something that eventually is over. Athletes make a great deal of money, but they can invest in some crazy things and lose it."

Sayers didn't. "I lost one time—a couple of thousand. The money I made, I still have most of it. I got good advice." He doesn't envy the salaries paid today. When he came out of Kansas, Kansas City of the AFL and Chicago pursued him. "Kansas City offered me more, but the competition was in Chicago, in the NFL." What he might have done to the AFL of the middle and late 1960s staggers the imagination.

He still regards ex-teammate Dick Butkus as probably the hardest hitter he can remember. "He played that way in practice, too. He made me a better player," he said, then smiled. "I probably made him better, too."

Sayers once danced and dodged to six touchdowns as a rookie against San Francisco. He suffered his first major injury against those same 49ers. But no one game stands out.

"It was just being able to be part of the game. You grew up hearing of Raymond Berry and Johnny Unitas and Jimmy Brown and then to get to play against them ... That was enough for Gale Sayers."

As a Kansas senior, he played at Syracuse against a sophomore named Floyd Little. "That was the day he got five touchdowns against us. I didn't score. They beat us 35-14 and he just went wild. It was one of those kind of days I had against the 49ers, breaking tackles, cutting just right."

Now it's racquetball when he can manage it, although he still has no weight problem. And he has no memory problem.

Evenings such as the one in the Waldorf help put a lot of things in proper perspective.

April 3, 1977, *Denver Post*

ALZADO'S MISSION OF MERCY, COMEBACK TRAIL MEET

"How long does it take to get to Brighton from here?"

Dark streaks of sweat stained the gray T-shirt and shorts Lyle Alzado wore as he walked into the Denver Bronco training room from the racquetball courts across the road.

"Thirty minutes unless it's you driving. Then it's 20," said equipment manager Larry Elliott.

Alzado checked the clock. Twenty minutes later, hair still wet from the shower, he had his Blazer on the interstate heading northeast. "I'm supposed to be there at 1," the defensive tackle said, handing across an envelope. "Here's the details."

More than 100 junior high school students were out there ahead, waiting to hear him. He had spent the morning lifting weights, running, playing racquetball, after starting with a 6:30 a.m. wake-up and an hour sports show on a radio station with defensive safety Bill Thompson.

Now the Blazer fled northeast on the bright, windy afternoon.

Even as a driver, Alzado was intense.

"Hostile," he said when asked how he planned to approach the 1977 season. "I'm going to win that job back," he said, and the car seemed to lurch ahead. His passenger's memory was triggered back to a Tuesday morning about midway through the 1976 season.

The league statistics had just arrived showing the Bronco defense among the league leaders. "I'm at an all-time low," Alzado had said. His leg was encased in a cast and he was using crutches. "They're so good, and I'm not part of it."

Four months later, the cast was gone. So were the crutches. The frustration remained.

"I remember when the draft was—Jan. 24, 1971. It started at 9 a.m. I was in college in Yankton, S.D. I got up at 5 that morning and went over to the athletic director's office and never left. I sat there all day. At 4 that afternoon I was still in

that same chair when the phone rang. It was Lou Saban. He said, 'Lyle, you are now a Bronco.' I was so happy I knocked the projector off a table running out. I broke the door. It was the happiest moment of my life. I was the 79th player taken."

He shifts in the car seat. "I feel as though I've got to win my job back all over again." The dry winter landscape flows past. "I remember when I was a rookie and Pete Duranko got hurt. I moved into the starting lineup."

The thought isn't finished. It didn't have to be. Duranko never got the job back. Alzado moved in and kept it until the opening play of the 1976 season, in Riverfront Stadium in Cincinnati. Somebody fell across his leg. The ligament tore. "I don't even remember how it happened."

He had tried to stay in, managed one more play and that was it. The season was ended for Lyle Alzado. And young Rubin Carter moved into his place and played so well that Alzado, as this particular late winter afternoon began, was now penciled in as a defensive end while Carter remains at nose guard.

"I'll play where they want me, but it's hard moving positions."

If winter plans prevail, Alzado will move back to end, marking the third straight year he has been asked to change positions. It will also mark the third head coach he has played under with Red Miller replacing John Ralston.

"I was in the 'Dirty Dozen,'" he says snorting. "We've been called everything. I don't care. We had to do what we felt was necessary. We just couldn't relate to [Ralston] as a head coach. People told me, 'Get out of town.' Some players didn't like it. Fine. I'm my own man. I stood for what I believed. It was hard to do. To say the least. I knew I was gone if he stayed. I asked Fred [Gehrke, general manager] to try and work out a deal for me."

He turns the Blazer into the school parking lot. Inside, the 6-3, 260-pound frame, leather jacket, the "Rocky" profile, attract immediate attention, especially from the office staff.

"Are you somebody?" a blond-headed youngster asks in some awe.

"I hope so," Alzado answers, grinning. July, August and September will answer it better in the Bronco training camp. In the meantime, there is the room down the hall, and all those faces. Alzado had spent some spare minutes—Elliott's estimate was right—quizzing the teachers about the group he would face. Broken homes? Reading problems? Truancy? Fighting? What's the age spread?

"I know where you're coming from," he begins, tossing the jacket over a chair. "Have any of you knifed a guy?"

He had their attention. There were no hands. There was also no coughing, shuffling, squirming or nudging. "I have. I thought that was the way things were." Spanish Harlem. Brooklyn. Long Island. The streets. "The jail scene, sleeping in the park on your own."

He tells of winning Golden Gloves fights, of bar battles, of Lawrence High School teammates now in jail. "I've never seen them more attentive," a teacher murmurs. Inside the room, Alzado is challenging them in another way: "If you'll raise your grades two levels, say from a D to a B, I'll personally pay for two tickets to a Denver Bronco game for you and a friend."

"Which game?"

"You choose."

"And if the whole class raises their grades that way, I'll charter a bus and bring you to Fort Collins for a day at our camp. But it's got to be two levels, and you've got, what, seven classes? OK. You've got to raise them two levels in either three or four of those classes. I'll let your teachers decide which."

Outside, back in the Blazer, he takes several deep breaths and slumps in the seat. "It's like coming down emotionally after a game. You don't know for a year whether you've done any good. But you've got to be on your toes every second. They've been lied to so much their whole lives, they know when you're tellin' the truth."

(A few minutes earlier, he had asked for questions. None had anything to do with academics. "How's your leg?" "Like new money." "Can you guys beat Oakland?" "I think we can." "Can you beat Pittsburgh?" "Pittsburgh? We always beat Pittsburgh. Pittsburgh who?" Then, turning serious, he challenges again. "There are a lot of things you can do without going to college. That's baloney that you can't be something unless you go to college.")

The road flies past again.

"I've got a lot to learn about the radio," he admits. "This morning I pronounced Bowie Kuhn's name like it was Kahn. Some guy called in and said, 'Hey, if you're gonna be on, learn how to pronounce it.'" Alzado shrugs and smiles.

"Why take these kind of assignments if they drain me like this? I take the time because I need it. I need to do it. I have to pay back the older people who helped me. I like to think those kids needed me today." There was no fee involved. It's not unique. Other Broncos do the same.

Children's Hospital is next. Three young burn cases greet him by name. "Where's your cast?" one asks.

"I got rid of it."

"Good."

He moves through several wards, including one containing leukemia patients. "I never know what to say. What do you say?"

(*"Our nickname was the Golden Tornadoes. Other teams were afraid—literally, they were afraid—to come in to play us. They didn't want to. We'd break 'em up. We won the championship. Now a lot of those guys are in jail. I know one, he was a 9.6 sprinter. He's not doin' nothing. Just layin' back, drinkin' wine and feelin' fine,' he tells me. When I got out, New Mexico State sent me home because of my police record. So did Kilgore Junior College in Texas. My coach finally got Yankton to look at me. I remember when I got off the bus out there, there were about three buildings. I looked around, and the coach came over and said, 'Come on, let's get a couple hamburgers.' I told him, 'Hey, I got no money.' He said, 'I'll buy.' I never wanted to leave that place."*)

He walks into a darkened room containing a youth in traction.

"Whatsa matter?" You don't like smilin'?" The youngster grins. Alzado autographs a picture, chats for a moment, goes back into the corridor. "Good. I got him to laugh."

In the next room, a wide-eyed kid watches him enter. "You with the Nuggets? Oops. Wrong team." This time Alzado laughs.

"You never know what to say," he repeats.

The volunteer chairman with him shakes her head. "You don't have to say anything. Just be there. Look at their eyes. They're this big."

The afternoon wears on. More rooms. More eyes.

There is a meeting later.

And tomorrow, more work on the knee.

July isn't that far off. Almost like a 20-minute drive to Brighton.

December 24, 1977, *Denver Post*

RED MILLER PLAYS DIFFERENT TUNE FOR BRONCOS

He strode through the interview room with a big grin on his face, walking past a number of writers and a waiting television camera. Grabbing a blue pen, he scribbled one word on the board:

"Playoffs."

Then Robert "Red" Miller, 50, laughed the laugh of a happy man.

All fall, as the Denver Broncos worked their way through a backbreaking schedule with all but flawless results, Miller had refused to speculate.

"We'll take them one at a time and see if there is something good at the end," he would say as the record grew from 5-0 to 6-1 to 10-1. Pittsburgh, Cincinnati, St. Louis, Baltimore all lay in their wake, but still Miller wouldn't say it.

Finally came Houston, and Miller raced into the delirious Bronco dressing room, waited for the press, and hollered, "Playoffs! I want to talk playoffs!"

A wait of 17 years, 11 weeks had ended. And ironically, it was Miller who was there in the old days, who finally returned to take the once-hapless Broncos to their first playoff and their first division title.

... And Miller, the son of an Illinois coal miner and grandson of a mule skinner, has parlayed a tough, professional approach and just the right human touches into a rapport with his club that is one of the major reasons for Denver's success this year.

It began almost immediately.

On the practice field at Fort Collins last summer, Miller, who has specialized in line play, got down to demonstrate against 275-pound Claudie Minor. Miller didn't bother to don a helmet, and the ensuing collision left blood streaming down his face.

"Coach," the shocked 6-4 tackle said, "coach, you're bleeding."

"Get down there again," Miller ordered, ignoring the blood that had his huge tackle aghast.

Miller is a man who gets involved, a fact that weighed against his predecessor, John Ralston, whom the players asked to be replaced last winter.

Miller has built a league-wide reputation as an offensive coach, and is given most of the credit for masterminding the New England offense's development the last four years. ...

But Miller also at one time had a self-acknowledged reputation as a man who could raise a little hell on occasion. He wondered if it was a factor in his never getting the No. 1 job he wanted. "I quit drinking about a year and a half ago," he said recently. "I haven't had a thing since."

But he doesn't let that keep him from relaxing. Miller is an accomplished pianist, especially ragtime.

At Denver's rookie show last summer, Miller named No. 1 draft choice Steve Schindler of Boston College and No. 2 choice Rob Lytle of Michigan to head up the program.

"Shouldn't a rookie coach be in the rookie show, too?" one asked.

Miller laughed. "Get a piano and the rookie head coach will be there." He was, and wowed them.

The feeling of mutual respect grew. Although the players had become disenchanted with Ralston, most of them had been brought into the organization by him, and Miller was quick to acknowledge this when he was named last Feb. 1.

... But none [of the new players] has had quite the total impact of the red-thatched native of Macomb, Ill., and standout guard from Western Illinois where he was named MVP for three straight years. He went on to six years of prep and college coaching before joining Lou Saban's first staff with the old Boston Patriots in 1960.

The apprenticeship was under way.

The onetime Denver guard, Bob McCullough, remembers Miller as an intense student even in the early years. "He's very innovative. Even back then, he'd hand-splice game films himself so we could see a series of the same play in different games. A lot of coaches will tell you whom to block on a certain play. It looks good on the blackboard, but when 22 people start moving out there, some blocks are impossible.

"I've seen Red on the practice field work for hours running through every lineman's assignment to make certain each block is possible. If it isn't, he'd change it. He won't ask the players to do anything he feels can't be done."

But he'll also demand every ounce of energy to accomplish something he feels is possible. ...

Miller has emotions to match his red hair. In Baltimore a year ago, New England won its final game, and Miller came running through the press box from the coaches' booth, shouting, "Where's the Sack Pack now?"

He ran on the field to protest a decision in Kansas City earlier this season, risking a penalty that could have hurt his club. Players cautioned him another time. "I know I've got to control that," he admits.

But it's hard. "My dad mined coal in Illinois. I helped in the summer. We had 10 children in the family. I was the second youngest. The food started up on the side of the table with the breadwinners. Then it was passed along according to age. Sometimes, there wasn't a lot left by the time it reached our end. Maybe that's why I'm hungry," he said.

His German-Scots-English bloodlines have produced a tough but compassionate man who isn't afraid to jump off the golf cart he uses to ride to various units during practice and show a 280-pound tackle how he wants it done. ...

"If Red had a uniform in his locker and it was legal, he'd play," insists Denver's Lyle Alzado. "He's done more for this team than anybody who's ever been here. It's amazing. He demands respect as a coach and he's also your friend. I don't know how he does it."

... But he's a lousy travel agent.

In Cincinnati, where Denver had just won its sixth straight, Miller lingered long after everyone else, finishing some interviews. When he got out to the curb, the team buses had left for the airport. The players relished an impromptu court when Miller finally made the plane.

But he wasn't through. The night Denver returned from Houston, where it had beaten the Oilers, then learned on the way home that Oakland's loss at Los Angeles had ushered Denver into the AFC West title, Miller enjoyed the celebration.

Then he walked through the lot to his car, turned the key, and nothing.

"It was dead," he recalled. "I hitchhiked a ride home with some fans."

They may send a limousine to take him to the stadium for the playoff.

Just in case.

December 10, 1978, *Denver Post*
LOVE STORY TOO SHORT FOR LEN, JACKIE DAWSON

This is a love story. It would be nice to say it has a happy ending, and in some ways, it does. It just ends too soon, for me, but you'll have to judge for yourself.

The fact the Kansas City Chiefs are in town for a big game makes it all the more poignant, which is not an emotion you normally use in terms of football. Bear with me a few paragraphs. They are necessary for what comes later.

No team, not even the Oakland Raiders, has so tormented Denver over the years. The wins over Oakland may have propelled Denver to the top the past two seasons, but it was the losses to Kansas City year after year that typified what Denver used to be. Awful.

It was 56-10 or 52-9, Mike Garrett, Otis Taylor, and there was Hank Stram, ordering his huge legions to onside kick, get another couple scores.

Denver fans hated them. They hated the Chiefs. And they hated—and if truth were known, probably secretly admired and wished they had—the architect of all those victories, the Kansas City quarterback, Len Dawson.

He was what Denver didn't have—the icy, poised field general, the total quarterback, with all the weapons at his disposal and absolute knowledge of how and when to use them.

Then the team faded, and Dawson faded. He had taken them to the heights in New Orleans in January 1970, defeating Minnesota in the fourth Super Bowl. It was a horrible week. His name was brought up in a gambling investigation by an eastern politician. It was unjust, unconscionable and never used again.

But it made a terrible week for Dawson, and for his wife, Jackie, and their children Lisa and Len Jr. The Dawsons had met in high school in Ohio, married in their sophomore year at Purdue and suffered through five years of neglect at the start of his pro career.

Jackie had encouraged him, even when Pittsburgh let him languish and his athletic gifts rusted. When Hank Stram got him in 1962, "he didn't even have a good spiral on the ball," Stram once recalled.

But it came rushing back with some patience, and he won championships and finally stood there on a small platform in New Orleans, arm around young Lenny, who looked up in near adoration as his dad talked to President Nixon by phone.

It was total exoneration.

And Jackie felt it was also time. "Quit. Quit now, quit on top," she urged. Len didn't. But by 1975, after Kansas City had worked its way through 16 right guards, he finally retired, moving over to radio and television chores he had performed for several years on the side.

Life was quieter in the Dawson household, less hectic than when stadium fans booed Jackie's husband, threw things at him and politicians tried to get themselves elected by smearing his name.

Then came 1976, and in the spring for some reason Jackie noticed occasionally that her right hand couldn't hold things firmly. A fork or a glass would slip.

So she went to the hospital for an exam, and suffered a stroke in the hospital.

The Dawsons' marriage had endured many crises but this was the biggest. There was some paralysis, some speech impairment. Most of all, there was a drastic adjustment in roles.

Len Dawson, all-pro quarterback, now became a tender and loving homemaker. He plunged into it with the same dedication and intensity that had marked him as a player.

"I couldn't boil water, I couldn't make tea," he once admitted of his culinary shortcomings.

Soon, he was comparison shopping, the kitchen was filled with gourmet cookbooks—he bought something resembling a music stand to hold them while he worked and studied—and he was proud of it. So was Jackie.

"I didn't look at the sports page first thing in the morning. I looked at the grocery ads," Dawson would say, smiling. The man who could freeze 270-pound tackles with a baleful stare in the huddle after a missed block now held forth on where to buy the best vegetables. He may once have been vaguely aware that a tomato was somehow involved in spaghetti sauce and Bloody Marys, but he now could tell dinner guests where to buy the juiciest tomatoes in town.

He tried, as unobtrusively as possible, to keep life's normal rhythms intact. He still worked in electronic journalism, traveling to weekend games for NBC, to New York in midweek to tape an NFL highlight film, some Kansas City radio work.

And he still went to Arrowhead Stadium to work out, but only at special times. "Today's the day I take Jackie to the hairdresser," he would tell a caller. It was not said in a resentful tone. Just matter of fact.

He would encourage, prod, make certain she got to the doctor, to rehabilitation sessions, and Jackie improved—to a point. "She has plateaued a little," he said not long ago. It discouraged her, but Len kept working at it.

He would talk with her, and they went out to dinner with friends. When he caught her favoring her left hand, he'd gently chide: "Jacqueline ..." and she'd sigh and switch to her right.

"He was her coach, just as she'd been his coach back in the days when his career was going bad in Pittsburgh and she encouraged him," a friend said.

"Boy, he's a slave driver," Jackie told friends one evening. "I woke up this morning and didn't feel like doing some exercises and he actually got mad at me. Can you imagine that? He got mad at me. I remember, in the early years, I'd get mad at him and encourage him when he'd get down."

Len was fixing breakfast for the two of them Thursday morning, waiting for Jackie to come downstairs from her shower. Gradually, it occurred to him she was taking longer than usual, and he went to check.

He found Jackie, 42, in the bathroom. How she died, nobody is certain. She may have suffered another stroke, or simply slipped and fell.

I just thought you'd like to know what it was like for Len and Jackie Dawson, and maybe say an extra prayer for each this morning.

November 8, 1981, *Denver Post*

HARAWAY HANGS 'EM UP
AFTER 44 YEARS WITH THE *POST*

Naw, Haraway. You don't get away that easily. You can't just slip off into retirement after 44 years with nary a word of mention.

You've traced and chronicled the growth of sports in this town since the days your dad bought a $100 season box at old Merchants Park and sawed off the entrance so your wheelchair would slide through. You've seen Bears Stadium grow out of an old city dump, then keep growing into 75,000-seat Mile High Stadium. You watched as the University of Denver football team flowered and then withered and died, and as Colorado moved up and into the Big Eight.

You have conducted a shameless love affair with every sport you've ever covered or watched, and you've inspired more of us than you'll ever know or dream of, just watching you function.

"Scribe." It has always seemed to be your favorite self-description. Nothing fancy. But accurate. A recorder. A viewer and observer and recorder, and one of the most memorable men I've met. And, dammit, I'm going to miss you and your damn crutches and your big, toothy grin and an outlook on life that life really doesn't deserve.

"I'm a fan who gets paid for doing what I'd pay to watch anyway," you once said. I believe it. Now, when *Denver Post* readers pick up Monday's edition, they'll be reading a sports section without Frank Haraway in it for the first time since June 27, 1938.

Not that you'll be absent from the city's press boxes, of course. You'll still string for *Sports Illustrated* and *The Sporting News,* and score for the Bears, and keep statistics for the Broncos and Nuggets. So it's not as if you'll disappear from the scene.

It's just that I won't have to try to keep pace with you and those jet-assisted crutches that you use so unfairly. I still remember the afternoon I tried to keep up as we both headed across downtown to a press conference and wound up a badly beaten second.

For those who might not have met you, maybe a couple of biographical notes would help. Your 44 years here mean you've been part of this paper for more than half its life and two-thirds of yours. You covered 4,285 Denver Bears baseball games—and had the box scores stored in file drawers to prove it. You covered the University of Colorado for 25 of those 44 years, and one of your great lines came in the 1960s when you wrote of a game in which the Buffaloes had fumbled away any winning chance, "The Blundering Herd."

Readers should also know you then worried about that lead for days, afraid it was unfair.

Haraway, you see, came from a different time, and maybe four years in bed and another four confined to a wheelchair with tuberculosis of the hips that left his legs paralyzed gave him a different perspective. Just moving and working were a joy. As a kid, he played baseball in a wheelchair—and hid the bruises on his legs when he couldn't get them out of the way of a ball. Haraway just refused to accept physical limitations. He used to keep two wheelchairs, "in case one got a broken spring" while quarterbacking the neighborhood football team. "God, it's a wonder I'm still alive," Haraway told a fellow worker once during a recital of all the things he did despite those balky legs. He held the state table tennis championship three times.

"But the point is, I'm sure my interest in sports had a lot to do with me getting over the illnesses of youth and getting to where I was able to lead a normal life with the minor exception of the crutches."

Haraway could do awesome things with them or in spite of them. Once, when they were starting to tear down the old DU Stadium, he was driving past it when he was struck with a wave of nostalgia. It was late, but he got out, and climbed all 87 rows to the top. There were another 13 steps leading to the press box on top of the west side. Frank climbed those, too, then sat there, all alone in the growing dusk, and thought of the games he'd seen in this stadium. "I sat there and started to cry, all by myself," he said. That's vintage Haraway.

Haraway loves life, and his role in it, and if all this sounds too good to be true, believe it. It's Haraway. We could probably never assign him to some rip-and-tear type of story. He's too much what Will Rogers said: "I never met a man I didn't like." I doubt Haraway ever has met somebody about whom he couldn't quickly find some good points to write about.

So, Frank Haraway, your final byline is atop a University of Denver hockey report in Sunday's papers.

Forty-four years are a long time to be doing anything. To have done it as well is remarkable.

For a two-wheelchair guy in a one-wheelchair world, Scribe, you did a helluva job.

November 15, 1981, *Denver Post*

BRONCOS JOE COLLIER SELDOM HAS TO DEFEND HIS CALLS

It's simple. He just paces like a caged bear for some three hours every Sunday afternoon—or Monday night—has little 5x7 note cards tucked into his waistband, and pretends he's a computer.

Most of the time, he is.

One national writer, in fact, recently nominated Denver Broncos defensive coordinator Joe Collier as the NFL coach of the year. Not a bad thought. His players view him almost in awe.

His wife, Shirley, like most football wives, becomes a virtual widow from July until January—February once, in 1978. His son, Joe, has literally grown up with the Broncos, working more training camps than most players ever survive, and now finishing a good career at Heritage High while still working the Denver bench on home games. The senior Collier, meanwhile, just goes through life with the bland appearance of a country parson—and the competitive disposition of a street thug. Collier was one of Northwestern's top athletes, and still is a ferocious presence on the racquetball court.

He is a football anomaly, having outlasted three head coaches while keeping his own post and even enhancing it. His reputation seems to grow by the season. He now has spent 13 of them in the Mile High City, watching Lou Saban, then John Ralston, then Red Miller come and go. Collier just goes on.

Today, you'll recognize him easily. He'll be the only Denver Broncos coach on the sideline wearing an orange baseball cap. That's for quicker visual search-and-find help for Randy Gradishar, the linebacker who takes Collier's wigwag signals and translates them into fronts, stunts, blitzes and coverages for his teammates.

They have a common reputation: Each is widely regarded as the best there is at his particular job. Denver, under Collier, has constructed—make that reconstructed—the NFL's best defense.

"He's a genius." I'd quote the player who said it, but that would require listing some 18 defensive players. Or maybe 45, to include the offense, too. Or even 55, to take in the other coaches.

Dan Reeves, the fourth head coach Collier has worked for here, still says the smartest thing he's done so far is to have kept Collier and his defensive staff intact last spring, when Reeves took over. Now, Reeves often doesn't even bother to watch when his defenders are on the field, trusting the whole operation to Collier and Co., while he, Reeves, searches out quarterbacks and receivers and linemen for counseling.

Collier, if anyone uses the word genius in his presence, just gets that shoulder-shaking, eye-squinting laugh like Pluto in the cartoons. No noise, just the outward signs. The whole proposition, Collier would say, is preposterous. Then he'll isolate himself with another roll of film and probably find something else that will come popping back into his computer brain during the height of the action to prove the word is, too, true. Against Minnesota, for instance, Collier had Perry Smith positioned perfectly to hurl the Vikings' last running play back just enough to make sure a potential field goal try was short.

Against Detroit, he had called a defense that sent defenders wide just when Billy Sims headed that way. Another snuff, another win, another correct guess by this man whom many regard as the league's top defensive strategist.

When he first came to Denver in the late 1960s, he helped assemble a team noted for its fierce pass rush. Then, in the mid-1970s, it was the linebacking. Denver became one of the first to perfect and polish the 3-4 defense in the modern era.

Now, it's situation defenses, complexity, sophistication.

And it's Collier in his orange baseball cap, wigwagging. "We didn't use to signal at all," he says. "In the old days, the middle linebacker called the signals. I never did at Boston, or Buffalo, or even here when I first came to Denver. Fred Forsberg was calling them. Teams didn't have the variety they show on offense now, didn't use the three receivers as much, motion wasn't a big thing. It just wasn't as difficult in the secondary. So things were simpler to call."

No more. But some things never change. "The championship teams are the ones that score 20 points and hold on. I played a whole career with a team [Buffalo] that scored 25 or 30 points and lost." That's O. J. Simpson. In all his great years, he played in only one—that's one—playoff game. Buffalo lost 32-14 to Pittsburgh in 1974.

Joe Collier has spent the past decade constructing a defense and a style that has permitted a Jon Keyworth, a Dave Preston, an Otis Armstrong, a Rob Lytle, a Larry Canada, a Jim Jensen and now a Rick Parros and a Tony Reed, all of them, a *chance* at a playoff or more.

None of them will wind up with a bust in the Hall of Fame in Canton, Ohio. That's no disgrace. Thousands of their contemporaries won't, either. But O. J. will. Yet he will never have made it to the final game.

Denver's defense has. It may again. And Collier will be the brain behind the scene, the one under that orange cap, behind those glasses.

So, listen: "I don't remember what year we started calling signals from the sideline. It just got to be where it was a little too much of a burden to train the guy each week. Remember Ray May? (For those who don't, May came from the championship Baltimore Colts, and taught Denver defenders to hold hands in the huddle.) We were signaling by then. I remember that because I discovered Ray was blind as a bat. He didn't tell me. He couldn't see me, let alone the signals, yet he never said a word to me that he couldn't see. He kept squinting, waving to repeat the signal." That gave Collier his first hint.

His shoulders shake and the eyes squint at the memory. Or at recalling how onetime cornerback Calvin Jones tipped off whether it would be zone or man coverage by the way he lined up. "We went two games before somebody from another team leaked it to us."

Shake. Squint. Silent laughter.

"We blow some, you know. Sometimes I signal wrong and sometimes Randy reads them wrong. Of 1,000 plays a year, we may blow 50."

Why do geniuses—geniusi?—remember failures, rather than triumphs? I don't know, either.

January 8, 1984, *Rocky Mountain News*

WITHOUT PHIPPS—NO BRONCOS

The year was 1965, and the Denver Broncos were within hours of becoming the Atlanta Broncos.

"It never came quite to that, although we got close," former Denver Bronco owner Gerald Phipps admitted once. "The closest was in 1965. If the gentleman from Atlanta hadn't been the kind of guy he was, and had been willing to buy 52 percent, which he could have done, they were willing to sell, he could have just come in and taken over the operation and moved it.

"Fortunately, he took the position he wouldn't buy 52 percent from the voting trust while Allan and I had 42 percent and were thoroughly unhappy with the deal.

"He said, 'Unless I can get yours, too, I won't buy.' It was the day after that that we closed the deal with the voting trust (which then controlled the club and was desperately trying to get out from under crushing debts) and got control of the thing. His name was J. Leonard Reinsch. He was president of Cox Broadcasting Co. Later that year the AFL awarded a franchise to him in Atlanta and the NFL came in and took it away."

I found the notes of this conversation tucked back in a drawer, yellowing, but still very much alive in the fabric of the local NFL franchise. It comes up because Gerald and Allan Phipps are to be honored as Citizens of the West at the Brown Palace Monday night, and because they each richly deserve it.

... Many of us have come lately to this wonderland of smog and creative snow removal. The Phippses were born to it, bred to it, raised in it, hooked on it. They are bone-deep westerners, despite eastern educations and national business ties and the rest. They embrace the whole thing with a genuine love.

They are vestiges of a vanishing breed, the paternalistic owners in pro sports.

"I miss the trips," Gerry was saying last summer at Mile High. He and Janet used to occupy the front seats, left, on United 5085, the traditional charter the club used to take. When Gerry and Janet flew 5085, Allan and Clara took a commercial flight. Then they'd swap. The couples rarely made the same plane.

If you had missed the game, you had only to inspect the faces in front row left boarding the plane afterward to know how it came out. Normally, in those years, it was bad.

"There was a crisis almost every day," Gerry recalls. None were small.

Yet they kept the Broncos here, and helped Denver maintain what was the most tenuous of fingerholds on major-league membership.

Without them, there would be no Broncos. There would be no 75,000-seat Mile High Stadium, and the lure it represents for major-league baseball. There would be, perhaps, no Nuggets, since they are housed in a 17,000-seat arena that most likely would not have been approved without the emotional voting surge inspired by the stadium bond defeat in 1967.

The Phippses kept breath faintly visible on the glass until the patient rallied. Without them, and what they managed to do, we would be an Indianapolis, civic nose pressed to somebody's pane, hoping.

They got the club for a relative song in that 1965 deal, and sold it for 30 times more when Edgar Kaiser arrived 16 winters later. But there was no guarantee of such success those frosty days before the NFL and AFL merged. It teetered on the brink of vanishing.

They did well. And because of them, so did the Denver sporting public.

May 1, 1987, *Rocky Mountain News*

Joy "TJ" brought to Broncos

will be missing next season

Tom Jackson is gone, and he turned out the lights on Camelot behind him yesterday. They won't be rekindled, not quite the same way, not again.

Jackson wore a dark gray suit, white shirt and one of those sincere ties. Yesterday, at Bronco headquarters, the 36-year-old linebacker could have been selling corporate bonds instead of announcing his retirement.

Fourteen years ago, on a smoggy summer night, it was a gray T-shirt, shorts and shower clogs. It was 2 o'clock on an early Sunday morning, the first weekend rookies had been allowed to leave training camp at Cal Poly in Pomona, Calif., like the first pass at boot camp.

Jackson and another rookie had passed. They spent the night playing pool instead in one of the dormitory recreation rooms. "I don't know if I had enough money to leave campus that weekend, anyway," he admitted yesterday. "Besides, it meant going to this bar and trying to drink with Charley Johnson. I decided I would be better off trying to sharpen my game."

Even then, Tom Jackson had the basic smarts.

He has come a long way from Cleveland and Louisville and that deserted campus in California, and yet, in other ways, he has never left. The joy of Jackson the rookie lingered with Jackson the veteran.

There is more sophistication now, layers of polish applied by two Super Bowls and three Pro Bowls and all those locker rooms where TJ became the man the media sought for quotes.

He can stand in front of a room full of cameras and television lights and remote units and comfortably trade quips and smile and deliver the great one-liners.

Miss him? Denver won't know until he isn't there on Sunday next year, until his name and analyses aren't there in the paper next morning, until he isn't on the sideline and something irreplaceable is missing as well.

Jackson did well yesterday afternoon. He didn't cloud, never choked up. It was his coach who broke.

In the back of the crowded amphitheater, it was linebacker coach Myrel Moore who had the bubbly eyes and raspy voice. Those who would characterize pro ball as a heartless thing needed yesterday for a glimpse of the other side.

"Yeah, I tried to talk him out of it," Moore conceded. "It was strictly selfish."

Moore came to Denver with the John Ralston staff in 1972, and Jackson arrived the next year. With the exception of three years, they have been together since. That's a lifetime in the pros.

Now, Moore has seen four of those "lifetimes" end, and his eyes glistened and reflected the TV lights in the front of the room.

Jackson. Rizzo. Swenson. Gradishar. They should go up on the ring of fame as an entry, not one by one.

From 1975 until age or injury began to whittle at this group, Moore had a quartet unmatched in the league. He knew it then. He knows it now. And he knows it was a special time, a special unit, not to be duplicated.

All except Rizzo made it to the Pro Bowl, and a case could have been made for the Merchant Marine Academy graduate.

Rizzo was the computer heart. Gradishar the analyst. Swenson delivered the big plays. Each was vital, and as a unit, they gave the Broncos Orange Crush its personality. But it was Jackson who furnished the passion, the flair, the sheer exuberance that enveloped them all, and made those years special ones for Denver—and for them.

"Yeah," Moore murmured, choking back more tears. "Just use those words. Exactly. You don't need their names. Big play. Analyst. Computer. Passion. Yeah. That's them. Good. Print that."

It was Jackson, that golden afternoon in Oakland en route to the Super Bowl in 1977, Denver at last beating the hated Raiders, who ran to the sideline and shook his fist at John Madden and defied all the ghosts Denver had exorcised that day:

"It's all over, fat man!" he shouted. Six weeks later, in Denver, his team 9-1, Jackson became the all-pro Moore had expected.

"It was against Baltimore. We were both 9-1, best records in football. It was a big game," and the Colts' Bert Jones was passing Denver silly.

"He had them up over midfield, and if they score, they win."

He was dinking in front of Jackson, short, stabbing little passes like banderillas in bullfighting, weakening the muscle to set up the kill.

"TJ'd been flirtin' with Jones all day, baitin' him. Jones had thrown three or four right in front of him. Big plays. Finally, on the drive, Baltimore goes back in the huddle and comes back out.

"They are going to throw the exact same pass. TJ sensed it. He got a jump on it and intercepted and went 65 yards. (Actually, it was 73.) The ball game was history."

And Denver's Orange Crush was on its way into legend country.

"That's the time he knew he was a pro and knew he was an all-pro."

And now he's a civilian.

"After this?" he said yesterday. "I'm probably going to go somewhere and have a drink."

Scotch and tears in private, with 14 years of replays sliding just inside the eyelids, is not a bad way to end it.

May 3, 1988, *Rocky Mountain News*

MANTLE'S TIME WENT BY TOO FAST

SALISBURY, N.C.—He sits at a table that has been hurriedly dragged from some storeroom and placed in the warm afternoon sunlight.

A folding chair is discovered and set behind the table.

"The line will be formed in this direction," a man shouts, waving order into a formless throng of a couple hundred people, each clutching a baseball or card or old picture. Many are youngsters, not fully aware of who it is sitting at that chair behind that table.

"Their daddies knew about me when they were 14, 15 years old. I guess that's it," he says. "It's flattering they would even still want my autograph."

When did Mickey Mantle get wrinkles on the back of his neck? Did his Yankee uniform always pooch like that around the waist?

"I can't remember a crowd like this," the security man directing traffic said. "We got no places left to park."

Soon, there are 4,500 packed into the picturesque little stadium down on the corner of the Catawba College campus. Hundred-foot pine trees form a dark green hitter's background around the outfield fence.

Mickey Mantle, Catfish Hunter and Willie Mays are advertised. So are Bob Costas and Paul Maguire of NBC. Costas is the 1988 sportscaster of the year, and this is his production, this exhibition game between his all-star Senators and the Catawba team. It is part of the annual National Sportscasters and Sportswriters awards program.

Catfish and Willie are no-shows, but Mantle flew in, kept his promise.

"I came because Costas and I are good friends," Mantle says, signing yet another baseball. "To Brandon," he writes. "To Matt," he scribbles on the next one.

When did Mickey Mantle get gray?

There are more people waiting for Mickey Mantle's signature at this little folding table far down the right field line than are watching Costas and his NBC all-stars warm up.

"Does it feel good to have those pinstripes on again?" a fan asks. Mantle signs and shrugs.

"They don't fit. It's kind of embarrassing."

When did Mickey Mantle become 56? Isn't there a law against it? If not, shouldn't we consider passing one? Mickey Mantle should always have the warm sun draped over those broad shoulders. He should be fixed permanently in the summer, like the Fourth of July and green grass.

"Naw, I won't play. I won't even take batting practice," he says. "I don't even go to old-timer games. It's all I can do anymore just to play a round of golf because of my knees."

When did Mickey Mantle develop that slow, limping walk? Pass that law. Quickly. I want to remember Mantle, hitting left-handed, and nobody could throw him out.

And now you're trying to tell me this is Mickey Mantle? He is 56? And he has farmer's wrinkles deep as some arroyo creasing the back of his neck? And he limps as he walks out to wave his cap during the introductions?

That's Mickey Mantle?

"When I was 24, 25, I thought it would last forever," he says, signing. "I thought it would never end." Another baseball is thrust across the table. "I was over the hill at 32. I played until I was 36, but the last four years weren't very good," the Yankee legend says.

"It was partly my head," he admits. "I didn't believe I had to take care of myself. The guys who took good care of themselves are the ones you see up in the statistics. But I'm not one of the old-timers who thinks the new guys aren't as good as us. They are."

He talks of free agency, of the decline of the Yankee dynasty, of making $32,000 the year he won batting's triple crown. He doesn't like four-hour games, and liked it better when you could identify players with teams—Musial meant the Cardinals, Williams meant the Red Sox, DiMaggio meant the Yankees. Or Mantle did. "Even with free agency, I think I'd still want to be a Yankee. But I'd go knock on George Steinbrenner's door, and when he opened it, I'd say, 'Hi Partner.'" Old joke, Mantle smiles.

"Basketball players soon will average $900,000," he is told.

"Average? That's more than I made in 18 years."

When did Mickey Mantle get old?

July 1, 1989, *Denver Post*
GEHRIG'S MEMORY TRANSCENDS 50 YEARS

He never denied his fate, nor did he ever even begrudge it.

"I'm not a headline guy," Lou Gehrig said one day in 1927. "I know that as long as I was following Babe Ruth to the plate I could have stood on my head and no one would have known the difference."

That year, Gehrig led the American League with 175 runs batted in—and Ruth hit 60 home runs. There was always this shadow quality to Lou Gehrig, the brilliance of the man and his career subdued by something else, or someone else.

In 1932, he became the first major leaguer in the 20th century to hit four home runs in one game. He got second billing on the next day's sports pages—to John McGraw of the Giants, who picked that particular day to retire.

Can it really be 50 years this Tuesday since Gehrig, 36, wiping his eyes, stood at home plate in Yankee Stadium and begged off the rest of his career?

"Today ... I consider myself ... the luckiest man ... on the face of the earth," he said in that halting, emotional farewell to the game, the fans, the world and maybe himself.

Almost 40 years later, his wife, Eleanor, said of her husband: "I had the best of it. I would not have traded two minutes of my life with that man for 40 years with another."

Everyone grows up with sports heroes, mystical, mythical even. Mine for some reason was Gehrig even though Iowa City, Iowa, was light-years from Yankee Stadium and I never saw the man play. Ruth was beyond any imagination, a godlike figure, somebody off baseball's misty Mt. Olympus, to be worshipped but not imitated. For some reason, Gehrig didn't create that aura. He was human. He dramatized what a mere mortal could do if he really worked at it. He was as dependable as tomorrow's sunrise.

You could look at Gehrig on the old black and white newsreel films on Saturday afternoon and think, "If I work hard, maybe." Gehrig inspired that. Ruth just inspired awe.

You figured Gehrig would last forever. He almost did. In some ways, he still is.

And then came July 4, 1939, and Gehrig, hitting .143 in just eight games to that point, told everybody goodbye. Two years later, just shy of his 38th birthday, he was dead. And you got up early the next day, peeked through the east window, just to make sure there had, indeed, been a sunrise that day, and the world had decided to go on as usual.

Fifty years later, I stare at sports pages filled with greed and corruption and accusations, and I wonder: How would Gehrig fit into today's baseball picture?

The year Ruth hit 60, the Babe also earned $70,000. Gehrig drove in 175 runs, had a league high 52 doubles and 47 homers of his own, and did it for $7,500, and smiled that deep, dimpled smile and never threatened to hold out or refuse to report the next spring.

What would he think, sitting in a modern clubhouse, staring at some teammates these days? What would Lou Gehrig bring on today's free agent market? Is there that much money in the Western world? He played every day. He played with flu and headaches and broken fingers and personal problems and worries. (There is no record he ever played with a pulled hamstring, however. I have this personal theory that old-time athletes did not have hamstrings. Hamstrings were invented about the time agents were invented.)

Then it began. Walking with Eleanor, he would stumble on curbs. He couldn't open a catsup bottle on a train, the man they knew as the Iron Horse, and Bill Dickey, across the table, had to look away, glance out the window. Joe DiMaggio, young and fresh and emerging, remembered standing to one side, watching in dismay as Gehrig missed 19 straight pitches at batting practice in spring training in 1939.

In the locker room, struggling to pull on his pants, he fell and had trouble getting back up.

It was called amyotrophic lateral sclerosis, and 13 Americans a day are diagnosed with the disease now named for Gehrig. A group of nerve cells and pathways in the brain and spinal cord degenerate, progressively paralyzing muscles. Eventually, the brain is left, staring out of a body that no longer works.

Gehrig took himself out of the lineup for the first time in 2,130 games on May 2, 1939, and then he walked slowly to the plate and the microphones at Yankee Stadium some two months later and officially said goodbye.

Nobody will ever top that streak. It is as unreachable as Joe DiMaggio's hitting streak of 56 straight. The circumstances of the game deny it now.

While you watch the fireworks Tuesday, or open a beer or spread the picnic blanket, think just a moment of that July 4 a half century ago, and the final appearance of Lou Gehrig at Yankee Stadium. And then think of George Steinbrenner and Wade Boggs.

Put things in perspective for yourself.

♦ ♦ ♦

Bob Martin was probably Dick's closest friend. The two Irishmen respected and admired each other's work, humor and ethics. For almost 10 years, beginning in 1976, they collaborated in making about 20 half-hour feature films for television.

People Productions was sponsored by Public Service Co. of Colorado and produced films on subjects ranging from the Children's Hospital Neonatal Ward to the Denver Symphony. Only a few were about sports.

In some respects, Bob and Dick's friendship was an unlikely one. Dick was from a big family, Bob an only child. Dick was a lifelong Roman Catholic. Bob said he forgot which religion it was he was supposed to belong to. If anything, Bob said, he was an agnostic. Dick was a registered Democrat, Bob definitely was not.

Surprisingly, they could talk religion, politics, sports or history and respect the other's viewpoint—perhaps because they were both avid readers and could back up their opinions with facts.

Dick was at the hospital with Bob's wife, Bev, the day Bob died, Feb. 25, 1990. Ironically, Dick probably already had the liver cancer that would take him a little less than three years later.

Dick wrote about Bob—other than brief mentions—three times. The first was when Martin celebrated 25 years as the Voice of the Denver Broncos, the second was an obituary and the third was when Bob was honored at Salisbury, N.C., during a sportscasters and sportswriters awards ceremony in 1990.

August 31, 1989, *Denver Post*

MARTIN CELEBRATES 25 YEARS
AS VOICE OF DENVER BRONCOS

He doesn't drink. That's one of Bob Martin's failings. No wine, no beer, no hard stuff. He has traveled through some of Europe's great wine country sipping Coca-Cola or mineral water.

"I just don't like the taste, " he told me once. I think he mentioned it while he was ordering wine for the table. He happened to know more about it than any of the rest of us, but that's nothing new. It's just one more of the surprises draping the 6-5 frame of Colorado's predominant broadcaster.

We have guys at the *Denver Post* covering cops who have never committed a crime, so I guess Martin ordering wine doesn't require he also drink the stuff.

He also rarely forgets. Anything. A name. A place. A date. A fact. It's a disgusting habit for any friend to have. I will get an occasional note or verbal nick for some misplaced grammar. Ah, well. Having Martin in your social circle is like having one of those disgusting neighbors who can fix anything, who are constantly turning their lawn into a living entry blank for House and Garden contests, and who never—ever—have a leaky faucet.

But there, I've got him. I have actually fixed a leaky faucet. My wife had to identify it, true, but I fixed it. Martin? Never. He will coldly criticize a dish in a restaurant, or dispassionately observe that the bow work of the principal fiddler seemed a bit off at the concert. But once past opening the door and turning lights on and off, he is helpless about the house. He once gave his wife, Bev, a power saw for Christmas. Bev is the handyman in that family.

The seeming aloof manner also masks one of Denver's most acute senses of humor. You must listen carefully at times in order not to miss it. His is a stiletto wit, not the broadsword that seems to mark the efforts of too many these days.

So, how has a guy with all these faults lasted 25 years as the official and unquestioned—for that matter, never even challenged—Voice of the Denver Broncos?

He is undoubtedly one of the most professional professionals I've encountered in this business. He comes prepared, helped by what can only be a near-photographic memory. It allows him to swallow a roster whole and spit it back out at all the appropriate times.

In all our years together, I've known him to lose his cool just once.

"The Broncos are going to the Super Bowl!" he screamed in disbelief that magical New Year's afternoon in 1978. "The Broncos are going to the Super Bowl!" For a guy who had waited as long as Martin, maintaining the annual Death Watch, it was more than excusable. Miracles should be treated with emotion.

Once, some years ago, we had a small television production company and turned out three or four half-hour documentaries each year. It was fun, a nice change of pace for us. We'd select some topic, usually nonsports, and share production chores with Russ Rayburn, a onetime KOA-TV cameraman who now has his own business. I'd write the script. Russ would film it. Martin would narrate with that one-of-a-kind delivery. We'd rent a sound studio.

"Amazing," I remember the sound engineer saying at the end of one taping session. "He comes in here for commercials, things like this, and I can hardly remember him ever having to do it over. He gets it perfect the first time every time."

And for 25 years, he's gotten the Broncos perfect, as well. He doesn't schmooze them. A dropped pass is a dropped pass, a blown assignment a blown assignment. It is the professional "they," never the amateurish "we" now in vogue among so many jocks-turned-broadcasters (and some broadcasters turned would-be jocks).

Martin could have been an accountant, a lawyer, a judge, a music critic. Instead, he's been a disc jockey (go ahead, play that image in your mind for a moment), a station owner, a symphony patron, art collector, political analyst, gourmand.

He's also starting his 25th season as the Voice of the Broncos, on KOA. A generation has grown up in this part of the United States believing his voice is the only official one. They are right.

Just don't ask him to describe the function of a pipe wrench.

February 26, 1990, *Denver Post*
BOB MARTIN, TRULY A MAN FOR ALL SEASONS

You're a good deal poorer this morning, Denver. I wonder if you really know yet just how much.

All of us lost something special when Bob Martin died yesterday. I'm not going to use vague words—like gallant and brave and determined—to describe the way he spent more than two years battling cancer.

They're the best I've got, but they would embarrass him. He operated on a more precise level.

He was a 6-foot-5 midwesterner who never finished college but could embarrass Ph.D.s with his almost photographic recall and the wealth and range of detailed knowledge he could bring to a dinner table. I think of him, and the word "competence" springs to mind. So does professional. ...

Again, the word "genius" would embarrass him, but it fit. He rarely forgot.

Anything. A name. A place. A date. A fact. Who played Othello in some West End production 10 years ago—and how well. It was a scarey quality to have in a friend, much like living next door to some demon gardener while you raised crabgrass.

He was the true Renaissance Man.

... Going to the Super Bowl as he did was an act of awesome will. We'll never know how much.

It would have been his 499th Broncos broadcast. It was his 25th year as Voice of the Broncos. If the team he covered played with the same willpower and determination and preparation he brought to his job, we would not be explaining four Super Bowl losses or early Nuggets fades from the playoffs.

He didn't drink and he didn't smoke. His only known vices were lip-burningly-hot coffee, chocolates, biographies, London and Republicanism. He had no tolerance for pretension or incompetence. There was also a shy reserve. Some mistook it for aloofness. Not so. When Martin made a friend, it was for life. ...

May 12, 1990, *Denver Post*

NO ONE SAYS "NO" TO MARY CARPENTER

His first clue—in fact, the only clue—came when the dinner check arrived at The Fort restaurant in Morrison, where Lynn Carpenter and his wife, Mary, had taken another couple to celebrate the Carpenters' 25th wedding anniversary.

Lynn tugged out his wallet and plopped a MasterCard on the bill.

"Oh, Lynn, I don't think I'd do that," Mary exclaimed.

Mary, it turned out, had used up the credit limit that little bit of plastic implies. No furs, understand. No glitzy gowns, no luncheons in the trendy places our city's oh-so-self-impressed glitterati like to gather.

No, Mary Carpenter had just charged $2,700 on their own card to buy airline tickets to take a bunch of kids east for a wheelchair games competition.

You have to know Mary Carpenter. Nobody who does will be surprised by this little tale. They will smile knowingly and chuckle and nod. "That's Mary," they'll agree.

And it is. Friday, with a November-like wind slashing across the track at Metro State, there she was, clipboard in hand. When they bury Mary Carpenter, it's likely they will do it having first found both her best dress and her best clipboard.

Mary was conducting the 12th annual Tournament of Champions, a track meet that reassures all of us that sanity still prevails in little, isolated corners of the sports world. There wasn't an agent in sight. Not a three-piece suit and a long-term contract to be found. Unfortunately, neither were any of this city's megabuck pro athletes there, either, helping, or just circulating and talking.

Too busy with high-profile celebrity golf tournaments, probably.

But it would have been nice if just one of our resident big-time jocks had spent a morning, lending encouragement or maybe even buying the ribbons so many of the competitors wore pinned proudly to the entry badges hung around their neck. Mary bought 'em.

They stood shivering, goose bumps visible on the thin legs poking beneath shorts. There were almost goose bumps on the steel braces holding many of those legs. The Tournament of Champions is for kids with things like cerebral palsy or spina biffida and the like. The Colorado School for the Deaf and Blind brings some 30 kids each year, and Mary Carpenter and Lynn—and Lynn's computer—spend some 60 hours carefully making sure kids with similar "challenges" are ranked against each other.

"Before the computer, she would be up all night the night before the meet," says Lynn. "Last night, she set a record. She was in bed by midnight."

This is Mary's life, it would seem. Winters, this mother of two grown boys conducts a weekly handicapped ski program at Winter Park, where she bribes the resident ski equipment folk with canisters of homemade cookies. "Our kids never have to wait. Their stuff is ready the moment we show up," one friend said Friday.

July, she is meet director for the 1990 Junior National Wheelchair games at Colorado State University. Before, in June, she'll have run her annual wheelchair summer camp, putting kids on horses for the first time in their young lives. Her other full-time job is as a physical therapist and adaptive physical ed teacher in Jefferson County.

Their two sons, Doug, 24, and David, 26, have inherited the basic Carpenter's bent for such unpublicized service to their fellow men. Doug is on a Peace Corps mission in the South Seas. David extended army service to take a paramedic course.

"Mary," the harried woman said, interrupting a conversation Friday. "Do you have extra volunteers? We need one on the obstacle course." Mary was away. "The people here at Metro are wonderful," she is saying over her shoulder. "Their students help, and so do kids from DU. It's not me. It's so many people."

But it's Mary who blindsides "donors" for sandwiches, help. A dozen years ago, 20 kids came to the first meet. There were 263 Friday.

"There is no way you ever say no to Mary Carpenter," a friend was saying Friday.

Apparently, there is no way Mary ever says no, either.

Happy Mother's Day, Mary Carpenter.

July 30, 1990, *Denver Post*

"THE CHIEF" HONORED WITH LIFE-SIZE STATUE

The statue is life-sized even if its subject is still bigger than that. It's bronzed, and at its base are two words that no old-time Denver sports fans need to have interpreted.

"The Chief."

The University of Denver commemorates 40 years of collegiate hockey this weekend, with more than 100 former players coming back for a weekend of dinners and dances and golf and lying and remembering.

For recent arrivals, it should be noted that DU once was to college hockey what UCLA once was to college basketball. And John Wooden was held in no more awe in his sport than Murray Armstrong was in his.

The Chief.

The statue that will be unveiled in front of the DU Arena this Friday afternoon as part of the gala weekend shows Armstrong in that tattered and famous old warm-up jacket he brought south with him from Canada in 1956, when then DU chancellor Chester Alter hired him away from selling hats and coaching hockey in Regina.

"I want a winner," Alter told his new coach.

He came to the right man. "If I don't give you a national championship in two years, fire me," Armstrong snapped back. Armstrong gave him a title—the first of five he would deliver. He also gave him the best college hockey team ever assembled, end the argument. He gave him magic, Friday and Saturday nights when a ticket to the 5,200-seat arena was the most prized possession in town for years.

Armstrong went into Western Canada and brought down that region's top players. He guaranteed them an education. In return, he demanded all their abilities, and he wanted them to graduate. Before it became institutionally fashionable, Armstrong was graduating every hockey player he recruited.

And he was winning five national championships and 10 Western Collegiate Hockey Association titles, and doing it with such insolent, taunting, marvelous style that the NCAA rewrote its rules to combat him. That's how good Armstrong was. That's how good he made DU become.

It's those players and their more modern counterparts who assemble this weekend.

You think of Alabama and you think of Bear Bryant. You think of Michigan and you think of Bo. You think of UCLA and you think of Wooden. And, if you've lived in Denver more than a dozen years, you think of DU and you think of hockey and Murray Armstrong.

For 21 years, until he retired in 1977 and he and Sis went to Florida and two-a-day golf, The Chief made DU hockey synonymous with success. ...

This will be a nice blend of the old and the new. There will be Glen Anderson of the Edmonton Oilers and their Stanley Cup successes. He played at DU in 1978. Mike Christy (1969–72) and Kevin Dineen (80–83) and Grant Munro (59–61) and George Konik and Cliff Koroll and Grant Dion.

Konik played on Armstrong's great teams of 1959–60 and and 1960–61. No better team has ever taken the ice on the collegiate level. They cursed themselves when the Soviets managed to come from behind and tie them. They beat the U.S. Olympic team (and the Swedes and West Germans). They laid waste to college hockey en route to back-to-back championships. The 1960–61 team averaged—averaged—7.6 goals per game as it went 30-1-1.

And this weekend, paunchier, balder, grayer, they reassemble to replay a frozen kind of Camelot when the question was never, "Would they win?" It was merely, "How much would they win by?"

I covered the Broncos and DU in some of those years. The seasons were more defined. Broncos from August to December. Since Armstrong never scheduled home games until January, it worked out perfectly. I would leave another tattered Broncos season, two wins, three, four, and pick up Armstrong and DU on their way to another championship.

It was the ridiculous to the sublime. I'll be in Tokyo this weekend, with a Broncos team that now measures losses as it once counted wins. But sometime soon, I'm going to drive to DU, and look at the statue, and remember magic time on the Hilltop, and the old hat salesman who made it all possible.

September 28, 1990, *Denver Post*

GARCIA WILL LEAVE LEGACY THAT COUNTS

Let's just mark it off to a chilling early autumn rain, maybe. But I've been thinking of legacies lately, of what a man leaves behind him, and watching television clips of one Michael R. Wise and one Kenneth Good and one Bill Walters and one Neil Bush.

I see a film clip of Messr. Wise striding toward an investigatory session where, later, he will take the Fifth more than a dozen times. He is smiling and confident and beautifully tailored and perfectly barbered.

Should we expect less from the former chairman of former Silverado Banking, Savings and Loan?

And then I think of a little guy named Joe Garcia. Don't wrack your brain. You don't know Joe. It's your loss, but you don't. For almost 50 years, Joe has never owned a suit that cost what Michael Wise's suit cost. Hell, his total suit costs for 50 years may not total what the one Wise wore.

Joe is retired now, just like Wise. My bet would be Wise is retired on more money than Joe Garcia has available. Joe spent his life working hard, for a salary. Then he went home, fixed some supper and, while the likes of Mr. Wise and his crowd were visiting the city's trendy and pricey restaurants, ordering the best wines, impressing each other with their largesse and style, Joe Garcia piled the few supper dishes in the sink and rushed to the gym.

He'd spend the next four or five hours working with kids. Then he'd go home, to bed. And he'd get up at 4:30 the next morning and start all over. He'd do this five days a week, and did it for 43 years.

"Oh, I don't know," he said yesterday when I asked him how many kids he figures he's helped train over all those decades. He thought awhile. "Maybe 5,000, maybe more."

Think of that, a little, while you watch the 5 o'clock news and see these dandies with nary a hair out of place explain how they looted life savings and it wasn't their fault.

For almost 50 years, Joe Garcia's life has been spent teaching kids how to box. I don't care if you don't like the sport. I happen to, even did a little of it as a kid.

"I love to train fighters," says Joe. "I don't mind if I don't work their corner at the fight. I like the idea of training them, and the idea of helping take them off the streets. I figure, if I can take 10, 13 kids off the streets four or five nights a week, I am accomplishing something."

He isn't getting his name in our society pages, of course, not like Mr. Walters has, or Mr. Bush, or Mr. Perfect Suit, or Mr. Good. He isn't even getting his name in the sports pages.

It doesn't bother Joe Garcia. That's the beautiful part. "I don't want any glory out of it. This is my relaxation." And those 5,000 fighters are his kids. He has never married.

He goes to the old gun club on the southwest corner of Sloan Lake, one he and others have helped convert into a gym. And he works there until 9 or 10 each night, getting kids ready for the Golden Gloves, or for a Golden Gloves Smoker coming up Oct. 13 at The Sports Complex, 5555 W. Evans Ave. They'll have to wait a bit to tell you how many fights. Depends on how many sign up. "Fourteen, 15, I suppose," says Garcia.

Channel 9 has this program, "Nine Who Care." I think that's it. This is my nomination for Joe Garcia and what he has done for the Golden Gloves and for 5,000 kids.

I'm a little up to here with football coach pretensions and player poutings and salary negotiations for sums of money that would run small cities or decent welfare programs.

... When you go, [to the Golden Gloves competition] look around. Find a little guy probably standing off to one side, smiling.

Say hello.

And then we'll talk more about who has really left a legacy.

March 27, 1992, *Denver Post*
ALI SHOWS THE RING'S GOOD SIDE

He was the late 20th century's Pied Piper. He still is. And if ever one wanted to measure the difference between what is good and what is evil in sports, Denver and Indianapolis offered all the evidence needed yesterday. In Indianapolis, former heavyweight champion Mike Tyson was sentenced to six years' hard time for rape. In Denver, former heavyweight champion Muhammad Ali brought traffic to a smiling stop at the intersection of Arapahoe and 18th streets, downtown. He was walking from a restaurant to U.S. Sprint's local offices.

He almost didn't make it. A cook came running from a nearby restaurant and into the intersection as the light changed. "I seen the champ!" he shouted. "I seen the champ!"

Upstairs, in Sprint's telemarketing division on the 13th floor, Ali shut down operations. All he did was show up. "The champ's here," it ran, like a flame through cellophane. Young adults who were in grade school when Ali fought his last fight in 1981 climbed over each other for a close-up view. The champ worked the room like some pro entertainer in a Las Vegas showroom. He told jokes, the same ones he had used on executives at a luncheon a little earlier. He did magic. He passed out autographs.

They were kids, those phone operators, when Ali was at his peak. Kids or younger when Ali ruled the world of boxing. The Thrilla in Manila and the classic in Zaire and the sadder ones that came later, at the end, when he should have been retired, are scanty memories. The battle with the feds during the Vietnam War is, at best, even flimsier.

But Ali as champion, Ali as symbol, Ali as maybe the most universally recognizable human on the planet, is still there, like a comet, dragging them down the halls and creating huge pods of humanity and laughter wherever he paused.

Contrast that legacy with what happened in Indianapolis. Tyson is sentenced. A career and a talent is wasted in his self-destructive path.

"No comment," Ali said when asked. But, later, outside, the irrepressible Ali surfaced when he was taking a picture with a Denver police officer. Slowly, with a grin, he raised his hands as if surrendering. "This is my Mike Tyson imitation," he whispered.

Only the fragile voice and the slower gait betray the Parkinson's symptoms that bother him now. They are Ali 1992. The eyes and the mind and the attitude are vintage 1965. He is self-conscious of his speech, declining most on-camera sessions.

But a glance at his schedule confirms the Ali of old is still there. He travels 100–125 days a year for charity. Abuwi Mahdi, his special assistant, says he signs 400 to 500 autographs a day. A decade after his last fight, the demand remains insatiable. You wonder, a decade from now, how many people will follow almost worshipfully to get Tyson's signature.

At lunch, Ali had done some magic tricks, and at one point had Mahdi take a video cassette to the back of the room and place it on a camera. He would, he promised, make it rise. So we all stared, and Ali stood at the podium, this slow, beatific smile spreading across that famous mug. "April fool," he finally said. "All you intelligent people, I convinced you that I might lift that."

He did. We all watched. We waited, and felt laughingly foolish at the end. But that's Ali. He has spent 50 years convincing all of us he can do absolutely anything, and do it with flare and class and a showbiz touch. "I controlled their minds," he said of his opponents. He called Sonny Liston "The Ugly Bear," Floyd Patterson was "The Rabbit," Joe Frazier became "The Gorilla."

And Ali became the world's Everyman, instantly recognizable on every continent. Oh, maybe the penguins on Antarctica had a problem. But an anecdote Mahdi related shows what happens anywhere Ali goes.

"We were in Zurich, at midnight, coming back from a jazz club to the hotel, and a car full of kids stopped. They weren't sure, but they thought it was him. He walked over and started talking." It took them another half hour to get home.

Ali is in town on behalf of the Muhammad Ali Foundation that funnels money into the Red Cross, United Negro College Fund, Save the Children, Special Olympics and Habitats for Humanity. These are the national charities. He has others on a local level. His association with Sprint brings 5 percent of that corporation's earnings in certain areas to the foundation for distribution.

"He gets stronger as the day goes on," Mahdi sighs. "We had to beg him to quit at 11:30 p.m. in Phoenix the other night. There were eight of us, and the rest were exhausted. He wanted to get something to eat and talk."

Ali has an 18-room home in Los Angeles and a smaller one on 90 acres in Michigan, some hour and a half from Chicago. Like his presence here on the day

Mike Tyson disappears from public view, that home represents a huge irony. It once belonged to Al Capone.

Why does the aura linger so long after the title expired? "He's genuinely kind," Mahdi says. "He is a loving individual. He doesn't discriminate. If you need the shirt off his back, he'll give it to you. He never says no, to anyone. In Phoenix, we were on a really tight schedule, riding to the next place, when the phone rang to let us know a convalescent home wanted him to come by.

"'We don't have time,' I told him. 'We'll make time,' he said. We spent an hour there and were late everywhere else the rest of the day."

"I work for Allah," he whispers when asked why he thinks his fame has outlasted his physical gifts. "If you praise God, He praises you." Argue? About then, the kids-turned-grown-ups on the 13th floor of the Sprint offices began to chant:

"Ali ... Ali ... Ali." All we needed was a ring and a time warp and a memory reborn. "I seen the champ," the cook had shouted. In Denver yesterday, nobody had to ask who that might be.

July 17, 1992, *Denver Post*

Buck was giant of old AFL

Go gently, Buck.

No more tears.

Buck Buchanan, 51, died of lung cancer yesterday. It took the damnable stuff two years to finally get him. The world of football has lost a giant in both the literal and figurative sense. He was as good as there has been, and for those of us who trace our writing ancestry back to the ancient days of the AFL, Buchanan typified the old Kansas City Chiefs.

Henry Stram, a fireplug of a man, loved huge linemen. He surrounded himself with guys like 6-7 Jim Tyrer and 6-5 Bobby Bell and the 6-7, 280-pound Buchanan. He loved putting all those sequoias up on the front row at warm-up time and letting the other club stare at them.

There are two major memories I have of Buchanan.

The first was January 15, 1967, the first Super Bowl. It was in the Los Angeles Coliseum, and it would finally bring the two leagues together. We would know, once and for all, if the haughty NFL was better than what it called The Other League.

The war was six years old by then, brutal and bitter and expensive, with no Marquis of Queensbury rules. Kidnapping was permitted. Cheating, lying, what-ever worked to get a top prospect was accepted.

Buchanan had been the AFL's No. 1 draft choice in 1963, coming out of Grambling. And he had endured all the old taunts and jeers of the NFL. Why not play in the good league? Maybe you couldn't play over here.

So, that mid-January day, he walked with his teammates down the tunnel toward the field—and this huge bear of a man had tears streaming down both cheeks. He was that emotionally involved. Now he'd prove it.

Later, when Jim Taylor came his way on one play, Buchanan picked Taylor up—and spiked him into the turf, head first.

My second vivid memory is a year ago about now, at Canton, Ohio. Buck was there as a member of the Hall of Fame, pro football's highest honor. His yellow Hall of Fame jacket hung loosely on him. He had already begun to lose a lot of weight. The ravages of the disease were evident, but he was still Buck.

Somehow, he knew I'd been ill, too, and we chatted for a few minutes at a luncheon for the new candidates. It was pleasant, reliving the old league, a time and a place and an attitude that died when the leagues merged in 1970. Something was lost then, especially the sense of team, and of league vs. league, of "us" vs. "them" on both sides.

There was an enormous sense of loyalty on the part of the players who came into the AFL in the early years. They were Don Quixotes, tilting at NFL windmills, forever questing. To play against the Green Bay Packers, the very image of the NFL at that time, was all they could ask.

It was the reason for those tears. "I'd never been that emotional before a game," Buchanan had told me once for a book I did on the Chiefs. "I really felt I could have hurt somebody and been glad I'd done it. I don't normally feel that way. Football's a game. I love to play and to win, but not to the point of hurting somebody. But at that time, I really wanted to hurt someone. On one play Elijah Pitts carried the ball, and when I hit him I said, 'You can't run this hole here, man!' He said, 'I'll be comin' back.' I said, 'Every time you come back, dammit, I'll be right here waitin' on you.' We kept it up throughout the game."

It's one more reason to feel sad this morning, knowing we have lost another member of that time and that place.

Buchanan could have played for any team, any time. That he played for the Chiefs was somehow fitting, since they came to represent the old AFL and what it was. They were stylish and innovative and tough. And they were huge, but none bigger than Buchanan until his old Grambling teammate, 6-9 Ernie Ladd, went to the Chiefs in Ladd's final years. At Grambling, Buchanan would eat a half dozen eggs "and seven or eight pieces of toast" for breakfast. But it was modest compared to Ladd, who held the school record of 56 pancakes at one sitting.

As pros—Ladd at that time was with the San Diego Chargers—when Kansas City would visit, Ladd would pick Buchanan up at the airport, take him to Ladd's home, "and put me in the stance. Then he'd show me tricks I could use on offensive linemen, like a step I could take to keep the center from blocking me."

It was a mood and a time that won't happen again, and Buchanan was an integral part of it.

Rest easy, Buck.

⚜   ⚜   ⚜

CHAPTER ELEVEN

NO MORE CHEAP CIGARS

✦   ✦   ✦

Liver cancer is the bottom of the ninth, two out, 10 runs down and nobody on base, but Dick kept the rally going more than two years. ...

At a going-away party for a mutual friend last summer [1992], several people approached Dick and Mary Kay, not to talk about the Broncos or even directly about his health but to tell him how much they'd enjoyed a column he had written about "Puppy," the name his grandson gave to the wig Dick wore after cancer treatments cost him his hair.

That's what satisfied: reaction to his craft, not his disease.

Everyone in this business respected Dick Connor. I'll further confess to envy. Cover an event when Dick was on press row and you'd wake up in the morning, turn to his column, then reread yours and wish you'd gone into the field of transmission repair.

—Mark Wolf, sports columnist, *Rocky Mountain News*

Dick Connor was dead. Richard James Connor, to be accurate. Connor knew all about accuracy. It was as much a part of his professional life as the paper his words were printed on.

He died at home. Cancer killed him. Cancer has had an easier time.

Connor fought every step of the way. For more than two years, cancer marched through his body and ultimately took a couple shots at his brain.

But his brain and his sense of humor remained in mint condition to the very end. The pain and the chemo and the effort to battle both slowed him down. But he was still writing and he was still Connor.

People die. It's one of life's merrier little pranks. Most people are re-membered—for a while. Some for longer than that.

It is suspected Connor may still be remembered when the Rockies are taking the field in their fifth World Series.

So the visitor from Elsewhere asks, "Who pray was Dick Connor?"

He was a writer, who chose to write about what Red Smith called "children's games." So did Smith. There was Smith and everybody else. Dick Connor came high in the latter category. He liked sports and you knew that when you read what he wrote.

And a whole lot of people read what he wrote, four days a week, and trusted what he said. That was the thing about Connor. Trust followed him around like a puppy dog.

—Gil Spencer, editor, *Denver Post,* **now retired**

Knowing Dick Connor meant you missed fewer of life's joys.

As a chronicler and critic of Denver sports for three decades, he framed people and events in the best available light.

With a patient and optimistic eye, Connor never tired of looking for what shined in the subjects of his writing. He allowed himself to be awed by both a Dikembe Mutombo dunk and a cloudless Colorado afternoon.

Doctors discovered cancer inside Connor in 1990. But he didn't waste time cursing the disease. The *Denver Post* columnist instead decided to stay happy and keep working until his death last December, at age 62.

"You are not entirely your own person," Connor once wrote in a letter of love to a teenage daughter. "You owe parts of your life to others, just as they do to you."

What I owe Dick Connor is this lesson: If a man knows how to live, he need not be afraid to die.

—Dedication page, 1993–94 Denver Nuggets Media Guide, by *Denver Post* sports columnist Mark Kiszla

⚘   ⚘   ⚘

For at least 15 years, I had been urging Dick to write a book about his experiences as a sportswriter and columnist. The book would be more a collection of anecdotes, impressions and people than a listing of columns.

He liked the idea—sort of—but wasn't sure anyone would be interested in it because it would not be a "kiss-and-tell" tome. That wasn't his style.

After he was diagnosed with cancer and the first shock wore down a little, he again talked about a book. Maybe his personal experience with cancer and how he chose to deal with it could be a "hook" to write about newspapering and sports, he said. He began writing impressions and notes to himself.

He decided to write for the paper about having cancer because he noticed the other writers watching him solemnly in the press box. He said they all knew he was dealing with this, but because cancer is cancer, everyone was afraid to talk about it. If he brought it out in the open, he thought everyone would be more comfortable. He even chose a title for the book: "No More Bad Wine, No More Cheap Cigars."

That was, in fact, one of the axioms he lived by those two years. Since both smoking and drinking are not exactly part of a cancer regimen, he decided to forego both—except for a glass of very good wine when we went out to dinner and an expensive cigar on rare occasions, primarily with his fellow sportswriters after a game.

The sense of humor and the courage he conveyed in the following columns were not an act. It was how he lived and inspired others to live.

If death can be beautiful, his was.

Our five children and I, his brother Bob and Father John McCormick were with him when he quit breathing.

Mark said, "Take the first star to the right, and go straight on 'til morning."

The quote from "Peter Pan" was fitting.

October 14, 1990, *Denver Post*

CANCER CALLS A COLD TIME-OUT FROM FANTASY WORLD

Well, at least I don't have to join millions of Americans and spend time worrying about someday getting cancer.

I've got it. The suspense is ended.

This week, I will be operated on at the University of Colorado Health Sciences Center. I don't know how long I'll be in the hospital, or even all the directions we're going to explore. Then, you'll be stuck with me four times a week again.

"I'm afraid it's bad news," Elroy Goebel said over the phone three weeks ago.

"Naw," I thought. "I'm not really hearing this." Three days earlier, all I had were some questionable results from blood tests at my routine annual physical and concerns over travel arrangements for the baseball playoffs and the World Series. Now I had a tumor on my liver. "Hepatoma," is the shorthand version.

I've known Dr. Goebel for maybe 25 years, from when both of us worked around the Denver Broncos. I was covering the team for the *Denver Post* and he was the team physician, and when we moved to Arvada we kind of kept in touch. His office wasn't far from our home, and he has been the family physician and a friend for longer than either of us cares to remember.

I had taken my regular physical in mid-August, a little after getting back from Tokyo. No symptoms. Oh, maybe fatigue at times, but what does that mean? I just turned 60. So I don't have experience at that, either. Is a little more fatigue part of it?

Still, the blood workups weren't quite right, and we agreed I'd watch my diet and lay off any wine or liquor and come back for another test in a month. The regular fall routine set in, the NFL opened, CU started, and I went to Champaign, Ill., and then came home and watched Denver beat Kansas City on Monday night.

That Monday morning before the game, on a whim, I decided it had been a month and called Goebel's office. There was an opening, and he examined me, and thought the liver was enlarged. "I'd like you to get an ultrasound," he said.

I went to St. Anthony's the morning after the Monday night game.

"We'll talk to your doctor, and he'll let you know," the St. Anthony's people said.

And that's when Goebel called later in the day and said there was bad news.

Since, it's been a CAT scan, and a magnetic resonance imaging test, and a nuclear scan and some other stuff, and enough blood withdrawn to satisfy Dracula. And it's been Mary Kay and me waiting for the phone to ring and jumping when it did.

And each time, what we hoped was some mistake has become something worse.

A peculiar detachment sets in, overlays the shock. No, you think. It isn't happening. There have been times sitting in those white, antiseptic rooms with straight-back chairs and tables with fresh layers of paper on them, listening to a doctor, that I have felt like a third person. I am somehow over to the side, watching this conversation, hearing it, but not being part of it.

They are talking, this doctor and this guy that looks like me, about somebody else.

"Surgery ... chemo ... primary site ... unusual in this country ..." Figures. I can't get something off the K-Mart shelf. I have to go and recruit some sort of designer bug. Strangely, they tell me, it may have been growing on my liver for four or five or six years. Or maybe just a few months. They don't know. Only now has it begun to send out signals, enough to finally track it down.

But there has been a great deal of luck, too. The Colorado Health Sciences availability is the biggest. It was simpler when we could call it University Hospital. So the hell with it, I will. They have the best people available, anywhere. It is one of the most exceptional resources in our nation, and not enough Coloradans recognize it for what it is.

The *Post* has been marvelous. "If you need to go somewhere for another opinion, we'll fly you there," my boss, Woody Paige, and our editor, Gil Spencer, said. It feels nice, to have that kind of backing. But it isn't necessary. University Hospital has it all.

Mostly, though, I'm blessed. Mary Kay and I have done a lot of hugging, and the kids have rallied around. I took myself off the travel list except for local games.

We drove to Wyoming a couple of weekends ago to watch the Air Force game. It was one of those idyllic September days that make natives out of the latest immigrants, and we stopped counting antelope when we got somewhere over 100. That Sunday, all the kids and grandkids came over for brunch, and we watched the Broncos-Bills game on TV.

I've got the best of everything, and odds at least as good as Denver someday winning a Super Bowl. No. Better. Oddly, I have never felt bad. Still don't, at least until the treatments began. I don't feel sick. But now I awake in the morning and see the sun coming through the window and have that momentary sense of peace— and then the memory comes back.

Cancer. I've got it. I'll be damned if I'm going to let it have me. Brave words. Do I believe that? Depends on the moment. Cancer does that. Your horizons shrink, and your emotions are put on a permanent roller coaster.

Certainly, your priorities change. Working helps, immensely.

I debated writing this, but finally decided it is what I do. I write. To some extent, I am a public figure, and we are always grousing about them being too secretive. Besides, maybe selfishly, it would help me come to grips with things, and at least explain my absences from the batting rotation here at the *Post*.

Going to Wyoming that day, and to Boulder the following Saturday, and then to Fort Collins was great therapy. So was covering the Monday night game with Cleveland. The drives were lovely, and we'd stuff Beethoven or Verdi into the tape deck and Mary Kay and I could talk—we've done an enormous amount of that—and watch the scenery. We could pretend it was normal, and it almost was for those few hours.

And watching the Broncos, anytime, and trying to write about what happens is the most satisfyingly distracting thing I can think of, except maybe counting downs for the Buffaloes.

I can't really believe it's happening, but it is. I've spent my adult life chronicling the fantasy world of sports. This is real life. And I'd appreciate a prayer if you've got one you aren't using.

October 24, 1990, *Denver Post*

LIFE ON THE WARD STOPS WHILE BRONCOS ON THE TUBE

Her name is Tracy Steinberg, and she works Sundays by choice. She is a nurse at University Hospital, where I have been spending my fall vacation of late, and she noticed I had the Broncos game on Sunday morning.

"Someday I'm going to do a paper on that," she said.

"What? The Broncos?"

"No. On what happens around here when they play."

Nothing happens, that's what. That's the point. Nothing. Nothing at all. Anywhere. For three hours, it is peaceful bliss.

"We get a lot of paperwork caught up," said Tracy. "I know the doctors are watching, too, because we don't get calls from them. They go off somewhere and watch. And the patients are all watching, and it just goes very quiet."

Curious, I decided to take a walk down the hall. Sure enough, virtually every set was tuned to Denver in Indianapolis. Sure enough, I couldn't find a doctor in view. Sure enough, the nurses were hunched over records, catching up.

"Oh, it's that way all over," said Dr. Ben Anderson a little later. "We get virtually no business in emergency OR during a Broncos game. I don't know if it's because fewer people are driving so there are fewer accidents or what. But you could chart it."

So I walked the hall, and heard people talking. Who is Blake Ezor? Who is Kevin Clark? When is Denver going to fold?

... And all up and down the corridor, it was quiet and peaceful.

But we waited. "Denver has been outscored 71-26 in the fourth quarter" one NBC graphic proclaimed. Denver is a team that has led every one of its games, and we knew what was coming there at Spa University, the fall vacation mecca of Colorado Boulevard.

Sure enough, from back in the shadows, the Colts capitalized on Denver's patchwork secondary and drew even at 17-17. Now the only question would be how

Denver would lose it, what exquisite anguish it would work on its followers for another week.

Not this time. Ezor chugged. Elway threw. Mark Jackson caught, or Mel Bratton, or Steve Sewell or Sammy Winder ran. And even through the cold surface of the tube, from two time zones away, you could see Denver decide this had all gone far enough.

"Someday," Tracy promised, "I'm going to do a paper. Last week, against Pittsburgh, I had six patients. All through the game, nobody rang. All the call buttons were quiet. We didn't get a single order phoned in from one of the doctors.

"But the second the game ended, all six buttons flashed on and the phone started to ring.

"All six patients wanted a pain pill."

December 24, 1990, *Denver Post*

CHRISTMAS MEANS HOPE

John Elway's final throw Sunday night, like one of those Christmas toys "any child can assemble," didn't quite fit.

Hole A never quite lined up with Hole B.

Neither did the 1990 season.

But let's not think about that this fine, crisp morning.

A year ago, I was flying home from San Diego Christmas Day. Nothing new. In this business, you don't have weekends or holidays. The NFL is no respecter of special holidays. ...

Christmas, for some reason, has come to be associated as much with airplane terminals as Midnight Masses. ...

Bowl teams traditionally spend Christmas in some gilded hotel. Colorado is making it a habit. Colorado State would like to.

We all have traditions to observe.

I started a new one for myself. I got out a batch of letters and cards yesterday, from all over the country, and reread them. They came in after I wrote a column in October about having cancer. This might seem a strange time to do an update, but I think it fits.

We'll all give special thanks today. I've still got cancer, understand, along with thousands of Americans who view this holy day with a different perspective. But the disease doesn't have to be the end of the world.

In my case, it has been something of a beginning. The letters were like some wonder drug. In some cases, I heard from friends, even classmates, I hadn't heard from in 40 years or more. In others, there were encouraging notes from total strangers, many of them also battling this thing in one form or another.

And I got to thinking that the common denominator in all those letters and all that advice was hope, which is really what Christmas itself is all about—hope, and love and peace.

I don't want this to be maudlin. I also got unsolicited cancer cures I'm not certain modern medicine will ever endorse—diets, exercises, ice treatments, heat treatments, tree bark, even standing on my head to redistribute the flow of blood. It was all well meaning, sincere. And I guess it worked for them or they wouldn't have recommended it.

But I decided at the outset I would put myself in the hands of the experts at the University of Colorado Health Sciences Center and University Hospital, and I have, with no regrets. And, maybe, it's working. They weren't able to go in and remove the tumor on my liver, but at least we figured out a treatment program that is creating a draw, and I'll settle for that.

Yesterday, Christmas Eve, I met Dr. Bill Robinson up on the eighth floor. The hospital was virtually deserted, offices locked, corridors dark. Bill gave me the biggest Christmas present I could want.

The numbers are edging toward the good side. And, while it was just one blood test, and it's too early to draw any real conclusions, there came a surge of Christmas hope. It was enough for me.

My autumn has been as odd and out of focus as that of the Broncos. Yesterday's encouraging numbers restored equilibrium. Maybe, down the road, they'll slide. I don't know. I just know that for now, for today, this morning, this moment, Bill Robinson delivered the Connor Family Christmas present with all the flourish of John Elway's final pass.

And this time, there were no yellow flags upfield. I hope your Christmas is as joyous as ours.

October 14, 1991, *Denver Post*

CANCER A WORD, NOT A SENTENCE

Happy anniversary!

It's been exactly one year since I wrote a column that began, "I don't have to worry about getting cancer anymore. I have it."

I still do. And the purpose of this column today is to let you know you can have cancer and live with it. I'm not saying by any means I enjoy the damn thing. But there is a little printed sign on the wall next to the scale in my doctor's office on the eighth floor at University Hospital.

"Cancer is a word, not a sentence," the sign reads. There is something a little profound in those seven words.

It's a beautiful credo for those of us who have this lousy affliction. I kept thinking about that sign after I saw it, and have generally kind of made it my battle cry. It's right. Cancer does not have to be a sentence. Admittedly, each case is different—in type, in severity, in prognosis. I'm talking only mine, but I have seen too many marvelous people over the past year not to have changed some opinions I once held.

Like many, I once associated cancer and death as automatic companions. No more. I have been increasingly astonished—and encouraged—at the number of people who live with cancer, and at the research and progress being made at places such as the Cancer Research Center at CU.

Since diagnosis a year ago, I've had two surgeries, been poked and prodded and measured and weighed and gulped an incredible number of pills and learned to shoot myself in the leg three times a week. If I ever get arrested, they'll bust me because of the pinpricks alone.

These aren't hobbies I had ever planned on taking up as I grew older. But they aren't a lot worse than trying to resurrect an old golf swing, either.

If those have become regular parts of my life in the last year, I have still been lucky enough to retain the other parts as well. I have gone to the Orange Bowl, the Super Bowl, the Final Four, the Kentucky Derby and the U.S. Open, and our family spent 10 glorious days on the Oregon coast this past summer. I haven't cut a thing out of my life except cigars, which I still miss when I write.

In fact, having cancer gives you a certain freedom. We were in the Stanford press box a couple of weeks ago when B. G. Brooks of the *Rocky Mountain News* lit up a cigar.

It smelled delicious. "Got another?" I asked.

He did, and he gave one to *News* columnist Bob Kravitz, as well. The three of us sat there on the balmy California evening, puffing, writing, when I saw the cloud we were building.

"You know," I told Kravitz, "we could get cancer from this." He broke up coughing and laughing.

I have gotten to the point that, sometimes, I can go clear past breakfast before remembering I have cancer. There was a point, a year ago, when it was all I could think of, when it dominated my thoughts and actually almost numbed my body.

How am I doing now?

Great. The cancer is still there. They couldn't get it out. But it hasn't grown, and in fact may have shrunk a bit. The latest blood reports—I go in to University Hospital once a month to get my oil changed, as I like to put it—show the cancer is absolutely stabilized.

"I know you'd like me to tell you it's going away," says Dr. Bill Robinson, my oncologist. "But this is good news, and we'll keep doing exactly what we are doing." As a matter of fact, I have been something of a guinea pig, in that they now are treating two other patients who have the same thing—hepatoma, or cancer of the liver—the way they are treating me "because you've been doing so well."

I know it sounds odd, in the circumstances, but I would not trade parts of this past year for anything. I have met marvelous people, and rediscovered what I knew all along, that Mary Kay and the kids and the grandchildren are all stronger and tougher than I am, and worth any amount of medicine or chemotherapy or needles in the thigh.

I have learned love, both given and received. I would not work anywhere else than where I do. The *Denver Post* backed me and the family to a degree that should be held up for other corporations to examine as a role model. I don't have to say that. I feel it.

I am working full-time, no restrictions, and enjoying it more than ever. I'm blessed by being able to work in sports, to go where the public goes to relax, and to be paid for doing so.

In fact, I think work was partly responsible for a quick recovery. I had two surgeries in 10 days last October/November. The second was on a Thursday before the Nebraska game. University Hospital doesn't have cable TV.

So I talked my way out that Saturday, and got home in time to see the second half on cable in the den. It was the good half, of course. And a week after, with Mary Kay lugging my portable computer because I wasn't supposed to tote anything heavier than six pounds or so, we started our new lives.

They are new, for both of us, because there are new realities you learn to live with. Mortality certainly is one. She spent two nights in an adjoining bed in the hospital when I had surgery, and not long ago, I was talking to a support group. One of the men said, "Don't you think it's harder on the loved ones?"

Absolutely. I remembered Mary Kay across the room, alert to any tiny variations in my breathing. The patient is the star of the show. All he or she has to do is endure. The family has to cope, to feel helpless, to wish they could do something more, and that is infinitely harder.

Cancer above all is not a private disease. In different ways, it affects everyone around the patient. Two of our grandchildren broke into tears at school not long after I was diagnosed. What's the matter? they were asked. "Grandpa's sick." I go to the hospital for my monthly checkup, and sit in the office, and see a couple across the way, clutching X-rays from some other doctor, obviously waiting for an exam and a second opinion, as frightened and uncertain as Mary Kay and I were a year ago.

But I also see people like myself, who have been through it, are still and who can walk out smiling and back to life. If there is any one thing that has surprised me, it is the number of people I have discovered who have survived cancer or coped with it, to go back to a more or less normal routine.

I received more than 1,000 letters and cards after that initial column. They are still in a big box in the garage, some unread, almost all unanswered. I am not being ungrateful. It is simply that part of the mental process I have built for myself is positive reinforcement. I try not to let negative thoughts intrude.

Of course it doesn't work all the time, but it's my trick with myself. For instance, unlike some patients I know who can tell me every medication, every procedure, and who may know more than many med students, I don't want to know.

Not everything. If I thought I should be expecting the cancer to move to the next stage, I would lie in bed at night like a child in a creaky house, wondering what is behind the moving curtain. I don't want to waste the rest of my life with that kind of anticipation. What will happen is out there, for someday. I'm not going to let knowledge of it ruin the days—hopefully years—between now and then. I'm concentrating on those, squeezing more out of them than ever before. Wrong. WE are concentrating. Mary Kay and I. We drove to Estes Park and listened to elk bugle a couple of weeks ago. It's something we've never done before.

We go to daily Mass, and breakfast with friends and relatives, and the day begins. We talk about it. I'm not saying I try to deny. That's not it at all. I just deny the damn thing affecting our lives more than it has to.

Like every cancer patient, I suppose, I live in a certain hope that someday Bill Robinson is going to call and say they've just found the magic bullet. I'm realistic enough to know that's not going to happen. Probably.

But I also buy lottery tickets.

August 2, 1992, *Denver Post*
TREATMENT ONE HAIRY EXPERIENCE

So, it has come to this:

I end the summer and start a new football season combing my hair with a washcloth. Actually, I can do it with the palms of my hands or my fingers, but the washcloth gives a slicker finish. Unless, of course, I lick my palms, which is bad manners in public. Besides, people tend to edge away.

A late spring bout with a neurosurgeon and some chemotherapy finished what nature had started several years ago. I woke up in University Hospital one morning with my head resting on a very hairy pillow. I knew it had been your basic white linen when I went to sleep, so I quickly looked in the mirror.

Who was that guy?

I looked like one of those tuft-eared creatures you see in zoos, and every time I touched my scalp with a brush, I harvested a new crop of old hair.

"It'll come back," the doctors assured me. They sounded too much like trustees for Silverado to suit me.

"If you'd like, we can give you a list of firms that make very nice hairpieces. Or you can just wait until it grows out again." I opted for raging vanity, and the morning Mary Kay drove me away from the hospital after nearly a month, we went straight to one of three places we had circled on the list.

Bingo. Chuck Gardner came up with a better head of hair than I had ever had. In fact, it was what I had always hoped to have, even if he did pretty much match the gray that had become a basic part of my persona. It was full and nicely shaped and didn't have that little open space at the back that was spreading on my own scalp.

I wondered: Would Dan Reeves recognize me? Doug Moe?

The wig made its debut at a Sigma Delta Chi banquet the next night. I think my boss recognized me, although it puzzled me why he kept introducing himself. I trotted it out again for a visit to Arapahoe Race Track. This time I'm sure I caught him staring curiously a couple of times. Or maybe it was the horses I announced I was betting.

Wigs have been part of civilization for centuries. They have found Egyptian mummies adorned with them. Now, all of a sudden, I was part of this ancient culture and not at all certain I wanted the membership card, thanks very much.

"You look good in it," my wife would say. Wives are supposed to say those things. I kept looking in the mirror. I didn't recognize this guy any more than I had the one without hair. Was I in some facial time warp here, wearing somebody else's profile?

There were strange looks in the office, quickly averted. Or maybe I just imagined them. Would they have been the same if I had arrived one morning looking like a newly shorn member of the American volleyball team, or a swimmer?

Gradually, the docs were proven right. My own hair started growing again, sprouting like the stubble left in a wheat field. "I think it's coming in thicker than before," my wife said. (See paragraph above, "Wives are," etc.)

I wore the wig anytime I left home, tore it off the second I came back through the door. It was like constantly wearing a hat, and I have never worn hats, even in winter. More, summer arrived. Heat. It was like wearing a fur cap.

Sitting on the deck one day, playing with my year-and-a-half-old grandson, I pulled the wig off. My grandson jumped backward in fright.

"It's OK," I said, holding out the hairy thing. He backed off more. Finally, I coaxed him into touching it.

"Puppy?" he said.

The wig was forever named. Puppy. "You wearing Puppy tonight?" Mary Kay would ask.

My own hair kept up its revival. It will never look as nice as Puppy, never be as full, as luxurious, as distinguished. But I can scratch my head, and it only takes five seconds to comb it in the morning. Two if I'm late.

I'm getting to like it, actually, this new, streamlined me. It's cool, and no bother at all on a windy day. You save money on shampoo, and can leave the blow-dry stuff to the pretty faces on television. One of the highlights of the summer came not long ago—I had to get a haircut again. Not a full-fledged, card-carrying one, understand.

"Just kind of neat it up," I said in the manner of a street person walking into an investment house and asking for the current short-term treasury rate. Danny Fiore, who once cut Elvis Presley's locks, is used to dealing with custom tailoring. He didn't even laugh.

I have gone from the Michael Jordan–U.S. swimmer–U.S. volleyball look to more the Clyde Drexler do.

And Puppy?

Puppy is retired—inactive, will not play again except maybe on state occasions—draped over a small statue of the Blessed Mother on Mary Kay's dresser. I'm not sure there isn't at least a minor sacrilege involved, but I figure if ever I need Puppy again, the association can't have hurt.

September 4, 1992, *Denver Post*

PUPPY'S LOOSE AGAIN, DOG-GONE IT

Puppy is loose in the land again. This is just a gentle warning.

You may recall that Puppy is a wig, a very nice wig. I got it to disguise a growing field of bare skin when chemotherapy and some neurosurgery combined to erase the hair on my scalp late last spring.

It was luxuriant, looked better than my homegrown stuff ever had.

But it was hot, and one day, playing with my 18-month-old grandson, I absently pulled the wig off. My grandson nearly went into shock. Eventually, I coaxed him into touching the wig.

"Puppy?" he said. The wig was named.

My hair grew back, sort of, and I've even considered carrying a pocket comb again. Then the neurosurgeons at University Hospital found another little spot, and they are going in to remove it this afternoon.

Puppy is back, at least on 24-hour recall. "We won't shave your head this time," the surgeon has assured me.

But they will poke a hole in it and take out the tumor, and it will confirm everything Dan Reeves ever thought about writers. Even a guy with a hole in his head—maybe even especially a guy with a hole in his head—can write a sports column.

"Just a few days," they have assured me. I may be home by Tuesday. The trouble with that timing is it messes up the first great weekend of the fall season, one I had spent all summer anticipating.

CSU at CU under the noonday sun tomorrow. Raiders at Broncos under the lights a day later. How can you ask for better starts to my favorite time of year? So I'll hope the TV works at the hospital, and that my eyes focus by noon Saturday and I'll watch the Rams and Buffs. By Sunday night it should be a snap.

I can't wait to see old Earle Bruce take a shot at Bill McCartney's new offense. ...

Personally, I'm relieved the golf tournament season is finished.

I have noted this trend, and brought it up with my boss.

It's not a big deal, really. I just told him if he ever again assigns me to a golf tournament I would have to kill him.

Lately, every time I go to cover a big tournament, I wind up with a hole in the head. It happened in April when I went to The Masters, came home and they zipped out a small tumor. Now I'm just finished writing about The International at Castle Pines and what happens?

Should I change my grip on my pencil, perhaps? Adjust a quarter turn or go to a slightly altered stance when I conduct an interview? Maybe I should switch to a Titlist pen?

Ah, well, we'll see.

Hopefully, by Tuesday I can be on our deck with Connor, our grandson, and we can inspect Puppy for any summer damage. Puppy has been up on a shelf in the bathroom, probably pouting.

Go Buffs. Go Rams. Go Raiders. Go Broncos.

Go Puppy. I get cheated out of the first big weekend of the football season and Puppy might have to make a comeback.

✢   ✢   ✢

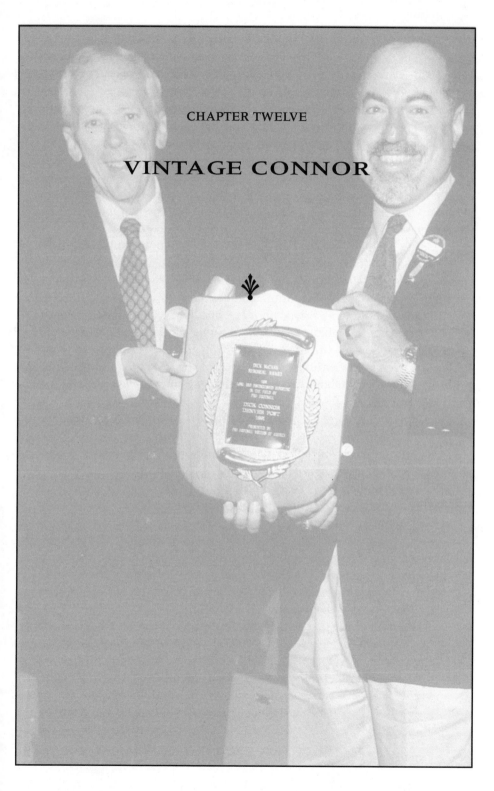

CHAPTER TWELVE

VINTAGE CONNOR

❧   ❧   ❧

With his keen perception and deft literary style he laid claim to a time and place. With unflagging good humor and astounding courage in the face of the cancer that finally took him, he commanded as much of a reader's respect as any columnist can in a job surrounded by volatile allegiances.

It says much for this man's grace under pressure that the Dick Connor Era, unlike those of too many athletes he chronicled, did not wane noticeably near the end and leave his fans wondering why he pressed on even as the ravages of chemotherapy took their dispassionate toll. Connor wrote many wonderful and memorable pieces, but even the best individual efforts pale in comparison to the astounding level of consistency.

On his bad days, and he had precious few of them behind a keyboard, his columns offered pleasant excursions into another realm. He seldom resorted to vitriolic diatribe—not often enough to satisfy the most virulent strain of sports fan—but confrontation was never his style. He gladly left that task to those who thrived on it and aimed instead for detail, nuance and the deft turn of phrase in pursuit of gentle persuasion.

His prose flowed with the kind of effortless ease that prompted readers and even fellow writers to conclude that this kind of work could not be difficult. Connor, bless his soul, did his colleagues no favor by making it look so easy.

—Kevin Simpson, columnist, *Denver Post*

No one in Denver journalism has been more honored by his colleagues. For 22 [out of 23] years, Dick Connor had been named Colorado Sports Writer of the Year.

But his colleagues weren't the only ones who admired Connor. His readers admired him as well.

During three decades of writing in Denver, Dick came to be trusted by his readers. They knew he would be fair, they knew he would be insightful, they knew he would be entertaining. They knew he would not be vindictive, they knew he would not be petty, they knew he would not be dull.

And he never let them down.

... His best writing had an elegance that cannot be taught. Such talent comes not from lessons; it comes from an intimacy with the language and from years of very hard, solitary work. ...

His family was blessed with his love for them. And we—his readers and his colleagues—were blessed with his love for the language.

—Chuck Green, *Denver Post* **editorial page editor**

❧   ❧   ❧

✤   ✤   ✤

Dick was often asked what he would have done if he hadn't been a sportswriter. He would love to have written novels, and admired those who did. But he couldn't plot.

He said covering politics would probably be his second choice on a newspaper because politics, like sports, has an abundance of human drama. He would definitely have been a writer of some kind—writing legal briefs if he had gone to law school, or writing and teaching history.

No one who knows him can picture him doing anything other than writing. He often said he preferred sportswriting because of its literary freedom. He never took advantage of that freedom.

The following columns don't fit into convenient slots. They are included because they are vintage Connor.

March 21, 1976, *Denver Post*

WELCOME TO HOUGHTON

CLICK.

"... Uh, we just aborted. We're going to taxi back to the other end of the runway and have the snowplow make a couple of runs and then we'll be on our way ... Uh, it's really no surprise to us that we aborted. We thought we'd make a run and see how the drifts were. It was just a little too much snow. But we'll get it plowed off and be on our way with no trouble. Just sit back and have another cup of coffee ..."

CLICK.

It's too bad there wasn't a jet pilot around to announce the Deluge.

The North Central voice last week sounded cheerful enough for a gray, snow-filled morning with the night-long storm still blotting out the nearby treeline in Hancock, Mich. Hemingway wrote about the area in "Up in Michigan." But he didn't have the Western Collegiate Hockey Association playoffs in mind.

University of Denver coach Murray Armstrong and his Pioneers were the last plane to leave the Houghton-Hancock area in the Upper Peninsula that day, because theirs was the only plane to make it in. The plane had arrived the night before.

Houghton isn't a place you go to without a good reason. The town died 40 years ago when copper mining did. Nobody bothered to tell the state. So it just sits there, symbolized by the 114-year-old Douglas House, which houses a few salesmen and visiting college hockey teams arriving to play Michigan Tech.

No other city in the WCHA (Western Collegiate Hockey Association) has quite the home edge as the Huskies. It takes seven hours to reach Houghton—at 11 p.m.—from Denver. As often as not, the arrival includes a couple of passes at the airport through a snowstorm. Ours did.

CLICK.

"... Uh, we were a little late getting away from Green Bay and the wind has shifted and we're getting a little local snowstorm here at the moment. Soooo, we're just going to take it around again ..."

CLICK.

Streams of snow slash past the window in the glare of the landing lights outside.

The second time is the charm. Fully 30 yards of runway remain between the plane and the row of red lights marking the end of the concrete and the start of the long sloping hill falling into the valley. It's another routine white-knuckle Hancock landing in a snowstorm, engines reversed, brakes jerking right from the moment of touchdown.

The bus outside is too hot. It's also too small for all the hockey equipment as well as players and others. Baggage is heaped in the seats. Players stand, or sit on suitcases. The windows frost over immediately. The wipers fight the heater to dominate conversation on the way into town.

Next day, the snow is reduced to occasional flakes floating down in a pale, weak sunlight. "Nice day," says the shopkeeper proudly. "Nothing wrong with this kind of day."

Outside the new ice arena on the hill, a graveyard rests under its winter blanket. Only the rounded tips of the stones above the snow. There's an image there. Maybe I'll think of it.

Murray Armstrong's sweet tooth lasts only until he can get across the street to the bakery. It is one of Houghton's salvations, just as the sign in the window is one of its greatest intrigues to a visitor: "Hot Pasties." I wonder if Sid King is aware of this. "It's sort of like a meat pie," I'm told. "And you pronounce it different."

... Maybe by next year Tech will have to come down off its hilltop and go to Denver for the playoffs. They'll stay at Writers' Manor instead of the Douglas House. There will be no hip-deep snow, no heatless rooms on a minus-12-degree night, no old-fashioned, cloth-covered phone lines, or icy linoleum bathroom floors, or steel shower stalls, or radiators that refuse to respond to kicking or swearing.

But there are drawbacks.

There are no bakeries advertising "Hot Pasties."

Houghton, after all, has some advantages.

❧   ❧   ❧

The following was first published on Jan. 19, 1980. It was reprinted on November 6 of that year after it was named best column in the annual Professional Football Writers of America national writing competition. The column was filed the day before the Super Bowl, and shortly after the Soviet Union invaded Afghanistan.

January 19, 1980, *Denver Post*

SUPER BOWL'S PROMOS "UNTHINKABLE" IN BACKWASH OF AFGHANISTAN

LOS ANGELES—After the headline, nobody needed strong coffee to shake the effects of a week of Super Bowling.

"U.S. Ponders the Unthinkable," the *Los Angeles Times* Friday morning edition proclaimed across the top of page one.

Deep in the innards of the Marriott Hotel near the Los Angeles airport, some 800 writers and broadcasters and cameramen were filing into the ball room, filling every chair, standing two or three deep across the rear of the room, lining the walls from front to back.

"The Soviet invasion of Afghanistan, and the possibility of additional moves against Iran or Pakistan, has given rise to grave concern among White House and other national security officials about the ultimate unthinkable possibility—war with the Soviet Union," the Times' *first paragraph read.*

Up front, television technicians switched on the lights and flooded the raised platform. Soundmen fiddled with microphones taped to the podium. Tape recorders were placed strategically, so as not to miss a word. Notepads were opened.

A major press conference was obviously imminent. But for them, the most unthinkable question was not whether an atomic war was imminent. It was whether or not Al Davis was going to move his Oakland Raiders to Los Angeles. Unthinkable Question No. 2 was whether or not instant replay of controversial officiating calls was feasible.

"Such a war, officials believe, almost certainly would become a nuclear war because the United States has concentrated on its nuclear capability rather than on matching the Soviet Union's massive strength in conventional warfare."

Pete Rozelle strode to the mass of microphones, into the wash of light from all the cameras. Tanned, confident, blue sport coat setting just the right note of sartorial splendor. He was, as always, a master at this sort of thing.

"Any questions?" No preliminaries. Get them quick. Laughter. Set the right tone early.

"Commissioner," the writer from Washington, D.C., began, "would you discuss the Jack Tatum case, Al Davis and the cross-ownership situation in Washington."

Rozelle smiled and did. All three. Smoothly, no notes. He had not read the book by Tatum, Oakland defensive back. Just excerpts. But he rejects the philosophy of violence in those excerpts. He needed more data on Davis' proposed move to the L.A. Coliseum. He hoped Davis would seek league approval. Otherwise—.

Without specifying, there seemed to be some unpleasant consequence lurking behind that "otherwise." As for Edward Bennett Williams' potential conflict of interests in sports ownerships, Rozelle said he hoped to get together and work it out soon.

"White House and other senior officials dealing with national security say that if the Soviet Union carries its expansionism into Iran or Pakistan, the United States will have little choice but to oppose it militarily."

Rozelle said one reason his National Football League has remained stable is that "we have not had a lot of team movement. The last was when the Cardinals moved from Chicago to St. Louis."

Afghanistan has had three governments in 20 months. Now it has the Russians. Iran has 50 American hostages. And the United States is talking about sending forces to protect Iran, and about not sending athletes to Moscow for next summer's Olympics.

It's no crazier, I suppose, than sitting in a crowded ballroom on the first sunny morning of a rainy week, talking about what effect moving a team from Oakland to Los Angeles might have, when the headline on the papers tucked under the various chairs hinted at the possibility that, maybe, perhaps, there might not BE an Oakland or a Los Angeles or a Moscow soon.

Q—Would you try to block it if Davis did not seek league approval and just arbitrarily moved his franchise to Los Angeles?

A—I would take every appropriate step to enforce the league constitution, which in effect, would be to try to block that move.

"'The United States would not at all be comfortable with the Soviet Union sitting on Iran's oil fields,' one Defense Department official remarked dryly as he considered the options this country would face if the Soviet Union continued its military advances."

At the podium, Rozelle was not comfortable with Al Davis. "He has to come before his peers and get 21 votes," Rozelle said.

The United States couldn't get the United Nations to even mention Russia by name in condemning its invasion.

"When officials discuss the military options now available to the United States, they use words like 'horrendous' and 'scary' and raise the spectre of World War III."

"We are delighted to see the sun this morning," Rozelle said to a question about whether or not the Rose Bowl field would be soggy for Sunday's game between Pittsburgh and Los Angeles. "We've been told all they needed was some wind and a couple of days of sun to dry out both the field and the parking lots, and it looks as though we are going to get both."

"The President has called the invasion the greatest threat to world peace since World War II and has said it is a steppingstone to their possible control over much of the world's oil supplies."

Early this week, outside a Los Angeles restaurant, a Cadillac was parked with a license plate reading OPEC 1. To cover the three news centers this week, the press corps has been logging more than 100 miles a day. Nobody has bothered to figure out what that comes to in numbers of quarts of oil or gallons of gasoline.

"U.S. military options to meet such a threat are severely limited by geography, manpower and equipment ... And it is when defense specialists contemplate U.S. readiness for such an operation against the Soviet Union—particularly in so distant a region as Iran or Pakistan—that the concern about where it might end becomes most grave."

Rozelle talked about instant replay, about artificial turf, expansion, Ed Garvey, travel, realignment, the image of the league.

Later, in the pressroom, writing this, the ballroom empty again, the television lights all gone, workers beginning to stack the chairs, the headline remains.

"U.S. Ponders the Unthinkable."

"Hey, you guys hear? The Pakistanis are massing at the border."

"Gimme the Russians and 10 points," somebody says.

"NBC is trying to get the rights to World War III."

"Who would do the color commentary?"

Somehow, it really wasn't very funny.

FINDING RESPITE WITH THE GREEKS

TARPON SPRINGS, Fla.—The rain and blustery wind outside made the room even warmer, cozier while the boats bobbed gently at the dock down the street.

The old men sat in their grizzled, day-old stubble of beards, under the flat, black fisherman's caps, and sipped the strong coffee out of tiny white cups.

The card game started later.

We had decided, three of us, that there had to be life outside the Super Bowl and its surrounding hysteria.

There was. It was here, in this old Greek fishing and sponge-harvesting center, an hour up the Gulf coast from Tampa.

It was not just a break from the glitter and gloss and gleam leading up to the nation's most grossly overpublicized game.

It was a trip to what we are, or were, as a nation.

The three of us in that warm coffee shop, the Dodekanese, were the only ones who couldn't speak Greek. That made us even. Several of the older men had been here for years and can't speak English. There is no need. They live in this totally Greek enclave. They shop at the Greek markets, attend the Orthodox Church, eat at Costas next door and years ago boarded the boats for two-week cruises into the Gulf to bring back sponges. The industry is all but dead on the Gulf coast now. So they come and sip coffee here. But English is still superfluous.

"In the early years, 1900, this whole street was lined with coffee shops like this," said Phillip Klimis. "I came here from the old country in 1947." He dove for sponges for a couple of years, then went north to Pennsylvania and worked in the steel mills until his closed in 1978, when he took retirement and moved back here.

Now he comes to the coffee shop, sips the hot, sweet mud, plays cards and listens to the talk of horse racing and whether or not Oakland—they don't call them Los Angeles—will beat Washington on Sunday.

"Jimmy the Greek picked Washington," somebody said.

"He don't know nothin'," Komino Haskas snorted. Komino is from the younger generation, although he, too, was born in Greece. "He ain't even Greek, is he?"

Komino is an avid Raiders fan, and goes to as many Tampa Bay Buc games as he can. He's also one of the rare eligible bachelors here, a mark of distinction almost as great as the old one of being captain of your own boat.

"I'll tell you," Komino says, looking fondly about the room. "They might not be able to speak English, some of them, but they can name you every quarterback in the National Football League." The coffee shop arguments are heated, vocal on this gray, dismal day when it's better to gather over the Greek espresso than to be outside.

Close your eyes, and you could be in some Mediterranean village, with the store sign names and even the songs on the jukebox lettered in the Cyrillic characters, the menus filled with octopus, grape leaves wrapped about some ancient Greek dish, Joe Theismann and Lyle Alzado just distant mythical figures, like minor deities on a misty Olympus.

"Tarpon Springs was once bigger than Tampa and St. Pete and all the others," says George Billiris. His business card proclaims him a "sponge merchant international."

His family goes back to generations of well-to-do sponge commerce in Greece and to the start of the business here. They have seen it all, even down to the present where only four boats remain.

"There once were 180, with an average of six men per boat. This was the sponge center of the world for a while."

Four movies and dozens of television scripts have been filmed here. In "Beneath the Twelve Mile Reef," Billiris was a stand-in for Gilbert Roland.

Now, only tourists flock to the steamy docks in summer, to look at a way of life that has all but vanished from this coast and continent. A local family created a major rift when it purchased and leveled the world's only remaining sponge exchange and rebuilt it as a tourist-oriented delicatessen. There are those here who will never forgive them.

"In 1946, The Disease came," says Billiris. "Overnight, it could leave the ocean floor black." It was the second visit of the mysterious killer. In 1939, "it only hit from 100 feet deep on out. It didn't come in. The one in '46 came all the way in to beach."

It signaled the start of the end.

There were a few spurts of sponge industry left, enough for a couple of new waves of immigrants from Kalymnos, a sparkling island in the Aegean eight miles from the Turkish coast. Kalymnos accounts for more than half the Greek community here, and for the close-knit feeling that pervades the place as much as the sea next door.

"The first wave of Greeks came before 1900, looking for a better way of life. It's a father-to-son trade. You started as the lowest form of life, a deckhand, and graduated up to be a diver and it was a big deal if you became a captain and boat owner. That made you Mr. Big in Tarpon Springs. The disease broke the chain. We lost the youth."

Komino works on air conditioning units. George Tyrikos has not gone down for sponges in more than six years. He is a painter. Their fathers came over together from Greece.

"There's no money in the sponge business anymore," says Komino. "I mean, what would you rather be? A doctor? A lawyer? A dentist? A pharmacist? Or a sponge diver? Most of the guys are going for the education."

Ted Watts, the Oakland cornerback, is a product of Tarpon Springs, where the team is named the Spongers, and the mascot wears a diving helmet.

"Manny Fernandez used to come up here to eat."

On the walls of a restaurant across the street, oils of old scenes line the walls, the now vanished wooden dock lined with sponge boats named Kalymnos and Symi and Eleni. "The world sponge industry is a $20 million annual one," says Billiris. "Americans account for only about $1.5 million now, the Bahamas maybe $2 million. The rest is in the Mediterranean."

"See that guy?" one says, pointing to a middle-aged man entering the shop. "He was one of the best divers when he was younger. Everybody in here was a diver. Everybody."

Around the room, the card games are going hard as noon arrives.

"I could stay down, no mask, no suit, for two or three minutes," Klimis says. Abruptly, you wonder how long John Riggins can hold his breath. "In the old country, we had one man who stayed down six minutes."

"Leroy Selmon's the greatest defensive end ever lived," Komino says, shifting back to football.

Somebody says no, it's Lyle Alzado.

"Alzado wears pantyhose."

They'll gather here Sunday, and you wonder what it will be like if Alzado sacks Theismann. What will it sound like in the Dodekanese Coffee Shop if Watts, the hometown hero, becomes a national figure by intercepting and scoring?

"I may come down in the middle of the third quarter and start collecting," Komino promises.

Outside, the wind gusts. Tampa and the Super Bowl seem a long way off

♦   ♦   ♦

The column that follows was one of a trio submitted for the Colorado Press Association's annual writing competition for 1986. It was awarded first place for personal columns. The other two appear in the "Golf" and "College Sports" chapters.

June 29, 1986, *Rocky Mountain News*

DRUG VICTIMS ARE TRAGIC, BUT THEY HAD A CHOICE

The headline on the front page of the *Rocky Mountain News* yesterday was stark enough:

Defensive back for Browns dies of cardiac arrest at 23.

It comes only a bit more than a week after Len Bias' death. His, too, was described initially as cardiac arrest. It was only later, when the autopsy was completed, that suspicions were confirmed.

Cocaine had shocked his system into shutting down. Will that be the eventual diagnosis for Cleveland's Don Rogers?

Maybe drugs had absolutely nothing to do with Rogers' death. But we are so conditioned now. An athlete dies. It is like one of those word association tests. "Athlete dead. Drugs."

Please don't use the phrase "recreational drugs" around me. There was nothing "recreational" about Len Bias' use. Recreational. The word seems to imply fun, a level of tolerance, of pleasure. There was no fun in what happened to Len Bias.

We in my business cater to that by using "recreation" as a modifier, thus draping it with some credibility.

"Recreational drugs," we write. It implies fun. It delivers Len Bias on a slab.

I hope every 10- or 11-year-old in the nation who would be an NBA star read those stories, the ones that claim Bias never used the stuff "except just this once." Once was too many. Certainly, Len Bias' death is a tragedy. More to the point, it was a waste.

Recreational my behind.

It has been interesting, reading all the stories, watching the newscasts, the posturing, the chest-beating, the finger-pointing in the wake of Bias' death.

They have all used the word "tragedy," and I suppose that is fitting. Anytime a future is snuffed out, there is an element of tragedy to it. I grieve for his parents, his family.

But it doesn't go much beyond that. Every politician with working instincts is pouncing on it, including those in the coaching profession and so-called educators who would duck any distant responsibility.

As a result, Len Bias is being elevated to a status in death he may never have achieved in life. That's the real tragedy, the fact we'll never know, will we?

From all accounts, he was a pleasant kid on the verge of great wealth, a talented basketball player who had been used by the University of Maryland, but who in turn had used Maryland as well.

He was caught in the euphoria of the whole thing, and somebody talked him into it "just this once." At least, that's the story we are told.

I am sorry for Len Bias. But there is a point missing in most of what has been written and said about him so far.

We have a long polished black wall in Washington that lists the names of our Vietnam War dead. They were individual tragedies, too. None got the headlines Len Bias has.

Children die of abuse every day. They may get a paragraph on the back page. Aren't they human tragedies?

Some ghetto youngster bereft of hope and overdosed on that "recreational" junk is every bit the loss Len Bias was. And we have national cemeteries filled with neat graves and crosses of youth from any number of generations who were given uniforms and no choice and sent away with a rifle.

As with Bias, we will never know what they might have done, might have accomplished for us all, and for themselves, had they lived.

That has always been the tragedy when a youth dies. We have the measure of a man or a woman who lives a normal span. We can see their achievements, their limitations. It is sad; and we miss them. But we have no idea where the horizon was for Len Bias, or for some kid on a bike struck and killed by a drunk.

All of this is leading to a point.

The soldier, the kid on a bike, the infant born with some defect that takes him even before he can recognize a sunset, none of them operate by choice.

Len Bias did.

That should be the true message for the kids reading about his death. That's what should be drummed home to them, when some slimy piece of human garbage plies them with that stuff.

Soldiers, true victims of whatever kind, have little choice.

Len Bias did.

Len Bias could have said "No."

May 28, 1989, *Denver Post*

MOVE FROM OLD BUILDING ELICITS FOND MEMORIES

Other faces, other bylines.

What you are reading this morning is the next to last edition of the *Denver Post* from our present home. I kept thinking of that this Memorial Day weekend, taking the back stairs up to the office where colleagues were busy stuffing the detritus of years, sometimes decades, into packing boxes.

We're moving, as you've been advised elsewhere today, I'm sure. To new digs, fancy ones, with views, new furniture, lots of glass and chrome and glitter befitting a major metropolitan daily. Uptown, big-time.

But I'm going to miss this place, the old one, the one that fits like 5-year-old shoes. The one where the stone steps are slightly bowed in the middle from so many feet wearing on them over so many years and where decades of marvelous newsmen and women worked.

It's a mixed bag for me. This is my second farewell to this building. The major part of my working life has been spent right here at 650 15th Street, and I sat in the office the other afternoon, remembering.

What would Jim Graham think of our business today? Graham? Nah. You're too young. Graham is—was—a sports columnist here. Graham came out of the Battle of the Bulge with frostbite, and I often thought it must have penetrated to his innards as well. He was a curmudgeon, a grumbler, a tilter at windmills and one of the nicest men I've known in this business. He had one of this city's best collections of opera recordings, and fancied himself an expert on wines. He and the Broncos' Allan Phipps used to get into long debates.

When Graham died, they found dozens and dozens of vintage years tucked in closets and under the bed. All were vinegar. Because of his war experiences, he kept the place at a minimum of 80 degrees. He wore paper clips as tie clasps, and gravy as tie patterns. He lived for the blunt question. "Did you jump or were you shoved?" he asked Lou Saban the morning Saban resigned as Broncos' head coach.

He died in San Francisco, out there to attend the start of the opera season. They found his body one morning, riding up and down in an elevator at his hotel where he'd returned from that evening's performance, proving columnists go to glamourous places but sometimes come to unexpected ends.

Graham. I watched Michael Knisely pack some files this week, and I thought of Graham, and how he refused ever to call Muhammad Ali by any name but Cassius Clay. And I thought of Harry Farrar, easily the most talented man ever to occupy these column spaces for the *Post*.

You never read Sam Pirkle? Poor child. Farrar, cloaked as Pirkle, could undress the high, the mighty and the pretenders as well as anyone in American journalism. Red Smith? I miss Pirkle, and I envy Farrar for his talent. Sometime, with a free moment, do yourself a favor. Go back and get a copy of an old *Post,* and read Pirkle nee Farrar.

We used paste and rulers and pencils and copy paper then. There was noise, the metallic symphony of typewriters that built and built as deadlines neared. We had a Western Union wire, and wire copy machines that would clatter to life, and a bell to signal when something big was breaking. Computers don't signal. You cannot reach into them and rip off the day's startling headline.

I miss it, that part. Like many of my generation, I have compromised but never quite surrendered to these new electronic marvels. I memorize the simplest of codes and functions and procedures, but I have no intention or desire of ever knowing why it is I do them or do them in a certain order.

It's enough that it works. When we first switched to the tubes, I used to write my column at home, on an old upright Smith-Corona (still on top of the file cabinet), and then bring it to the office and type it in. I couldn't think on those damn tubes.

I think of the days when we actually had copy boys who went for coffee and snatched late stories out of the typewriter as you finished a page, or a half page if it was really getting late.

I remember the great flood of '65, and how frustrating it was for me. I had just come over from the *News* and had no permanent assignment, and here was one of the biggest stories in Denver history and I wasn't part of it. I watched them working by candlelight on the desk down on the second floor, and wandered around hoping somebody would need an extra body.

I started covering the Denver Broncos the year (1966) they went through three coaches and two general managers, a player rebellion, a quarterback strike, fights on the practice field and shoving matches and food fights on the plane on the way home. They also got marooned by fog in San Diego. I wondered why I had never pursued the law or archeology, two other early interests.

You could smoke then. Some still chewed. Swearing was allowed, and nobody brought running shoes, little silky shorts and bean sprouts to the office.

I wonder: Who will be the first to spill coffee on the carpet in the new joint? The ghostly laughter will be familiar. And why do I hear "Aida" in the background?

<hr>

June 2, 1989, *Denver Post*

MIXED SIGNALS CONFUSE KIDS

The subject today, students, is signals.

Not the "Hup One, Hup Two!" kind, please understand.

Mixed signals.

As in, that rollicking band of happy-go-lucky beer drinkers on Miller Lite, the ones who can't decide if it tastes great or fills less. Either way, it looks like the only possible way we should be spending our spare moments.

I defy you to look at almost any sporting event on television and miss this merry group. Of course, if you'd rehearsed as long as they must on the product, you'd be happy, as well.

As in, Rick Pitino, who resigned from Providence protesting the only place he ever really wanted to be was back in New Yawk City, now resigns from the Knicks protesting the only place he ever really wanted to be was back out in a rural, academic setting.

As in, in Dallas, the Mavericks are asked permission for the now-coachless Knicks to talk to Dallas coach John MacLeod about maybe coming to the big city to replace the departed Pitino, who is in Kentucky accepting a seven-year, $105,000 contract to take over that tainted program and make it well again. The $105,000, of course, is merely the tip of the iceberg, perhaps a 10th of what this Al Pacino look-alike will harvest annually there amid the splendor of the bluegrass.

And, while we see these signals, we are hammered with incessant advertisements: Don't drink and drive. Preferably, don't drink period. Don't take drugs. Say no. Isn't booze a drug? Doesn't it numb, warp, twist and addict, too?

And we glorify it, give it a good-ol'-boy glamour, a respectability that tells teenage viewers and younger, "Hey, it's OK. Have a good time. In fact, have another." Almost on the same page, we are reading stories of one-car accidents, fatal ones, or of some guy gone berserk under the influence.

What are we saying here?

We preach loyalty and integrity while we practice all the gypsy vices in sports. A suburban Denver linebacker signs with Miami because he likes Jimmy Johnson's style. Then Jimmy Johnson heads for Dallas, which has just fired the man who coached it to five Super Bowls, more than any other coach. Johnson can change. The kid can't.

Signals? What's a kid to believe?

The panic quality that greeted the surgeon general's threat against booze advertisements was centered on its possible effect on commercial endorsements of sports events. Whatever would we do for a Super Bowl, or the World Series, or the NBA playoffs without the Masked Marauder?

I'd like to suggest maybe they'd endure, anyway. If it's too bad, they might even play the World Series and the Super Bowl where they belong, in daylight. And they might finish the NBA finals before June 20. The NBA season, if it goes the full seven, will end two days after the U.S Open is decided, and 10 days after we know whether or not Sunday Silence has won the Triple Crown.

TV has warped things that much, and done it by taking money from sponsors that include the surgeon general's booze-making targets.

We preach conditioning, health, exercise and a happier, longer life, and we grab a captive television audience by the eyeballs with clever commercials lauding the pleasures of a brew. (Understand here, I drink the stuff. Understand, too, I like it. Understand, once again, I'm now old enough to know what it can do. Is a 14-year-old watching the NBA finals?)

There would be sports after booze, just as there have been sports after cigarettes.

As for coaches jumping contracts, I have fewer problems there. Loyalty is a two-way lane, and the reason a coach is being hired is always rooted in the fact another one has just been fired. Pitino, I understand, always wanted a New York job, but when he got one, he discovered he didn't like the pro life as well as he did the college one.

I'll accept that, along with the proviso that a million bucks a year will let him have Mindy's cheesecake flown down daily to Lexington. John MacLeod has been working at Dallas on a handshake agreement with an owner who, in February, intimated he ought to fire the guy.

What loyalty does that build in MacLeod, who is struggling to right a team with one key man in drug rehab—watched too many commercials?—another pouting, others hurt.

Take the job, MacLeod. Good for you, Pitino. Enjoy the countryside before the suffocating pressure gets to you, as well.

When they stop firing, then I'll hone my sense of outrage at coaches jumping to better jobs one step ahead of the alumni or the owner.

But the signals? We just ousted the Speaker of the House for the first time in our history. The major signals I've been noticing of late are full of very loud static.

September 22, 1989, *Denver Post*
NO OUTRAGE FOR ME

An editor who had retired from one of the big eastern dailies once remarked that columnists should always write from a sense of outrage.

He must have meant in summer and winter for sports, and politics anytime.

Constant outrage leads to headaches, ulcers and gas. And I'm not certain it always leads to the best columns, either. Somewhere, there ought to be room for just enjoying life.

That's where spring and fall enter the equation. Who can be mad in my business, standing on the clubhouse verandah at Augusta National in April, staring out on that lush, rolling course with its banks of brilliant new flowers with a whole new year ahead? If that triggers dismay, outrage, see your doctor.

Or spring training. The clack of palm fronds in the soft, warm breeze, sun on the face, players who are still speaking to each other and to the press, games that don't count and forecasts that count even less. No night games. Especially that. What's not to like?

Outrage is easy when it's 90 degrees and the humidity matches it in the midst of a seven-game losing streak in July, or when the windchill is minus 30 and the NFL's not-so-instant replay crew is taking one interminable delay after another to make decisions in December. It comes naturally then.

And it's no trouble at all when some coach is fired as scapegoat for what his players failed to do, or some player is dumped because a coach was too stupid or ineffective to put him in the right situation or develop his ability.

But late September? With the leaves turning, and hay fever season blessedly over, and you can see your breath again in the early morning? The best time of all is just ahead:

October, the playoffs, the World Series, the meat of the college seasons, the appetizers for the pros. Nobody has been fired yet, and even the 0-2 teams can look at the rest of the schedule and hope. The casualty count hasn't mounted, and the weather is still perfect for tailgating on a Saturday or Sunday afternoon.

Locally, it's a vintage year so far. I don't even mind munching on a few invectives from the outrage times. As long as they are low-fat, noncaloric, I deserve to eat my words. Yes. Dan Reeves obviously made some good decisions, and I suspect his 1989 edition is one that will get better, not flatten out or decline, as the season goes on. So here's a toast, not a roast, for the pride of Americus [Ga.].

Bill McCartney, like Reeves, has stubbornly stood his ground, and he and the Buffs are winning their way, the right way. He had the guts to throw his starting cornerbacks off the team just before the start of the year. It may still hurt him at times, but he followed his convictions.

"I want Coach Mac to know that he can wake up in the morning and he can suspend a couple of kids if they are not willing to meet expectations of the university," CU president Gordon Gee said the week before the season opener.

"And we are not going to judge him solely by what is happening out there on the field. I suspect there are very few programs in the country where the coach would feel comfortable doing that."

Outrage? Thunderous applause is due, instead. For McCartney, for Gee, for a school that would challenge all the prevailing wisdom that winning is the only object. Just so long as they remember it is an object, of course.

September and October are not made for rage. I still get nostalgic thinking of the years our kids were playing or cheerleading in high school, of the drives to little towns on Friday night, homing in on the big lights on tall poles to find the field, then shivering and yelling and waiting in long lines at the booster group concession stand for coffee.

It was invariably terrible coffee and tremendous Friday pleasure.

Sports are supposed to be that—pleasure, fun, diversion, a way to forget the other elements of life, the sad parts, the outrageous parts. The bad times come naturally, with no effort. And it takes no columnistic genius to note that cheating is bad and losing is not desirable and ugly people seldom win beauty contests.

The trick lies in separating human duplicity from human frailty. You properly get outraged only at the first. Anything less is just needless heavy breathing in print. Taking a called third strike with the bases loaded comes under the second. So does dropping a pass in the end zone. A coach who deliberately plays an injured kid qualifies as an example of the first. The Chicago Cubs and Kansas State in October—any October—are examples of the second.

"Avoid fried foods which angry up the blood," Satchell Paige once cautioned. "If your stomach disputes you, lie down and pacify it with cool thoughts."

Paige obviously was a September man, an October man, a springtime man, and would have made a lousy columnist, by that eastern editor's measurement.

Me? Give me now, anytime.

May 6, 1990, *Denver Post*

DERBY WINNER'S JOY UNBRIDLED

LOUISVILLE, Ky.—Weep no more, my lady. Not unless they are long overdue tears of joy.

So it took 53 years of trying. So you became 92 in the process. So your trainer, Carl Nafzger, had to call the race for you because you couldn't see over those standing in front of you.

Wheelchairs don't let you sit too high.

Wait no more, my lady. It all came true on a May afternoon that seemed to open itself just in time for you and for your horse, Unbridled.

And, at the end, Mrs. Frances Genter of Bloomington, Minn., could only listen as Nafzger screamed.

"I couldn't see, so Carl made the call for me," she said later. "He said, 'He's sixth ... he's fifth ... he's going to win it.'"

A week of rain miraculously ended an hour before the race. A day-long drizzle lifted, the temperature went from 46 to 54 and the sun came out. It created and island of blue directly over Churchill Downs almost on cue as 128,257 conducted that traditional weep-out, singing, "My Old Kentucky Home" as the horses paraded in front of the grandstand.

At the end, there is that haunting refrain, "Weep no more, my lady." An omen, maybe?

At 3:30 p.m. in Denver, your 3-year-old was a 10-1 longshot, largely ignored on a day and a week devoted almost exclusively to Mister Frisky and Summer Squall.

At 3:45, your horse with the recycled name and the onetime bull rider as a trainer and the hand-me-down rider with the reluctant whip was prancing in the winner's circle.

It was Unbridled, coming out of the final turn as if launched from a slingshot, his jockey taking one peek backward, shooting past Summer Squall and the desperately coaxing Pat Day and winning by 3 1/2 lengths.

And it was Mrs. Genter, 92, wheeled across the track and into that horseshoe of roses to end the longest vigil yet. Art Rooney had to wait 40 years for an NFL title, and, like you, he missed one of his team's great moments. He was in an elevator when Franco Harris made the Immaculate Reception.

Which is the better story—Unbridled, the name reincarnated from that of an earlier Genter horse that died almost 40 years ago, or this tiny old woman with the long, long dream?

"This is such a thrill. I'm really, really thrilled," said the woman, who with her late husband Harold, founded Toastmaster and later became the first lady of Florida thoroughbred breeding.

They got into the horse business in 1939—and not until this week did she get to come to Churchill Downs on the first Saturday in May as an owner.

There were chances, of course. But there are some 48,000 thoroughbreds foaled each year, and only 15 lined up in the sudden burst of sunlight yesterday.

The original Unbridled was one of the top 2-year-olds in 1949, but didn't make it to the 1950 Kentucky Derby and died at 3. Five other Genter colts were Derby quality, but for one reason and another, failed to make this magic weekend in the bluegrass country.

The family grew and left, her husband died and she remarried and the years flew. The breeding business in Florida grew apace. But always, on Kentucky Derby day, she came as a spectator, never into Section 318 on the third floor of the clubhouse, where owners and trainers are closeted.

Then, when she did, her trainer called the race she couldn't see.

"I told her, 'You just won the Kentucky Derby, Mrs. Genter,'" Nafzger said afterward. And what did she say? "Ohh!"

Unbridled, ridden by Craig Perret after Day opted for Summer Squall, had reduced his owner to one squeaky, delighted response.

He had blitzed a field by coming from as far back as 12th, and if they'd gone longer, he would have won bigger.

Yesterday, Perret talked of seams opening just at the right moments, "and I was at the right place at the right time."

So, at last, was Mrs. Frances Genter.

August 3, 1990, *Denver Post*

LAND OF ACTION BEFORE THE SUN RISES

TOKYO—Dabadabadababababa.

Sorry. It's as close as I can come to what the Japanese auctioneer in black, knee-high rubber boots sounded like at 6 o'clock of a Friday morning.

I can't understand American auctioneers, either. It must be the breed.

Your Denver Broncos still slept the sleep of the innocent—or the jet-lagged. Presumably, they were all home when I left the hotel at 4:30.

The Tokyo fish market is supposed to be the largest in the world. It doesn't get quite the play of the Ginza or the Geisha or the Imperial Palace. But it's bedrock Tokyo, a must-see.

"But you must be there before 5," the man at the information desk had said. "It's over by 6."

So I went into the gray, muggy dawn and got into one of Tokyo's magnificent cabs—the doors open automatically, the drivers wear ties and white gloves, and if you have the desk clerk write out your destination, you'll get there.

You hear it before you see it, or smell it. The sound kind of builds, blending into a smorgasbord of horns, engines, shouts.

And there it is, blocks of long, low sheds, hurrying workmen, whizzing carts being towed by what sound like motor scooters.

"We came to experience the culture," Seattle's Chuck Knox had told a press conference the day before. For some reason, no Broncos or Seahawks were visibly experiencing this particular culture. Not at 4:45 a.m.

Walk past the ice house. Next to the docks, maybe two blocks away down long, narrow aisles, it's the most critical spot in the whole place. Walls of ice, whole bergs of the stuff, are being sawed and chipped and shaped and whisked off to all corners.

Watch your step. One of those motor-scooter carts may run you down. Or one of the old-fashioned ones, a 10-footer with wheels at the back and a reed mat on the bed and a man in front, in undershirt, handkerchief wrapped about his head, pulling the cart loaded six- and seven-high with boxes full of iced fish. Dan Reeves should put every lineman into one of these traces and make him pull for a week instead of conditioning drills.

Outside, rows of trucks are waiting. One, a small semi, has its driver, head back, mouth open, sound asleep.

But where are the fish? So far, it's ice, and Styrofoam cartons, and noise. I pick an aisle and start toward the river. There they are.

In an area roughly the size of three football fields, there are thousands of them, four and five feet long, mostly tuna and dolphin and some salmon and shark to untrained South Platte River eyes.

They are frozen solid, just off the factory boats, and a kind of ground mist is enveloping the area as it rises from the carcasses. Hundreds of men are walking down the rows in their Japanese "Wellies," poking with picks, peeling back flaps of flesh, grading.

The sun is finally beginning to tip some buildings nearby.

Speak English? I ask a man sitting on a three-step platform at the end of an acre of fish. No. But he taps his watch and motions with his hand. Stay, he indicates.

I wait. And at 5:45, a siren goes off. Then, one after another, a hundred handheld bells begin to ring through the knee-high fog in the shed. Now I know what the man was doing with his hand, simulating a bell ringing.

All the inspection stops. The men who had been going down the rows, peering into the gutted fish with flashlights, assemble on the platform. Each tugs on a leather cap, his official badge of office.

And the auctioneer, clipboard in hand, begins a wild, agitated act, jumping from one foot to the other, waving, shouting. It is over in 15 minutes. Everything is sold. Your Denver Broncos even may have eaten some of it last night.

I walk back through the sheds. Abruptly, those hundreds of empty cubicles now are filled with squid in long metal tanks and shrimp and clams and fish, all on beds of ice. If it lives in the sea and is edible, it's here this Friday morning. Restaurant buyers are making their way down the aisles by now.

One is munching on some raw fish he holds in butcher paper.

It's 6 a.m. and full daylight, and the almost frenetic pace has slowed. The man at the desk was right. Get there early.

I head for the street to hail a cab, past the white semi. The driver is exactly where I left him, still snoring amid the bedlam. Obviously, he, too, had listened to the man at the desk.

<hr>

January 13, 1991, *Denver Post*

COWBOY HAS RADAR DETECTOR, WILL TRAVEL

He had been up all night, riding an airplane from Calgary to Portland, Ore.

He was rushing to make an afternoon rodeo in a city near the Oregon city of roses. And he was late.

"There was a problem with the plane, and when I landed, I rushed outside and there was one cab left at the curb. It was old, and the driver had to weigh 300 pounds.

"I told him where I needed to go. 'Well, I dunno,' he said. So I kept slapping $20 bills on the dashboard. It cost me $80 to get 80 miles an hour.

"I dug a radar detector out of my luggage and put it on the dash, and I got in the backseat and started changing into my work jeans and spurs, and he went barreling along, and when we got there, there were two horses left.

"One was mine."

Dave Appleton laughed as he stirred a bowl of oatmeal at his hotel late this week before heading for the Coliseum and that afternoon's rodeo.

"I won."

Welcome to the life of a cowboy, 1990-style.

You listen to this transplanted Australian, the 1988 all-around champion, a Coors Shootout titlist, a 30-year-old with a firm grip on his life and his future as well as his present. And you contrast his life with that of another athlete, an NFL one, for instance, or a major-league baseball player.

I know one former Nugget who once called the Nugget office in June and asked how to get an airplane ticket. He didn't know. It had always been done for him.

Rodeo cowboys laugh at such stories. They are the last of a self-reliant breed that has long since died in team sports. On the rodeo circuit, you take care of yourself. "We're the last of the Mohicans," says Appleton. He has tried travel agencies. "They last about three weeks. I can ride in three rodeos the same day. We all do. And you have to have Plan A and Plan B and Plan C and Plan D. For the same day."

He made $121,000 his best year, when he was the best there is. The last two years, his friend and travel colleague, Ty Murray, has seized that all-around title. But it's typical of the cowboy life that Murray, Appleton and Cody Lambert have formed this informal triumvirate, traveling and working together. "I make arrangements and Cody helps and Ty makes all the money," Appleton says.

Appleton came to the United States in 1980. "I was 20, and I didn't know a soul."

Now, he's one of the Professional Rodeo Cowboys Association stars, is bringing out his own line of shirts (The Lone Roo Collection, part of the Roper line, by the Karman Western Apparel on Wazee St., and Akubra Hats. End of commercial).

He rode by car-light in Australia, where rural rodeos might last past dusk and patrons were asked to circle the ring and turn on headlights. "All you can see is this dusty haze hanging in the light beams, and every once in a while you see some legs go through the lights."

It conditioned him for moments like the Cowboys' Christmas, the July 4 feeding frenzy when a man might be booked into three arenas an airplane ride apart on the same day. It's nothing to compete, pack, drive all night, compete, pack and drive again. All expenses are yours. And it costs to enter.

Appleton, a 4-handicapper, looks at golf with a certain pro envy. Phil Blackmar, the 100th man on the PGA Tour earnings list for 1989, earned $140,949. A year earlier, as the best cowboy there was, Appleton missed that total by just under $20,000.

"I'd like to see us get to where our 50th or 60th guy would be making $60,000 or $70,000, and the winner would have the potential of $500,000." It's a dream he knows is hard to realize.

"The biggest difference between rodeo and, say, basketball, is that when the game is over, mom and dad and the kids can go out in back and find a hoop and pretend they are Michael Jordan. When the rodeo ends, it's hard to find a bull and pretend to be Ty Murray, or a bareback horse and pretend to be me."

So it's back to the road, and being what he loves—a rodeo cowboy. Even if it means a week that includes Cheyenne, then Hill City, Kans., then Casper, then Dodge City, then Phillipsburg, Kans., then Deadwood, then Casper again. Driving all the way.

"I called a place in Phillipsburg. It was only a three-hour ride from Dodge, and I knew we needed a good night's sleep. 'We have one room left. It has two beds,' the guy said. 'The queen size is $45. The king size is $50. It depends on which bed you sleep in.'

"I slept in the king and made it up next morning but he caught me."

January 15, 1991, *Denver Post*

WAR'S STARK REALITY WILL BE PUNCTUATED BY PLAYING OF GAMES

It was a bit of graffiti scrawled on a subway wall in New York that caught my eye sometime back in the early 1970s. "Old soldiers never die. Just young ones," it read.

It's funny, isn't it, what lingers in the mind and then surfaces at appropriate times? E. B. White once wrote that "the time not to become a father is 18 years before a war." I have a quiet sense of relief this morning that my three sons are well past that age.

Somehow, writing about games didn't seem to fit this morning's word menu. Understand: I think the distraction of games will be more important than ever very shortly, and I am not one of those who piously thinks every game should be canceled. We will need those brief hours and those games to relieve the awful reality of the rest of the day and night.

We won't shut down movie theaters, or concert halls. We shouldn't close stadiums or arenas, either. More on that in a moment.

But for now, this particular morning, this particular day, just hours from the United Nations deadline in Kuwait, I wondered what life was like on the Air Force Academy campus. We take it for granted, except in these moments. Twenty years ago, being a cadet was not fashionable. ROTC cadets had to sneak to formation in civvies on state campuses.

This time, there is a curious resignation to the whole thing. We are going to war. And 60 miles south of Denver, plastered majestically against the Front Range on a 17,000–acre reservation, the Air Force Academy sits as one of three of the most distinct campuses in the nation.

What was yesterday like for them? Fisher DeBerry, coach of the football team that just beat Ohio State in the Liberty Bowl, was on the road like his colleagues all over the country. He was recruiting. J. T. Kokish, the linebacker, is getting ready for the East-West Shrine game. The basketball team was preparing for last night's home game against Doane College, and the hockey team was working on its half of the field house.

Life went along roughly normal down the hill, on the athletic side.

But up the hill, in the dorms, the dining room, the vast parade-ground area?

"It was basically all anyone was talking about," hockey goalie Mike Blank said in a phone interview. "Our table in the dining room is normally not too vocal, but that was the whole topic of conversation at breakfast. And it's about all you hear walking to class."

A B-52, symbol of another war, is poised to greet visitors as they drive up the hill from Interstate 25. The cemetery reminds us of even more wars, other airmen, ones who wore fleece-lined jackets and flew B-17s over Germany, or even older ones, who dared steer canvas-sided aeroplanes over trenches in France.

There is no escaping it at the AFA. It's the very reason for its existence. I doubt, really, that the conversation at Colorado or Colorado State or Wyoming was a great deal different. If you are male, and 20, or 19, or 21, Saudi Arabia and Iraq and Kuwait are going to be more prominent in your thinking this morning than who leads the WAC in basketball or whether the UPI vote on the national championship means as much.

The world is about to intrude grotesquely on your life and that is a shock over oatmeal and toast.

It's just that at the Air Force Academy, as at West Point and Annapolis, the purpose for attending is so vastly different. They knew from the start that such a morning could come.

"We knew when we came here that it was different," Blank said. "This just brings that realization a little closer. We were aware of what we might have to do. It is always in the back of your mind."

Now, they inspect passersby a little more closely. Terrorism is a distinct possibility on such a reservation, more so than on other campuses. Blank, like so many AFA cadets, plans on a career in the air. So he'll have a one-year flight school facing him after graduation this spring.

"I guess someone at West Point would face a quicker obligation," he said of immediate service in the Middle East.

As for canceling games, this future airman sees no reason. "That would just mean he has won," he said. "Cancel the Super Bowl? It would mean he has succeeded in making us change our way of life. No, I don't think we should stop any games."

Neither do I. There is no danger anyone will confuse one with the other.

January 30, 1991, *Denver Post*

GOLDEN GLOVES TRAINS KIDS FOR MORE THAN BOXING

The contrast was as dramatic as it's possible to imagine.

I had just flown 1,500 miles from the land of palms and sea and the mind-numbing excess of a Super Bowl week. Corporations thought nothing of reserving the trendiest restaurants for 200 of their favored clients.

Tickets were going for $1,000. Thirty-second ABC commercials sold for $800,000.

And now it was early Monday evening, and I was pulling up outside the one-story building on the southwest corner of Sloan Lake. It used to be a gun club. For the past year and a half, it has been the training site for kids who want to learn to box.

Snow hissed against the stucco sides of the building. Inside, it sifted through a broken pane in one of the windows.

A heater kept the room warm, and an electronic device signaled a one-minute pause after fictional rounds. It helped keep a pace to the evening.

"Some of the guys just left," said Joe Garcia. He is 68, and you have read about him in my columns for several years. I think he does, by himself, more good than 90 percent of the bureaucrats ever accomplish in keeping kids pointed in the right direction.

He's never made a dime from it. Joe Garcia is a giver, not a taker.

Now, on this snowy late January night, he watches 12-year-old Jamie Barnes, who is shadow boxing in a ring that is four years older than he is. "Don't be lookin' down, Jamie," Garcia calls out over the sound of the heater and the wind coming off the lake and slamming against the building. "What I tell you? Don't be lookin' down."

He watches, nods in satisfaction. "We took him to Prescott [Ariz.] not long ago. He won a bronze. We had two bronzes and a silver. And one of the fighters from Rude Park won a gold. He'll go on to the nationals in Iowa."

All the committee meetings and learned speeches and sociological studies in the world don't accomplish what Joe Garcia and his friends do in this gym from 6 to 9:30 p.m. five nights a week, every week of the year. "We had 17 kids in here last Friday night," Garcia says.

"They don't even have to want to box in tournaments," he says. "If they just want to work out, learn to box, they're welcome." But don't waste his time, or those of kids who do. Garcia, who won 19 of 21 amateur fights and went 22-5 as a pro before and after World War II, was still getting in the ring until he had a hip operation six years ago.

"They couldn't hit me."

Beside him, Mike Quintana, 48, watches two novice super heavyweights, Gale McGee, 21, of Wheat Ridge, and Rod Silva, 22, of Edgewater. They were teammates on Jefferson High School football teams, and work together as drillers for Ground Exploration. Neither has had a fight.

Quintana once boxed for Garcia, back in the early 1960s, and went undefeated in 30 amateur bouts before he enlisted in the Marines and fought with the lst Marine Division in Vietnam. Later, he served as a guard at Chino State Prison in California.

"Elbows in," he shouts at Silva, who is laboring the heavy bag that is wrapped in masking tape to keeps its innards inside. Silva grunts and hits, grunts and hits. "You had 75," Quintana calls out. Seventy-five blows in 30 seconds. The last dozen were stingless, off arms left spaghettilike from muscle fatigue. Seventy-five in 30 seconds. If he was a commercial, he would have cost $800,000 on ABC Sunday night.

"We work them hard," says Garcia. "I try to get kids off the street, work 'em hard and they go home all tired out."

... There are no league officials, no strutting superstars. Just some kids in sweat clothes with holes in them, and two men who give lovingly of their time.

"We don't make a dime," says Quintana. They spend them, though. Coming back from Prescott with seven people packed in his Jeep Cherokee, he gassed up the final time at Raton, N.M.

"After we paid for the gas, we had 15 cents left among us," he says. I left, wondering how many Giants and Bills went home from Tampa with 15 cents left in their pockets.

What would be worth $1,000 a ticket?

It was the priciest Super Bowl so far. And the best. "The price is holding," the guy on the elevator at the Tampa Hyatt said shortly after noon on game day. "I'm still getting $700 for low end zone."

Normally, by kickoff, it's possible to get a Super Bowl ticket for almost face value outside a gate when the pro scalpers still have a handful. But not XXV. Allegedly, tickets were still going for $300 at the halftime intermission, and choice seats commanded $1,800. Face value was $150.

Riding to the game that day, I started thinking—is any sporting event worth, say, $1,000? Any? Ever? Can you think of any single game or race or boxing match or shotput or pole vault in history for which you would pay $1,000 to watch?

Me, either. None.

But, as we drew closer to the stadium that afternoon, I started listing events I might be willing to pay $1,000 to become a silent, invisible, witness.

For instance, since this is Sunday, church day, I would pay $1,000 to stand in the crowd and hear the Sermon on the Mount. And I'd pay $1,000 to watch Moses descend the fog-shrouded mountain with the Ten Commandments in his arms. Would he really look like Charlton Heston?

Those are the events that would be worth that kind of money.

I would love to have seen Edison at the moment his tinkering convinced him the incandescent lightbulb was more than just a theory, that it actually worked. And I would pay to have been on the North Carolina strip of beach in 1903 when the Kitty Hawk lifted from the dunes and launched the era of flight. That would have been worth $1,000, that moment.

What else?

It's all subjective. You probably have your list ... Maybe for some of you, there are sporting events that you'd be willing to pay that sum to watch in person.

It wouldn't be the day the Four Horsemen are born. Not the game. It wasn't the game, after all. It was what Grantland Rice wrote about Notre Dames' 13-7 win over Army on Oct. 18, 1924, the image he created in words, that immortalized the Notre Dame backfield. Maybe—maybe—I'd pay $1,000 to sit in the press box and watch him type the most memorable sports phrase in history: "Outlined against a blue-gray October sky, the Four Horsemen rode again."

So, as long as we are on scribblers, I'd also pay to watch Shakespeare at work with a crow quill and a candle. Did his lips move as he wrote? Did he sound the words, voice them out loud as they would have to be spoken later on the stage? Or did he stare off into space like most of us do at times, stand, scratch, twitch, go get a glass of water and do anything to postpone the actual writing?

Ditto being a dust mote in the room where Beethoven or Mozart spun their genius. What were their little composing quirks? Did the end of the day see a ream of scores wadded and crumpled in the corner of the room, or was it all, as Mozart said, as if he saw the notes in his head and just had to copy them down on paper?

I'd pay $1,000 to attend The Last Supper, and to peek into Washington's cabin on the coldest night at Valley Forge and glimpse his despair. It would also be worth the price to watch a returning general being feted in Rome. Would he, too, look like Charlton Heston? Or would he look like James Mason? I'd like to see what Genghis Khan's battle tent looked like, be there when Brendan the Irish monk (not Columbus) bumped ashore in the New World. Or when the *Mayflower* dropped anchor and they stood there, staring at the dark shoreline, wondering.

A friend says he'd pay $1,000 to be in Hitler's bunker at the finish, and another says she'd go to the bank and write a check if she could stand outside the Winter Palace in St. Petersburg and watch the Russian Revolution begin.

Make your own lists. Just know this:

I'd pay bleacher seat prices, $1 or so, to go back and see if Babe Ruth really did call his shot, and to hear a Knute Rockne halftime oration, or stand and watch Hitler's face as Jesse Owens won again and again and again in Berlin in 1936.

But I wouldn't pay one single nickel for any single moment in any single Super Bowl.

May 2, 1991, *Denver Post*
ALL'S QUIET AT DINARD'S STALL DURING DERBY HUBBUB

LOUISVILLE, Ky.—It is 5:30 of a clear, cool, windy morning and the most prominent feature at Churchill Downs at this hour is a full moon.

Birds have set up an awful twittering in the nearby trees, a stable cat is still prowling and out on the fabled track itself, the morning can be heard rather than seen.

"Huff ... huff ... huff," comes the breathing of a horse from the dark. You can hear the pounding of hooves on the dirt, detect dark forms beyond the rail. Across the track, the twin spires are floodlit reminders this is a special place, a special week.

The 117th Kentucky Derby is three days away, and even the backsiders can't quite get a grip on this one. Nobody knows. Not for absolute, chalk-perfect sure.

A year ago, Summer Squall and Mr. Frisky were locks, right? Of course, Unbridled won, but we all learned later it would have been different if Summer Squall hadn't spooked at the head of the stretch and Mr. Frisky hadn't come into the race with a throat infection that went undetected until two weeks after the Derby. Of course.

"Look out," a leadout boy calls. The crowd waiting to talk to Strike the Gold's trainer, Nick Zito, parts. "Horse coming out," somebody calls.

"He'll kick, that one," the groom murmurs. Nobody argues. Meanwhile Zito is sponging Strike the Gold and steam rises from the son of Alydar, who keeps trying to nip his handler.

Everybody around Strike the Gold is in an ugly mood as the light strengthens. He has worked a slow 51 2/5 seconds for a half mile, and Zito is in no mood to talk, although later he will say he liked the workout. Strike the Gold is snapping at anything handy, and Zito walks away from the waiting writers.

The coffee has arrived at the press building, and the forms in the darkness gradually take shape as the light grows and a radio declares "it is 7:13 and we could have rain later this morning."

The little knots of writers and cameras grow around Best Pal and Strike the Gold and Fly So Free, and in the long rows of stalls, horses' heads poke out, ears forward, as they wait for breakfast or a workout.

One place that isn't crowded is barn 41, stall 22. Over there, near one edge of the rows of barns, Dick Lundy stands all by himself, watching. There is a wistful quality to his isolation.

It wasn't supposed to be this way. This is the stall once occupied by Sunday Silence (1989 winner) and before that by Ferdinand (1986) and last year's favorite, Mr. Frisky. Lundy's Dinard would have been one of this week's favorites, but exactly a week ago, it was discovered that Dinard had a torn suspensory ligament behind his left front knee.

Lundy has never saddled a horse in this most famous of horse races. Now, he still won't.

"It will take about three months," he says, watching the crowd about Strike the Gold in the next barn. "No surgery. It will just take time to heal, but we anticipate 100 percent recovery."

Recovery won't be quite the same for his emotions, he admits.

"I have two horses running Friday. It's the only reason I'm still here. Certainly, you'd like to be in the heat of this thing. I thought we had one of the horses that had a real chance at it. I still do. I still think he's as good a 3- year-old as there is in the country.

"How many times do you come to the Kentucky Derby with the favorite and get knocked out the week before?"

The sun is up now, washing shed row and the piles of straw, the horses being hosed off, and Lundy's quiet little corner of this early morning world.

"He's right there," he says of Dinard waving at the first stall. Inside, the Santa Anita Derby winner looks as dejected as his trainer. Dinard's head is down.

Lundy coaxes him with a carrot. For a moment, not even that lures Dinard. Finally, he turns his head, stretches his neck, nibbles, but he doesn't move his feet.

"It should be interesting," Lundy says of Saturday. "It's wide open. But it's kind of hard to drop out and just stand and watch like everybody else.

"This is the first horse I've had that really even deserved to come here."

Beyond, Fly So Free is being led back to his barn. His half mile was clocked in 46 3/5. Lundy watches the growing parade of hangers-on. It could have been his.

He feeds Dinard another carrot. It's at least something to do on a quiet May Day morning.

Magic HIV positive? Say it isn't so

No. There is no other real reaction to yesterday's news out of Los Angeles. Denial is the dominant one.

There has to be some mistake, a test tube switched, something, even as you know it's true. You are reminded of the little boy outside the courthouse when Shoeless Joe Jackson emerged after being banned from baseball:

Say it isn't so, Joe. Say it isn't so, Magic.

I was all but finished with a column on a totally different subject when sports editor Woody Paige called a little after 2 p.m.

"I don't know what you are writing for tomorrow," he said, "but Magic Johnson is retiring. He has been diagnosed with AIDS." (That was the initial report, changed when the details emerged at a later press conference in Los Angeles.)

Flu, the news reports out of L.A. had kept saying, explaining Magic's absence from the Lakers' lineup as the new season got under way. He had missed three straight games.

Flu.

Magic. AIDS. Is there any more improbable linkage than those two nouns? The man whose joie de vivre and dazzling passes and continent-spanning grin marked a whole sport, a whole decade, indeed a generation, is HIV positive.

That, as Johnson's dramatic late afternoon press conference disclosed, is the true diagnosis. He has been tested positive for the HIV virus. He does not have AIDS. He will quit basketball. He will become a spokesman for safe sex. And the rest of us will be left stunned, and wondering, and more than a little wistful.

Could there be a more appropriate spokesman? We have lost something very special in a world that gives us very few such personalities. But maybe we have gained something in the battle with AIDS. No, Magic is not gone as an individual. He'll live his life, as he promised. And perhaps he can give us something of the old magic in a new way, convince kids that sex carries consequences much greater than chewing gum or choosing the next movie. He is now Exhibit A.

You can get an argument in any sports bar in America, indeed, in many drawing rooms and living rooms and work stations. Who most marked the National Basketball Association in the 1980s—Magic or Bird?

You didn't need second names. They had transcended mere identification. It was instant. There was one Magic. There was one Bird, just as, now, there is one Michael. Only a few in any generation ever manage that.

Magic. I saw them together for the first time in Salt Lake City in 1979 in the NCAA Championships, the final game of the Final Four, Magic and Bird, in the dream matchup. Magic's Michigan State team won, and I can still see the almost beatific smile from center court as it ended. Then, for the next decade, working on opposite coasts, they were linked by their brilliance and the almost inevitable march toward their annual June showdown for the league championship.

My other most personal memory was of the playoffs in The Fabulous Forum in 1989, when Magic was hurt and Detroit won its first title. He limped off, quite literally into the shadows leading to the dressing rooms, and the pastel-emotioned Hollywood crowd sounded more like midwestern steelworkers as they chanted his benediction:

"Magic! ... Magic! ... Magic!"

"Is it true?" my daughter asks over the phone. She had been driving somewhere and heard a bulletin over her car radio. On KOA, Andrea van Steenhouse, the noted Denver psychologist, tells listeners how to treat this with their children.

Magic is, after all, a giant, a role model, and it's hard to imagine the impact this announcement will have on kids who saw him on cereal boxes and shoes and television. He was an American hero. What is he now? An American victim? In the United States of the late 20th century, we don't think of industrialists or playwrights or composers. We think of Desert Storm figures, and rock stars, and athletic stars when we select our heroes.

And, of those latter, nobody dominates more than Earvin Johnson Jr., 6-9, 215, 32 years old, three times league MVP, five times the leader who helped the Lakers to an NBA championship, newly married, ambassador, showman—HIV virus.

He was Michelangelo with a basketball. But now? How? When?

Johnson didn't specify, his doctor wouldn't say, or didn't really know. Standing before that assembly of microphones and lights and questions, he said the widespread understanding is "Only gay people can get it. Here I am saying it can happen to anybody."

It has. It has happened to Magic.

June 3, 1992, *Denver Post*

SARAJEVO OF THE OLYMPICS GONE FOREVER

The magic is gone, laughter replaced with tears, cheers with screams, joy with fear.

Just eight years ago, Sarajevo was a place of happiness, of a light snow drifting into the floodlit plaza for the evening medal presentations. It was a place where we sat one night with two Soviet bobsledders who had lost that day. They were each 30 years old and uncertain how much longer they could remain on the national team. We drank a lot of Pivo that night.

It was a place where John Husar of the *Chicago Tribune* and I went to a little cafe near the press center, and were presented with one menu. John held up two fingers, thinking he was signaling for another menu. The waiter showed up with two bowls of beg soup and kept bringing food until we finally decided he thought John had meant two of that night's specials.

It was a place where the people were fantastic in their eagerness to make the Olympic Games work. I worked for the *Rocky* in those years, and roomed with Mike Madigan in a high-rise apartment building that was completed barely in time for our arrival. We were, obviously, the first occupants in AB II, Dobrinja, flat No. 7.

I still have my rooming card with its official stamp. I've kept it, thinking someday I would like to go back with Mary Kay and look up whatever family might be living where Mike and I lived that winter of 1984. It would be fun, I thought.

Sarajevo is—was—a lovely city, set in a circle of mountains, half East in its culture, half West. You could hear muzzeins calling the faithful to prayer, or you could walk on a Sunday morning to an unheated Catholic church. The old market was a marvelous mix of goods, many handworked. I remember walking past the mosque one afternoon and seeing row after row of shoes lined up, waiting for their owners to emerge. And right in the middle of this sea of dark shoes was a pair of white Adidas.

I won't be going back to Sarajevo. Nor will I try to show Mary Kay the beauties of Dubrovnik, that wonder city on the Adriatic coast.

The daily headlines tell of shelling, death, ethnic murder. Furman Bisher of the *Atlanta Journal-Constitution* and I rented a car one morning and drove through the Balkans to Dubrovnik. He spun us 360 degrees on one mountain road, but luckily a plow had been through and heaped up a wall of snow that kept us from going over the edge.

Dubrovnik was worth the trip. It had survived centuries of assault, survived Napoleon, Hitler, the Austrian occupation. All had left it as it was, a whole city that seemed to come untouched from the early Middle Ages. It was a civic work of art set next to the Adriatic. It had towering walls, watchtowers, stone streets so old they had worn smooth and shiny under feet that may have included the sandals of Romans.

Notice I use the past tense. The headlines tell of Serbs shelling Dubrovnik, hitting the tower. They tell of Serbian guns in the hills around Sarajevo, the same hills that once echoed with cheers for Olympic skiers and sledders, lobbing shells into the market so many of us strolled in that happier time. Once, on a recent newsreel, I glimpsed a street that struck a memory. I'm sure it is the one Furman and I were on to rent the car for Dubrovnik.

But we won't be going back, just as Sarajevo will never recapture the spirit of 1984. It is dead, gone, and the world is poorer for that. Yugoslavia, already impoverished, had done everything it could to make those games work, and they succeeded. It was three weeks of fairy tales in that exotic East-West setting, and now it is rubble.

The Olympic torch is out, replaced by flames stirred by centuries of ethnic enmity and hatred. For one brief period eight years ago, they managed to submerge those ancient feuds in a common cause. We measured days in gold and silver and bronze medals. Now they are measured in corpses.

If this seems an odd topic for a June morning when Denver is celebrating its first-ever major-league baseball draft, it shouldn't. Sports have never been more than a veneer, a happy veneer to be sure, but nothing more. Eight years ago, the world watched Sarajevo with fascination and pleasure. We all cranked out stories of games and triumphs and cultures.

We walked across the bridge and over to the spot where the assassin had stood and fired the shot at Archduke Ferdinand that triggered World War I. And then we walked up the hill to the ice arena for the skating and hockey. Refugees huddle there in that building now—unless it, too, has been reduced to piles of shattered glass and brick.

Is our old apartment building still standing? Who lives there in flat No. 7, and how are they faring? I spent years wanting to go back and find out. No more. I just wish them well. The Sarajevo I once knew is the one I want to remember, even if it isn't the real one anymore.

July 11, 1992, *Denver Post*
Sports coverage changes over 100 years

It's funny how historic things seemed somehow, well, smaller at the time and then grow with the telling.

There is a wire service story in the *Denver Post* of Saturday, Oct. 1, 1927, that serves as a case in point. It is the day after Babe Ruth hit his 60th home run.

"Gave Up Hope of Breaking Record," the big top headline proclaimed. And, over the story itself:

"Babe Ruth's Dream Comes True;
Homerun No. 60 Breaks Record"

The story goes on for about a dozen paragraphs, but nowhere is there a single word from the great man himself. No obligatory, "Well, it was a curve that hung out over the plate and I just got the meat of the bat on it." Nothing.

"The baseball season has ended successfully for Babe Ruth," the un-bylined story began. "In the next to last game of the Yanks in the American League season, Babe produced home run number sixty Friday, establishing a new record for a season."

No bells, no whistles, no spotlights. Just the facts, ma'am.

"While some 8,000 fans got a thrill, Ruth crashed the ball into the bleachers to erase his old mark of fifty-nine first achieved by himself in 1921 and tied Thursday.

"Babe has been pulling for the new mark for six years. The veteran pitcher, Zachary, of the Senators had the distinction of hurling the ball which made the dream come true. It happened in the eighth inning with one strike and one ball on the Babe."

So much for history. The rest of that day's sports page was taken up with advance stories heralding the start—please note the date, Oct. 1—the start of the college football season.

By Oct. 1 these years, college teams are four games into their seasons. If the Babe had been on a 60-homer pace this season, he would be followed by hordes of writers and cameramen trying to put every word on tape or paper.

The two facts illustrate the changes in the sports pages over the past decades, and the changes in the way we pursue a story.

The *Post* has harbored some exceptional writers over the years, but sports weren't always one of the featured sections. In fact, in 1900, the day's sports budget was happily contained in one page toward the back of the paper. There wasn't a single byline.

By the war years, there might occasionally be two pages on a weekend, but the fare was hardly what we take for granted these days. "Colorado Laundry Team Is Crowded Out of First Place in State Bowling Meet by Navarre Hotel Team's Great Work," our lead headline proclaimed one February day in 1918.

Two years later, the war over, it was "Ministers Hopelessly Outclassed by Boulder," on a football story of a CU win over the University of Denver. By then, we were beginning to identify the writers. This story was by Charles E. Lounsbury: "Boulder 31, Denver U. 0, which tells the story of a crushed crowd of Ministers and their hopeless fight against a perfect scoring machine at Broadway Park Saturday afternoon. Although it was a conference contest, with neither side the favorite at the beginning, Boulder took the offensive from the first blow of the whistle, holding it until the end. Surprise attacks followed in such rapid succession that the befuddled Denverites stood helpless and allowed plays to skirt their ends, crash through their line and pass over their heads."

Bill McCartney and his crew should do as well this fall.

If there is a distinguishing difference from the early years of sports journalism and now, it would be the present emphasis, not on what happened, but on why and how, and what the participants think about it.

As noted, Babe Ruth can hit his 60th home run and that day's wire service writer did not think it worthy of getting a personal comment from the Babe himself.

Today, television and radio have changed that. People no longer have to wait until the next day to find out who won. But they will eagerly wait to find out what others thought of what they saw or heard. Much of our modern emphasis thus has moved to the dressing room and away from the press box itself.

When I started chronicling the Broncos so many years ago, I would often be the only writer, or one of just a couple, to visit the dressing room after a game. It was still common practice for a writer to stay in the press box and never see a coach or player for comment.

Today, at huge events, officials have had to ration access to the dressing room because of the sheer numbers of those trying to get a word or two from the star or the goat.

We've been blessed with some outstanding characters here at the *Post*. Otto Floto led the early parade. He was as much a promoter as a writer. Jack Carberry used to take an oversized legal sheet of newsprint, roll it into his old typewriter and proceed to write from one edge of the page to the other, all the way from the top to the bottom. When he ran out of paper, he ran out of that day's comment.

Harry Farrar served several sentences as the *Post's* featured writer, due in no small part to his fictional alter ego, Sam Pirkle. Between them, they savaged the pompous and pricked the egotistical in establishing a huge audience in the region.

Jim Graham once fought with George Patton, and suffered frostbitten toes. As a result, his east Denver apartment was kept at hothouse temperatures, and when Graham died while attending the San Francisco opera one year, friends went to the apartment to help straighten out his affairs. He had fancied himself an expert on wines, and collected them. But he then stored them in closets, under the bed and behind chairs, and the heat had turned them to vinegar.

We have grown from a single page to a whole section of our own, complete with marvelous color and graphics, and our scope has gone from state bowling to focusing worldwide.

But, sometimes, you still wonder if they didn't have more fun. The day after Ruth's 60th, Westbrook Peggler went out to Yankee Stadium to watch the final game of that season.

"Having hit sixty home runs already, Mr. Babe Ruth waggled his hitter with great earnestness in his last ball game of the season," Pegler wrote. "But the only time he reached base was the first of his four times at the plate when he walked, showing much reluctance and disgust about it, too."

Pegler then narrates a scene at third base before the game, with New York officials all gathered to congratulate Ruth on his feat. Who were they, Pegler asked the Babe.

"I do not know," he quotes Ruth in reply. "Just write that a number of unanimous gentlemen were there." Pegler wrote it precisely as the Babe said it.

♥   ♥   ♥